Swimming Science V

International Series on Sport Sciences
Volume 18

Series Editor

Chauncey A. Morehouse, PhD
The Pennsylvania State University
University Park, Pennsylvania U.S.A.

Swimming Science V

Bodo E. Ungerechts
Kurt Wilke
Klaus Reischle

Editors

Human Kinetics Books
Champaign, Illinois

Library of Congress Cataloging-in-Publication Data

International Symposium of Biomechanics and Medicine
   in Swimming (5th : 1986 : Bielefeld, Germany)
   Swimming science V.

   (International series on sport sciences,
ISSN 0160-0559 ; v. 18)
   "Proceedings of Vth International Symposium of
Biomechanics and Medicine in Swimming, held in Bielefeld,
Federal Republic of Germany, July 27-31, 1986"—T.p.
verso.
   Bibliography: p.
   1. Swimming—Physiological aspects—Congresses.
2. Human mechanics—Congresses. I. Ungerechts,
Bodo, E., 1948-   . II. Wilke, Kurt. III. Reischle,
Klaus, 1940-   . IV. Title. V. Title: Swimming
science 5. VI. Title: Swimming science five.
VII. Series.
RC1220.S8I574   1988   612'.044.   87-4002
ISBN 0-87322-108-7

Developmental Editor: Laura E. Larson
Production Director: Ernie Noa
Projects Manager: Lezli Harris
Assistant Editor: Phaedra A. Hise
Proofreader: Janet Beals
Typesetter: Theresa Bear
Text Design: Keith Blomberg
Text Layout: Denise Peters
Printed By: Braun-Brumfield, Inc.

ISBN: 0-87322-108-7
ISSN: 0-160-0559

Printed in the United States of America

10 9 8 7 6 5 4 3 2 1

Human Kinetics Books
A Division of Human Kinetics Publishers, Inc.
Box 5076, Champaign, IL 61820
1-800-DIAL-HKP
1-800-334-3665 (in Illinois)

Contents

Symposium Organization

This conference was organized through the efforts of

Abteilung Sportwissenschaft, Universität Bielefeld,
(Prof. Dr. Klaus Willimczik, Dean of the Faculty)

and supported by:
Deutscher Schwimmverband (DSV)

under the auspices of:
International Society of Biomechanics (ISB)
Working Group Biomechanics of Sport—WGBS—ISB—ICSSPE—
UNESCO

Local Organizing Committee

Bodo E. Ungerechts (Chairman)
Renate Schubert
Detlef Kuhlmann
Kerstin Twellmeyher
Stefan Koch
Jan P. Clarys (Advisory Member)

Scientific Committee

K. Wilke (Chairman)	Cologne
J. Clarys	Brussels
H. Gros	Stuttgart
L. Gullstrand	Stockholm
G. de Groot	Amsterdam
P. Hollander	Amsterdam
J. Klauck	Cologne
A. Mader	Cologne
U. Persyn	Leuven
K. Reischle	Heidelberg
B. Ungerechts	Bielefeld
K. Willimczik	Bielefeld

Preface

This volume contains the presentations of the Vth International Symposium of Biomechanics and Medicine in Swimming held in Bielefeld, Federal Republic of Germany from July 27 to 31, 1986. In addition to the oral and poster presentations, two new activities were introduced during this symposium: the demonstration and operation of measuring devices and the awarding of the "Archimedes Award" made possible through the generosity of L. Lewillie, Jean-Claude de Potter, and Jan Clarys, the organizers of the first Symposium in Biomechanics in Swimming held in Brussels in 1970. Both activities were very well received and hopefully will become a permanent part of future congresses.

The Bielefeld symposium was a continuation of the series of swimming conferences, "Biomechanics in Swimming." An attempt was made to include the medical and physiological aspects of swimming that were initiated at the Amsterdam symposium in 1982. This combination revealed a need for joint experimental approaches for the overall advancement of swimming, as well as a need for interdisciplinary research.

The topics and quality of the contributions are continuations of the foundation provided by the former congresses, which demonstrated the status of research and in turn challenged researchers to solve unanswered questions. After 16 years of swimming research, some trends can be recognized. There is a tendency to replace the descriptive analysis of swimming movements with a hydrodynamic analysis to provide a better understanding of the structure of acting forces. Different methods have been employed in the calculation of forces using an integrative model based on theoretical and empirical data or measuring forces directly during free swimming. In combination with physiological data, these methods provide greater scientific information concerning the effectiveness of swimming in general and of individual techniques. Perhaps this trend will considerably influence future methods utilized in teaching and training for swimming.

The Archimedes Award was presented to Luc van Tilborgh for his contribution concerning the propulsive and resistive forces in breaststroke swimming, an outstanding presentation of research was carried out at the Aquatic Institute in Leuven, Belgium.

The success of this International Symposium in Biomechanics and Medicine in Swimming was possible only through the joint efforts of the Local Organizing Committee, the Scientific Committee, and the sponsors.

The high scientific standards, however, must be attributed to the willingness of the participants to present and to discuss the results of their research. On this occasion the editors would like to thank the participants for their contributions to this conference. Special thanks must be given to C.A. Morehouse, Series Editor of the International Series on Sport Sciences, for his help with the editorial work and for his advice given to nearly every author.

Keynote Address

The Status of Research on the Biomechanics of Swimming

James G. Hay

The purposes of this chapter are (a) to evaluate the present status of research on the biomechanics of swimming and (b) to identify important questions for which answers are still needed. Also considered is the time that a swimmer takes to complete an event—the ultimate measure of the swimmer's performance. This *event time* equals the sum of the times taken starting, stroking, and turning. Each of these times is discussed here in turn.

Starting Time

The time spent starting may be considered to be the sum of the time from the starting signal being given until the feet leave the block or the wall (the *block* or *wall time*), the time from the feet leaving the block or wall until the hands first make contact with the water (the *flight time*), and the time from the first contact with the water until the swimmer begins kicking and/or stroking (the *glide time*).

Numerous studies have been made of the techniques used in starting. These studies fall into three categories:

- Descriptive studies based on gross measures of starting technique—for example, block time, flight time and distance, and glide time and distance (East, 1970; Miller, Hay, & Wilson, 1984)
- Comparative studies in which the relative merits of different techniques are evaluated (Hay, 1985; Zatsiorsky, Bulgakova, & Chaplinsky, 1979)
- Studies of factors influencing success in the use of a given technique (Guimaraes & Hay, 1985; Yoshida & Saito, 1981; Zatsiorsky et al., 1979).

The descriptive studies have usually involved the analysis of films taken at major competitions. These studies have yielded some useful information, but the conditions under which the data must be gathered are so restrictive that there is little hope that anything of great value can be obtained in this manner. If anything further is to be obtained by analyzing the starting techniques used in competition, it will most likely be through the use of technologies other than cinematography.

One of the most frequently asked questions in sports coaching is, Which of these two techniques is better? This is a question that has spurred hundreds of analyses. At least 15 studies, for example, have been conducted in an attempt to answer that question with respect to the grab start and the starts that preceded it historically. These studies are usually flawed because no control is exercised over the influence that differences in the amount of practice or in the complexity of the techniques involved have on the results obtained. As a consequence, such studies almost invariably show that the most practiced and/or the least complicated technique yields the best result. Indeed, only when a new technique leads to a better result despite being more complex and less practiced than the old one can any useful conclusion be drawn from a study of this kind (Hay, 1983). This, of course, is only a remote possibility.

Although very few studies have been aimed at identifying the factors that influence success in the use of a given starting technique, two of these deserve comment. In the first, Yoshida and Saito (1981) studied the grab starts of 3 female swimmers (aged 12 to 16 years) and 9 male swimmers (aged 17 to 24 years) who were candidates for the Japanese national team to the 1980 Olympic Games. They found that:

- the time from the starting signal being given until the subject's center of gravity was 5 m from the wall—the start time—was significantly correlated with times to 25 and 50 m, apparently confirming the importance of the start to performance over these distances;
- the horizontal velocity at takeoff and the glide velocity were significantly correlated with the start time but not with each other, suggesting that both were independently important in determining start time; and
- height and weight were significantly correlated with the start time and with each of the other variables already mentioned.

At first inspection, these findings appear to confirm what might have been expected. However, when these and other measures were correlated by this author with the start time with height and weight partialled out, none were found to be significantly correlated at even the .10 level of confidence. Assuming that the purpose of such studies is to identify characteristics of technique that have a significant influence on the result (and not to determine the influence of anthropometric variables), it seems only reasonable to suggest that these latter influences should be controlled, at least insofar as it is feasible to do so. In fairness to Yoshida and Saito, however, their study has been selected for mention here because it is a convenient example of the point at issue. It is by no means the only study in which no control is exercised over the influence of anthropometric differences among subjects. Indeed, such differences are rarely controlled in studies of this kind.

The second study (Guimaraes & Hay, 1985) deserves comment because it challenges some long-held beliefs about starting techniques. This study involved an analysis of the grab-starting techniques used by 24 high school swimmers, who were asked to perform a series of starts with a glide to touch a bulkhead 9 m from the start. When the variables measured were correlated with the start time, with the heights and weights of the subjects partialled out, the results showed that:

- the glide time was overwhelmingly the most important of the block, flight, and glide times (the partial correlation coefficient of $r = .97$ indicated that the glide time accounted for no less than 95% of the variance in the start time);
- the glide distance varied little from subject to subject and was not significantly related with the start time; and
- the average gliding speed was highly correlated with the glide time.

These results, coupled with the fact that the horizontal velocity at entry was not significantly related to the start time, suggest that the most important determinant of a successful grab start is not what takes place on the block or in the flight prior to entry, but what the swimmer does to minimize the resistive forces during the glide. The results suggest further that a shift in emphasis is needed in practice—a shift from an emphasis on position and actions on the block and in the air to an emphasis on minimizing the resistance encountered during the glide. The Guimaraes and Hay study needs to be replicated and expanded first, however. Only when this has been done can the suggested shift in emphasis be recommended with confidence.

Turning Time

Very few studies have addressed the techniques used in turning. Of 336 studies on swimming techniques cited in *A Bibliography of Biomechanics Literature* (Hay, 1981), only 20 were devoted to turning techniques. Of the 152 papers published in the proceedings of the first four International Symposia on the Biomechanics of Swimming, only two were devoted to this topic. Furthermore, of the total of 21 studies from the two sources mentioned, no less than 17 involved the comparison of two or more techniques and the attendant design limitations previously mentioned.

The reason for this unsatisfactory state of affairs is not hard to find: No simple, convenient, and versatile methods are available for the study of turning techniques, and few investigators have been sufficiently motivated to conduct analyses with the difficult, inconvenient methods (like three-dimensional cinematography) that are available. Under these circumstances, little progress will be made until someone takes the initiative and fully exploits available methods or develops new methods for this purpose. This is virgin territory, simply waiting for someone with the energy and the commitment to develop it.

Stroking Time

The time that a swimmer spends stroking is determined by the distance and the average speed of the swimmer over that distance. The distance involved is primarily dictated by the distance of the race, the average speed by the average stroke length (or distance per stroke), and the average stroke frequency (or stroke rate). The swimmer's average speed is equal to the product of these two factors:

$$S = SL \times SF,$$

where S = the average speed, SL = the average stroke length (or the distance traveled during the course of one complete stroke cycle), and SF = the average stroke frequency (or the average number of strokes per second).

Relationships Among SL, SF, and S

Several studies have been conducted to determine the effect of various factors on SL and SF and thus on the resulting S. These studies are often very confusing because the results in one appear to be exactly the opposite of those in another. Thus, if one notes how swimmers increase speed when moving down from 200 m to 100 m—usually by increasing SF and decreasing SL—one might conclude that the emphasis in training should be on increasing SF and decreasing SL. Then, if one examines the difference between a group of fast swimmers and a group of not-so-fast swimmers and notes that the faster swimmers have longer SLs, one might conclude that the emphasis in training should be on increasing SL. Some execeptions aside, the truth of the matter appears to be that (a) to increase S in the short term (for example, to "kick" at the finish of a race), one should strive to increase SF, and (b) to increase S in the long term (for example, over the course of a season), one should strive to increase SL.

Monitoring SL, SF, and S

Few attempts appear to have been made to develop procedures that will allow coaches and others to determine SL, SF, and S easily during practice and competition. A simple analog stroke watch has been described in the literature (Hay, Guimaraes, & Grimston, 1983), and at least one—a sophisticated digital device—is available commercially (Nielsen-Kellerman Co., 1066 High Vista Trail, Webster, NY, 14580). Although such watches are useful in the absence of anything better, they will never be entirely satisfactory until they are capable of recording not only SF (arguably the least important of the three parameters of interest) but also SL and S.

With this in mind, a series of devices has been developed to record all three parameters. The first two generations of these so-called Swim-Stroke Computers were designed to be carried in the hand as the operator walked along the pool deck recording the times for a specified number of strokes and for the swimmer to traverse a known distance. Once the operator had completed the four keystrokes involved, the microprocessor-based device computed the average SL, the average SF, and the average S; entered then on a six-digit display; and stored them for later retrieval. The latest versions of this system eliminate the need to move up and down the side of the pool and are thus much more appropriate for gathering data during competition. They also include four hand-held units linked directly to a microcomputer, so that the performances of four swimmers can be recorded simultaneously.

Propulsive Forces

The average stroke length is determined by the forces exerted on the swimmer: the *propulsive forces* that drive the swimmer forward through the water in reaction to the movements the swimmer makes and the *resistive forces* that the water exerts on the swimmer to oppose that motion. The mechanism by which swimmers generate propulsive forces has long been a topic of debate, most of which has focussed on the propulsion generated by the arms. Various theories have been advanced in the course of this debate.

Propulsive drag theory. This theory, the first to be widely accepted, posits that swimmers propel themselves through the water by pulling and pushing the hands directly backward. This action, it is argued, evokes from the water a reaction that drives the body forward.

Although the propulsive drag theory was accepted for decades, it is now known to be contrary to the evidence in many instances. The reason for the acceptance and subsequent long reign of the propulsive drag theory is not difficult to find. It lies in the choice of reference frames and particularly in the choice of a reference frame that is moving at a variable rate, rather than an inertial reference frame that by definition is moving at a zero or constant rate. Consider, for the sake of example and simplicity, the case of a freestyle swimmer who performs a vertical, straight-arm pull in which the arm moves through 45° in each 0.1 s. The motion of the arm, relative to the shoulder (S), and the path followed by the hand (H) are shown in Figure 1a. If the shoulder is stationary, the drag forces exerted on the hand would act in a direction tangential to the path followed by the hand, and the forward horizontal components of these drag forces serve a propulsive function. The shoulder, however, is moving forward, relative to the side of the pool, with a velocity approximately equal to the horizontal velocity of the swimmer's center of gravity (Figure 1b). The combined effect of the motion of the shoulder (relative to the side of the pool) and the arm (relative to the shoulder) produces a hand path in which the stroke cycle is completed with the hand farther forward than it was at the beginning and in which the motion of the hand is predominantly in a vertical (rather than horizontal) direction (Figure 1c). Thus, the very shape of the hand path severely limits the swimmer's ability to use drag as source of propulsion from the arms.

Propulsive lift theory. The propulsive lift theory was unveiled 16 years ago at the First International Symposium on Biomechanics in Swimming

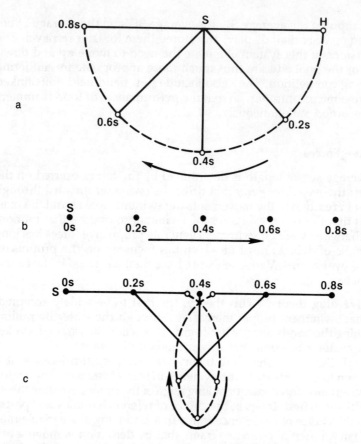

Figure 1 (a) motion of arm and hand (H) relative to shoulder(s); (b) motion of shoulder relative to side of pool; (c) motion of hand (dashed line) relative to side of pool.

in Brussels. On that occasion, Counsilman (1971) reported that the hand paths of world-class swimmers involved significant lateral (or sculling) motions and thus deviated from the straight-line pull generally advocated at that time. Counsilman's findings and his suggestion that these lateral motions of the hand enabled the swimmer to use lift forces for propulsion, spurred numerous studies of the question (Barthels & Adrian, 1975; Schleihauf, 1974, 1976, 1979, 1984; Schleihauf, Gray, & DeRose, 1983; Valiant, 1980; Wood, 1979). These studies revealed that (a) propulsion from the arms in swimming is derived from a combination of lift and drag forces and (b) one or the other of these forces is the dominant influence in some strokes and at some phases within a given stroke. Thus, for example, lift forces dominate in the breaststroke, and lift and drag forces each dominate at different phases in the front crawl (Schleihauf, 1979).

The person who has made the greatest contribution to existing knowledge of the role of lift and drag forces in propulsion from the arms in swimming is Schleihauf (Hay, 1983). Schleihauf's approach involved three steps:

1. Submerging a model of a hand in an open-water channel and measuring the lift and drag forces exerted on it under a wide range of flow conditions
2. Using three-dimensional cinematography to determine the hand paths, hand speeds, and hand orientations used by the subject
3. Combining the results of the previous two stages to determine the magnitudes and directions of the lift and drag forces exerted on the hands throughout the stroke

The approach taken by Schleihauf assumes that the forces acting on the hand under conditions of unsteady flow (i.e., under conditions where the flow velocity varies as a function of time) are effectively the same as those that act on the hand under steady flow conditions (like those under which Schleihauf's data were gathered in his open-channel experiments). To determine whether this approach was valid, Schleihauf (1979) conducted a number of experiments in which subjects were filmed performing vertical sculling and tethered swimming trials against known external loads. The supportive, or propulsive, forces were computed using the Schleihauf method, and the mean value of these forces was compared with the external load. Although the published results of these experiments were generally supportive, the lack of direct measures of the instantaneous forces that could be compared with the corresponding computed values has left the issue unresolved. More work must be done before the validity of this approach or the error bounds associated with it can be established.

Vortex theory. Several recent papers describe the behavior of the water in response to the swimmer's actions. Firby (1975) has written on the significance of the wave patterns created by the motion of a swimmer. Colwin (1984, 1985a, 1985b) has described the mechanisms associated with the generation of starting, bound, and tip vortices in swimming and has drawn attention to the role that circulation plays in the production of propulsive lift. Ungerechts (1987) has noted a lack of cross-flow from the dorsal to the plantar surface of the foot during dolphin and flutter kicks and has suggested that the propulsive forces produced by the legs cannot, therefore, be due exclusively to drag forces. He has also described the formation of vortices with horizontal axes at the points where the feet reverse the direction of their motion in a dolphin kick.

Analyses of the creation and shedding of vortices have led to the suggestion that the swimmer's propulsion can be attributed, at least in part, to such phenomena. Consequently, coaches and scientists occasionally discuss something called *vortex theory*—a theory that one must assume links the formation and shedding of vortices directly to the generation of propulsion. To date, however, no one has set forth a coherent account of how the generation and/or the shedding of vortices actually serves to propel a swimmer forward.

It is well known in fluid mechanics that the generation of a starting vortex and the circulation that is set up around the immersed body as a consequence are prerequisites to the creation of lift forces. This, however, is a far cry from a comprehensive theory of swimming propulsion. Indeed, for now at least, the term vortex theory must be considered a misnomer. There is no such theory. At best, there are a number of interesting ideas about the flow around a swimmer that might eventually lead to the development of such a theory. Even this, in my view, is not very likely. Instead, I expect that continued efforts to visualize, record, and understand the flow around a swimmer will lead not to a new theory of swimming propulsion but to an increased understanding of existing theories.

Although the concepts discussed by Colwin and Ungerechts deserve close scrutiny, very few methods are available that permit the flow around a swimmer to be visualized. Ungerechts has done some preliminary work using a dye injection procedure to visualize the flow around the feet in a dolphin kick. Tagori (1985a, 1985b) and Tagori, Masunaga, and Okamoto (1985a, 1985b) have done preliminary work using surface oil and tufts techniques to visualize the flow around a life-size model of a swimmer and around a swimmer performing in a flume. Colwin (1984) has suggested that shadow photography may have some merit as a means of visualizing the flow around a swimmer.

We have also been experimenting with a variety of methods of visualizing the flow around a swimmer. In the course of this work, the bulk of our attention has been devoted to the tufts technique—a technique in which short lengths of plastic tubing are attached at one end to the suit or skin of a swimmer and their motion observed as the swimmer performs. Although several things remain to be done, the results to date have been encouraging, and we look forward to eventually developing a simple, effective system for the purpose.

Resistive forces.   In swimming, the resistive forces to which the swimmer is exposed while stroking are often referred to as the *active drag*. This term is used to distinguish between the drag experienced when stroking and that experienced when being towed in some fixed position. The latter is referred to as the *passive drag*.

Much effort has been expended over the years in trying to determine the magnitude of the resistive forces to which a swimmer is exposed as he or she moves through the water. Numerous investigators (see Clarys, 1976, 1979; and Miller, 1975) have conducted studies to determine the passive drag experienced by a human body. Still others (Clarys, 1976, 1979; Di Prampero et al., 1974; Hollander, Groot, & Ingen Schenau, 1987; Hollander, Groot et al., 1986; Schleihauf, 1984; Schleihauf et al., 1983; Vaart, Savelburg, Groot, Hollander, & Ingen Schenau, in press) have embarked on the even more demanding task of determining the magnitude of the active drag.

With few exceptions, studies of the passive drag exerted on a swimmer have yielded results that are remarkably consistent. When a body is towed in a prone position, the passive drag varies approximately with the square of the velocity at which the body moves (Clarys, 1976), ranging from about 30 N (at 1 m/s) to about 120 N (at 2 m/s) (Clarys, 1976, 1979).

Consistency is not a feature of the results obtained in studies of active drag. Indeed, one could say that there is something of a controversy concerning the magnitude of the active drag experienced by a swimmer performing the front crawl stroke—the only stroke for which there appears to have been any serious effort to determine the active drag. At the heart of this controversy are the methods used to determine the active drag. These fall into two broad categories: *indirect methods*, used by Di Prampero et al. (1974) and Clarys (1978, 1979); and *direct methods*, used by Schleihauf (1984), Hollander et al. (1985, 1986) and Vaart et al. (1986). The indirect methods have yielded values for the active drag that are up to 3.1 times greater than for passive drag, at the same velocity of the swimmer (Clarys, 1976, 1979; Di Prampero et al., 1974; Rennie, Pendergast, & Di Prampero, 1975). The direct methods have yielded values that are less than the passive drag in two instances (Hollander et al., 1985; Vaart et al., in press), about the same as the passive drag in one other (Hollander et al., 1987), and about 1.3 times the passive drag in yet another (Schleihauf, 1984).

The measurement of the resistive forces to which a swimmer's body is subjected is of considerable interest to sport biomechanists for both theoretical and practical reasons. To obtain a thorough understanding of the mechanics of human locomotion in water and to provide useful information to practicing teachers, coaches, and swimmers, appropriate procedures must first be developed for measuring the forces involved. One can hardly expect to evaluate a swimmer's ability to minimize resistance and recommend ways in which this might be improved, if one cannot even measure the forces involved with some degree of accuracy.

Conclusion

Biomechanical analyses of swimming techniques are more difficult to perform successfully than the corresponding analyses of almost any other sports technique. This difficulty is due to (a) the media in which the techniques are performed, (b) the distortions produced by turbulence and wave action, (c) the need to record simultaneously in two media, and (d) the problems introduced by the entrapment of air in the flow. All these problems are unknown to biomechanists working in most other areas of sports biomechanics. In addition, almost all swimming techniques involve three-dimensional motion. The planar, two-dimensional analyses so widely used in studying many other sport techniques are thus rarely useful in swimming.

The difficulties inherent in this situation have not been noticeably relieved by the technological developments that have had a profound impact on many other fields in recent years. Indeed, research on the biomechanics of swimming has been virtually untouched by technological developments over the last decade or so. This is surely not how it should be. What is clearly needed is for researchers to be much more alert than in the past to the opportunities that developing technologies provide and to take advantage of those opportunities without delay.

Despite their importance, neither the complexity of the task nor the lack of appropriate technology is the major impediment to progress in the understanding of the biomechanics of swimming. The lack of scientists able and willing to devote their energies to the task warrants this dubious distinction. Although some progress in swimming research has been made over the last decade, the rate of such progress is unlikely to increase until the number of trained researchers who are active in the field increases. Those who wish to see an improvement in swimming research in the years ahead would thus do well to consider what might be done to attract established scientists to the field and to identify and train young scientists with a proven interest in swimming.

References

Barthels, K.M., & Adrian, M.J. (1975). Three-dimensional spatial hand patterns of skilled butterfly swimmers. In L. Lewillie & J.P. Clarys (Eds.), *Swimming II* (pp. 154-160). Baltimore: University Park Press.

Clarys, J.P. (1976). *Onderzoek naar de hydrodynamische en morfologische aspekten van het menselijk lichaam.* Unpublished doctoral dissertation, Instituut voor Morfologie, Brussels.

Clarys, J.P. (1978). Relationship of human body form to passive and active hydrodynamic drag. In E. Asmussen & K. Jørgensen (Eds.), *Biomechanics VI-B* (pp. 120-125). Baltimore: University Park Press.

Clarys, J.P. (1979). Human morphology and hydrodynamics. In J. Terauds & E.W. Bedingfield (Eds.), *Swimming III* (pp. 3-41). Baltimore: University Park Press.

Colwin, C. (1984). Fluid dynamics: Vortex circulation in swimming propulsion. In *ASCA Yearbook* (pp. 38-46). Fort Lauderdale, FL: American Swimming Coaches Association.

Colwin, C. (1985a, July-August). Essential fluid dynamics in swimming. *ASCA Newsletter*, pp. 22-27.

Colwin, C. (1985b). Practical application of flow analysis as a coaching tool. *ASCA Newsletter*, pp. 5-8.

Counsilman, J.E. (1971). The application of Bernoulli's principle to human propulsion in water. In L. Lewillie & J.P. Clarys (Eds.), *First International Symposium on Biomechanics in Swimming, Waterpolo and Diving proceedings* (pp. 59-71). Bruxelles: Université Libre de Bruxelles Laboratoire de l'Effort.

Di Prampero, P.E., Pendergast, D.R., Wilson, D.W., & Rennie, D.W. (1974). Energetics of swimming in man. *Journal of Applied Physiology,* **37**(1), 1-5.

East, D.L. (1970). Swimming: An analysis of stroke frequency, stroke length and performance. *New Zealand Journal of Health, Physical Education and Recreation, 3,* 16-27.

Firby, H. (1975). *Howard Firby on swimming.* London: Pelham Books.

Guimaraes, A.C.S., & Hay, J.G. (1985). A mechanical analysis of the grab starting technique in swimming. *International Journal of Sport Biomechanics, 1,* 25-35.

Hay, J.G. (1981). *A bibliography of biomechanics literature.* Iowa City, IA: Author

Hay, J.G. (1982). The most significant research of the past decade: Biomechanics. In *The academy papers* (pp. 20-26). Reston, VA: The American Academy of Physical Education.

Hay, J.G. (1983). Biomechanics of sport—Exploring or explaining. In G.A. Wood (Ed.), *Collected papers on sports biomechanics* (pp. 1-21). Nedlands: University of Western Australia.

Hay, J.G. (1985). *The biomechanics of sports techniques.* Englewood Cliffs, NJ: Prentice-Hall.

Hay, J.G., Guimaraes, A.C.S., & Grimston, S.E. (1983). A quantitative look at swimming biomechanics. *Swimming Technique, 20*(2), 11-17.

Hollander, A.P., Groot, G. de, & Ingen Schenau, G.J. van. (1987). Active drag of female swimmers. In B. Johnson (Ed.), *Biomechanics X-B* (pp. 717-724). Champaign, IL: Human Kinetics.

Hollander, A.P., Groot, G. de, Ingen Schenau, G.J. van, Toussaint, H.M., Best, H. de, Peeters, W., Meulemans, A., & Schreurs, A.W. (1986). Measurement of active drag during crawl arm stroke swimming. *Journal of Sports Sciences, 4,* 21-30.

Hollander, A.P., Schreurs, A.W., Meulemans, A., Best, H. de, Groot, G. de, & Ingen Schenau, G.J. van. (1985). Measurement of effective hand propulsive force during "front crawl swimming." In *Abstract Book, 10th International Congress of Biomechanics, Arbete och Hälsa, 14,* 111.

Miller, D.I. (1975). Biomechanics of swimming. In J.H. Wilmore & J.F. Keogh (Eds.), *Exercise and sport sciences reviews* (pp. 219-248). New York: Academic Press.

Miller, J.A., Hay, J.G., & Wilson, B.D. (1984). Turning techniques of elite swimmers. *Journal of Sports Sciences, 2,* 213-223.

Rennie, D.W., Pendergast, D.R., and Di Prampero, P.E. (1975). Energetics of swimming in man. In J.P. Clarys & L. Lewillie (Eds.), *Swimming II* (pp. 97-104). Baltimore: University Park Press.

Schleihauf, R.E. (1974). A biomechanical analysis of freestyle. *Swimming Technique, 40,* 89-96.

Schleihauf, R.E. (1976). A hydrodynamic analysis of breaststroke pulling proficiency. *Swimming Technique, 12,* 100-105.

Schleihauf, R.E. (1979). A hydrodynamic analysis of swimming propulsion. In J. Terauds & E.W. Bedingfield (Eds.), *Swimming II* (pp. 62-69). Baltimore: University Park Press.

Schleihauf, R.E. (1984). *The biomechanical analysis of swimming propulsion in the sprint front crawlstroke*. Unpublished doctoral dissertation, Columbia University Teachers College, New York.

Schleihauf, R.E., Gray, L., & DeRose, J. (1983). Three-dimensional analysis of hand propulsion in the sprint front crawl stroke. In A.P. Hollander, P.A. Huijing, & G. de Groot (Eds.), *Biomechanics and medicine in swimming* (pp. 173-183). Champaign, IL: Human Kinetics.

Tagori, T. (1985a). Water flow around human body at breaststroke swim. *Journal of the Flow Visualization Society of Japan, 2*, 36-37.

Tagori, T. (1985b). Water flow around human body at crawl stroke swim. *Journal of the Flow Visualization Society of Japan, 2*, 38-39.

Tagori, T., Masunaga, K., & Okamoto, H. (1985a). Water flow on the surface of human body in submerged condition. *Journal of the Flow Visualization Society of Japan, 2*, 34-35.

Tagori, T., Masunaga, K., & Okamoto, H. (1985b). Water flow on the surface of human model in floating condition. *Journal of the Flow Visualization Society of Japan, 2*, 32-33.

Ungerechts, B.E. (1987). On the relevance of rotating water flow for the propulsion in swimming. In B. Jonsson (Ed.), *Biomechanics X-B* (pp. 713-716). Champaign, IL: Human Kinetics.

Vaart, A.J.M. van der, Savelberg, H.H.C.M., Groot, G. de, Hollander, A.P., & Ingen Schenau, G.J. van. (in press). A quantification of drag in front crawl swimming. *Journal of Biomechanics*.

Valiant, G.A. (1980). *The contributions of lift and drag force components of the hand and forearm to a swimmer's propulsion*. Unpublished master's thesis. Dalhousie University, Halifax, Canada.

Wood, T.C. (1979). A fluid dynamic analysis of the propulsive potential of the hand and forearm in swimming. In J. Terauds & E.W. Bedingfield (Eds.), *Swimming II* (pp. 62-69). Baltimore: University Park Press.

Yoshida, A., & Saito, S. (1981). An analysis of the starting form in competitive swimming. *Health and Sport Science, 4*, 49-54.

Zatsiorsky, V.M., Bulgakova, N.Z., & Chaplinsky, N.M. (1979). Biomechanical analysis of starting techniques in swimming. In J. Terauds & E.W. Bedingfield (Eds.), *Swimming II* (pp. 199-206). Baltimore: University Park Press.

PART I

PROPULSION AND
RESISTANCE

Fundamental Mechanics Applied to Swimming: Technique and Propelling Efficiency

Gert de Groot
Gerrit Jan van Ingen Schenau

In the application of fundamental mechanics to human swimming, three major approaches can be distinguished in the literature:

- Kinematic analysis of swimming strokes, instantaneous speed, and so forth, (e.g., Bourgeois, 1983; Hoecke & Gruendler, 1975; Kent & Atha, 1975; Reischle, 1979)
- Propulsive or resistive force analysis (e.g., Barthels, 1979; Clarys, 1979; Di Prampero, Pendergast, Wilson, & Rennie, 1974; Schleihauf, 1979; Ungerechts, 1979)
- Analysis and simulations with the help of biomechanical models (e.g., Jensen & Blanksby, 1975; Toussaint et al., 1983)

In the application of modeling, swimming lags well behind land-based sports (Adrian, 1983). A reason for this might be that the external forces are difficult to measure (Plagenhoef, 1971). However, the same basic problems exist in land-based sports where, just as in swimming, the opposing drag forces and push-off forces must be measured (Di Prampero, Cortili, Mognoni, & Saibene, 1979; Hoes, Binkhorst, Smeekes-Kuyl, & Vissers, 1968; Ingen Schenau, Boer, & Groot, in press; Pugh, 1970; Williams & Cavanagh, 1983). So it is suprising that the application of fundamental mechanics in human swimming is still in its infancy compared with other sports, such as cross-country skiing, cycling, and speed skating. In contrast to these specifically human types of locomotion, swimming is an activity that is performed by other animals; the extensive and thorough literature on fish swimming is available to researchers on human swimming.

The purpose of this contribution is to discuss some general aspects of modeling in endurance sports and to apply one approach deduced from the literature on fish swimming to a problem that has so far been ignored in human swimming: the influence of swimming technique on efficiency.

General Models

The choice of a model in research on human locomotion depends on the purpose of the study in combination with the input variables that can be measured. The types of models can roughly be divided into (a) *multisegment models* and (b) *whole-body diagram models*. Multisegment models are used when internal forces, moments, power, and so forth are to be calculated and for simulation purposes. With known external forces or kinematic data, unknown variables are calculated using Newtonian or Lagrangian equations of motion. However, an important problem in the application of multisegment models is caused by the approximation of the segments by rigid links. This means that only net values of forces, moments, power production, energy state, and the like can be derived. As soon as individual muscles and ligaments are incorporated into such models, the unknown variables can no longer be solved due to the well-known indeterminacy problem (more unknown variables than equations—Miller, 1979). Many criteria have been used to solve this problem, but none have been very realistic. With the present state of the art, relating muscle activity directly to propulsive force or power output in one causal relationship seems impossible. Nevertheless, the application of multisegment models might at least provide a qualitative interpretation of muscular activity and the coordination of muscles in swimming when the moments in the joints are compared with the electromyographical recordings of muscles that pass over those joints.

When combining mechanics and energetics in endurance sports, segment models are hampered by several uncertainties. These problems concern the efficiency of positive and negative work, the amount of energy that can be stored in and reutilized from elastic structures, and the transfer of energy between segments (Williams, 1985; Williams & Cavanagh, 1983). Fortunately, in swimming these problems can be avoided to a large extent by taking the whole swimmer as one free-body diagram. In such an approach the energy liberation $\dot{E}$ of the swimmer is directly related to the external power P_o produced by the swimmer according to

$$P_o = \dot{E} \, e_m \tag{1}$$

where e_m = the mechanical efficiency, the ratio between mechanical power production and the energy equivalent of metabolic power. Although e_m obscures some of the uncertainties mentioned for multisegment models, the literature on fish swimming demonstrates that this relatively simple approach can be of real value in improving the knowledge about those factors determining human swimming performance.

The basic mechanical tools in this approach involve a power equation and a force equation. As in all endurance sports, part of the external power is used to overcome friction (P_d). In swimming, this part—P_d—is lost to friction, pressure drag, and waves. A second part, P_k, is lost when masses of water that are accelerated as a result of the push-off acquire kinetic energy. At constant speed the power equation is

$$P_o = P_d + P_k \tag{2}$$

The force equation used in the remaining part of this article is based on the simple statement that at constant speed the mean propulsive force (F_p) should be equal to the mean resistive force (F_d). Based on hydrodynamic theories derived from the literature on fish swimming (Alexander & Goldspink, 1977; Lighthill, 1975; Webb, 1975; Wu, Brohaw, & Brenner, 1975), it will be shown that swimming technique is closely related to the relative magnitude of P_d and that this is an important determinant of swimming speed.

Fundamental Relationships

In all types of endurance sports propulsive force F_p of the athlete (mass: M_1) is obtained by pushing off against a second body (mass: M_2). The action force (F_a) causes a backward change of momentum of M_2. The rate of change of momentum equals

$$F_a = M_2 \frac{\Delta w}{\Delta t} \tag{3}$$

with Δw the increase in velocity of M_2 as a result of F_a. The reaction force, F_p, is used to accelerate the athlete and to oppose frictional forces. If M_2 were at rest initially, the kinetic energy given to M_2 equals

$$E_k = \frac{1}{2} M_2 \Delta w^2 \tag{4}$$

As long as $M_2 > M_1$, this flow of energy from M_1 to M_2 is negligible. In sports like running, cycling, and speed skating, M_2 is the entire earth and therefore no energy is lost as a result of this principle of propulsion. In swimming, however, M_2 is the amount of water. In fact, one can state that propulsion during swimming can only be obtained by driving water backward (Alexander, 1975). With every stroke a certain amount of water with a "virtual mass" M_w (Lighthill, 1975) gets a backward velocity change Δw. Hence, the mean propulsive force per unit time is calculated using

$$F_p = f M_w \Delta w \tag{5}$$

where f = the stroke frequency. Then the flow of kinetic energy to the water (with zero velocity, initially) is

$$P_k = f \frac{1}{2} M_w \Delta w^2 \tag{6}$$

Because the minimal amount of power necessary to maintain a certain swimming speed (v) equals the mean frictional losses or "drag losses," this power, P_k, can be regarded as wasted power. The useful power (P_u) at constant swimming speed (v) equals

$$P_u = F_p \, v \tag{7}$$

This power is used to compensate for the frictional losses, (P_d). Neglecting (small) speed fluctuations

$$P_u = P_d = F_p v = \tfrac{1}{2} \varrho \, v^3 \, C_D \, A_p \tag{8}$$

because the drag force (F_d) can be described by

$$F_d = \tfrac{1}{2} \varrho \, v^2 \, C_D \, A_p \tag{9}$$

At a given drag coefficient (C_D) and frontal area (A_p) for the entire body of the swimmer, Equations 5 and 9 suggest that maximal speed is obtained by giving a large mass of water a large change of momentum at a high stroke frequency resulting in a high propulsive force. From a physiological point of view, one might argue that maximal power output (P_o) rather than propulsive force will be a major factor in determining performance. However, as already explained, this power output does not directly determine the speed because a certain amount P_k is wasted. Then

$$P_o = \tfrac{1}{2} \varrho \, v^3 \, C_D \, A_p + P_k \text{ or } v^3 = k_1 \, P_o - k_2 \, P_k \tag{10}$$

with k_1 and k_2 being constants. From these equations, maximal swimming speed should be achieved by a technique that gives a propulsive force that is optimal with respect to the relative values of P_d and P_k. In fish swimming the fraction P_d of P_o, which is useful in driving the fish through the water, is called *propelling efficiency* or *Froude efficiency* (Alexander & Goldspink, 1977; Lighthill, 1975; Webb, 1971). Expressed in Δw and v, this propelling efficiency equals

$$e_p = \frac{P_d}{P_d + P_k} = \frac{1}{1 + \tfrac{1}{2} \dfrac{\Delta w}{v}} \tag{11}$$

Maximal swimming speed can be achieved by a swimming technique where optimal propelling force is obtained with an optimal propelling efficiency. As stated already by Counsilman (1968), in such a technique the amount of water (the virtual mass) against which the push-off takes place should be as large as possible. In other words, Δw should be small with respect to v, which can only result in a sufficiently high propulsive force if much virtual mass is involved. This can be achieved by a large distance covered by the limbs (e.g., S shape). From hydrofoil theories applied in studies on fish swimming (Alexander & Goldspink, 1977; Lighthill, 1975), it can be deduced that these requirements of a high propulsive force with less wasted power can also be met, in part, by a proper use of lift forces on the limbs. This means that the analyses of lift and drag forces on lower arm and hands as published by Schleihauf (1979, 1983) can be related to propelling efficiency.

Lift, Drag, and Propelling Efficiency

Propulsive Force Derived From Drag

As indicated by Schleihauf (1979, 1983), the forces acting on the forearm and hand during swimming can be subdivided into lift forces and drag forces. Drag forces have the same nature as the well-known drag force on the entire body as the result of the forward velocity of the swimmer. If a swimmer wants to create a propulsive reaction force on the hand and arm, he or she can simply push the hand and arm backward in the water. Figure 1 shows a schematic representation of this process. As illustrated there, a swimmer has a forward velocity v (to the left); the arms and hands (presented as a flat plate) have a backward velocity u with respect to the water (to the right). The hand velocity with respect to the swimmer's body is $u + v$. In front of the flat plate (the hydrofoil), the water is pressed together while a wake with low pressure is formed behind the plate. According to Bernouilli's law, the difference in pressure $p_1 - p_2$ is proportional to the so-called dynamic pressure $\frac{1}{2} \varrho u^2$. The drag force on the plate is proportional to $\frac{1}{2} \varrho u^2 S$ in the frontal area. The actual drag force (D) is further dependent on a dimensionless constant, the drag coefficient (C_D), which depends on the geometry and streamline of the hydrofoil. Therefore,

$$D = \frac{1}{2} \varrho u^2 S C_D \tag{12}$$

In many publications S symbolizes the wetted area or the so-called *plane area* (about 0.5 times the wetted area) with the corresponding adjustments of C_D. To achieve a large propulsion force the hydrofoil should be moved fast backward. However, this also results in a large amount of wasted power P_k, because

$$P_k = D u = \frac{1}{2} \varrho u^3 S C_D \tag{13}$$

By using drag forces only, one can make a first approximation of the propelling efficiency in human swimming. Let us assume a uniform backward velocity (u) during the entire stroke and let the uniform forward velocity of the swimmer be v. According to Toussaint et al. (in press), the opposing drag force on the entire body equals

$$F_d = \frac{1}{2} \varrho v^2 C_{DB} A_p \tag{14}$$

where C_{DB} = the drag coefficient of the entire body and A_p = the cross-sectional area of the body. The mean propulsive force (F_p = D) equals the mean opposing drag force F_d:

$$\tfrac{1}{2}\, \varrho\, u^2\, C_D\, S = \tfrac{1}{2}\, \varrho\, v^2\, C_{DB}\, A_p \text{ or } u/v = \sqrt{\frac{C_{DB}A_p}{C_D\, S}} \qquad (15)$$

Using Equation 15, the propelling efficiency of this type of "straight backward" swimming can be calculated:

$$e_p = \frac{F_d\, v}{F_d\, v + F_p\, u} = \frac{1}{1 + \sqrt{\dfrac{C_{DB}\, A_p}{C_D\, S}}} \qquad (16)$$

This equation shows that for this swimming technique, e_p is dependent on the drag coefficient and plane area of the hand and arm. This dependency is confirmed by Toussaint et al. (1983), who showed that swimmers of a high performance level have a significant larger hand and arm surface than swimmers of a lower performance level. With the help of data from the literature, a rough estimation can be made of the magnitude of e_p in this type of swimming. With respect to active drag on experienced male swimmers, Toussaint et al. (in press) showed mean values of C_{DB} = 0.67 and A_p = 0.09 m². Schleihauf (1979) measured a drag coefficient for the hands of C_D = 1.4 for the position indicated in Figure 1. This value was based on S as plane area. This plane area is approximately equal to S = 0.018 m² for male swimmers. Values of C_D for the forearm have not been published yet, but this value clearly will be lower than for the hand. For a symmetric cylinder, a value of C_D = 0.8 seems reasonable. The plane area is estimated at S = 0.02 m². Then the propelling efficiency for this arm stroke is e_p = 0.45. Given the assumptions made, this value can be seen as a minimum value for human swimming.

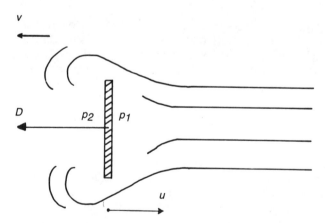

Figure 1   Propulsive reaction force D, proportional to pressure difference p_1-p_2, induced by backward velocity u. The swimmer's forward velocity is indicated by v.

Propulsive Force Derived From Lift and Drag Forces

As soon as a hydrofoil is placed at an angle with respect to the direction of its displacement, two different forces can be distinguished (see Figure 2). The first force (D, the drag force) is caused by the same phenomenon as explained previously and can be described by the Equations 12 and 13 with a corrected value for C_D. The second force (L, the lift force) is caused by a difference in pressure above and below the hydrofoil. This pressure difference is caused by a difference in velocity of the water between the parts of the water that flow over the hydrofoil and the water that passes under it. This difference in velocity is caused by the difference in distance that the parts of water must cover. According to Bernouilli's law, this difference in velocity causes a difference in pressure that is responsible for the lift force (L). This force is at right angles to the direction of u. L is described by

$$L = \tfrac{1}{2}\, \varrho\, u^2\, C_L\, S \tag{17}$$

where C_L = the lift coefficient, which is strongly dependent on the angle of attack (α). At $\alpha = 0$ lift is zero. With increasing α, lift increases to a maximum whereas above a certain optimal α_o, lift decreases again due to an effect called *stalling* (Alexander & Goldspink, 1977). Schleihauf (1979) showed that the human hand can generate an optimal lift coefficient of $C_L = 1.0$ at an angle of attack of about 40°. At this angle, C_D appears to be $C_D = 0.8$. Though L is at right angles to the direction of u, the generation of lift also causes some waste of energy to the water (Alexander, 1975; Alexander & Goldspink, 1977; Lighthill, 1975). This occurs because the downward force from the hydrofoil to the water, which is opposite to the lift force, causes a change of momentum of some mass of water. This

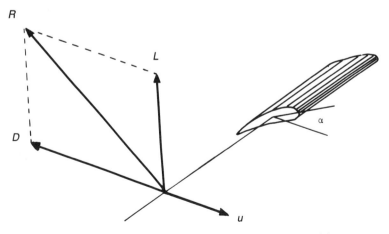

Figure 2 Lift (L) and drag (D) forces and vector sum (R) as generated by moving a hydrofoil with velocity u at a pitch angle α.

means that water that was at rest gets kinetic energy. Alexander and Goldspink (1977) show that the water affected by the hydrofoil can be approximated by the amount of water enclosed by a circle with diameter s, which is equal to the span of the hydrofoil and in this example approximated by the length of the lower arm (s = 0.25 m) and hands (s = 0.20 m). Per unit time an amount of water ¼ π ϱu s² passes through this circle (u is the velocity of the hydrofoil with respect to the water). Let the change of velocity of the water in the downward direction (opposite to L) be Δw. Then

$$L = \tfrac{1}{4} \pi s^2 \varrho\, u\, \Delta w \tag{18}$$

The rate at which this water gets kinetic energy then equals

$$P_{kl} = \tfrac{1}{8} \pi s^2 \varrho\, u\, \Delta w^2 \tag{19}$$

Elimination of Δw yields

$$P_{kl} = \frac{2 L^2}{\pi s^2 \varrho\, u} \tag{20}$$

This waste of power is called *induced power* (Alexander & Goldspink, 1977). An estimation of the optimal propelling efficiency in human arm propulsion is made by the (rather unrealistic) assumption that during the entire stroke, a technique is used that generates a resultant propulsion force with optimal forward direction (Figure 3). It is further assumed that this resultant force is generated at an optimal lift coefficient (hand at 40° to the direction of movement of the hand). At this optimal angle of attack, Schleihauf (1979) showed that the lift/drag ratio for the hand equals C_L/C_D = 1.75. Because no data concerning the lower arm have been published,

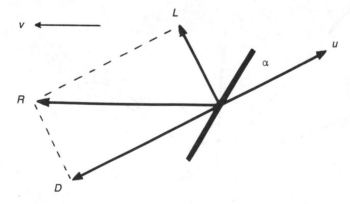

Figure 3 Lift and drag forces as in Figure 2, but with optimal orientation of R in the direction of the swimmer's speed v.

the drag coefficient and the lift/drag ratio for the lower arm must be estimated. Under the same angle of attack the drag coefficient is likely to be slightly lower than the value of $C_D = 0.8$ at $\alpha = 90°$ previously mentioned. At $\alpha = 40°$, C_D is estimated at 0.6. The lift/drag ratio will be smaller than for the hands. For sidewards movement this ratio will not exceed 1.0. However, for the sake of simplicity in the first approximation, a mean ratio for both hand and arm of 1.4 is taken in the calculation of e_p. The propelling efficiency is now calculated from

$$e_p = \frac{F_d v}{F_d v + P_{kD} + P_{kL}} \tag{21}$$

where P_{kD} and P_{kL} are the powers wasted to the creation of drag and lift, respectively, on both hand and forearm. This e_p can only be calculated if a relation is derived between v and u. This relation again is derived from the equality of the mean propulsive force, $R = \sqrt{D^2 + L^2}$, and the mean opposing force, F_d. Given all the assumptions, a value of $e_p = 0.56$ is calculated for this optimal technique.

It should be emphasized that this example shows that P_{kD} is 5 to 6 times larger than P_{kL}. This strengthens the fact that propulsive force is much more efficiently derived from lift forces than from drag forces. Unfortunately, one cannot create a lift force without a drag force, but obviously swimmers should use a technique that leads to a maximal lift/drag ratio.

These examples show that maximal speed in swimming is not only dependent on the magnitude of the propulsive forces. The best techniques seem to be those that lead to large lift/drag ratios. A last remarkable result of such a technique that can be deduced from these idealized examples concerns the stroke frequency. At a given forward swimming speed (v), the stroke frequency of a swimmer will to a large extent be determined by the backward component of the speed of hand and arm (u). At the given angle of attack and lift/drag ratio, the backward component of u in the second example is only half the value of u that was calculated for the straight backward technique. This means that at the same forward speed, the technique using lift and drag allows much longer strokes at a relatively low stroke frequency. Long strokes (large distance per stroke) seem to be a property of elite swimmers (Craig, Skehan, Pawelczyk, & Boomer, 1985; Toussaint et al., 1983).

Propelling Efficiency in Actual Swimming

The examples given are meant to illustrate the significance of the relation between swimming technique and propelling efficiency. In actual swimming techniques, the propelling efficiency will be lower than the predicted values because a continuing push-off force is hardly possible. From Equations 16 and 21 it can be learned that at the same mean propelling force the waste of energy is larger using shorter strokes with high peak forces than when longer strokes with a more uniform force pattern are employed. If, for example, the straight backward technique of the first example is performed with short intensive strokes that last a half cycle time (push-off force twice the mean opposing force), the propelling efficiency decreases to $e_p = 0.37$. A factor that also will affect the actual propelling efficiency is the fact that the arms do not only move in a position seen as optimal in hydrofoil dynamics. This holds for the angle of attack (Schleihauf, 1979) as well as for the position of the arm with respect to the direction of the movement of the arm. The actual maximal propelling efficiency of experienced swimmers, then, will be 0.50 or slightly higher for freestyle swimming and lower than 0.50 for other styles. Recently, the first experimental values of e_p during human front crawl swimming were obtained (Toussaint et al., 1988), which are in good agreement with the theoretical values mentioned here.

These values are lower than the maximal values reported for fish swimming. Webb (1971) reports values of $e_p = 0.15$ for swimming of trout at a slow speed (at 20% of maximal speed), up to $e_p = 0.80$ at maximal speed. At speeds of one body length per second (comparable with elite human swimmers), fish show values between 0.50 and 0.60 (Webb, 1971). For saithe and mackerel, Videler and Hess (1984) report maximum values of approximately $e_p = 0.75$. That fish can reach higher e_p values than humans is most likely due to their relatively larger surfaces of parts of the body (in particular the fins) that can contribute to propulsion in relation to the low C_{DB} values of their entire body. McMurray (1977) showed that the overall efficiency (product of mechanical efficiency and propelling efficiency) in human swimming is increased if swim fins are used.

As can be deduced from hydrofoil dynamics, however, not only the surfaces of fins determine propelling efficiency. In fact, long slender hydrofoils are much more efficient than hydrofoils with the same surface but shorter span and larger chord. This property is expressed by the so-called *aspect ratio*, the ratio between the span and the mean chord. The fastest marine animals appear to have sickle-shaped tailfins with a high aspect ratio (Lighthill, 1975). Probably due to the relatively high aspect ratio of lower arm and hand, humans can reach a propelling efficiency that is remarkably high for a creature not especially built for swimming.

Because swimming speed is a function of both an optimal mean propelling force and an optimal propelling efficiency, both of these aspects will have to be combined in a single model in order to predict an optimal swimming technique with respect to the transformation of energy liberation into speed.

References

Adrian, M.J. (1983). Biomechanics and mathematical modelling. In A.P. Hollander, P.A. Huijing, & G. de Groot (Eds.), *Biomechanics and medicine in swimming* (pp. 142-153). Champaign, IL: Human Kinetics.

Alexander, R.M. (1975). *Biomechanics*. London: Chapman and Hall.

Alexander, R.M., & Goldspink, G. (1977). *Mechanics and energetics of animal locomotion*. London: Chapman and Hall.

Barthels, K.M. (1979). The mechanism for body propulsion in swimming. In J. Terauds & E.W. Bedingfield (Eds.), *Swimming III* (pp. 45-54). Baltimore: University Park Press.

Bourgeois, M. (1983). A general computing method for obtaining biomechanical data in swimming. In A.P. Hollander, P.A. Huijing, & G. de Groot (Eds.), *Biomechanics and medicine in swimming* (pp. 96-102). Champaign, IL: Human Kinetics.

Clarys, J.P. (1979). Human morphology and hydrodynamics. In J. Terauds & E.W. Bedingfield (Eds.), *Swimming III* (pp. 3-41). Baltimore: University Park Press.

Counsilman, J.E. (1968). *The science of swimming*. Englewood Cliffs, NJ: Prentice-Hall.

Craig, A.B., Skehan, P.L., Pawelczyk, J.A., & Boomer, W.L. (1985). Velocity, stroke rate and distance per stroke during elite swimming competition. *Medicine and Science in Sports and Exercise*, **17**, 625-634.

Di Prampero, P.E., Cortili, G., Mognoni, P., & Saibene, F. (1979). Equation of motion of a cyclist. *Journal of Applied Physiology: Respiratory, Environmental, and Exercise Physiology*, **47**(1), 201-206.

Di Prampero, P.E., Pendergast, D.R., Wilson, C.W., & Rennie, D.W. (1974). Energetics of swimming in man. *Journal of Applied Physiology*, **37**, 1-5.

Hoecke, G., & Gruendler, G. (1975). Use of light trace photography in teaching swimming. In J.P. Clarys & J. Lewillie (Eds.), *Swimming II* (pp. 194-206). Baltimore: University Park Press.

Hoes, M.J.A.J.M., Binkhorst, R.A., Smeekes-Kuyl, A.E.M.C., & Vissers, A.C.A. (1968). Measurement of forces exerted on pedal and crank during work on a bicycle ergometer at different loads. *International Zeitschrift für Angewandte Physiologie*, **26**, 33-42.

Ingen Schenau, G.J. van, Boer, R.W. de, & Groot, G. de (in press). Biomechanics of speed skating. In C.L. Vaughan (Ed.), *Biomechanics of sport*. Boca Raton, FL: CRC Press.

Jensen, R.K.K., & Blanksby, B. (1975). A model for upper extremity forces during the underwater phase of the front crawl. In J.P. Clarys & J. Lewillie (Eds.), *Swimming II* (pp. 145-153). Baltimore: University Park Press.

Kent, M.R., & Atha, J. (1975). Intracycle kinematics and body configuration changes in the breaststroke. In J.P. Clarys & J. Lewillie (Eds.), *Swimming II* (pp. 125-129). Baltimore: University Park Press.

Lighthill, J. (1975). *Mathematical body fluid dynamics*. Philadelphia: Society for Industrial and Applied Mathematics.

McMurray, R.G. (1977). Comparative efficiencies of conventional and superswimfins designs. *Human Factors*, **19**(5), 495-501.

Miller, D.I. (1979). Modelling in biomechanics: An overview. *Medicine and Science in Sports and Exercise*, **11**(2), 115-122.

Plagenhoef, S. (1971). *Patterns of human motion, a cinematographic analysis.* Englewood Cliffs, NJ: Prentice-Hall.

Prampero, P.E. di, Cortili, G., Mognoni, P., & Saibene, F. (1979). Equation of motion of a cyclist. *Journal of Applied Physiology: Respiratory, Environmental, and Exercise Physiology, 47*(1), 201-206.

Pugh, L.G.C.E. (1970). The influence of wind resistance in running and walking and the mechanical efficiency of work against horizontal or vertical forces. *Journal of Physiology, 213,* 225-276.

Reischle, K. (1979). A kinematic investigation of movement patterns in swimming with photo-optical methods. In J. Terauds & E.W. Bedingfield (Eds.), *Swimming III* (pp. 127-136). Baltimore: University Park Press.

Schleihauf, R.E. (1979). A hydrodynamic analysis of swimming propulsion. In J. Terauds & E.W. Bedingfield (Eds.), *Swimming III* (pp. 70-109). Baltimore: University Park Press.

Schleihauf, R.E. (1983). Three-dimensional analysis of hand propulsion in the sprint front crawl stroke. In A.P. Hollander, P.A. Huijing, & G. de Groot (Eds.), *Biomechanics and medicine in swimming* (pp. 173-183). Champaign, IL: Human Kinetics.

Toussaint, H.M., Helm, F.C.T. van der, Elzerman, J.R., Hollander, A.P., Groot, G. de, & Ingen Schenau, G.J. van. (1983). A power balance applied to swimming. In A.P. Hollander, P.A. Huijing, & G. de Groot (Eds.), *Biomechanics and medicine in swimming* (pp. 165-172). Champaign, IL: Human Kinetics.

Toussaint, H.M., Groot, G. de, Savelberg, H.H.C.M., Vervoorn, K., Hollander, A.P., & Ingen Schenau, G.J. van. (in press). Active drag related to speed in male and female swimmers. *Journal of Biomechanics.*

Toussaint, H.M., Hollander, A.P., Groot, G. de, Ingen Schenau, G.J. van, Vervoorn, K., Best, H. de, Meulemans, A., & Schreurs, W. (1988). Measurement of efficiency in swimming man. In B.E. Ungerechts, K. Reischle, & K. Wilke (Eds.), *Swimming science V* (pp. 45-52). Champaign, IL: Human Kinetics.

Ungerechts, B. (1979). Optimizing propulsion in swimming by rotation of the hands. In J. Terauds & E.W. Bedingfield (Eds.), *Swimming III* (pp. 55-61). Baltimore: University Park Press.

Videler, J.J., & Hess, F. (1984). Fast continuous swimming of two pelagic predators, saithe (*pollachius virens*) and mackerel (*scomber scombrus*): A kinematic analysis. *Journal of Experimental Biology, 109,* 209-228.

Webb, P.W. (1971). The swimming energetics of trout II. Oxygen consumption and swimming efficiency. *Journal of Experimental Biology. 55,* 521-540.

Webb, P.W. (1975). Hydrodynamics and energetics of fish propulsion. *Bulletin of the Fishing Research Board of Canada, 190,* 1-159.

Williams, K.R. (1985). The relationship between mechanical and physiological energy estimates. *Medicine and Science in Sports and Exercise, 17,* 317-325.

Williams, K.R., & Cavanagh, P.R. (1983). A model for the calculation of mechanical power during distance running. *Journal of Biomechanics, 26,* 115-128.

Wu, T.Y.T., Brohaw, C.J., & Brenner, C. (1975). *Swimming and flying in nature.* New York: Plenum Press.

Active Drag Related to Body Dimensions

Peter A. Huijing
Huub M. Toussaint
Rick Mackay
Kees Vervoorn
Jan Pieter Clarys
Gert de Groot
A. Peter Hollander

During this century, a great deal of attention has been given to the presupposed relationship between body shape and dimensions and hydrodynamic resistance (Alley, 1949; Amar, 1920; Clarys, 1976, 1979; Clarys, Jiskoot, Rijken, & Brouwer, 1974; Counsilman, 1951; Gadd, 1963; Jaeger, 1937; Jurina, 1972, 1974; Karpovich, 1933; Klein, 1939; Liljestrand & Stensstrom, 1919; Lopin, 1947; Miyashita & Tsunoda, 1978; Onoprienko, 1967; Safarian, 1968; Schramm, 1960, 1961; Tews, 1941; Tilborg, Daly, & Persijn, 1983; Zaciorski & Safarian, 1972). However, only Clarys (1976, 1979) related drag for actively swimming subjects (active drag) to anthropometric variables. Contrary to expectations, Clarys (1976, 1979) found only few correlations between active drag and anthropometric variables, which forced him to conclude that the shape of the human body has hardly any influence on active drag and that other factors are therefore more important.

Given the fact that some argue that drag force is directly proportional to the product of velocity squared and a constant of proportionality, which among other things is dependent on the (projected) area of the body exposed to flow (Rouse, 1946), one would expect at least some relationship between this variable and drag. The development of a new method of determining active drag (MAD system) (Hollander et al., 1986) warranted a reevaluation of this relationship, which was the aim of the present work.

Methods

Active Drag

A total of 17 well-trained male swimmers participated in this study as subjects. In a 25-m pool they swam, with a pull buoy supporting their legs, minimally six lanes at a variety of speeds, while making use of a system designed to measure active drag (MAD). This system is described

31

extensively elsewhere (Hollander et al., 1986). Basically, it provides the swimmer during each stroke with the opportunity to push off with the hand against a fixed pad rather than against accelerating water (i.e., propelling efficiency = 1). As the pads are connected to a force transducer, time history of propelling force exertion can be recorded. The mean propelling force is equal to the mean drag force if velocity of swimming may be assumed to be constant. The distance between pads was 1.35 m, and they were fixed 0.8 m below the water surface, which, after getting habituated to swimming on the system, caused the swimmers no apparent difficulty. The force signal was low-pass filtered (Krohnhite, 30 Hz, 21 db/octave), digitized (sampling frequency 100/Hz) real time, and stored using an Apple 2E microcomputer. Mean drag was calculated from the time integral and exertion time. Mean drag for each swimming speed was calculated by averaging mean drag for the middle 13 strokes of a lane. Swimming speed was calculated for these strokes as well. Individual swimming speed drag data were least square fitted with the following function:

$$F = A \cdot v^2 \tag{1}$$

where F represents drag, v swimming speed, and A the constant of proportionality, which was used as characterizing variable for the speed drag relationship. The drag coefficient was calculated for a speed of 1.25 m/s according to:

$$C_d = \frac{F}{\frac{1}{2} \varrho \, v^2 A_p}$$

where ϱ represents the density of water and A_p the body cross-sectional area exposed to flow.

Anthropometry

The following anthropometric variables were measured directly on the body: body height and weight, biacromial distance, arm length (i.e., distance between acromion and most distal part of the hand), upper and lower arm lengths (i.e., distance between acromion and caput radii, distance from caput radii to processus styloideus radii, respectively), hand length (i.e., distance from processus styloideus radii to most distal part of the hand), leg length (i.e., height of trochanter major above ground), upper and lower leg lengths (i.e., distance from trochanter major to lateral knee cleft, lateral knee cleft to most saggital point malleolus lateralis, respectively), foot length (i.e., distance from dorsal aspect of calcaneus to most distal part of foot), thorax depth both at maximal inspiratory and expiratory positions (i.e., horizontal distance from sternal angle to the spinous process), and maximal upper arm and upper leg circumferences.

From photographs, maximal body cross-sectional area (Clarys, 1978) was determined in three positions: with arms along the body (APAL), and with one (AP1AH) and two arms (AP2AH) extended above the head. Of these, AP2AH was used as an estimate of A_p. From these variables length/breadth ratio (L/B), length/depth ratio (L/D), and breadth/depth ratio (B/D) as well as the length/thickness ratio $(L^2/AP2AH)$ were calculated according to Clarys (1979).

Statistics

Pearson's product-moment coefficient of correlation was calculated for anthropometric variables and active drag as well as for the relationships between different anthropometric variables.

Results

A typical example of the relationship of swimming speed to active drag is shown in Figure 1. Table 1 shows relevant results of correlation calculations. Note the relatively high and significant coefficients of correlation between projected body area measurements and proportionality coefficient A (Equation 1) as well as the lower but significant coefficient of correlation between body height and this variable. The almost total absence of significant coefficients of correlation between drag coefficient (C_d) and anthropometric variables is also noteworthy.

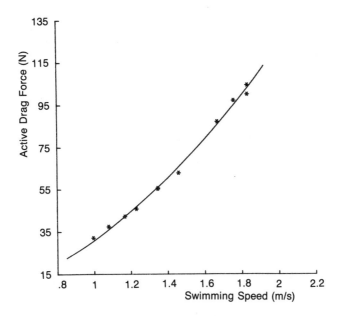

Figure 1   The relationship of swimming speed to active drag.

Table 1   Coefficients of Correlation Between Body Dimensions and Drag Variables

Variables	C_d	A	AP1H	AP2H
Body weight	0.29	0.82*	0.87*	0.89*
Body height	0.10	0.55*	0.51*	0.66*
Biacromial distance	−0.04	−0.06	0.13	−0.06
Bitrochanter distance	0.49*	0.74*	0.65*	0.65*
Arm length	0.05	0.54*	0.52*	0.67*
Upper arm length	0.02	0.36	0.33	0.47
Lower arm length	−0.22	0.26	0.38	0.50*
Hand length	−0.21	0.23	0.32	0.44
Leg length	0.13	0.57*	0.49*	0.65*
Upper leg length	0.13	0.46	0.34	0.50*
Lower leg length	0.14	0.38	0.27	0.40
Foot length	−0.21	0.33	0.39	0.57*
Thorax depth inspiration	0.21	0.21	0.22	0.15
Thorax depth expiration	0.17	0.20	0.38	0.15
Upper arm circumference	0.13	0.49*	0.63*	0.57*
Upper leg circumference	0.25	0.74*	0.86*	0.82*
Body surface	0.29	0.82*	0.87*	0.89*
Skinfolds	0.42	0.41	0.41	0.27
$L^2/\text{AP2AH}$	−0.18	−0.55*	−0.63*	−0.61*
L/B	−0.39	−0.48	−0.49*	−0.36
L/D	−0.10	0.22	0.17	0.35
B/D	0.11	0.45	0.44	0.51*
APAL	0.31	0.74*	0.85*	0.77*
AP1AH	0.21	0.84*	1.00*	0.91*
AP2AH	0.22	0.87*	0.91*	1.00*

*$p \leqslant .05$.

A number of other anthropometric variables yield rather high and significant coefficients when correlated with proportionality coefficient (A). This is indicative of some relationship between these variables and active drag as measured with the MAD system. When a significant coefficient of correlation was found between anthropometric variables and active drag, it was always accompanied by significant coefficients of correlation between the one- and two-handed versions of the projected body area measurements. Not only does this relationship exist qualitatively but also quantitatively: Very high and significant coefficients of correlation were found between active drag and anthropometric variables, on the one hand, and the value of coefficients of correlation between anthropometric variables and both the one-handed and two-handed versions of projected body area, on the other hand (i.e., Table 1, Column 2 vs. Columns 3 and 4, $r = .97$ and $r = .96$, respectively).

Discussion

It should be kept in mind that the methods employed in the present study (i.e., fitting swimming speed and drag data with a quadratic function and using proportionality coefficient A as a variable for active drag) are sensitive for skin friction as well as viscous pressure drag (Miller, 1975). No conclusions can be drawn regarding wave drag (Miller, 1975) using the methods employed, even though the wave drag is included in the measurements performed in this study.

The most striking result of the present work was the fact that, in contrast with Clarys (1976, 1979), significant correlations were shown to exist between selected anthropometric variables and a variable characterizing drag of the actively propelling swimmer.

Especially notable were the high degree of correlation of maximal body cross-section with drag as well as the lower but significant correlation between body height and drag found in the present study. Both relationships are known from ship hydrodynamics (midship cross-sectional area and ship length) (Clarys, 1979; Rawson & Tupper, 1976) but could previously not be shown to exist for swimmers (Clarys, 1976, 1979). A very likely reason for this discrepancy in results was the considerable difference in magnitude of active drag found. Clarys (1976) reported values of approximately 150 N, whereas in the present study values of approximately 70 N were found at a swimming speed of approximately 1.5 m/s (see also Hollander et al., 1986). In the present study, active drag was actually measured using the MAD system, whereas Clarys (1976) obtained estimates of this variable by manual extrapolation. The MAD results for active drag are of the same order of magnitude as those calculated by Schleihauf, Gray, and DeRose (1983) for natural swimming. A difference in magnitude of active drag by itself cannot explain the lack of correlation reported by Clarys (1976); also, no systematic difference should exist between Clarys's drag estimates and the MAD results of this study.

In addition to a high degree of correlation between maximal body cross-section and active drag, significiant correlations were also found between several other anthropometric variables and drag. As all these variables showing such correlations correlate with maximal body cross-section as well, these relationships likely contribute heavily to the findings. However, a direct relationship between these anthropometric variables and active drag, as is most likely the case for body height (see also Rawson & Tupper, 1976, for a ship hydrodynamics parallel) cannot be excluded on the basis of the present results.

References

Alley, L.E. (1949). *An analysis of resistance and propulsion in swimming the crawl stroke.* Unpublished doctoral dissertation, University of Iowa, Iowa City.

Amar, J., (1920). *The human motor*. London: Routledge and Sons.

Clarys, J.P. (1976). *Onderzoek naar de hydrodynamische en morfologische aspekten van het menselijk lichaam*. [Investigation into hydrodynamic and morphological aspects of the human body] . Unpublished doctoral dissertation, Vrije Universiteit, Brussels.

Clarys, J.P. (1979). Human morphology and hydrodynamics. In J. Terauds & E.W. Bedingfield (Eds.), *Swimming III* (pp. 3-41). Baltimore: University Park Press.

Clarys, J.P., Jiskoot, J., Rijken, H., & Brouwer, P.J. (1974). In R.C. Nelson & C.A. Morehouse (Eds.), *Biomechanics IV*, (pp. 187-196). Baltimore: University Park Press.

Counsilman, J.E. (1951). *An analysis of the application of force in two types of crawl strokes*. Unpublished doctoral dissertation, University of Iowa, Iowa City.

Gadd, G.E. (1963). The hydrodynamics of swimming. *New Scientist*, **19**, 483-485.

Hollander, A.P., Groot, G. de, Ingen Schenau, G.J. van, Toussaint, H.M., Best, H. de, Peeters, W., Meulemans, A., & Schreurs, A.W. (1986). Measurement of active drag during crawl arm stroke swimming. *Journal of Sport Science*, **4**, 21-30.

Jaeger, L.D. (1937). *Resistance of water as limiting factor of speed in swimming*. Unpublished master's thesis, University of Iowa, Iowa City.

Jurina, K. (1972). Comparative study of fish and man. *Theorie Praxe Telesne Vychovy*, **20**, 161-166.

Karpovich, P. (1933). Water resistance in swimming. *Research Quarterly*, **4**, 21-28.

Klein, W.C. (1939). *Test for the prediction of body resistance in water*. Unpublished master's thesis, University of Iowa, Iowa City.

Liljestrand, G., & Stensstrom, N. (1919). Studien über die Physiologie des Schwimmens [Studies on the physiology of swimming]. *Scandinavian Archives of Physiology*, **39**, 1-63.

Lopin, V. (1947). *A diagnostic test for speed swimming the crawl stroke*. Unpublished master's thesis, University of Iowa, Iowa City.

Miller, D.I. (1975). Biomechanics of swimming. *Exercise and Sport Science Review*, **3**, 219-248.

Miyashita, M., & Tsunoda, R. (1978). Water resistance in relation to body size. In B. Eriksson & B. Furberg (Eds.), *Swimming medicine IV* (pp. 395-401). Baltimore: University Park Press.

Onoprienko, B.I. (1967). Influence of hydrodynamic data on the hydrodynamics of swimmers. *Theory and Practice in Physical Education USSR*, **4**, 842-847.

Rawson, K.J., & Tupper, E.C. (1976). *Basic ship theory: Vol. 2*. London: Longman.

Safarian, I.G. (1968). Hydrodynamics characteristics of the crawl. *Theory and Practice in Physical Education USSR, 11*, 18-21.

Rouse, H. (1946). *Elementary mechanics of fluids*. New York: Dover.

Schleihauf, R.E., Gray, L., & DeRose, J. (1983). Three-dimensional analysis of hand propulsion in the sprint front crawl stroke. In A.P. Hollander, P.A. Huijing, & G. de Groot (Eds.), *Biomechanics and medicine in swimming* (pp. 173-183). Champaign, IL: Human Kinetics.

Schramm, E. (1960). Die Abhangigkeit der Leistungen im Kraulschwimmen vom Kraft-Widerstand Verhaltnis. [The dependence of performance in the crawl stroke on the strength/resistance ratio]. *Wissischaft Zeitschrift der Deutsche Hochschule Korperkultur Leipzig, 3*, 161-180.

Tews, R.W.J. (1941). *The relationship of propulsive force and external resistance to speed in swimming*. Unpublished master's thesis, University of Iowa, Iowa City.

Tilborg, L. van, Daly, D., & Persijn, U. (1983). The influence of some somatic factors on passive drag, gravity and buoyancy forces in competitive swimmers. In A.P. Hollander, P.A. Huijing, & G. de Groot (Eds.), *Biomechanics and medicine in swimming* (pp. 204-217). Champaign, IL: Human Kinetics.

Zaciorski, V.M., & Safarian, I.G. (1972). Untersuchungen von Factoren zur Bestimmung der maximalen Geschwindigkeit im Freistillschwimmen [Investigations on factors determining maximal speed in freestyle swimming]. *Theorie und Praxis in Korperkultur, 8*, 695-709.

Contribution of the Legs to Propulsion in Front Crawl Swimming

A. Peter Hollander
Gert de Groot
Gerrit Jan van Ingen Schenau
Roel Kahman
Huub M. Toussaint

Because swimming is performed with both arms and legs, the question is often raised, to what extent do the arms or legs contribute to swimming speed? Although it is generally accepted that in front crawl swimming a greater part of the propulsion results from the arm stroke (Adrian, Singh, & Karpovich, 1966; Holmer, 1972), many instructors still spend a lot of time in drilling the leg kick of the crawl stroke, indicating leg kicking's relative importance at least during sprint swimming.

Evidence for the contribution of leg action to swimming speed is derived from indirect methods using towing (Counsilman, 1968) or measuring oxygen consumption (Holmer, 1974) or the speed that can be achieved by swimming with arms or legs only (Bucher, 1975; Karpovich, 1935). From these kinds of experiments the power delivered by the arms while swimming arm stroke only cannot be assumed to be the same as when the legs are additionally involved in propelling the body.

In the present study, the system to measure active drag (MAD system) (Hollander et al., 1986) was used to study the contribution of the legs to propulsion in front crawl swimming and to discover whether the power delivered by the arms is the same in swimming with and without leg kicking.

Methods

The subjects in this study were 7 female and 11 male swimmers of national and Olympic level. Mean propulsive forces of the arms were obtained by using the MAD system during a front crawl-like activity. The MAD system (Hollander et al., 1986) consists of a variable number of push-off pads mounted on a 23 m long horizontal rod attached via a computer-linked force transducer to the wall of a swiming pool, 0.8 m below the water surface.

Propelling forces of the arms in front crawl swimming can be measured during each stroke. At a constant speed and using the arms only, the mean propelling force equals total drag at any given speed. Each subject was requested to swim 10 lanes at 10 different velocities between 1.0 and 2.0 m · s⁻¹. In order to keep the body in a horizontal position and to prevent leg kicking, the legs were fixed together and supported by a pull buoy. From these 10 lanes the individual relationship between drag (F_d) and speed (v) was calculated for each subject and expressed as values for a and n in

$$F_d = a \cdot v^n \tag{1}$$

At maximal speed during arm swimming over 25 m, the power delivered by the arms (P_a) was calculated according to

$$P_a = F_d \cdot v_a \tag{2}$$

The subjects also performed one lane at maximal speed (v_{a+l}) swimming the whole stroke on the MAD system. The power produced by the arms (P_a') was calculated:

$$P_a' = F_p \cdot v_{a+l} \tag{3}$$

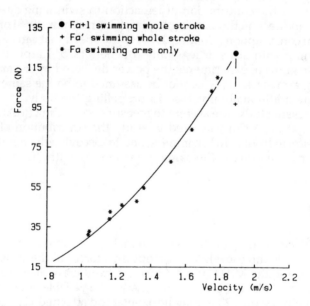

Figure 1 From 11 observations (*) the relation between swimming speed and force was calculated. The force necessary to swim at maximal speed (●) was calculated by extrapolation. The measured arm force (+) at maximal swimming speed using both arms and legs is also indicated.

Using the individual relation (Equation 1), drag during swimming the whole stroke at maximal speed (v_{a+l}) was calculated. The total effective power produced by the arms and legs together (P_{a+l}) at speed v_{a+l} was calculated (see Figure 1) according to Equation 2. The effective power delivered by the legs (P_l) was calculated by subtraction:

$$P_l = P_{a+l} - P_a'$$ (4)

Results

Individual values for drag, swimming speed, and the relation between these two variables for 1 subject are given in Figure 1. The values for a, n, v_a, v_{a+l}, P_a', P_{a+l}, and P_l are given in Table 1. The mean value of maximal swimming speed on the MAD system using arms only (v_a) was 1.72 m • s^{-1} (ranging from 1.51 to 1.91 m • s^{-1}). Swimming the whole stroke, the mean speed increased 0.07 m • s^{-1} or 4% (ranging from -0.02 to 0.17 m • s^{-1}).

The mean value for the effective power of leg kicking at maximal speed (P_l) was 14.6 W or 11.7% (ranging from -9.8 to 37.8 W). Hence, the relative contribution of the effective power delivered by the legs relative to

Table 1 Values for Variables for Individual Subjects

Subject	Gender	a	n	v_a	v_{a+l}	P_a	P_a'	P_{a+l}	$dP = P_l$
1	m	18.8	2.40	1.83	1.90	153.5	142.2	167.4	13.9
2	m	16.3	2.47	1.72	1.83	108.0	110.9	133.0	25.0
3	m	22.6	1.83	1.78	1.95	121.1	137.9	149.6	28.5
4	m	20.9	2.38	1.82	1.94	163.0	174.5	196.1	33.1
5	m	17.8	2.46	1.78	1.86	132.4	134.2	153.2	20.8
6	m	23.8	2.01	1.75	1.88	132.9	142.7	158.9	26.0
7	m	26.0	2.31	1.68	1.69	142.4	110.5	148.6	6.2
8	m	20.3	2.41	1.84	1.82	166.3	140.8	156.5	-9.8
9	m	22.5	2.09	1.88	1.85	154.5	142.7	151.2	-3.3
10	m	26.6	2.07	1.91	1.92	197.2	189.8	196.9	-0.3
11	m	22.5	2.41	1.84	1.90	186.5	161.6	200.7	14.2
12	f	26.0	1.54	1.57	1.65	83.4	85.0	93.2	9.8
13	f	25.2	1.49	1.56	1.62	73.6	80.4	83.1	9.5
14	f	23.1	2.08	1.55	1.64	90.7	96.7	104.6	13.9
15	f	22.5	2.20	1.64	1.66	109.1	96.7	113.9	4.8
16	f	15.2	2.74	1.67	1.81	102.4	99.5	139.5	37.1
17	f	20.6	2.11	1.70	1.82	109.2	104.8	133.0	23.8
18	f	19.6	1.95	1.51	1.59	67.6	57.4	77.8	10.2
Mean				1.72	1.79	127.4	122.7	134.7	14.6

total power to overcome drag ranged from -6 to 27%. Mean power output using the arms only (P_a) was 127.4 $\pm$ 37.8 W, whereas the power output of the arms during swimming the whole stroke (P_a') was 122.7 $\pm$ 34.7 W.

Discussion

In this study, the contribution of the legs to propulsion in swimming was studied. The total power output of the legs will actually be much higher than the figures presented in Table 1 because the propelling efficiency of the legs will be substantially lower than 1.0 (Groot & Ingen Schenau, 1987). This is a consequence of the fact that only part of the power delivered by the body is used to overcome drag. Another part of the power produced is lost by accelerating water masses (Toussaint et al., 1983; Groot & Ingen Schenau, 1988). Using the MAD system and swimming with arms only, no energy was lost in accelerating water masses: The swimmer was pulling and pushing against fixed pads. As a result, a somewhat higher speed was attained in swimming using the MAD system than during real arm swimming. Hence, the increase in both speed and effective power due to leg kicking may be underestimated. In the present experiments, the result of adding the leg kick was increased swimming speed, although the difference was rather small (approximately 4%). Power output of the arms was thus unaffected by the addition of leg kicking when swimming at maximal speed.

Further, because in sprint swimming performance faces no serious central limitations, the addition of leg kicking may make a useful albeit small contribution to power output. However, in longer distance events, the relatively low propelling efficiency of leg compared with arm work may imply that the addition of leg work may be counterproductive in performance terms if there are central limitations (e.g., oxygen transport) on power production.

References

Adrian, M.J., Singh, M., & Karpovich, P.V. (1966). Energy cost of leg kick, arm stroke, and the whole crawl stroke. *Journal of Applied Physiology, 21*, 1763-1766.

Bucher, W. (1975). The influence of leg kick and the arm stroke on the total speed during the crawl stroke. In J.P. Clarys & L. Lewillie (Eds.), *Swimming II* (pp. 180-187). Baltimore: University Park Press.

Counsilman, J. (1968). *The science of swimming.* Englewood Cliffs, NJ: Prentice-Hall.

Groot, G. de, & Ingen Schenau, G.J. van. (1988). Fundamental mechanics applied to swimming: Technique and propelling efficiency. In B.E. Ungerechts, K. Reischle, & K. Wilke (Eds.), *Swimming science V* (pp. 17-29). Champaign, IL: Human Kinetics.

Hollander, A.P., Groot, G. de, Ingen Schenau, G.J. van, Toussaint, H.M., Best, H. de, Peeters, W., Meulemans, A., & Schreurs, A.W., (1986). Measurement of active drag during crawl arm stroke swimming. *Journal of Sports Science, 4,* 21-30.

Holmer, I. (1972). Oxygen uptake during swimming in man. *Journal of Applied Physiology, 33,* 502-509.

Holmer, I. (1974). Energy cost of arm stroke, leg kick, and the whole stroke in competitive swimming. *European Journal of Applied Physiology, 33,* 105-118.

Karpovich, P.V. (1935). Analysis of the propelling force in the crawl stroke. *Research Quarterly, 6,* 49-58.

Measurement of Efficiency in Swimming Man

Huub M. Toussaint
A. Peter Hollander
Gert de Groot
Gerrit Jan van Ingen Schenau
Kees Vervoorn
Henk de Best
Ton Meulemans
Willem Schreurs

In some competitive sports like rowing and swimming, an interesting phenomenon occurs in the generation of the propulsive force. That is, the push-off cannot be made against a fixed object but against water, which will give way. The propelling force is thus generated by giving masses (M) of water a velocity change (Δv). These water masses acquire a kinetic energy change ($\frac{1}{2} M \cdot \Delta v^2$) and, as a result, consume part of the external power the swimmer delivers.

The energetic consequences of this phenomenon have been studied more extensively in the field of animal locomotion, for example, in fish (Webb, 1971). In human swimming, however, this power loss in the generation of the propulsive force has been overlooked. When calculating efficiency of swimming humans, only the ratio of power needed to overcome drag and the power equivalent of the measured oxygen uptake was taken into consideration (Adrian, Singh, & Karpovich, 1966; Holmer, 1972; Pendergast, Di Prampero, Craig, Wilson, & Rennie, 1973; Di Prampero, Pendergast, Wilson, & Rennie, 1974). In this study, the power that is lost to the water when generating propulsive forces during swimming is estimated. This power loss is then taken into account when the propelling efficiency (e_p) is defined and calculated as the power needed to overcome drag (P_d) divided by the total external power (P_o), that is, power needed to overcome drag and power lost in the generation of the propulsive force (P_k) (Groot & Ingen Schenau, 1987; Toussaint et al., 1983):

$$e_p = P_d/(P_d + P_k)$$

Methods

To measure power needed to overcome drag alone (P_d) and to prevent power losses due to kinetic energy flow to the water ($P_k = 0$), the subjects swam along a series of push-off pads attached to a 23-m long horizontal rod mounted 0.8 m below the water surface in a 25-m pool. A second rod with push-off pads was placed 1.25 m beside the first, enabling the subject to swim in both directions (see Figure 1). A detailed description of this so-called MAD system is given by Hollander et al. (1986). This enabled the swimmer to push off from fixed points along the length of the pool. At one end of the pool, the rod was connected to a force transducer linked to an on-line computer using a 12-bit analog-to-digital converter (ADC) operating at a sample frequency of 100 Hz. This enabled the propelling force at each pad to be measured.

At constant swimming speed, the mean propulsive force equals the mean opposing drag force. As the time needed to cover the distance between the first and last pad was measured, average velocity could be calculated. The subject was instructed to swim 10 lengths over the MAD system at different but constant speeds, once with and once without a mouthpiece. In this way, two drag-velocity curves were constructed (see Figure 2). For a more detailed description of the construction of drag-velocity curves readers are referred to Huijing et al. (1988).

When measuring $\dot{V}O_2$ during MAD swimming, power is the product of force times velocity, and thus P_d can be calculated for a known velocity using the drag velocity curve (see Figure 2). Because no power is lost to the water ($P_k = 0$) using the fixed push-off pads (MAD system), oxygen uptake ($\dot{V}O_2$) reflects the power needed to overcome drag alone (P_d), whereas the $\dot{V}O_2$ of swimming free will reflect the total power required (i.e., $P_d + P_k$). Thus, at a specific swimming velocity, the power loss to the water can be calculated from the difference in the power equivalence of the oxygen uptake according to

$$P_k = (P\dot{v}O_{2free} - P\dot{v}O_{2MAD}) \cdot e_m$$

where $P\dot{v}O_2$ equals the power equivalence of the oxygen uptake and e_m the mechanical efficiency.

The power needed to overcome drag (P_d) while swimming the MAD system is measured together with the oxygen uptake repetitively at different constant velocities. The mechanical efficiency (e_m) is estimated by the slope of the regression line between P_d and the power equivalence of the oxygen uptake ($P\dot{v}O_{2MAD}$).

Mechanical power equivalence (Watts) for oxygen uptake (l/min) was estimated using the formula

$$P\dot{v}O_2 = \frac{1}{60} \cdot \dot{V}O_2 \cdot 10^3 \cdot (4.2 \cdot (4.07 + RER))$$

where RER equals the respiratory exchange ratio.

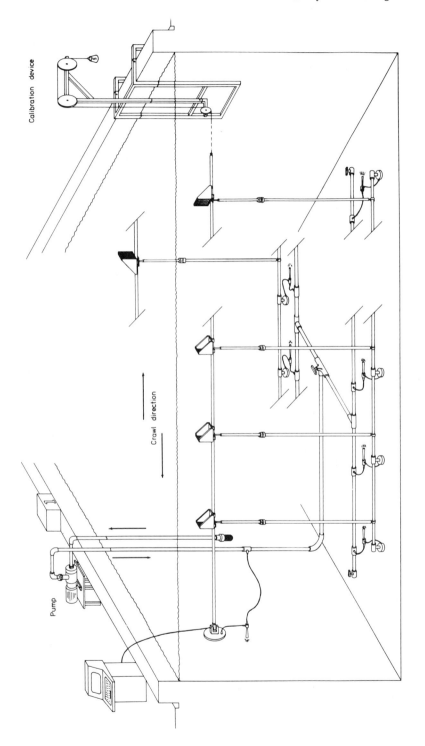

Figure 1 Diagram of the MAD system used in this study.

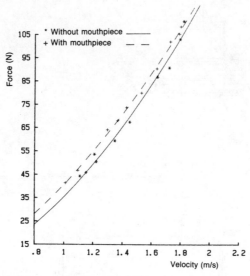

Figure 2 Drag-velocity curve showing the difference in drag swimming with and without mouthpiece.

To measure the power lost to the water (P_k) the subject swam 400 m at a submaximal constant velocity using arms alone on two separate trials: once free and once using the push-off pads. Four Douglas bag collections were made over the last 200 m by which time a steady state response had been attained. Oxygen uptake was assumed to reflect total energy requirement at the submaximal exercise levels studied. It was calculated from O_2 and CO_2 concentration, measured with a Mijnhardt oxylyzer (UG64) and a Mijnhardt capnolyzer (UG55), and the volume of the expired air was measured with a dry gas meter. In this way, P_d and P_k could be measured and the propelling efficiency (e_p) calculated from the formula:

$$e_p = P_d/(P_d + P_k).$$

The estimation of mechanical efficiency in one subject required three to four measurements of P_d and $\dot{V}O_2$ swimming 400 m on the MAD system. Consequently, the measurements were done on separate days to prevent subjects from becoming fatigued.

Results

Full data on one subject (male, age 25 years, weight 91 kg, height 1.92 m, Olympic participant in 1976, 1980, 1984) are presented. As power equals force times velocity and drag force is dependent on the square of velocity, power in swimming relates directly to the cube of swimming velocity.

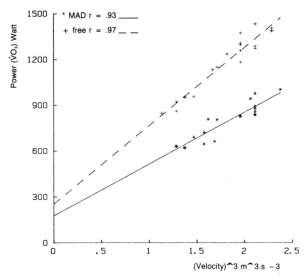

Figure 3 Power equivalence calculated from oxygen uptake data in relation to the cube of swimming velocity.

The power equivalences calculated from oxygen uptake data are therefore presented in relation to v^3 (see Figure 3).

Both in MAD and free swimming, $P\dot{v}o_2$ was highly correlated with v^3 ($r = .92$, $r = .97$, respectively). The relationship in MAD swimming is given by:

$$P\dot{v}o_{2MAD} = 326.9\ v^3 + 195$$

By extrapolation this suggests an oxygen uptake at zero velocity having a power equivalence of 195 W, which corresponds well with a value measured with the subject floating at rest of 169 W. P_d was calculated using the drag-velocity curve (with mouthpiece) presented in Figure 2. Figure 2 shows that drag was hardly influenced by the mouthpiece used in these experiments to measure oxygen uptake.

Mechanical efficiency was calculated from the regression of:

$$P\dot{v}o_{2MAD}\text{ on }P_d: (P_d = 0.089 \cdot P\dot{v}o_{2MAD} - 2.89,\ r = .85)$$

resulting in an e_m of 8.9%. Values for the respiratory exchange ratio ranged from 0.71 to 0.95 with a mean of 0.82. From values for P_d and P_k the propelling efficiency was calculated. The propelling efficiency was to some extent dependent on swimming velocity ($r = -.84$, $p \leqslant .01$, Figure 4). A mean propelling efficiency of 58% was obtained at an intermediate swimming velocity of 1.2 m/s.

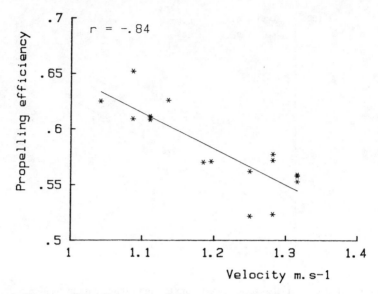

Figure 4   The propelling efficiency in relation to swimming velocity.

Discussion

These results closely agreed with the values for propelling efficiency calculated using the model presented by Groot and Ingen Schenau (1988). The obtained value for the mechanical efficiency (9%) seems to be rather low compared to values reported, for example, in arm cranking (15%; Toussaint et al., 1983). In part, this may be due to the extra work the respiratory muscles must do in order to overcome the slightly higher hydrostatic pressure on the lungs. It might also result from the power that the subject must deliver in making turns at the end of the pool, as well as the energy cost of the recovery phase in swimming where the arm must be supported against gravity. However, because these conditions exist in both MAD and free swimming and because there is close similarity between EMG signals (Clarys et al., 1988) in both forms of swimming, it seems reasonable to assume that the mechanical efficiency will also be the same and thus can be used in the calculation of P_k. In the literature, data on overall efficiency (the product of mechanical and propelling efficiency) are presented. The product of the presented values for e_p and e_m is 5.4%. This is comparable to the values reported by Holmer (1972) and Adrian et al. (1966), although efficiency is to some extent dependent on velocity—a finding previously reported by Klissouras (1968) for the dolphin stroke over a comparable velocity range.

In competitive swimming, the ability to swim faster arises from the capacity to reduce drag (F_d), to increase the propelling force (F_p), and to perform at a high propelling efficiency (e_p). The significance of the approach presented here is that contrary to expectation no correlation appears to exist between drag and swimming performance (Hollander et al., 1986) or between maximal oxygen uptake and maximal swimming performance (Holmer, 1983; Toussaint et al., 1983). However, there is unanimous agreement that proficient swimmers are much more economical in their oxygen uptake than less skilled swimmers (Anderson, 1960; Holmer, 1972; Karpovich & Millman, 1944). This suggests that propelling efficiency is a very important performance-determining factor.

Acknowledgments

We want to thank our students Anita Beelen, Anne Rodenburg, Wilma Knops, Thomas Janssen, and Mark Kluft for their cooperation in the process of data collection and Tony Sargeant and Bodo Ungerechts for critically reviewing this manuscript.

References

Adrian, M.J., Singh, M., & Karpovich, P.V. (1966). Energy cost of leg kick, arm stroke, and whole crawl stroke. *Journal of Applied Physiology*, **21**, 1763-1766.

Andersen, K.L. (1960). Energy cost of swimming. *Acta Chirurgica Scandinavica (Suppl.)*, **253**, 169-174.

Clarys, J.P., Toussaint, H.M., Bollens, E., Vaes, W., Huijing, P.A., Groot, G. de, Hollander, A.P., & Cabri, J. (1988). Muscular specificity and intensity in swimming against a mechanical resistance (surface EMG in MAD-and free swimming). In B.E. Ungerechts, K. Reischle, & K. Wilke (Eds.), *Swimming science V* (pp. 191-199). Champaign, IL: Human Kinetics.

Di Prampero, P.E., Pendergast, D.R., Wilson, D.R., & Rennie, D.W. (1974). Energetics of swimming in man. *Journal of Applied Physiology*, **37**, 1-5.

Groot, G. de, & Ingen Schenau G.J. van. (1988). Fundamental mechanics applied to swimming. In B.E. Ungerechts, K. Reischle, & K. Wilke (Eds.), *Swimming science V* (pp. 17-29). Champaign, IL: Human Kinetics.

Hollander, A.P., Groot, G. de, Ingen Schenau, G.J. van, Toussaint, H.M., Best, H. de, Peeters, W., Meulemans, A., & Schreurs, A.W. (1986). Measurement of active drag forces during swimming. *Journal of Sport Sciences*, **4**, 21-30.

Hollander, A.P., Toussaint, H.M., Groot, G. de, & Ingen Schenau, G.J. van. (1985). Active drag and swimming performance. *New Zealand Journal of Sports Medicine*, **13**, 110-113.

Holmer, I. (1972). Oxygen uptake during swimming in man. *Journal of Applied Physiology*, **33**, 502-509.

Holmer, I. (1983). Energetics and mechanical work in swimming. In A.P. Hollander, P.A. Huijing, & G. de Groot (Eds.), *Biomechanics and medicine in swimming* (pp. 154-164). Champaign, IL: Human Kinetics.

Huijing, P.A., Toussaint, H.M., Mackay, R., Vervoorn, K., Clarys, J.P., Groot, G. de, & Hollander, A.P. (1988). In B.E. Ungerechts, K. Reischle, & K. Wilke (Eds.), *Swimming science V* (pp. 31-37). Champaign, IL: Human Kinetics.

Karpovich, P.V., & Millman, N. (1944). Energy expenditure in swimming. *American Journal of Physiology, 142*, 140-144.

Klissouras, V. (1968). Energy metabolism in swimming the dolphin stroke. *Internationale Zeitung für angewendte Physiologie und einschlislich Arbeitsphysiologie, 25*, 142-150.

Pendergast, D.R., Di Prampero, P.E., Craig, A.B., Wilson, D.R., & Rennie, D.W. (1977). Quantitative analysis of front crawl in men and women. *Journal of Applied Physiology, 43*, 475-479.

Toussaint, H.M., Helm, F.C.T. van der, Elzerman, J.R., Hollander, A.P., Groot, G. de, Ingen Schenau, G.J. van. (1983). A power balance applied to swimming. In A.P. Hollander, P.A. Huijing, & G. de Groot (Eds.), *Biomechanics and medicine in swimming* (pp. 165-172). Champaign, IL: Human Kinetics.

Webb, P.W. (1971). The swimming energetics of trout II. Oxygen consumption and swimming efficiency. *Journal of Experimental Biology, 55*, 521-540.

Propulsive Techniques: Front Crawl Stroke, Butterfly, Backstroke, and Breaststroke

Robert E. Schleihauf
Joseph R. Higgins
Rick Hinrichs
David Luedtke
Cheryl Maglischo
Ernest W. Maglischo
Anne Thayer

This article includes a hand propulsive force analysis of 12 female and 14 male swimmers from the 1984 U.S. Olympic team. Summary statistics of pulling motion and hand propulsive forces are presented in each of the four competitive strokes. Further, a detailed example of model stroke technique is presented for one subject in each stroke to clarify the relation between pulling motion, hand angle of pitch, and propulsive force.

Methods

All filming took place at the Mission Viejo Olympic training camp, about 3 weeks prior to the 1984 Summer Olympic Games. Swimmers were filmed in their first and second strokes, with the exception of individual medley swimmers who swam all four strokes. The current report presents statistics for samplings of (a) 36 sprint freestyle (100- and 200-m race pace), (b) 12 butterfly, (c) 17 breaststroke, and (d) 23 backstroke data sets (where a data set is defined as the results of single-arm/two-camera stroke analysis).

Prior to filming, each subject was photographed with a 35-mm still camera (to determine anthropometric measures), and black tape markings were attached to each hand. Swimmers swam from 2 to 8, 25-m swim trials at race pace during filming; each film trial was followed by an easy 25-m swim to the starting position. Successive trials were started when the swimmer stated that he or she was sufficiently rested to conduct the next time trial.

Film data were collected by four Locam cameras operating at a 66 fps. Each camera was housed in custom-made underwater housing and was connected to an above-water battery-powered control panel. Cameras were positioned to simultaneously collect front, right-side, and two bottom views on each 25-m swim trial. The cameras were held in place underwater by rigid supports similar to those described in Schleihauf, Gray, and DeRose (1983). A scale reference, background pool markings, and a cable (temporarily suspended along the center of the swimmer's lane) were used in the analysis of camera location data. Biomechanical analysis of the film data (front and bottom view only) was conducted as specified in Schleihauf et al. (1983), with the exception that hand-force computations were adjusted to take into account finger spread and negative hand pitch (back of hand lead) propulsive effects.

The three-dimensional fingertip-pulling pattern data were analyzed to define three linear measures: depth (x coordinate), width (y coordinate), and length (z coordinate). Each linear measure was computed as the difference between the maximal and minimal fingertip coordinate values along the x, y, and z dimensions. The stroke starting and ending points were defined as beginning at hand entry and ending at hand exit from the water in freestyle, butterfly, and backstroke. The breaststroke pull duration began at the instant of hand separation on the outward press and ended when the hands nearly touched at the beginning of the underwater recovery motion. Each individual's pulling dimension data were rescaled as a function of arm length to express all linear measures with respect to a 6-ft (1.83-m) tall swimmer. The elbow angle at the point of maximal flexion was computed from shoulder, elbow, and wrist three-dimensional coordinate data.

The hand effective resultant force (RE) curve (the component of the hand resultant force vector aimed in the forward direction) was analyzed to yield three statistics:

- Diagonality index—the average angle between the negative hand line of motion and the forward direction at the first, second, and third largest points of RE force production
- Lift drag index—the average ratio of lift to drag force at the largest three occurrences of RE force
- Force distribution index—the average location of the largest three RE forces expressed as a percentage of the total time duration of the underwater phase of the arm pull

Results and Discussion

Pull Dimension/Pulling Motion Summary Data

The pulling dimension data are shown in Table 1. The diagonality index data presented in Table 2 show that breaststroke involved nearly pure sculling motions (a pure side-to-side or up-and-down hand motion would generate a diagonality index of 90°, whereas the remaining strokes employed diagonality measures between 40° and 60°. Backward propulsive

Table 1 Summary Statistics: Pulling Dimension Data

Stroke	Depth (cm) Mean SD	Width (cm) Mean SD	Length (cm) Mean SD	Elbow angle (deg) Mean SD
Freestyle	69.8 ± 8.4	37.1 ± 8.1	64.5 ± 9.7	93 ± 11
Butterfly	59.4 ± 6.8	46.7 ± 7.1	48.0 ± 6.9	82 ± 11
Backstroke	61.5 ± 11.9	68.8 ± 7.4	58.2 ± 10.9	66 ± 11
Breaststroke	32.0 ± 7.6	77.7 ± 7.9	−20.8 ± 9.4	66 ± 11

Table 2 Summary Statistics: Pulling Motion Data

Stroke	Diagonality index	Lift-drag index	Force distribution index
Freestyle	59 ± 13	1.04 ± 0.28	0.82 ± 0.07
Butterfly	44 ± 21	0.95 ± 0.39	0.81 ± 0.06
Backstroke	47 ± 17	0.77 ± 0.21	0.58 ± 0.13
Breaststroke	81 ± 9	1.25 ± 0.21	0.65 ± 0.13

hand motions (with a diagonality index of 0.0) were not evident in the sample.

The lift-drag ratio index data show that lift force predominates over drag force in breaststroke. In freestyle and butterfly, lift and drag force appear to be about equally important during the most propulsive portions of the stroke. Backstroke swimmers seem to use drag force more than lift force (i.e., sculling motions are less important than in breaststroke).

The force distribution index data show that the largest effective propulsive forces occur near the end of the arm pull in freestyle and butterfly. In breaststroke, the largest forces occur about two thirds of the way into the pull (at the midpoint of the inward scull motion [see Schleihauf, 1979]). Backstroke involves large hand-force production just past the midpoint of the arm pull. Unlike freestyle and butterfly, the shoulder roll at the end of the pull in backstroke appears to detract from the hand speed and propulsive force generated on the water during the finish of the stroke.

Models of Skilled Technique: Front Crawl Stroke

Data for Rowdy Gaines are shown in Figure 1. During the midportion of the bottom view, instantaneous pulling data are given in Figure 1a. The lift (L), drag (D), and resultant (R) hand-force vectors are indicated

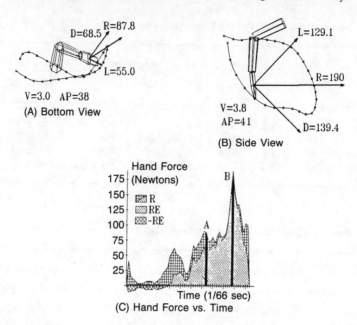

Figure 1   Gaines, front crawl stroke. (A) Bottom view, midstroke; (B) side view, finishing sweep motion; (C) hand resultant/effective resultant force curves versus time.

(magnitudes are given in Newtons) in the illustration. In addition, the hand speed (*V*) is shown in meters per second, and the hand pitch (*AP*) is shown in degrees. Note that three-dimensional force vector data are illustrated, and forces not entirely contained in the plane of the paper appear shortened. For example, the *L* vector is aimed both forward and upward (into the paper for a bottom-view illustration), and its length is shortened. The hand force produced at a given instant may be compared to the remaining forces produced in the pull by reference to the hand force curve (Figure 3e) shows three large pulses of *RE* force (Frames 22, 40, and 51). Instantaneous values near the first force pulse are shown force curve shows both the total hand force produced and the effective hand force. For Gaines, the hand-force production was small in the begining and middle of the pull and greatly increased during the last one third of the pull.

Figure 1b illustrates the instant of peak hand-force production. Note that the *R* force was directed nearly straight forward, and thus, the *R* and *RE* values were nearly identical in magnitude (Figure 1c).

Models of Skilled Technique: Butterfly

Matt Gribble's butterfly is illustrated in Figure 2. The stroke data bear a resemblance to freestyle (Figure 1) with the exception that the pull is wider (see Table 1), and thus the inward scull motion is more prolonged

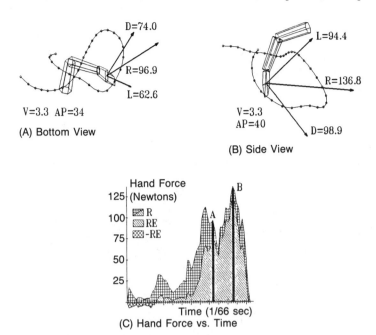

Figure 2   Gribble, butterfly. (A) Bottom view, inward scull motion; (B) side view, finishing sweep motion; (C) hand resultant/effective resultant force curves versus time.

(see Figures 1a and 2a). The finishing portion of the pull (Figure 2b) shows an approximately equal interaction of lift and drag forces in the generation of the largest hand force. Some of the sample butterflyers used less lift force, more drag force, and straighter back-pulling motions than those employed by Gribble. Thus, the sample diagonality and lift drag index values are less in butterfly than in freestyle.

Models of Skilled Technique: Backstroke

Data for Betsy Mitchell are shown in Figure 3. Inspection of the hand-force curve (Figure 3e) shows three large pulses of RE force (Frames 22, 40, and 51). Instantaneous values near the first force pulse are shown in Figure 3a. During this phase of the pull the hand force is aimed nearly straight forward. Later in the stroke (Figure 3b) larger hand force was created, although some force was "lost upward" (it could be that the upward component was important in the generation of shoulder roll). The bottom view (Figure 3c) shows that hand force was also lost to the side. Finally, Figure 3d shows an effective upward hand motion at the very end of the arm pull. Mitchell turned the palm up, slightly extended the wrist, and was able to create effective hand propulsion just prior to the hand exit. Most of the backstrokers in the sample created no effective propulsion during this phase of the pull.

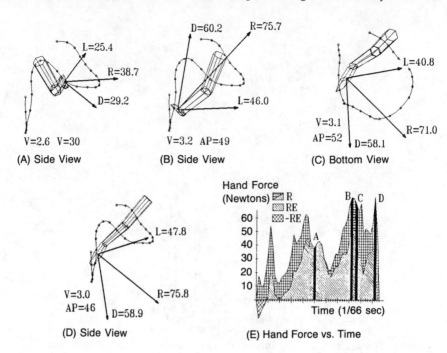

Figure 3 Mitchell, backstroke. (A) Side view, midstroke; (B) side view, downward sweep; (C) bottom view, inward sweep; (D) side-view, upward sweep; (E) hand resultant/effective resultant force curves versus time.

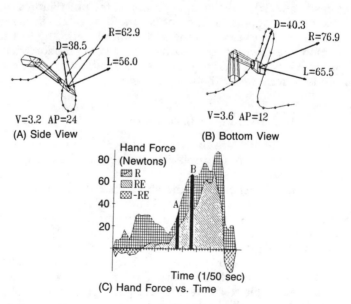

Figure 4 Rhodenbaugh, breaststroke. (A) Side view, downward sweep; (B) bottom view, inward scull motion; (C) hand resultant/effective resultant force curves versus time.

Models of Skilled Technique: Breaststroke

Data for Kim Rhodenbaugh are shown in Figure 4. The downward sweep of the hand (Figure 4a) shows an effective production of propulsive force in spite of the fact that the net z-dimension hand motion was forward. The inward scull portion of the pull (Figure 4b) shows exceptionally effective force production, primarily due to a hand line of motion that was inward and slightly backward, coupled with a small angle of pitch.

Conclusions

In each of the four competitive swimming strokes swimmers employed curvilinear pulling patterns in which diagonal pulling motions played an important role in propulsion. The lift drag index values indicated that, in general, lift force predominated drag force in breaststroke, lift and drag were about equally important in freestyle and butterfly, and drag predominated lift in backstroke. The force distrubtion index values indicated that the largest hand forces occurred near the end of the pull for most freestyle and butterfly swimmers. Breaststroke and backstroke swimmers seemed to employ the largest hand forces near the middle of the arm pull.

References

Schleihauf, R.E. (1979). A hydrodynamic analysis of swimming propulsion. In J. Terauds & E.W. Bedingfield (Eds.), *Swimming III* (pp. 70-109). Baltimore: University Park Press.

Schleihauf, R.E., Gray, L., & DeRose, J. (1983). Three-dimensional analysis of swimming propulsion in the sprint front crawlstroke. In A.P. Hollander, P. Huijing, & G. de Groot (Eds.), *Biomechanics and medicine in swimming* (pp. 173-184). Champaign, IL: Human Kinetics.

The Relation of Peak Body Acceleration to Phases of Movements in Swimming

Bodo E. Ungerechts

The question of the manner in which propulsion in aquatic surroundings is produced by repeated cyclic actions of body parts concerns physiological, hydrodynamic, and functional/morphological aspects. Only if one succeeds in taking all these factors into account may a more satisfying answer be found than is currently available.

The objective of this article is to discuss the functional/morphological and hydrodynamic causes (some temporal aspects) of the acceleration related to swimming movements during the breaststroke. The intracyclic acceleration of a swimming body is the sum of the resultant braking and propelling forces and is basically the origin of swimming speed.

The movement of a swimming body can be described as periodically changing. In competitive swimming these intracyclic fluctuations are considered to limit swimming performance and depend on the swimmer's skill (Toussaint et al., 1983). This might imply that basically the fluctuations can be omitted as is possible when driving a car. A car's shape is designed to produce less resistance. The mechanics of the engine are not affected by the air flow, whether it is laminar or turbulent. Engine work and air flow, then, have nothing in common. Because the swimmer acts as a self-propelling body, the propelling part and braking area are not separated as in a car.

In self-propelling bodies, propulsive forces depend on the change of the body form, its frequency, and its amplitude, so changing shape must be taken into account. The resistive forces can be attributed to the same parameters. The combinations of movement, shape, and type of flow are determinants of the amount of propulsion. Muscular activity alone will not produce any propulsion.

The same "undulating" body simultaneously produces resistive and propulsive forces, a situation that cannot be compared to a rigid car with a steady flow. In contrast, self-propelling bodies create a nonsteady flow. Hydrodynamic studies reveal that the flow along an "undulating" body is a fluctuating flow (Ungerechts, 1983), and the research indicates that this fluctuating flow influences the boundary layer along the body.

In breaststroke Barthels (1979) compared the propulsive mechanism of the breaststroke kick with the mechanism of the sculling hands, the so called *lift force handle*. Barthels points out that "the feet are sculling and remain in a vertical section of water while the body moves forward in response to leg extension" (p. 53), creating a *force wall*

If a force wall can be produced, then the peak acceleration depends on the functional properties of the knee extensors, that is, their temporal development of forces or moments, respectively. On the other hand, the question remains, Do the upper and lower extremities create the "force wall" according to the same hydrodynamic principles?

Subjects and Methods

A total of 36 breaststrokers (13 females and 23 males) from four different West German swim clubs participated in this study. Among them were the best performers in the 100- and 200-m breaststroke. The swimming speed ranged between 1.30 m/s and 1.57 m/s in males and between 1.00 m/s and 1.39 m/s in females. They were asked to swim 15 m at sprint speed, and 16-mm films were taken orthogonally from above from a 5-m platform at 55 fps.

From every second frame of the film, the displacement of the hip joint was digitized. This point was chosen as a reference in order to simplify comparison to former displacement/speed-time curves. The coordinates of the hip joint and times of the beginning of different phases in the leg action were recorded simultaneously as follows: (a) maximum knee flexion at the end of the recovery phase; (b) at the point of full knee extension, which was assumed to be the end of the outward sweep; and (c) at the final inward sweep of the leg action.

The coordinates of the hip joint were processed by a computer program using a smoothing procedure with third-degree polynomials over seven points to calculate the first and second derivatives from displacement data (Fritz, 1979).

The plots of acceleration-time curves (see Figure 1) were used to identify the peak acceleration and the time when it occurred. This time was related to time when the legs started the kicking action and the time when the legs were extended and had reached their outermost position of the dihedral shape.

Results

The point of peak acceleration was related temporally to the point of maximal knee flexion and maximal knee extension (see Figure 2). The peak accleration, ranging from 6 to 8 m/s^2, was achieved during the leg kick action, 137 ms (s = ± 65 ms) after the beginning of the outward motion of the legs. This part lasted 209 ms (s = ± 46 ms). The peak value occurred on an average 72 ms (s = ± 40 ms) before the legs reached their outermost position, just starting the inward motion. This result supported the observation of Maglischo (1982) who stated that "the outward sweep ends when the legs are nearly extended" (p. 149). The peak acceleration was assumed to coincide with the change of feet direction.

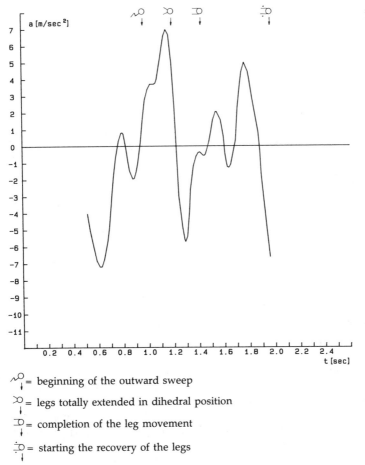

$\curvearrowleft\hspace{-0.5em}\circ$ = beginning of the outward sweep

$\circ\hspace{-0.5em}\curvearrowright$ = legs totally extended in dihedral position

$\circ\hspace{-0.5em}\leftarrow$ = completion of the leg movement

$\circ\hspace{-0.5em}\leftarrow$ = starting the recovery of the legs

Figure 1 The acceleration-time curve of the breaststroke swimmer, derived from the displacement of the hip in combination with the phases of leg movement.

Discussion

Although the "roughness" of the acceleration curves was evident, the comparison indicated that peak acceleration occurred during the leg kick near the point of the turning phase of the feet. Remarkably, this was true for swimmers who were technically instructed in different ways.

What is the explanation for this combination of movement phase and maximal acceleration? At least two forces acting on the center of gravity must be taken into account: (a) the rotation force due to the displacement of the mass of the lower limbs and (b) the reaction to flow forces.

Assuming the force wall does exist, the effect of the leg kick could be compared to the push-off from the wall (e.g., after a turn). According to Hüellhorst, Ungerechts, and Willimczik (1988), the duration of stretch-

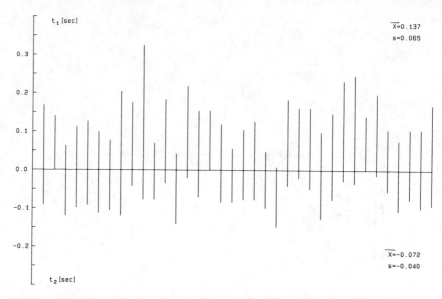

Figure 2 Duration and point of maximum acceleration during leg extension. Each line represents the duration of leg extension for one swimmer. t_1 = beginning and t_2 = end of leg extension. Maximum acceleration occurred at 0.0.

ing the legs with feet at the wall lasts 199 ms, which is quite similar to the duration of the outward sweep during the kick (206 ms).

Takahashi, Yoshida, and Tsubakimoto (1983) investigated force-time variables during the push-off from the wall. They observed that the peak forces occurred 72 ms before release from the wall and pointed out that peak forces of the knee extensors appeared at approximately the same knee joint angle, irrespective of the surrounding location of the body in space. In the breaststroke, the highest acceleration occurred 137 ms after the beginning of the kick and 72 ms before the legs were fully extended.

Conclusions

On the basis of these functional/morphological similarities of the leg extensors and their effect on body propulsion, the existence of a force wall can be hypothesized. But does that also indicate that the flow that creates the force wall is comparable to the situation of the sculling hands, as evidenced by the effect of the lift force? The question is, Are the hydrodynamic conditions (i.e., the angle of attack and the flow velocity) such that the body is pushed forward at maximum acceleration?

Although the flexibilities of breaststrokers' feet are remarkable, it is questionable that the swimmers can adapt the position of the feet to the flow conditions (as is done with the hands) to create the largest propulsive forces in the swimming direction. Because all swimmers accomplished

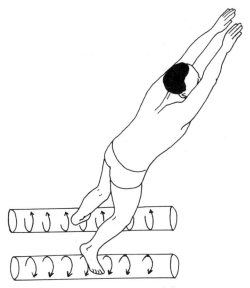

Figure 3 A representation of a pair of vortices assumed to be formed as a breaststroke swimmer completes the outward sweep and starts the inward sweep of the leg kick.

their maximal body acceleration during the same period of the leg kick, perhaps a principle other than the lift concept based on steady flow is the cause of the peak acceleration.

The other principle that may explain a high thrust production is the so-called *vortex theory*. This theory considers the relevant parameters involved in nonsteady flow (e.g., that the flow along the feet is influenced by the body). Inspection of the flow of fast swimming vertebrates or diving swimmers doing the butterfly kick by flow-visualizing technique revealed that the water is set into rotation when the rear body part changes direction (Ungerechts, 1985). The rotating water associated with propulsion can be called *vortex gust*. As a gust is formed, momentum is transferred to the fluid and in reaction, its "impulse" accelerates the body. In breaststroke the transition from outward to inward sweep of the legs might create vortex, as shown in Figure 3.

Both functional/morphological and hydrodynamic factors cause peak acceleration by the creation of effective flow that coincides with the properties of the leg extensors. In practice, therefore, emphasis should be placed on the turning motion and on developing greater feet flexibility.

References

Barthels, K.M. (1979). The mechanism for body propulsion in swimming. In J. Terauds & E.W. Bedingfield (Eds.), *Swimming III* (pp. 45-54). Baltimore: University Park Press.

Fritz, M. (1979). *Berechnung der Auflagerkräfte und der Muskelkräfte des Menschen bei ebenen Bewegungen aufgrund von kinematischen Aufnahmen* [Measurements of human movement forces determined by cinematographic analysis]. Bochum, F.R.G: Ruhr-University.

Hüellhorst, U., Ungerechts, B.E., & Willimczik, K. (1988). Displacement and speed characteristics of the breaststroke turn. In B.E. Ungerechts, K. Reischle, & K. Wilke (Eds.), *Swimming science V* (pp. 93-98). Champaign, IL: Human Kinetics.

Maglischo, E.W. (1982). *Swimming faster*. Palo Alto, CA: Mayfield.

Takahashi, G., Yoshida, A., & Tsubakimoto, S. (1983) . Propulsive force generated by swimmers during a turning motion. In A.P. Hollander, P.A. Huijing, & G. de Groot (Eds.), *Biomechanics and medicine in swimming* (pp. 192-198). Champaign, IL: Human Kinetics.

Toussaint, H.M., Helm, F.C.T. van der, Elzerman, J.R., Hollander, A.P., Groot, G. de, & Ingen Schenau, G.J. van. (1983). A power balance applied to swimming. In A.P. Hollander, P.A. Huijing, & G. de Groot (Eds.), *Biomechanics and medicine in swimming* (pp. 165-172). Champaign, IL: Human Kinetics.

Ungerechts, B.E. (1983). The validity of the Reynolds number for swimming bodies which change form periodically. In A.P. Hollander, P.A. Huijing, & G. de Groot (Eds.), *Biomechanics and medicine in swimming* (pp. 81-88). Champaign, IL: Human Kinetics.

Ungerechts, B.E. (1985). Considerations of the butterfly kick based on hydrodynamical experiments. In S.M. Perren & E. Schneider (Eds.), *Biomechanics: Current interdisciplinary research* (pp. 705-710). Dordrecht, Netherlands: Nijhoff.

Estimation of Breaststroke Propulsion and Resistance-Resultant Impulses From Film Analyses

Luc Van Tilborgh
Eustache J. Willems
Ulrik Persyn

In this study, the position of the total body center of gravity (cg) during breaststroke swimming was estimated from film analysis, using a personalized computer model of the human body (adapted from Hanavan, 1964). This allowed for a calculation in each movement phase of the impulses resulting from the difference between propulsion and resistance. Individual variations in a breaststroke movement cycle, which correlated significantly to swimming performance and to hip velocity fluctuation (Persyn, 1974; Persyn, Vervaecke, Thewissen, & Verhetsel, 1981), were then directly related to these resultant impulses. Mainly the new-look, undulating style was anlayzed and compared to the commonly used style of breaststroke swimming.

Methods

Subjects

A total of 23 German breaststrokers were filmed (16 mm, 40 fps) at different swimming velocities from the front and side views underwater. To provide them with immediate feedback, they also completed the test battery of the "Leuven Evaluation Center for Swimmers" (Persyn, Hoeven, & Daly, 1979). In this article, the performances of only 9 male swimmers from this group (aged 14.5 to 20.5 years; breaststroke performance 100 m: 1.06.1 to 1.13.7, 200 m: 2.23.5 to 2.33.1) are discussed with respect to their sprint velocities.

Modified Hanavan Model

A total of 26 body measurements were taken to define the personalized computer model. The original model of Hanavan (1964) was first modified by Stijnen, Spaepen, and Willems (1980), the lower torso being divided into two segments. To apply this modified model to swimmers, two further adaptations were needed. First, the thorax was considered independent from the shoulders, reducing the average error in localizing the cg (compared to using a force plate) by 3.8 mm (12.6%). In all, 12 subjects were investigated in nine body positions, using raw data from Peeraer (1984). A second adaptation took into account the nonhomogeneity of the trunk, using data from Parks as cited in Plagenhoef (1971). This led to a further improvement of 1.47 mm (4.9%). The total improvement was thus 5.27 mm (or 17.5% of the error in the model as adapted by Stijnen et al.).

Film Analysis

Marks were fixed on the joint axes and on the head; the thorax, abdomen, and pelvis were identified with tape markings as described by Stijnen et al. (1980). Both 16-mm front and side views were used to delimit the movement phases: leg spreading and squeezing, arm spreading and squeezing, and first and second parts of the arm and leg recovery (Persyn, Maeyer, & Vervaecke, 1975).

For calculation of impulses, only side views needed to be digitized. As the movement was considered symmetric, only one arm and one leg were used. Head and shoulder position during breathing had to be estimated from contour graphs of the swimmer. This estimation was guided by the simultaneous above and underwater video tapes that were made so that immediate advice on techniques could be provided.

Calculated Parameters

To obtain velocity and force curves, the first and second derivative of the displacements of the cg were calculated using a digital differentiation filter (Usui & Amidror, 1983). In addition, the impulses resulting from the difference between propulsion and resistance were calculated for each movement phase. Because these could be calculated directly from the first derivative, the impulses were more reliable than the forces.

Results

For 50-m sprint pace, the work needed to accelerate the body from its lowest to its highest velocity per breaststroke cycle amounted to 92 J on the average in this sample. Power lost to fluctuation was thus calculated to be 79 W.

Persyn (1974) found that within top-level swimmers the hip continued to accelerate during the squeezing phases of the arms and legs and therefore induced a lift propulsion. When the average impulse per phase was calculated for the present swimmers on the basis of the displacements of the cg, the impulse during leg squeezing was 4 times greater than that during leg spreading (averages for the sample: 46 Ns and 11 Ns, respectively; see Figure 1). The fact that the greatest hip acceleration was seen

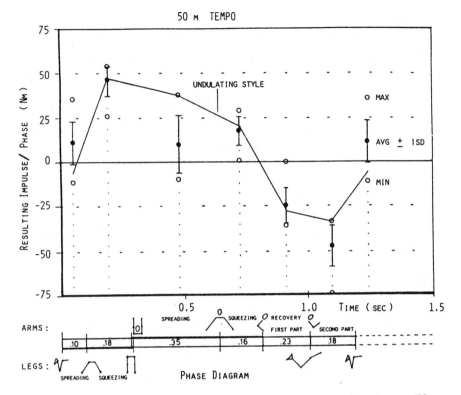

Figure 1 Resulting impulses per movement phase for male breaststroke swimmers (N = 9). The durations indicated in the phase diagram are averages for the entire sample.

during the (backward) spreading phase of the legs was more of a result of inertia than of propulsion.

During the squeezing of the arms a larger impulse also resulted than during the spreading (17 and 12 Ns, respectively). Taking into account the large water resistance during this phase caused by the body inclination and the large trunk velocity, there had to be a great deal of propulsion in order to obtain a positive resulting impulse during arm squeezing.

Of course, the most useful application of the method is the treatment of individuals. As an example, some results are given for the one swimmer in the present sample who used the new-look, undulating breaststroke. Of course, care should be taken not to generalize results from only one swimmer. This swimmer showed the least velocity fluctuation of the cg in the sample (Pearson coefficient of variation, 18.8%; range of other subjects 19.2 to 24.4%). In the 1972 Olympic Games, one swimmer who used a similar technique also had the flattest velocity fluctuation curve of the hip (Persyn, Maeyer, & Vervaecke, 1975). In the recovery phase, the swimmer was able to maintain the highest cg velocity (0.80 m/s; range of other subjects, 0.50 to 0.74 m/s). The resistance impulse during the second part of the recovery, the hip flexion, was only −34 Ns (range of other subjects, −39 to −77 Ns). (See Figure 1, note deepest point of the full line.)

Most typical in the new-look breaststroke is the body undulation, which is characterized by an upward hand displacement during the spreading phase—from deep (piking) to close to the water level. Although being one of the weaker swimmers in arm isometric strength, the swimmer being described demonstrated the largest impulse in the sample during this phase (37 Ns; range of other subjects, −9 to 24 Ns). Is this a result of the longer movement path (and thus duration) of the arm spreading and/or of reduced resistance through body undulations, as hypothesized for the butterfly (Persyn, Vervaecke, & Verhetsel, 1983)? Another remaining question is whether the negative impulse during the leg spreading is typical for the downward leg action of undulating breaststroke, or whether it was specific for this individual. It might also be the consequence of the relatively high translation velocity that this swimmer was able to maintain during the recovery phase.

Discussion

Film analysis using a personalized computer model of the human body is a rather time-consuming way of investigating swimming. However, it seems to be a valuable tool for gathering data on time-space parameters in connection with propulsion and resistance resultant impulses in various movement phases. When a sufficient amount of these data can be brought together in a computer database, reducing the movement analysis to a few key positions and reconstructing the movement with simulation may be possible in the future. This would make the method of greater practical use, especially when personal computer graphic animations can be used for showing simulated results.

Acknowledgments

We would like to acknowledge the help of Bodo Ungerechts (University of Bielefeld, Federal Republic of Germany) for bringing these swimmers together in the "Bundesleistungszentrum Warendorf" and for his cooperation in the experiment. We also greatly appreciated the help of V. Stijnen, who took the measurements and gave advice in the use of the computer model.

References

Hanavan, E. (1964). *A mathematical model of the human body* (Technical report AMRL-TDR-64-102). Wright-Patterson Air Force Base, OH: Wright Air Development Center.

Plagenhoef, S. (1971). *Patterns of human motion.* Englewood Cliffs, NJ: Prentice-Hall.

Peeters, L. (1984). *Het gebruik van versnellingsmeters in de analyse van bewegingen* [The use of accelerometers in movement analysis]. Unpublished doctoral dissertation, Catholic University, Leuven, Belgium.

Persyn, U. (1974). Technisch-hydrodynamische benadering van de bewegende mens in het water uitgaande van "The Science of Swimming" van Counsilman [Technical-hydrodynamic approach of moving man in water, on the basis of "The Science of Swimming" by Counsilman]. *Hermes (Leuven)*, **8**, 33-136.

Persyn, U., Maeyer, J. de, & Vervaecke, H. (1975). Investigation of hydrodynamic determinants of competitive swimming strokes. In L. Lewillie & J.P. Clarys (Eds.), *Swimming II* (pp. 214-222). Baltimore: University Park Press.

Persyn, U., Hoeven, R., & Daly, D. (1979). An evaluation procedure for competitive swimmers. In J. Terauds & E.W. Bedingfield (Eds.), *Swimming III* (pp. 182-195). Baltimore: University Park Press.

Persyn, U., Vervaecke, H., Thewissen, M., & Verhetsel, D. (1981). Observatiestudies als voorbereiding tot het verbeteren van de schoolslag van doorsnee zwemmers [Observation studies as preparation to the correction of average breaststroke swimmers]. *Hermes (Leuven)*, **15**(1), 43-55.

Persyn, U., Vervaecke, H., & Verhetsel, D. (1983). Factors influencing stroke mechanics and speed in swimming the butterfly. In H. Matsui & K. Kobayashi (Eds.), *Biomechanics VIII-B* (pp. 833-841). Champaign, IL: Human Kinetics.

Stijnen, V., Spaepen, A., & Willems, E.J. (1980). Models and methods for the determination of the center of gravity of the human body from film. In A. Morecki, K. Fidelus, K. Kedzior, & A. De Wit (Eds.), *Biomechnics VII-A* (pp. 558-564). Baltimore: University Park Press.

Usui, S., & Amidror, I. (1983). Digital differentiation filters for biological signal processing. In H. Matsui & K. Kobayashi (Eds.), *Biomechanics VIII-B* (pp. 1207-1214). Champaign, IL: Human Kinetics.

Patterns of Velocity in Competitive Breaststroke Swimming

Albert B. Craig, Jr.
William L. Boomer
Partricia L. Skehan

In competitive swimming, increased velocity is associated with an increase in stroke rate and a decrease in the distance traveled per stroke cycle (Craig, Boomer, & Gibbons, 1979; Craig & Pendergast, 1979; Craig, Skehan, Pawelczyk, & Boomer, 1985; Pai, Hay, & Wilson, 1984). The velocity, which is the product of stroke rate and distance per stroke, can increase only if the increase of the stroke rate is proportionally greater than the decrement of the distance per stroke. In the breaststroke the decrease of the distance per stroke with increasing stroke rates is greater than in other stroke patterns (Craig & Pendergast, 1979). It has also been reported that the fluctuations in velocity are greater in the breaststroke than in the other competitive strokes (Craig & Pendergast, 1979).

Previous documentation of the variations in velocity and the temporal relations within this competitive stroke pattern have been limited to one or two individual swimmers (Bober & Czabanski, 1975; Kent & Atha, 1975; Schleihauf, 1979). Publications were not found that indicated the temporal and velocity changes during the stroke cycle for a range of stroke rates.

Methods

The 12 male swimmers involved in this study were members of the University of Rochester Varsity Swimming Team. They were all competent but not particularly skilled in swimming the breaststroke. Their average physical characteristics were as follows: height, 183 cm; weight, 75 kg; age, 19 years. The average time to swim the 100-yd (91.4-m) breaststroke in competition was 1:07 (range, 59.6 to 74 s).

Velocity and distance during repeated swims of the length of the pool (22.9 m) were recorded by methods that have previously been described (Craig & Pendergast, 1979). A fine (0.25-mm diameter), malleable stainless steel wire with no appreciable elasticity was attached to a belt worn by the swimmer. This wire was pulled from the "swim-meter," which was fixed to the end of the pool. A fishing reel on this device was adjusted to produce a 0.25 to 0.30-kg drag on the line. The wire passed over a small wheel attached to a direct current generator, which gave a voltage output directly proportional to the swimmer's velocity. The line also passed over another wheel that had slots corresponding to 0.1-m distance traveled. The electronic circuit provided a suitably amplified signal each time a light signal fell on a photosensitive diode mounted by the side of this wheel. These velocity and distance signals were recorded on a two-channel polygraph using a paper speed of 12.25 cm/s.

During each swim, the subject was instructed to keep his stroke rate as constant as possible. Five repeated swims were made using progressively increasing stroke rates for each. The rate for the first swim ranged between 20 to 30 strokes per minute, and the last trial at maximal speed was swum using 50 to 60 strokes per minute. The recorded pattern of velocity during the stroke cycles varied widely from subject to subject. In order to identify the different fluctuations in these records, the subjects were requested to swim at moderate speeds while their motions were video taped. The video picture also included a simultaneous view of the polygraph channel used to record velocity. By playing back the tape at slow speeds it was possible to identify the movements that had produced the fluctuations in the velocity records.

From each swim at least four and usually five stroke cycles were assessed. The stroke cycles chosen for measurement were those following the first complete stroke cycle after surfacing from the push-off. In most cases it was noticed that this first stroke cycle had a slower velocity than subsequent strokes.

The following measurements of each stroke cycle were made, and the results were averaged from each separate swim. The measurements of time were resolved to 0.01 s and those of velocity to 0.025 m/s.

- *First deceleration (D-1)*. The time from the maximal velocity associated with the leg action to the minimal velocity before the arm action.
- *Acceleration associated with the arm action (AcA)*. The time from end of D-1 to the peak velocity caused by the arm action.
- *Second deceleration (D-2)*. Time from the end of AcA to the minimal velocity before the leg action.
- *Acceleration associated with the leg action (AcL)*. Time from the end of D-2 to the maximal velocity associated with the leg action.
- *Minimal velocity before the arm action (V1)*. The velocity at the end of D-1.
- *Maximal velocity associated with the arm action (V2)*. The velocity at the end of the AcA.
- *Minimal velocity before the leg action (V3)*. The velocity at the end of D-2.
- *Maximal velocity associated with the leg action (V4)*. The velocity at the end of AcL.
- *Average distance per stroke*. The number of distance marks on the record from the first to the last stroke measured multiplied by 0.1 m divided by the number of strokes and expressed as m/stroke.
- *Stroke rate*. The total time for the strokes measured divided by number of strokes and expressed as strokes per minute.

• *Mean velocity during the stroke cycle.* The product of the distance per stroke and the stroke rate and expressed in m/s.

Results

As shown in Figure 1 there was a reciprocal relationship between stroke rate and the distance traveled with each stroke. This relationship was quantitatively the same as previously reported (Craig & Pendergast, 1979).

The temporal relationships within the stroke pattern are illustrated in Figure 2. The four columns within each category indicate the average results in the range of stroke rates of 20 to 30, 30 to 40, 40 to 50, and 50 to 60 strokes per minute. As the stroke rate increased, D-1 and to a lesser

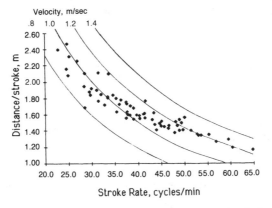

Figure 1 The relationship of stroke rate and distance per stroke. Each swim is plotted. The isopleths indicate the velocity.

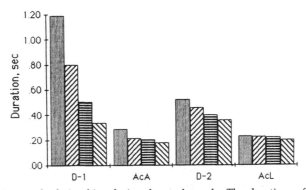

Figure 2 Temporal relationships during the stroke cycle. The durations of the different parts of the stroke cycle as defined in the text are shown in each category. The columns within each category represent average values for the stroke ranges of 20 to 30, 30 to 40, 40 to 50, and 50 to 60 strokes per minute.

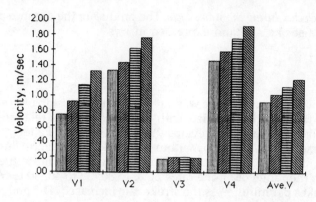

Figure 3 Velocities during the stroke cycle. The velocities at different points in the stroke cycle as defined in the text are shown, and the average velocity for each cycle is also indicated. The columns within each category represent average values for the stroke ranges of 20 to 30, 30 to 40, 40 to 50, and 50 to 60 strokes per minute.

extent D-2 decreased (Figure 2). In contrast the time used for AcA and AcL remained quite constant over this three-fold change in stroke rate.

Because the arm action began earlier in the stroke cycle, V1 and V2 increased with stroke rate (Figure 3). However, the increase of the velocity resulting from the arm action (i.e., the difference between V1 and V2) was not significantly related to the stroke rate. The minimal velocity during the stroke cycle (V3) occurred when the hips and the knees were flexed in preparation for the leg action. Although the velocity of some swimmers was momentarily zero at this point, the average was 0.2 m/s. The leg action produced a velocity (V4) that was directly related to the stroke rate.

Discussion

The stroke cycle during breaststroke swimming was characterized by two periods of deceleration and two periods of acceleration. As neither decelerations nor accelerations were linear, calculating mean values for these periods was not possible. However, by dividing the change in velocity by the time period, an "index" of the rate of change was calculated that probably approximated the magnitude of the rate of change in velocity. The first deceleration was characterized by an index of −0.60 m/s/s in the range of stroke rates of 20 to 30 strokes/min to −1.8 m/s/s in the 50 to 60 strokes/min range. Comparable values for the second deceleration were −2.2 and −4.4 m/s/s. A similar calculation for the acceleration of the arm action indicated no relationships to the stroke rate and averaged 2.3 m/s/s. The leg action produced values of 5.6, 6.0, 7.1, and 8.7 m/s/s for the different groups of stroke rates.

The results from this group of male swimmers indicated that the increase of velocity with increasing stroke rate was to a major extent related to the timing of the different movements. The periods of D-1 and D-2 both decreased as the stroke rate increased, but the periods AcA and AcL were relatively constant. The lack of relationship of the index of acceleration due to the arms with the stroke rate suggested that there might be a limitation in the propulsive force that these swimmers developed during this part of the stroke cycle. By contrast, part of the increased velocity could be accounted for by an increase of propulsive force related to the leg kick.

The movement patterns in the breaststroke have changed radically in the past 10 years, and during competition today one can observe different styles. A limitation to the current study was that despite individual variations within the group all were coached by one person. To some extent this coach's views of the best stroke pattern might have influenced some of the results. These swimmers were encouraged to emphasize the speed and the power of the adduction phase of the arm action. This approach could account in part for the lack of relationship of the acceleration index of the arm pull with the stroke rate.

However, despite these possible limitations the breaststroke swimming style apprarently was dependent on precise timing. It is commonly observed that competitive times of some breaststrokers may vary greatly within a short time. If the swimmer's "timing is off," he or she may have a very poor race. These observations suggest that the mechanics of swimming may be more critical in the breaststroke than in other competitive stroke styles.

References

Bober, T., & Czabanski, B. (1979). Changes in breaststroke techniques under different speed conditions. In J.P. Clarys & L. Lewillie (Eds.), *Swimming II* (pp. 188-193). Baltimore: University Park Press.

Craig, A.B., Jr., Boomer, W.L., & Gibbons, J.F. (1979). Use of stroke rate, distance per stroke, and velocity relationships during training for competitive swimming. In J. Terauds & E.W. Bedingfield (Eds.), *Swimming III* (pp. 263-272). Baltimore: University Park Press.

Craig, A.B., Jr., & Pendergast, D.R. (1979). Relationship of stroke rate, distance per stroke and velocity in competitive swimming. *Medicine and Science in Sports*, **11**, 278-283.

Craig, A.B., Jr., Skehan, P.L., Pawelczyk, J.A., & Boomer, W.L. (1985). Velocity, stroke rate, and distance per stroke during elite swimming competition. *Medicine and Science in Sports and Exercise*, **17**, 625-634.

Kent, M.R., & Atha, J. (1975). Intracycle kinematics and body configuration changes in the breaststroke. In J.P. Clarys & L. Lewillie (Eds.), *Swimming III* (pp. 125-129). Baltimore: University Park Press.

Pai, Y.-C., Hay, J.G., & Wilson, B.D. (1984). Stroking techniques of elite swimmers. *Journal of Sports Sciences*, **2**, 225-239.

Schleihauf, R.E., Jr. (1979). A hydrodynamic analysis of swimming propulsion. In J. Terauds & E.W. Bedingfield (Eds.), *Swimming III* (pp. 70-109). Baltimore: Univeristy Park Press.

PART II

STARTS AND TURNS

Three Types of Grab Starts for Competitive Swimming

James E. Counsilman
Brian E. Counsilman
Takeo Nomura
Motohiro Endo

Coaches and athletes are constantly searching for methods of improving athletic performances. In swimming, particularly in the sprint events, the start plays a crucial role in determining the outcome. Various starting techniques have undergone experimentation. Since 1967, when Hanauer introduced the grab start, most of the effort has been confined to comparative studies of this technique with other conventional starts. Many of these studies have shown the grab start to be superior to all others (Bowers & Cavanagh, 1975; Hanauer, 1972; Lowell, 1975; Roffer & Nelson, 1972). It has been almost universally adopted as the start of choice except during relay takeoffs when it is considered more advantageous to use the wind-up start.

Performance of the grab start consists of placing both feet on the front edge of the starting block and grasping the front edge with both hands. The hands may be between the feet or outside the feet, the former technique being the most common. At the sound of the gun, the swimmer pulls him- or herself downward and forward, diving into the water with the body inclined at an angle of 15 to 30° with the surface of the water and the hands and head lower than the feet.

The next step in the evolutionary process of the start was to experiment with various angles of entry. When the grab start came into popular use, the body was actually inclined as stated above, but the term *flat start* came to be associated with it. This term will be used in this article because it is commmonly accepted, although in fact it is a misnomer.

Because the hands enter the water first with the rest of the body entering the water slightly in back of this point, many coaches and swimmers believed the flat start caused more resistance than would an entry that allows the body to enter at the same point at which the hands enter. They began experimenting with a technique that they described as permitting the body to follow the same opening in the water that the hands had created. It was called variously the *hole-in-the-water start*, the *scoop start*, the *sailor dive*, the *spoon start*, the *no-resistance start*, and the *pike start*. To accomplish it, the swimmer was instructed to leap upward and to pike at the hips when he or she attained maximum height. The effect would be to incline the body steeply toward the water at an angle of about 45°. The hands would enter steeply and the rest of the body would follow at the same angle. The shortening of the radius of rotation when the body assumed the piked position (jacknife) would permit the body to rotate in a forward direction so the desired angle of entry would be obtained. In this article that start will be called the *scoop start*.

Although many swimmers at the national and international level still use the flat start, a film study of the last three outdoor U.S. Senior Championships indicated that an increasing number have adopted the scoop start with a deeper angle of entry.

A third type of start that has gained in popularity since 1980 is referred to as the *track start*. U.S. Olympic Champion Rowdy Gaines was one of the first of the world-ranked swimmers to adopt this start, and American Dara Torres influenced its acceptance when she set a world record for the 50-m freestyle using it.

The track start is nearly identical to the flat start with regard to the angle of entry into the water. It is also like all the grab starts except that one foot is placed near the back end of the starting block, as in the starting position of a track runner—hence the name track start.

Subjective observation of competitive swimmers using the track start seems to indicate that although it should enable the swimmer to enter the water at a steep angle of 45° or greater, nearly all the swimmers employing it actually entered the water at an angle of approximately 35°.

Many coaches and swimmers believe the scoop start to be the fastest of the three described above, but no research could be found that compared the speed of the three starts.

Purpose of Study

The purpose of this study was to compare the three starts: the scoop start, the flat start, and the track start. In all three of these starts the grab position was used by all subjects. Two groups were studied: Group A consisted of 37 male college swimmers and Group B of 121 male and female swimmers, aged 10 through 17 years.

Methodology and Presentation of Data

Group A

To make a comparison of the three starts by male college swimmers of national caliber, the Indiana University Varsity Men's Team of 37 swimmers was tested. Each swimmer practiced each start 100 times over a period of 4 months, after which each swimmer was timed for three 12.5-yd freestyle trials of each type of start. The stopwatch—calibrated in one hundredths of a second—was started upon the command to go (a whistle), and the watch was stopped when the swimmer's head crossed a black line on the bottom of the pool, which indicated 12.5 yds. If the swimmer had a fast start or "jumped the gun," that trial was disqualified. The mean averge time of these three trials was assigned as that particular swimmer's score for that particular start.

The mean times were as follows: (a) scoop start, 4.37 s; (b) track start, 4.25 s; and (c) flat start, 4.16 s. Of the total number of 37 subjects, 31 were fastest when using the flat start, and 6 were fastest when using the track start. Not a single swimmer was fastest when using the scoop start. This study, however, was inconclusive because the swimmers who took part had been using the flat start for years, performing this type of start perhaps thousands of times. It is possible that they could not become as proficient in doing a new type of start merely by performing it a fraction of the number of times they had practiced another start. This factor was also operative in some of the other research that has compared different types of swimming starts for speed.

Group B

Another approach in comparing the speed of the three starts was made by testing young swimmers, aged 10 through 17 years. The total number of swimmers was 121; 55 male swimmers between the ages of 11 and 17 years and 66 female swimmers between 10 and 16 years of age. These swimmers were participants in a swimming stroke analysis clinic held at Indiana University in the summer of 1984. Each child spent 5.5 days in the program. On the first night the swimmers were shown a film demonstrating the three starts. A verbal description of each start was given at a meeting of all the swimmers. They then practiced each start three times a day for the next 4 days. On the 5th day, all were timed for each start, and simultaneous under and out-of-water video tapes were made of each of the time trials.

As previously mentioned a swimmer is usually faster at one starting style than another because he or she has been practicing that specific start for a longer period of time. For this reason after the first session in which the three starts were described and shown to the swimmers on film and before the actual practice of the starts began, the swimmers were asked to list which of the three starts they were accustomed to using. The results were as follows: (a) scoop start—males, 38%, females, 54%; (b) track start—males, 12%, females, 14%; and (c) flat start—males, 40%, females, 32%. It was considered that this information would generalize trends to a great extent in spite of the possible limitation already mentioned.

Three elements—time, angle, and distance—were selected as the parameters to be studied. The items were as follows: time for 5-yd distance, time for 10-yd distance, takeoff angle, angle of the body upon entry into the water, distance from the starting platform to the point at which the head entered the water and to the point at which the head broke the surface of the water after the dive, and the depth to which the swimmers penetrated the water.

The diving well at the outdoor Indiana University swimming facility with a depth of 16 ft was selected as the site for the research. A starting platform 30 in. in height from the surface of the water was installed at the side of the pool. Two high-speed rotary video cameras were used to photograph each of the swimmer's trials from out of the water and from under the surface of the water. The cameras were placed 18 yd from the subjects. Grid lines underwater on the side wall of the pool were used to determine how deep the swimmer's body penetrated under the surface, the horizontal distance it covered, and to help determine the angle of entry of the body into the water.

Each subject's standing height and score on the standing vertical jump were measured in inches and recorded. Each swimmer reported his or her best time for the 100-yd freestyle during the previous year.

After practicing each dive three times per day for 4 days, each swimmer performed each of the three starts twice on the 5th day. Each trial was timed and video taped and then analyzed for the variables measured. Figure 1 shows that the times for 10 yd using the flat start and the track start were quite similar for both males and females. All of the age groups recorded slower times for the scoop start with the exception of the 10-year-old girls. A similar trend was recorded in the time for 5 yd.

Figure 2 displays a relatively high correlation between the time for 10 yd and the time for 100 yd of freestyle in both males and females. Although the start contributes somewhat to the ultimate speed with which a swimmer covers 100 yd, other factors are also operating, such as status of training, endurance, stroke mechanics, and so forth.

Figures 3 and 4 indicate a high correlation between vertical jump data and height and time for the 10-yd distance among male swimmers. These particular relationships did not exist among the female swimmers.

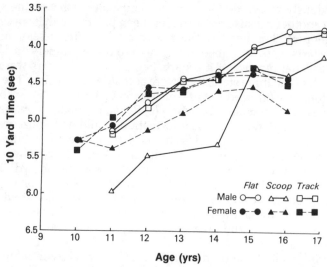

Figure 1 10-yd time for each age, sex, and starting style.

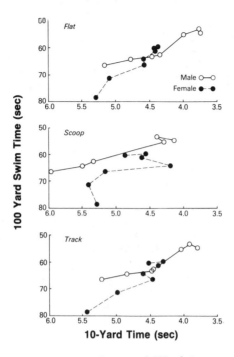

Figure 2 The relationship between 10-yd time and 100-yd time.

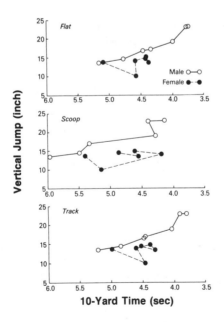

Figure 3 The relationship between 10-yd time and vertical jump.

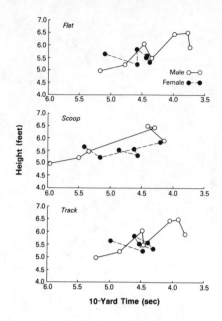

Figure 4 The relationship between 10-yd time and the swimmers' height.

Figures 5 and 6 display the takeoff angles and entry angles, respectively. The highest takeoff angle occurred in the scoop start. This was especially evident among male swimmers for whom the average takeoff angle of the scoop start was 17.64 ± 11.65°, the flat start was 5.08 ± 8.51°, and the track start was 7.40 ± 10.95°. Among women swimmers the mean takeoff angle of the scoop start was 3.42 ± 8.56°, the flat start was 0.56 ± 7.15°, and the track start was 0.77 ± 7.81°.

The angle of entry into the water (see Figure 6) was always greater in the scoop start than in the flat or track starts in all age groups with the exception of the 10-year-old females. The mean entry angle for the male swimmers, when doing the scoop start, was 47.36 ± 7.66°, for the flat start was 31.02 ± 7.50°, and for the track start was 34.48 ± 7.83°. For the women the angle of entry for the scoop start was 47.11 ± 6.75°, for the flat start was 36.25 ± 7.85°, and for the track start was 35.77 ± 6.54°.

Figure 7 depicts the distance from the edge of the pool to the point at which the head entered the water. The average distance for the scoop start among males was 9.96 ± 1.08 ft, for the flat start was 10.29 ± 1.23 ft, and for the track start was 9.72 ± 1.14 ft.

These figures reveal that a greater distance in the air was achieved by the flat start compared to the other two starts. This difference in distance, however, was not statistically significant. A similar pattern can be observed in the women's data in which no statistical significance was found among the distances in the three types of start: in the scoop start the mean was 8.97 ± 0.81 ft, the flat start, 9.03 ± 0.69 ft, and the track start, 8.64 ± 1.75 ft.

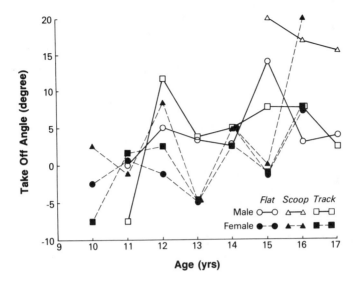

Figure 5 Takeoff angle for different age, sex, and starting style.

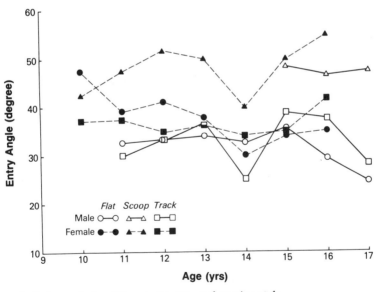

Figure 6 Entry angle for different age, sex, and starting style.

The claim by proponents of the scoop start that it impels the swimmer further out over the water before the head enters the water is not apparent in the group studied here, inasmuch as there was not a statistical difference in the distance covered in the air by any of the three starts.

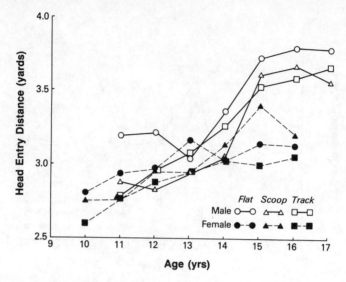

Figure 7 Head entry distance for different age, sex, and starting style.

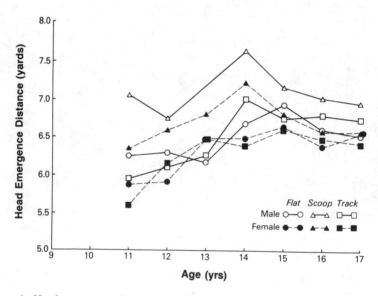

Figure 8 Head emergence distance for different age, sex, and starting style.

Figure 8 displays the distance from the edge of the pool to the point at which the head emerged from underwater after the dive. The average distance for the male swimmers was 22.50 ± 1.04 ft for the scoop start, 21.21 ± 1.04 ft for the flat start, and 19.70 ± 1.81 ft for the track start. Among female subjects the distance was 21.51 ± 1.68 ft for the scoop

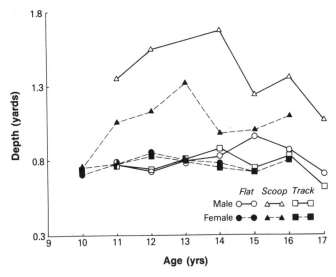

Figure 9 Depth for different age, sex, and starting style.

start, 20.43 ± 1.77 ft for the flat start, and 20.18 ± 1.86 ft for the track start. In both male and female swimmers the scoop start covered the greatest distance underwater. However, a big difference was not observable in any starting style among the 15-year or older subjects.

Figure 9 shows the depth to which the subjects penetrated the water after the start. The depth was almost identical in the flat and track starts among both male and female swimmers. Performance of the scoop start resulted in the deepest penetration beneath the surface of the water in all age groups and particularly among male swimmers. The average depth achieved when performing the scoop start among males was 3.99 ± 1.08 ft, when performing the flat start was 2.43 ± 0.51 ft, and when performing the track start was 2.31 ± 0.45 ft.

For females the following means were obtained: for the scoop start, 3.24 ± 0.69 ft; for the flat start, 2.24 ± 0.39 ft; and for the track start, 2.31 ± 0.36 ft. When doing the scoop start, 88% of the subjects went deeper than 3.1 ft, and 10% went deeper than 4.5 ft.

Discussion

The primary limitation of any study involving such physical skills as the competitive swimming racing start is that the subjects will be more skilled in one of the techniques than in the others.

In the first phase of this study employing 37 collegiate male swimmers (Group A), this factor may have been significant in determining the results. The two starts taught by the coach and practiced by the swimmers—the flat start and the track start—proved to be superior to the scoop start in time for the 12.5 yd distance. The mean time to achieve the distance for the three starts was 4.16 s for the flat start, 4.25 s for the track start, and 4.37 s for the scoop start.

In order to minimize the effect of acquired skill, a second study was devised. Group B consisted of 55 male swimmers, aged 11 to 17, and 66 female swimmers, aged 10 to 16. After being shown films of the three starts, the swimmers were asked which of the three starts they customarily used in competition and practice. The majority of Group B subjects indicated that they customarily used the scoop start. Despite this fact, after a total of only 12 practice trials of each of the three starts over a 4-day period, the flat start and the track start proved to be superior with respect to time for 5 and 10 yd.

The steepness of the angle of entry and the depth of penetration beneath the surface of the water are significant sources of safety hazard when the scoop start is performed in a pool that is less than 4.5 ft deep. It is a fact that many accidents have resulted from the use of the scoop start, ranging from chipped teeth to spinal injuries. Several cases in which an accident resulted in quadriplegia have come under litigation, and multimillion dollar settlements have been paid. Because most multipurpose pools place the starting blocks at the shallow end of the pool, where the depth of water is usually 3.5 ft, the use of the scoop start is not advisable. This is particularly true for male swimmers, who submerged to an average depth of 3.99 ft. The average depths for males when using the other two starts were 2.43 ft for the flat start and 2.31 ft for the track start.

Conclusion

It is the recommendation of these researchers that the scoop start not be used in shallow pools of a depth of less than 4 ft, particularly from starting blocks 30 in. in height from the surface of the water or more. Even at the depth of 4.5 ft potential hazard exists if the swimmer misjudges the depth of his or her dive.

If, as this study demonstrates, the scoop start is not faster than the starts that are characterized by shallower entries, it is essential that this information be promulgated among coaches and competitive swimmers in order to eliminate the use of this potentially dangerous technique.

References

Bowers, J.E., & Cavanagh, P.R. (1975). A biomechanical comparison at the grab and conventional spring starts in competitive swimming. In J.P. Clarys & L. Lewillie (Eds.), Swimming II (pp. 225-232). Baltimore: University Park Press.

Hanauer, E.S. (1967). The grab start. Swimming World, 8(6), 5, 42.

Hanauer, E.S. (1972). Grab start faster than conventional start. Swimming World, 13(4), 8-9.

Lowell, J.C. (1975). Analysis of the grab and conventional start. *Swimming Technique*, **13**(2), 66-69.

Roffer, B.J., & Nelson, R.C. (1972). The grab start is faster. *Swimming Technique*, **9**(4), 101-102.

Displacement and Speed Characteristics of the Breaststroke Turn—A Cinematographic Analysis

Ulrich Hüellhorst
Bodo E. Ungerechts
Klaus Willimczik

The amount of time spent in turning in swimming events, especially in long-distance races, is astonishingly high. Thayer and Hay (1984) found that, for example, 39% of the total race time in the 200-m breaststroke event was spent on turning. They used short-time measurement to record the time for the whole turning phase including the approach, the turn, and the glide. Quite a few previous investigations used different distances before and after the actual turn (Fox, Barthels, & Bowers, 1963; Scharf & King, 1964). Most of these investigations, however, intended to compare different turning techniques. Chow, Hay, Wilson, and Imel (1984) were the first who did not take arbitrary distances to the wall (distance-in, distance-out) as a basis of their measurements. With the help of high-speed films they determined both distances for each swimmer individually according to the cycles of swimming. *Distance-in* was defined as the horizontal distance between the vertex of the head of the swimmer and the wall at the beginning of the last stroke before initiating the turn; *distance-out* was defined as the distance from the wall to the end of the first stroke after the turn. From these distances they computed the time for the two subphases of the turn and the total time for turning.

Up to the present, none of the investigations referred to the center of gravity (cg) and consequently no continuous curves of the displacement and speed of the cg exist. The aim of this study was to make a differentiated analysis of the breaststroke turn on the basis of displacement and speed curves of the center of gravity.

Procedures

Turns of 8 elite swimmers were filmed from a lateral view using a 16-mm high-speed camera. The analysis included the period from the beginning of the last stroke before executing the turn to the beginning of the underwater arm stroke. Filming from a lateral view it was possible to define characteristic body positions each swimmer passed through during the breaststroke turn. In this way displacement curves and the calculated speed could be interpreted not only for the whole turn but also for separate phases. On each of the displacement curves, six points were marked indicating the characteristic body positions during the turn. These positions were the following: (a) ▲ beginning of arm recovery, (b) △ beginning of the leg kick, (c) ◆ hands touching the wall with the body fully extended, (d) ◇ trunk in a normal position, (e) ■ beginning of the push-off, and (f) □ last contact with the wall. When evaluating the distances, times, and speeds, one should remember that the swimmers were asked to execute the turns according to their individual styles. Only those turns were analyzed in which the incoming swimmer touched the wall with the legs fully extended. The question as to how imperfect timing in approaching the wall affected the times for the distinct phases of the turn or for the turn as a whole was not considered.

For detailed treatment it was necessary to divide and characterize the turn into distinct phases (see Figure 1):

Phase 1: The approach. An optimal approach to the wall avoids a too-long and thus too-slow glide before the swimmer's hands touch the wall.

Phase 2: The turn. The actual turning motion of the swimmer takes place between the moment when the hands make the first contact with

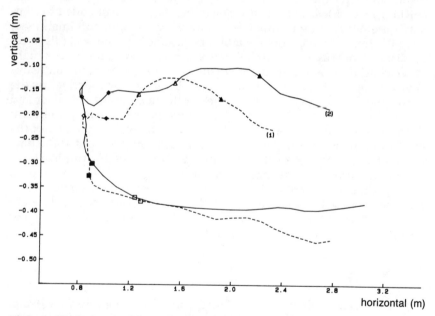

Figure 1 Displacement of the center of gravity. ▲ = beginning of arm recovery, △ = beginning of the leg kick, ◆ = hands touching the wall with the body fully extended, ◇ = trunk in a normal position, ■ = beginning of the push-off, □ = last contact with the wall. ---- Subject 1, —— Subject 2.

the wall and the start of the push-off. This rather complex movement involves a rotary movement around two axes of the body, which serves to change the swimmer's direction. It can be divided into two subphases. The first subphase extends from the first contact with the wall until the trunk is in a vertical position. The second subphase extends from this position until the start of the push-off. Ideally, the time needed to execute the movement must be reduced to a minimum, while at the same time one must optimally prepare for the subsequent push-off.

Phase 3: The push-off. The push-off phase is of particular importance because errors that are made in this phase (path of acceleration not optimal, push-off too slow, wrong angle during push-off) negatively affect the push-off velocity.

Phase 4: The glide.   An essential factor for achieving good transition from the turn to the swimming phase is the choice of the proper point for starting with the underwater arm stroke. In all graphics presented, the ends of the curves coincide with the beginning of the underwater arm stroke.

The more important criteria for executing the turn quickly are (a) a short time for completing the movement from the moment when the swimmer's hands touch the wall to the end of the push-off and (b) a high velocity of push-off. In the present study, the quickest turn measured $t = 1.20$ s and $v = 2.23$ m/s. The mean values were $t = 1.39$ s and $v = 2.12$ m/s; the slowest result was $t = 1.56$ s and $v = 1.86$ m/s. In the following section, interindividual differences during distinct phases of the turn will be discussed on the basis of the displacement curves and the calculated velocity of the center of gravity.

Results

For purposes of discussion, 2 subjects with representative motion patterns of turns were chosen.

The Turning Phase

Concerning the first subphase of the turn, two structurally different types in the displacement of the center of gravity were distinguishable. (see Figure 1). Some graphs showed a relatively high peak in the displacement curve, whereas other graphs showed a rather flat displacement curve, indicating that the center of gravity was moving downward without prior upward movement. Both turns illustrated were relatively quick ($t = 1.20$ s and $t = 1.33$ s) and a high velocity was attained during the push-off ($v = 2.25$ m/s). The subject who completed this part of the movement most quickly showed a displacement curve of the latter type.

It is open to question whether this peak in the curve, which always showed a distinct rise of the center of gravity, was useful to the swim-

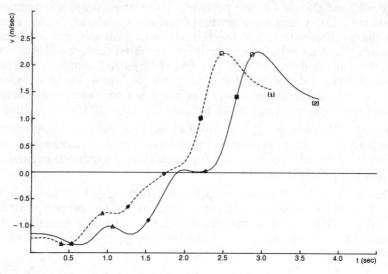

Figure 2 Component of velocity in swimming direction. ▲ = beginning of arm recovery, △ = beginning of the leg kick, ◆ = hands touching the wall with the body fully extended, ◇ = trunk in a normal position, ■ = beginning of the push-off, □ = last contact with the wall. ----- Subject 1, _____ Subject 2.

mer in minimizing time for this phase or in the subsequent phases of the turn. Considering the velocity curves (resultant, vertical, and horizontal swimming direction) in conjunction with the displacement curves, one can observe that this displacement curve had some effect on the curve of velocity.

In all these cases, the graph of the velocity component in the swimming direction showed that the velocity of the center of gravity varied about 0 m/s over a rather long period of time. An example is given in Figure 2 (Curve 2). In contrast to this, Curve 1 of Figure 2 shows a straighter course. In this case, less time was needed for the total phase of the movement.

The resulting velocity curves in Figure 3 also exhibited differences though both curves were similar to a large extent. They were different only in the fact that in Curve 2 a longer period of low velocity was included. In the vertical direction, the late beginning of the higher velocity was very noticeable again. The gain in time for Subject 1 compared to Subject 2 cannot be generalized. There seemed to be a compensation for the longer course of the center of gravity by a higher velocity in vertical direction.

The Push-Off Phase

There were also differences in the push-off angle, which varied between 0 and 13.1°. A larger angle implies that the center of gravity was still moving downward during the push-off. Subjects completing a rather quick turn (see Figure 1) did not execute the push-off from a horizontal

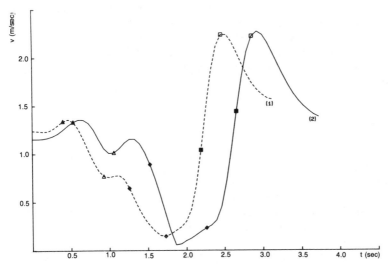

Figure 3 Resultant velocity. ▲ = beginning of arm recovery, △ = beginning of the leg kick, ◆ = hands touching the wall with the body full extended, ◇ = trunk in a normal position, ■ = beginning of the push-off, ▢ = last contact with the wall. ----Subject 1, ___ Subect 2.

position but from angles of about 7.5°. This can be attributed to the fact that the swimmers wanted to begin the push-off as soon as possible. They started the push-off before the upper arm was completely submerged and extended. The center of gravity was moving downward because the arm was not brought in front of the head until the push-off movement started. Those subjects performing a horizontal push-off waited until their arms were completely underwater, which means that they needed more time for the phases before the push-off. Moreover, these swimmers attained the highest speed in swimming direction—about 2.25 m/s. Therefore, the variations of the push-off angle between 0 and 13.1° appeared to have no effect on the push-off velocity. Correlation between push-off velocity and push-off time or path of push-off were not significant ($r = .27$ and $r = .50$, respectively).

The Gliding Phase

The end of the displacement curve coincided with the moment the swimmer started the underwater arm stroke. This point was up to the discretion of each swimmer. When the swimmer perceived his speed in swimming direction was low enough he started the underwater arm stroke. Almost all swimmers started the arm stroke at about the same speed (1.42 m/s). Two swimmers began the underwater stroke at 1.26 m/s. If these values were compared with the maximum speed during the last swimming cycle before the turn, the velocity at the beginning of the underwater armstroke for most of the subjects was only 0.05 m/s higher than the maximum speed during the last cycle. Only 2 swimmers began the underwater arm stroke so early that their velocity at this moment was 0.58 m/s and 0.33 m/s, respectively, higher than the maximum speed in the last cycle. The graph of the velocity showed the negative effects of corrections in direction on speed during the gliding phase. As soon as such corrections were necessary, the horizontal velocity plainly increased compared to the normal course.

Conclusion

In summary, this pilot study showed surprising similarities in the displacement curves in spite of individual differences. Variations could be observed in the difference between incoming level and push-off level. Distinct differences were noted in the displacement curve of the first subphase of the turning movement. However, no advantage was evident in either one of the two types of turns with regard to minimizing time for this phase.

The results showed that there was no negative effect on the push-off velocity if the swimmer started the push-off before his arm, which was moved above the surface, was submerged and extended completely. The swimmers performing this variation attained the highest push-off velocity. That meant that during this stage there was an opportunity to save time by starting the push-off early.

The effects of the push-off angle on the push-off velocity were not evident as long as there were no corrections of direction necessary during the gliding phase.

References

Chow, J.W., Hay, J.G., Wilson, B.D., & Imel, C. (1984). Turning techniques of elite swimmers. *Journal of Sports Science, 2*, 241-255.

Fox, E.L., Barthels, R.L., & Bowers, R.W. (1963). Comparison of speed and energy of two swimming turns. *Research Quarterly, 34*, 322-326.

Scharf, R.J., & King, W.H. (1964). Time and motion analysis of competitive freestyle swimming turns. *Research Quarterly, 35*, 37-44.

Thayer, A.L., & Hay, J.G. (1984). Motivating turn and start improvement. *Swimming Technique, 21*, 17-20.

PART III

KINANTHROPOMETRY

Estimation of Sprint Performances in the Breaststroke From Body Characteristics

Daniel Daly
Ulrik Persyn
Luc Van Tilborgh
Dirk Riemaker

In a previous study, equations for 100- and 400-m crawl performance estimations were developed from factor scores calculated from 18 anthropometric, 6 flexibility, and 5 strength measures and $\dot{V}O_2$ intake (Daly, Tilborgh, & Persyn, 1984). The error in estimation was around 3% for varying distances and crawl patterns. In this study equations were developed for the 100-m breaststroke with the intention of making field diagnoses, using a personal computer. A smaller number of easy measures was selected, and the factor scores were no longer calculated. In addition, the time-consuming $\dot{V}O_2$ intake test was eliminated.

Procedures

For the purpose of performance estimation, data from 121 men ($M = 15.5$ years, range 10.8 to 22.7 years) and 126 women ($M = 14.5$ years, range 10.0 to 18.0 years) were used. Belgian, West German, and Dutch elite swimmers were obtained from the archives of the Leuven Evaluation Center for Swimmers (Persyn, Hoeven, & Daly, 1979).

Information Selected for the Investigation

Swimming performance. The individual swim times for 100-m breaststroke were obtained from the published statistics of the various swimming federations and checked in a questionnaire. The mean times for the 100-m breaststroke were 1:20.3 ($SD = 7.3$ s) for the men and 1:25.3 ($SD = 5.6$ s) for the women. These times were transformed into European point scores (Coen, 1978) to provide a normal distribution for statistical analysis.

To describe the performance level by age, the sample was compared to the performances of the best American swimmers according to age group (Daly et al., 1984). The performance levels of the age groups were equivalent; however, the women performed slightly better than the men (men: $M = 66.7\%$, $SD = 12.6\%$; women: $M = 71.4\%$, $SD = 12.8\%$).

Body characteristics.   Following Pearson correlation studies (with analytical strokes, swimming with arms or legs alone, as well as total stroke) and factor analysis, five anthropometric, four flexibility, and four strength measures were selected. These are shown in Figure 1, and their means and *SDs* are given in Table 1.

Statistical Analysis

Statistical analysis was performed using the BMDP statistical package (Dixon, 1981):

1. Descriptive statistics were obtained and Pearson product-moment correlation coefficients were calculated between body characteristics

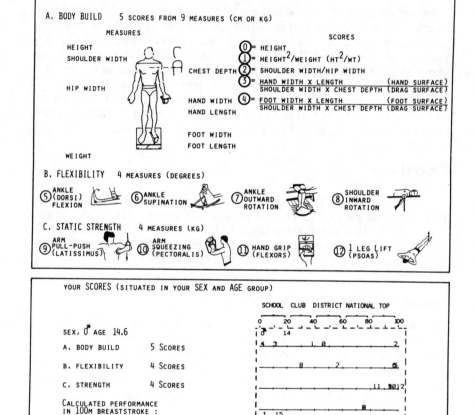

Figure 1   Performance estimation profile for 100-m breaststroke.

Table 1 Statistical Data for Body Characteristics of Total Sample in 100-m Breaststroke

Characteristic	Men M	Men SD	Women M	Women SD	Pearson r Men	Pearson r Women	Multiple R Men	Multiple R Women
Body build								
Height (cm)	172.57	11.35	163.60	8.60	.52***	.37***	X	X
Height²/weight	493.68	52.23	516.27	52.44	-.50***	-.21*	X	X
Shoulder width (cm)/hip width (cm)	1.64	0.11	1.57	0.10	.23*	.09	X	
Hand surface (cm²)/drag surface (cm²)	0.20	0.02	0.19	0.03	-.36***	-.24*	X	
Foot surface (cm²)/drag surface	0.31	0.04	0.30	0.05	-.49***	-.25		
Flexibility								
Ankle outward rotation (deg)	92.62	16.57	102.06	15.15	-.05	-.28**	X	X
Ankle supination (deg)	60.13	17.62	67.98	14.40	.17	.02	X	X
Ankle dorsiflexion (deg)	19.55	5.55	20.08	5.81	-.00	-.04		
Shoulder inward rotation (deg)	80.14	9.46	81.11	10.83	-.03	.06		
Strength								
Arm pull-push/weight (kg)	0.55	0.09	0.46	0.08	.22*	.11	X	X
Arm squeezing/weight (kg)	0.50	0.08	0.39	0.07	.29**	.18	X	X
Hand grip/weight (kg)	0.71	0.11	0.57	0.09	.19	.09	X	
1 leg lift/weight (kg)	0.28	0.05	0.25	0.05	.04	-.04		
R							.63	.60
R²							.40	.36
M time (m:s)							1:19.20	1:25.19
M error (s)							5.2	4.52
Range (s)							31.80	27.80
M error (%)							7.10	5.31
M error/range (%)							17.80	16.70

Note. X represents characteristics included in the regression equations.
*p = .05. **p = .01. ***p = .001.

(body build, flexibility, and strength) and 100-m breaststroke performances.

2. All possible subsets multiple regression was used to obtain performance estimation equations in the total sample from body characteristics and chronological age. In this step, equations for all combinations of estimators were calculated. The user then selected the equation that was sufficiently accurate and the most logical. This gave the best chance of succesfully applying the regression equations in groups outside the studied sample (Kerlinger & Pedhazur, 1973).

3. All possible subsets multiple regression was also used to obtain performance estimation equations in diverse age groups. Overlapping age groups of 3 years were formed. A performance for a 12-year-old, for example, was estimated with the equation found from the 11-, 12-, and 13-year-old group. This overlapping decreased the chance of faulty performance estimations for swimmers on the extreme borders of their age groups. Even with the age grouping, chronological age was retained as an independent variable.

Results

Total Sample

The Pearson rs between the 100-m breaststroke performance and body characteristics are given in Table 1. The surprising significant negative r between performance and height^2/weight and hand and foot surfaces (per drag) resulted from their relationship to chronological age. The influence of chronological age was controlled in the multiple regression analysis by including it as an independent variable.

The factors included in the multiple regression analysis for the total sample are also shown in Table 1. The total variance in performance explained by body characteristics was 40% for men and 36% for women with a mean error in performance estimation of 5.6 s (7.1% of the total time for the swim) and 4.5 s (5.3%), respectively (17.8% and 16.7% with respect to the range of performances).

The presence of ankle supination in both regressions can be noted, although this variable had shown no significant Pearson r. Ankle dorsiflexion (selected on the basis of correlations with kicking performance) (Vervaecke, 1983) did not significantly correlate with total stroke performance and was also not entered here into the multiple regression equations. Perhaps the new breaststroke style, with its downward kick, allows the sole of the foot to be placed in a propulsive position during leg squeezing without the extreme dorsiflexion needed in the more commonly used style with a more horizontal kick.

Age Groups

The results of the multiple regression analysis for six age groups of males and five age groups of females are shown in Table 2. Despite the age

Table 2 Results of Multiple Regression Analysis for Body Characteristics in 100-m Breaststroke

Characteristic	Male age groups						Female age groups				
	11-13	12-14	13-15	14-17	15-17	16+	11-13	12-14	13-15	14-16	15-17
N	18	30	43	38	34	22	39	60	69	45	26
M age	13.0	13.7	14.8	15.4	16.2	18.0	13.1	13.8	14.5	14.9	15.9
Chronological age	.09	.03		.07		.02		.02	.03		.08
Body build											
Height			.12	.07	.04	.27			.03		
Height²/weight		.04	.06	.08	.07			.03			
Shoulder width/hip width							.12	.02		.20	.09
Hand surface/drag surface	.27	.10			.04	.02		.06	.09	.17	.18
Foot surface/drag surface	.33	.18				.01		.08	.08		.04
Flexibility											
Ankle outward rotation			.07	.07	.25	.33		.09	.16	.07	.09
Ankle supination		.13	.05	.06			.04	.02		.05	.06
Ankle dorsiflexion											
Shoulder inward rotation	.20					.20		.04			.09
Strength											
Arm pull-push/weight	.32	.20					.09	.10			
Arm squeezing/weight	.10		.06	.02		.10	.22	.02	.03		
Hand grip/weight	.20	.09		.04	.03	.07	.02	.03		.07	.37
1 leg lift/weight										.04	.32
R	.83	.73	.71	.71	.75	.93	.62	.65	.56	.61	.82
R²	.68	.53	.50	.50	.57	.87	.39	.42	.32	.37	.67
M time (m:s)	1:22.5	1:22.3	1:20.5	1:19.4	1:18.5	1:16.0	1:26.7	1:25.4	1:24.9	1:24.1	1:23.2
M error (s)	8.1	7.1	4.1	3.9	3.8	2.4	4.2	4.4	4.2	4.0	2.9
Range (s)	31.8	31.8	22.1	22.8	25.2	25.9	19.8	27.1	27.1	27.1	17.2
M error (%)	9.8	8.6	4.1	3.9	3.7	2.4	4.9	5.1	4.9	4.7	3.5
M error/range (%)	25.5	22.2	18.6	17.1	14.9	9.4	21.4	16.2	15.4	14.7	16.7

Note. The decrease in explained variance when the particular measure was left out of the regression is given.

grouping, the chronological age was still entered into a number of the regression equations. It should be interesting to study groups of 1-year classification when sufficient subjects are available.

Height²/weight was entered into the performance estimation equations in all age groups of males with the importance clearly increasing with age (negative relationship). The hand and foot surfaces (per drag) were also frequently entered into the estimation equations. This was not due to a relationship with chronological age, as was seen previously, because age as a factor was now also present in the same regression equation. As with the height²/weight, this had a negative relationship. From this, one can conclude that an increase in drag surface is not a hindrance because this is also accompanied by an increase in muscle mass.

Perhaps most surprising here is the presence of the strength variable, 1 leg lift. This variable showed no significant r, nor was it entered into the previous regression analysis. One can assume that, when the age (size) factor is eliminated, the more interesting (relevant) estimators become apparent.

In general, these equations give more accurate performance estimations than when using just one equation for the total sample (men: 5.1 s, 6.4%; women: 4.1 s, 4.7%). Further, the accuracy of the equations for men increases greatly as age increases. The older swimmers had better techniques and their training backgrounds were more homogeneous, reducing the contributions of these factors to the variance. The females usually reached top-level performances chronologically earlier than the males. This may explain their lower mean error in performance estimations.

Discussion

A personal computer program has been developed in which the individual measurement results and estimated performances, by age group, are displayed in animations and graphs. The swimmer receives a hard copy of the results, which can be attached to his or her profile, as shown in Figure 1.

Further work on performance estimation is being done. A major change has been made in the independent variables. One global score is now obtained for the arms, one for the legs, and one for the trunk (streamline). This replaces the separate score for each anthropometric, flexibility, and strength characteristic. One can assume that characteristics can compensate for one another. In fact, two swimmers with completely different profiles can achieve the same performance.

References

Coen, G. (1978). *Schwimmsportliche Leistungstabelle* [Comparative performance tables for swimming]. Berlin: Bindlach.

Daly, D.J., Tilborgh, L. van, & Persyn, U. (1984, July). *Prediction of the appropriate pattern for crawl swimming in women.* Paper presented at the Olympic Scientific Congress, Eugene, OR.

Dixon, W.J. (Ed.). (1981). *BMDP statistical software*. Berkeley: University of California Press.

Kerlinger, F.N., & Pedhazur, E.J. (1973). *Multiple regression in behavioral research*. New York: Holt, Rinehart and Winston.

Persyn, U.J.J., Hoeven, R.G.C., & Daly, D.J. (1979). An evaluation procedure for competitive swimmers. In J. Terauds & E.W. Bedingfield (Eds.), *Swimming III* (pp. 182-195). Baltimore: University Park Press.

Vervaecke, H. (1983). *Somatische en motorische determinanten van de sprintsnelheid en van de bewegings uitvoering bij elite zwemmers* [Somatic and motor determinants of the sprint velocity and the movement in elite swimmers]. Unpublished doctoral dissertation, Catholic University of Leuven, Belgium.

The Relationship of Biological Factors to Swimming Performance in Top Polish Junior Swimmers Aged 12 to 14 Years

Henryk Kuński
Ayna Jegier
Anna Maslankiewicz
Elzbieta Rakus

Only a few reports are found in the literature that concern the relationship between progress in swimming performance and dynamics of change of chosen biological parameters. On examining prospectively some swimmers, Oelschläger (1969) indicated a close relationship between progress in sport competition and increase of heart size and physical efficiency. Keul, Lehmann, Dickhuth, and Berg (1980) observed a correlation similar to Oelschläger's in males who specialized in running and swimming distances requiring performances of over 2 minutes duration. However, the progress of sport performances has been observed with a constant level of oxygen uptake in Polish senior (Kuński & Sztobryn-Rutkowska, 1982) and top Swedish swimmers (Eriksson, Holmer, & Lundin, 1978). As Martinosov, Bulgakova, Statkjawiczjenje, Filmonova, and Chebotarieva (1984) stated, the progress of sport performances in female swimmers at the ages of 11 to 16 is mainly related to an increase in the morphological and functional aspects of the organism. According to Bulgakova and Voroncov's (1978) view, the basis for anticipating a swimmer's performance should be stability of features, which do not change under the influence of training and are controlled by genetic factors, namely skeletal diameters, ankle flexibility, and the results of long-distance swimming.

The main aim of this investigation was to find in what way changes in chosen biological parameters affect the progress of swimming performance in junior swimmers aged 12 to 14 years.

Subjects

Over 2 years, longitudinal studies were carried out with 74 female swimmers at the age of 12 to 13 and 70 male swimmers at the age of 13 to 14, who were the elite of the Polish junior swimmers. The female swimmers were divided into nine subgroups: 100-, 200-, 400-, and 800-m freestyle; 100- and 200-m breaststroke; 200-m butterfly; and 200- and 400-m individual medley. The male swimmers were divided into six subgroups: 100-m freestyle; 100-m backstroke; 200-m breaststroke; 100-m butterfly; and 200- and 400-m individual medley. It was possible to categorize each of the swimmers in one or more the subgroups, depending on their swimming specialties. The Polish ranking and the coaches' opinions were the other criteria utilized for this division.

Methods

A carefully standardized anthropological program that included the following measurements was carried out: standing height, body weight, lean body mass, Rohrer index, upper and lower extremity length, shoulder and hip width, and skinfold measurements according to Pařizkova.

Physical work capacity (PWC_{170}) was measured using a mechanically braked bicycle ergometer (Monark) at a pedalling rate of 60 rpm. Heart rate was monitored from electrocardiogram tracings. Swimming performances were evaluated by means of the best time in the special swiming distance in a 50-m pool during the summer. The progress of swimming abilities was estimated based on differences in times observed after one or more special distance swims during the competitive seasons. Conventional methods were used in the statistical processing in order to determine coefficients of correlation. The significance level was taken as $\alpha = .05$.

Results

The relationship between increase in biological parameters and progress of sports performance was analyzed according to swimming specialization. The coefficients of correlation for the 74 girls are listed in Table 1. They show that a positive relationship exists between changes in several biological parameters and progress of swimming performance, especially in the 800-m freestyle and 400-m individual medley. Increases in height, body weight, and length of extremities are related to the progress of swimming performance. Also, females with a small increase in thigh girth and percentage of body fat achieve better results. A lack of relation was observed between PWC_{170}/kg and improved performance.

The coefficients of correlation for the 70 males are listed in Table 2. A positive relationship exists between changes in several biological parameters and progress in swimming performance, especially in the 100-m freestyle, 200-m breaststroke, 100-m butterfly, and 200-m individual medley. In the 100-m freestyle, the greater progress is, the greater the increase in height, body weight, lean body mass, upper extremity length, shoulder width, and thigh girth, and the better the swimming performance. Body fat should decrease, however, if performance is to improve. It is interesting that there was a similar tendency in the 200-m breaststroke. In the 100-m butterfly, the greater the increase in height, lean body mass, upper and lower length of extremities, hip width, and PWC_{170}/kg,

Table 1 The Relationship Between Progress in Swimming Performance (Time of Swimming) and Increases in Biological Parameters for Top Polish Junior Female Swimmers

Variable	Freestyle				Breaststroke		Butterfly	Medley	
	100 m $N = 13$	200 m $N = 9$	400 m $N = 17$	800 m $N = 19$	100 m $N = 17$	200 m $N = 19$	200 m $N = 11$	200 m $N = 21$	400 m $N = 16$
Body height	−.73	−.64	−.55	−.57					−.80
Body weight	−.55	−.89						−.39	−.68
Lean body mass	−.74			−.62				−.30	
Rohrer index			+.52						
Upper extremity length				−.55					−.80
Lower extremity length				−.48		−.56			−.68
Shoulder width							−.52		−.72
Hip width					+.45				
Thigh girth			+.94	+.50	+.57	+.51	+.31		
% body fat			+.94	+.55	+.26	+.33		−.49	
PWC₁₇₀/kg				−.39					

Note. Only statistically significant correlation coefficients are given. A negative correlation coefficient indicates a positive relationship except for thigh girth and % body fat.

Table 2   The Relationship Between Progress in Swimming Performance (Time of Swimming) and Increases in Biological Parameters for Top Polish Junior Male Swimmers

Variable	Freestyle 100 m N = 9	Backstroke 100 m N = 12	Breaststroke 200 m N = 14	Butterfly 100 m N = 11	Medley 200 m N = 7	Medley 400 m N = 11
Body height	−.70		−.78	−.70		−.58
Body weight	−.68		−.61		−.92	−.75
Lean body mass	−.83		−.58	−.59	−.82	
Rohrer index					−.72	
Upper extremity length	−.77		−.52	−.92		
Lower extremity length		−.47		−.93	−.48	
Shoulder width	−.86		−.68		−.74	
Hip width				−.70		
Thigh girth	−.49		−.95			−.58
% body fat	+.75			+.61		
PWC₁₇₀/kg		−.85		−.71		−.55

Note. Only statistically significant correlation coefficients are given. Except for thigh girth and % body fat, a negative correlation coefficient indicates a positive relationship.

the better was the swimming performance. Significant correlations were found between performance (swim time) body weight, lean body mass, lower extremity length, and shoulder width in the 200-m individual medley.

In summary, this prospective study indicated that the relevant influence of progress in swimming performance was positively related to changes in several biological parameters. It should be noted, however, that many of the correlation coefficients, although statistically significant, were not high enough to be utilized for the purposes of prediction of performances in swimming.

References

Bulgakova, N.Z., & Varoncov, A.P. (1978). O prognozowanii sposobnostej w plawanii na osnovie longitudinalnych issledowani. *Teoria Praktika Fiziczeskoj Kultury*, **7**, 37-40.

Eriksson, B.O., Holmer, I., & Lundin, A. (1978). Physiological effects of training in elite swimmers. In B. Eriksoon & B. Furberg (Eds.), *Swimming medicine IV* (pp. 177-187). Baltimore: University Park Press.

Keul, J., Lehmann, M., Dickhuth, H.-H., & Berg, A. (1980). Vergleiche von Herzvolumen, nomographisch ermitteler Sauerstoffaurnahme und Wettkampfleistung bei Ausdauersportarten. *Deutsche Zeitschrift für Sportmedizinhe*, **30**, 148-154.

Kuński., H., & Sztobryn-Rutkowska, M. (1982, June) *Repeated assessment of aerobic work capacity and blood glucose and FFA concentrations in swimmers*. Paper presented at the Fourth International Symposium of Biomechanics and Medicine in Swimming, Amsterdam.

Martirosov, E.G., Bulgakova, N.Z., Statkjawiczjenje, B.V., Filimonova, I.J., & Chebotarieva, I.V. (1984). Polowoj dimorfizm niekotorych morfofunkcjonalnych pokazatelej i sportivnych dostizenij w plawanii. *Teoria Praktika Fiziczeskoj Kultury*, **3**, 16-18.

Oelschläger, H. (1969). *Vergleich zwischen spiro-ergometrischen Befunden und tatsächlichem Leistungvermögen in Training und Wettkampf*. Unpublished doctoral dissertation, University of Leipzig.

Pařizkova, J. (1962). Mezeni podilv aktivni kmoty a zuku v lidskem zele a jeko vyznam ve sportovni praxe. *Teoria a Praxe Telesne Vyokovy*. **10**, 273-279.

The Relationship of Anthropometric Measures to Different Types of Breaststroke Kicks

Reinhard Nimz
Ursula Rader
Kurt Wilke
Werner Skipka

In breaststroke swimming the kick has an important influence on propulsion. Therefore, teaching and using the most effective type of breaststroke kick are both necessary and desirable. At the moment the whip kick is the most effective type of breaststroke kick (Counsilman, 1977; Maglischo, 1982). This form is characterized by limited braking resistance and big traction areas, which can be used for propulsion (Völker & Wilke, 1974). The use of a whip kick seems to be very difficult because often it results in an uneconomical kick when performing the breaststroke.

The purpose of the present investigation was to determine whether anthropometric values as well as functional angles of amplitude for movements within the lower limb region were determining factors for a certain type of breaststroke kick. For that purpose, the flexibility of joint movements observed during a regular breaststroke kick were determined. This research was confined to three symmetrical types of kicks: whip kick, wedge kick, and a kick with plantar flexed feet.

Methods

This investigation was conducted with 24 male and female subjects, aged 18 to 30 years. Only those subjects who clearly showed one of the three investigated types of kicks were arbitrarily selected. All subjects had at least been swimmers for 10 years, so the subjects assumably had consistent movement patterns. The selection and classification in the three categories were done by the investigation leader observing the subjects. The group was divided into 9 whip-kick swimmers, 8 wedge-kick swimmers, and 7 swimmers who had a kick with plantar flexed feet.

The examined anthropometric and functional values within the lower limb region were chosen with regard to the relevance for the breaststroke kick. The following anthropometric data were obtained: length and circumference of lower limbs and widths of knees and ankles of both legs.

The maximal angles of amplitude flexion of the functional joint movements were measured: rotation angles (outward rotation in the knee joint, pronation of the feet, and endorotation in the hip joint) and flexion angles (flexion in the knee joint, dorsiflexion of the feet). All maximal amplitudes were measured during active movements of the subjects. The determination of the anthropometric values followed the descriptions by Tittel and Wutscherk (1972). Statistical significance was tested using the analysis of variance (Winer, 1971).

Results

The determination of the lengths, widths, and circumferences of the lower limbs showed no significant differences among the three examined groups (see Table 1). All amplitudes of the selected joint movements revealed generally the tendency that the swimmers with plantar flexed feet had, in relation to the other types of kicks, smaller flexibility (see Table 2). This reduced flexibility was less pronounced in the angles of

Table 1   Anthropometric Values of Breaststroke Swimmers With Different Types of Kicks

Value	Whip kick M	SD	Wedge kick M	SD	Plantar flexed feet M	SD
Length of the upper leg (cm)	53.0	4.5	51.2	3.1	52.4	4.2
Length of the lower leg (cm)	39.8	4.0	37.5	3.5	38.8	5.9
Width of the knee joint (cm)	11.3	0.6	11.3	0.3	11.7	1.3
Width of the ankle joint (cm)	7.4	0.6	7.0	0.5	7.6	0.6
Maximum circumference of the upper leg (cm)	54.6	2.3	54.8	2.9	54.9	4.8
Maximum circumference of the lower leg (cm)	36.8	1.8	36.6	2.6	37.3	2.2

Table 2   Functional Angles Amplitudes of Breaststroke Swimmers With Different Types of Kicks

	Whip kick M	SD	Wedge kick M	SD	Plantar flexed feet M	SD
Flexion in the knee joint	129.5	5.8	127.8	5.3	125.9	6.2
Dorsiflexion of the foot	70.5	8.3	72.2	5.5	69.8	5.1
Outward rotation in the knee joint	29.2	5.0	32.3	6.2	27.7	5.6
Pronation of the foot	13.5	5.7	15.6	5.2	10.6	4.3
Endorotation in the hip joint	33.9	8.0	31.6	6.7	28.7	6.6

floxion but displayed a statistically significant difference ($p < .05$) in the sum of rotation angles. Swimmers with whip or wedge kicks failed to exhibit uniform flexibility. The flexibility of the wedge-kick swimmers was either equal (sum of the flexion angles) or similar (sum of rotation angles) to the flexibility of the whip-kick swimmers (see Figure 1).

Regarding the right-left differences of flexion at the knee joint, there was a significant difference ($p < .01$) for the entire group. On the right side, higher values were obtained than on the left side. Viewing the pronation of the feet, the entire group showed significantly higher amplitudes of movement on the left side than on the right side. This could not be demonstrated separately for each group. The other amplitudes of movement showed no significant differences between the right and left sides.

In some attributes of flexibility, sex-dependent differences in the three types of breaststroke kicks were demonstrated (see Figure 2). This could

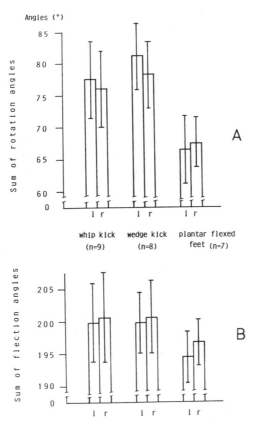

Figure 1 Flexibility of the left (l) and right (r) side within the lower limb region of breaststroke swimmers with different types of kicks. (A) Sum of rotation angles (outward rotation in the knee joint, pronation of the foot, endoration in the hip joint); (B) Sum of flexion angles (flexion in the knee joint, dorsiflexion of the foot).

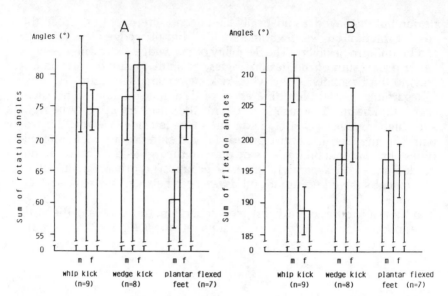

Figure 2 Flexibility of male (m) and female (f) breaststroke swimmers with different types of kicks. (A) Sum of rotation angles (outward rotation in the knee joint, pronation of the foot, endoration in the hip joint); (B) Sum of flexion angles (flexion in the knee joint, dorsiflexion of the foot).

be determined for the whip-kick swimmers. The male swimmers, contrary to the other groups, had greater amplitudes of movement than the female subjects. In the other two groups, the female subjects showed better flexibility. This behavior can be seen in Figure 2, especially in the angles of flexion, where the flexibility of the female whip-kick swimmers was less marked.

Discussion

The results indicate that joint flexibility within the lower limbs influences the performance of the breaststroke kick. The swimmers with plantar flexed feet who were not able to swim a regular breaststroke kick showed less flexibility in relation to the whip-kick and wedge-kick swimmers. The fact that this difference was significant in the rotational movements indicated that swimmers with plantar flexed feet cannot produce these movements because of reduced flexibility. The selected rotational movements—outward rotation in the knee joint, pronation of the foot, and endorotation in the hip joint—are in this combination typical for breaststroke swimming only and not for ordinary movements.

Swimmers with a plantar flexed feet kick fundamentally have no dorsiflexion of the feet. This investigation did not reveal a significant difference between the swimmers with plantar flexed feet and the other two groups. Indeed the swimmers with plantar flexed feet had the smallest amplitudes of movement but the whip kick swimmers had on an average a negligibly better flexibility. So it cannot be hypothesized that this failure of dorsiflexion of the swimmers with plantar flexed feet was related to their flexibility. The reason for this could be deficits in local perception or motor control problems.

By viewing both the regular types of breaststroke kick swimmers, it was established that no homogeneous tendency is evident in the determined amplitudes of movement. The obvious presumption that swimmers with the difficult type of whip kick need better flexibility cannot be corroborated. In some attributes of flexibility (outward rotation in the knee joint, pronation and dorsiflexion in the feet), the amplitudes of movement for the wedge-kick swimmers are higher than for the whip-kick swimmers.

The investigation showed that the ineffective type of wedge kick cannot be explained by lack of flexibility. Other explanations must be provided, such as the manner and the development of the learning process.

The results of this investigation also indicate that no outstanding flexibility is necessary for swimming the whip kick. For this reason, a small reduction in flexibility (at least concerning the female swimmers) should not be a handicap to learning the effective type of whip kick in breaststroke swimming.

References

Counsilman, J.E. (1977). *Competitive swimming manual.* Bloomington, IN: Author.

Maglischo, E.W. (1982). *Swimming faster.* Palo Alto: Mayfield.

Tittle, K., & Wutscherk, H. (1972). *Sportanthropometrie.* [Sport anthropometry]. Leipzig: Barth.

Völker, K., & Wilke, K. (1974). Zur Mechanik der Beinbewegung im Brustschwimmen [On the mechanics of leg movement in the breaststroke]. *Praxis der Leibesübungen, 15,* 167.

Winer, B.J. (1971). *Statistical principles in experimental design* (2nd ed.). New York: McGraw Hill.

Physiological Characteristics of Japanese Elite Synchronized Swimmers

Miwako Takamoto
Yoshio Nakamura
Miwako Motoyoshi
Yoshiteru Mutoh
Mitsumasa Miyashita

Synchronized swimming requires a high degree of artistic movement. Its performance was formerly so graceful and sophisticated that most of the routine events were comprised of floating and movement of the arms to music. However, it has become dynamic and powerful and is now a competitive Olympic event. Sychronized swimming has aroused scientists' interest, and several studies report data on Canadian and American synchronized swimmers. Synchronized swimmers in Japan have also been playing an important part in the world; however, knowledge and data on Japanese synchronized swimmers are limited. Thus, the purpose of this study was to investigate the physical and physiological characteristics of Japanese elite synchronized swimmers.

Methods

The study consisted of two tests (Tests 1 and 2). All subjects were fully informed of risks and the discomfort of the test procedures and consented to participate.

Test 1

A total of 23 elite Japanese synchronized swimmers participated in Test 1 from August to September, 1983. Nine were members of the 1983 Japanese National Team, and the others were close to national caliber.

Body composition, maximal oxygen consumption ($\dot{V}O_2$max), and vital capacity (VC) were measured on all subjects. Muscle fiber distribution was studied on 14 subjects. Body density was determined by underwater weighing (Behnke & Wilmore, 1974), and lean body mass (LBM) and relative fat (% fat) were also estimated (Brozek, Grande, Anderson, & Keys, 1963). Residual lung volume (RV) was measured in the water following the underwater weighing by use of the oxygen dilution method (Rahn, Fenn, & Otis, 1949).

$\dot{V}O_2$max was determined by a conventional incremental cycle ergometer test using a Monark bicycle. Work load was set so that the subject would reach exhaustion within 18 to 20 min. $\dot{V}O_2$max was expressed in three ways: liters per minute (l/min), mililiters per kilogram of weight per minute (ml/kg/min), and liters per kilogram of weight in water per minute (l/kg/min)—$\dot{V}O_2$max, $\dot{V}O_2$max/w, and $\dot{V}O_2$max/ww, respectively.

Standard spirometric techniques were used to measure VC on a spirometer (TKK, Takei, Tokyo) with the best of three trials selected for analysis.

Sample biopsies of muscle (Mutoh, Sadamoto, Miyashita, Katayama, & Mori, 1983) were obtained from the vastus lateralis muscle and cryostat-cut samples were stained for myofibrillar adenosine triphosphatase after preincubation (Padykula & Herman, 1955). Fibers were classified as Type I, Type IIa, and Type IIb (Brooke & Kaiser, 1969), and cross-sectional area of each muscle fiber was determined.

Test 2

A group of 15 Japanese elite synchronized swimmers, including one 1982 Japanese National Team member, participated in Test 2. Muscular power output was measured in October, 1982. Six Japanese adult females were measured as controls.

Cybex II (Lumex, New York) was used to determine the peak torque during isokinetic knee extensions. The subjects performed two to five maximal contractions at angular velocites of 0, 30, 60, 120, 180, 240, 300°/s, with the best peak torque of each trial speed selected for analysis. The subjects then performed 50 continuous knee extensions at an angular velocity of 180°/s. Average peak torque (MET) of the 50 repetitions was calculated.

Performance scores of the swimmers were obtained from compulsory figure performance scores of the 1983 Japan National Championship in Test 1 and the averaged scores of the 1982 Japan National Indoor Championship and the National Championship in Test 2. Pearson correlation coefficients and partial correlation coefficients between the measured variables and the scores were calculated.

Results and Discussion

Physical Characteristics and Aerobic Capacity (Test 1)

Table 1 lists comparative data on the physical characteristics and aerobic capacity of the subjects, Japanese female nonathletes and U.S. and Canadian synchronized swimmers. Compared to Japanese female nonathletes, the subjects of the present study were somewhat taller but were lower in weight and percentage fat. Compared to U.S. and Canadian synchronized swimmers, the subjects were smaller in body size and lower in percentage fat, which resulted in a lower lean body mass (LBM) of the subjects.

Table 1 Comparative Data on Physical Characteristics of Synchronized Swimmers and Japanese Female Nonathletes (Mean ± SD)

	N	Age (years)	Height (cm)	Weight (kg)	% fat	LBM (kg)	VC (l)	$\dot{V}O_2$max (l/min)	$\dot{V}O_2$max/w (ml/kg/min)
Present study	23	18.0 ± 2.9	159.4 ± 3.9	49.4 ± 4.2	21.3 ± 3.1	38.8 ± 2.9	3.65 ± 0.41	2.15 ± 0.23	43.2 ± 5.5
Japanese female non-athletes (Taguchi, Ueda, Hata, Yamaji, & Miyashita, 1976)	16	21.6 ± 2.8	157.4 ± 5.4	51.6 ± 6.6	24.1 ± 10.3	38.9 ± 4.1	—	—	—
1982 U.S. National Team (Roby, Constable, & Lowdon, 1983)	13	20.1 ± 1.6	166.2 ± 6.2	55.8 ± 6.7	24.0 ± 4.8	42.3 ± 3.8	4.40 ± 0.54	2.43 ± 0.16	43.2 ± 4.2
1977 Canadian elites (senior)(Poole, Crepin, & Sevigny, 1980)	22	17.5 ± 1.8	165.1 ± 6.1	56.4 + 4.9	—	—	4.07 ± 0.62	2.47 ± 0.31	44.0 ± 4.4

Ichikawa and Miyashita (1980) reported that the $\dot{V}O_2$max of female nonathletes was lower when measured with a bicycle ergometer compared with a treadmill test (18 to 20 years, 33.2 ± 4.3 vs 39.2 ± 5.1 ml/kg/min). The subjects of the present study were tested by a bicycle ergometer and produced higher $\dot{V}O_2$max values compared with both values of the female nonathletes. The subjects of the present study were similar in $\dot{V}O_2$max/w (ml/kg/min) to the other synchronized swimmers who were measured on a treadmill. Mean $\dot{V}O_2$max/w of the 1983 National Team members was 47.4 ± 2.5 ml/kg/min, which was higher than those of the U.S. and Canadian synchronized swimmers (Table 1). Therefore, the Japanese synchronized swimmers were slimmer and had higher aerobic capacities than nonathletic Japanese females.

Muscle Fiber Composition (Test 1)

As shown in Table 2, the subjects of the present study had a higher percentage of Type I fibers than female nonathletes (Type I 50%, Type IIa 30% to 35%, Type IIb 15% to 20%; see Houston [1978] and Nygaard [1981]). However, cross-sectional fiber areas of the subjects were similar to those of nonathletes. The characteristics, higher percentage of Type I fibers and tenuous muscle fibers of the subjects, were previously observed in endurance-trained male and female long-distance runners and competitive swimmers (Costill et al., 1976; Jansson & Kaijser, 1977; Nygaard & Nielsen, 1978). Training is not believed to convert Type I fibers into Type II fibers; hence, it has been suggested that the percentage of fibers is established early in life and that a high percentage of Type I fibers in athletes results from selection (Costill et al., 1976).

Muscular Power Output (Test 2)

Compared to the controls, the synchronized swimmers were similar in height (159.6 ± 5.9 cm vs. 160.0 ± 4.6 cm) and weight (51.3 ± 7.1 kg vs. 51.2 ± 6.4 kg) and were younger (16.1 ± 2.1 years vs. 24 ± 2 years). There were no statistically significant differences in peak torques at any speed nor in MET between the swimmers and the controls. Poole, Crepin, and Sevigny (1980) reported similar results in Canadian elite synchronized swimmers who were typical of female nonathletes. Figure 1 shows the

Table 2   Muscle Fiber Distribution and Fiber Area of 14 Synchronized Swimmers (18.1 ± 2.7 Years)

Fiber trait	Type I	Type IIa	Type IIb
Distribution (%)	59.7 ± 8.7	29.6 ± 5.8	10.1 ± 8.0
Cross sectional area (μm^2)	4,083 ± 747	3,639 ± 496	2,920 ± 678

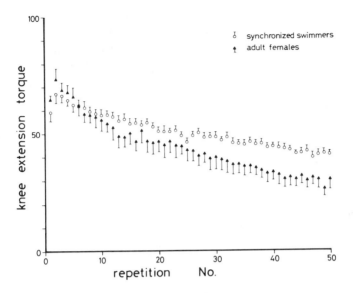

Figure 1   Change of peak torque in 50 knee extension repetitions in subjects and controls.

change of peak torque values when the subjects performed 50 knee extensions. Peak torque decreased with repetitions in both the swimmer and the control groups; however, the decline in peak torque of the swimmers was not as high as the controls. The initial peak torque (maximum) was nearly equal in both groups, whereas the last torque (minimum) was significantly higher in swimmers than controls ($p < .01$). Miyashita and Kanehisa (1979) reported that peak torque of knee extensor muscles for girls at 210°/s increased with age only from 13 to 14 years; beyond 14 years peak torque did not increase. Hence, synchronized swimmers were assumed to be similar to nonathletes in muscular force in a single exertion but had higher muscular endurance, which could be reinforced by the fact that synchronized swimmers had a higher percentage of Type I fibers (the results from Test 1). Thorstensson & Karlsson (1976) reported a linear correlation between muscle fatigability and percentage of slow-twitch (Type I) fibers.

Correlations of Physiological Profiles With Performance

Age, height, VC, V̇O₂max/ww, peak torque at every speed, and MET were significantly related to compulsory performance scores (see Table 3). Age correlated best with the scores, which suggests the importance of not only experience and development of skills but also growth and maturity. The partial correlation coefficient ($r_{12 \cdot age}$), excluding the effect of age, was still significant in all the variables except for VC and V̇O₂max/ww (Table 3).

Table 3 Correlation Coefficient (r_{12}) and Partial Correlation Coefficient ($r_{12} \cdot$ age) Excluding the Effect of Age Between Performance Scores and Variables

Variable	N	Pearson's correlation coefficient (r_{12})	Partial correlation coefficient ($r_{12} \cdot$ age)
Age (years)	23	.82*	—
Height (cm)	23	.70*	.54*
VC (l)	23	.60*	.41
$\dot{V}O_2$max/ww (l/kg/min)	21	.63*	.29
Peak torque of knee extension			
300°/s	14	.76*	.70*
100°/s	14	.79*	.69*
0°/s	14	.75*	.73*
MET	14	.76*	.69*

*$p < .01$.

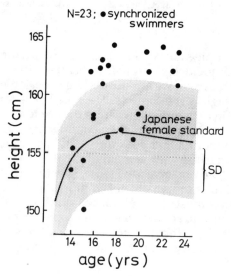

Figure 2 Height versus age of subjects and Japanese female standard. (Data from Iizuka, Nichimaru, & Nagata, 1980.)

As shown in Figure 2, from 12 to 14 years subjects' heights corresponded approximately with that of Japanese female standards, increasing with age. Beyond 14 years, subjects of the present study exceeded the height standard of Japanese females. Thus, two explanations for such a high correlation between height and scores (r_{12}, $r_{12} \cdot$ age) are growth and/or selection. In general, Japanese synchronized swimmers had slim bodies, high aerobic capacities, high muscle endurance, and slow-twitch fiber types of muscles.

The correlation between scores and muscular power output was far beyond the effect of age (Table 3), which might suggest that muscular power is important and may be developed in ways other than synchronized swimming. Consequently, dryland muscular training is recommended for synchronized swimmers.

References

Behnke, A.R., & Wilmore, J.H. (1974). *Evaluation and regulation of body build and composition.* Englewood Cliffs, NJ: Prentice-Hall.

Brooke, M.H., & Kaiser, K.K. (1969). Some comments on the histochemical characterization of muscle adenosine triphosphatase. *Journal of Histochemistry and Cytochemistry, 17,* 431-432.

Brozek, J., Grande, F., Anderson, J.T., & Keys, A. (1963). Densitometric analysis of body composition: Revision of some quantitative assumptions. *Annals of New York Academy of Sciences, 110,* 113-140.

Costill, D.L., Daniels, J., Evans, W., Fink, W., Krahenbuhl, G., & Saltin, B. (1976). Skeletal muscle enzymes and fiber composition in male and female track athletes. *Journal of Applied Physiology, 40,* 149-154.

Houston, M.E. (1978). The use of histochemistry in muscle adaptation: A critical assessment. *Canadian Journal of Applied Sport Sciences, 3,* 109-118.

Ichikawa, T., & Miyashita, M. (1980). Aerobic power of Japanese in relation to age and sex. *Hungarian Review of Sports Medicine, 21,* 243-253.

Iizuka, T., Nichimaru, T., & Nagata, A. (Eds.). (1980). *Physical fitness standards of Japanese people.* Tokyo: Fumaido.

Jansson, E., & Kaijser, L. (1977). Muscle adaptation to extreme endurance training. *Acta Physiologica Scandinavica, 100,* 315-324.

Miyashita, M., & Kanehisa, H. (1979). Dynamic peak torque related to age, sex, and performance. *Research Quarterly, 50,* 249-255.

Mutoh, Y., Sadamoto, T., Miyashita, M., Katayama, M., & Mori, T. (1983). A new instrument for percutaneous muscle biopsies. *International Journal of Sports Medicine, 4,* 289-290.

Nygaard, E. (1981). Skeletal muscle fiber characteristics in young women. *Acta Physiologica Scandinavica, 112,* 299-304.

Nygaard, E., & Nielsen, E. (1978). Skeletal muscle fiber capillarization with extreme endurance training in man. In B. Eriksson & B. Furberg (Eds.), *Swimming medicine IV* (pp. 282-293). Baltimore: University Park Press.

Padykula, H.A., & Herman, E. (1955). The specificity of the histochemical method for adenosine triphosphatase. *Journal of Histochemistry and Cytochemistry, 3,* 170-195.

Poole, G., Crepin, B.J., & Sevigny, M. (1980). Physiological characteristics of elite synchronized swimmers. *Canadian Journal of Applied Sport Sciences*, **5**, 156-160.

Rahn, H., Fenn, W.O., & Otis, A.B. (1949). Daily variations of vital capacity, residual air, and expiratory reserve including a study of the residual air method. *Journal of Applied Physiology*, **1**, 725-736.

Roby, F.B., Constable, S.H., & Lowdon, B.J. (1983). Physiological characteristics of champion synchronized swimmers. *The Physician and Sportsmedicine*, **11**, 136-147.

Taguchi, S., Ueda, K., Hata, Y., Yamaji, K., & Miyashita, M. (1976). Maximal oxygen uptake and its relationship to body composition of nonathletes and athletes (swimmers), with special reference to total body potassium. *Japanese Journal of Physical Education*, **21**, 19-26.

Thorstensson, A., & Karlsson, J. (1976). Fatigability and fiber composition of human skeletal muscle. *Acta Physiologica Scandinavica*, **98**, 318-322.

PART IV

MUSCLE FUNCTION

Muscular Mechanics and Neuromuscular Control

Dietmar Schmidtbleicher

Hypothesis of Hypertrophy

In the practice of training, some still believe that strength training merely calls for changes in enzymatic quantity or quality within the muscle, which ultimately results in muscle cross-section increases.

Results of ergophysiological and training research on the optimal training stimulus for the greatest possible strength increases appear to come from two distinct sources:

- The *tension stimulus theory*, created by Rasch and Pierson (1964) and Hettinger (1968) stipulates that maximal tension results in the most effective rate of strength increases.
- In contrast, the so-called *ATP-debt theory* from Meerson (1967, 1973) suggests that training with submaximal loads (15 reps in 20 s per set) done repetitively results in the highest strength increases.

In this second method, the muscle tension is considerably lower. Recent findings by Goldspink (1978) indicate that even in completely exhausted musculature no adenosine triphosphate (ATP) debt could be detected. According to this research, a debt situation can only occur as the result of a lessened ATP flux-rate, and this is very unlikely. Yet with submaximal repetitive loads, very high increases in strength can be achieved.

The apparent contradiction in the two research findings, in terms of training methods, is either nonexistent, or both theories are extremely well based. From a certain threshold upward, the muscle reacts with the same adaptation. Or, different physiological adaptation mechanisms lead to the same externally measurable results in relation to strength increases.

Research by De Lorme and Watkins (1953), in which the volume of training was kept constant and the muscle tension (intensity) was changed, showed that strength increases can be achieved with higher intensities. Based on these results, however, one can favor neither the tension nor the ATP debt theory, because the duration of training is also an important factor. Although muscle hypertrophy resulting from strength training is known to exist (Costill, Coyle, Fink, Lesmes, & Witzmann, 1979; Gordon, 1967; Jakowlew, 1975), how this process occurs is not yet clear. Satellite cells located on the muscle fiber are probably stimulated to split

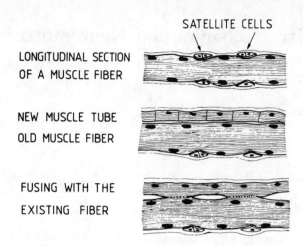

Figure 1 Hypertropy theory of Mauro (1979).

through tension stimulus (Mauro, 1979). These satellite cells build new *muscle tubes* parallel to the existing muscle fibers, which then fuse with the existing muscle fibers (see Figure 1). Some researchers have hypothesized that the new muscle tube can eventually become a new fiber. This probably occurs when further hypertrophy of an already thickened muscle fiber initiates supply (i.e., circulation) problems.

In this case, one would be dealing with a real proliferation of muscle fibers, which is called *hyperplasia*. But there is considerable doubt whether hyperplasia can occur in a fully matured human muscle (Bischoff, 1979; Ontell, 1979). It is assumed that the very small injuries (microtraumas) of the muscle fibers are stimulus for the splitting of satellite cells. This stimulus causes sarcoplasmic components to diffuse out of the cell, which in turn stimulates the splitting of satellite cells.

Neuromuscular Factors

Aside from muscle hypertrophy, maximal strength can be increased by other means. The adaptation of the nervous system to the training stimulus plays an important role here. From the classical cross-innervation studies by Buller, Eccles, and Eccles, (1960a) in the 1960s and a number of subsequent works, we know that the specific fiber typing of muscle (as mainly fast- or mainly slow-twitch fibers) depends on the consistency of those nerve cells in the spinal column that innervate the corresponding muscle (see Figure 2). In 1904 Sherrington, the famous British neurophysiologist, defined the basic element of nerve and muscle as the motor unit (MU). The MU consists of: (a) motoneuron, (b) axon, (c) motor endplates, and (d) the muscle fibers that were activated from one motoneuron.

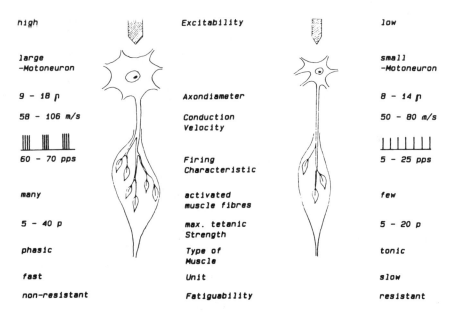

high	Excitability	low
large -Motoneuron		small -Motoneuron
9 - 18 ɲ	Axondiameter	8 - 14 ɲ
58 - 106 m/s	Conduction Velocity	50 - 80 m/s
60 - 70 pps	Firing Characteristic	5 - 25 pps
many	activated muscle fibres	few
5 - 40 p	max. tetanic Strength	5 - 20 p
phasic	Type of Muscle	tonic
fast	Unit	slow
non-resistant	Fatiguability	resistant

Figure 2   Fast and slow motor units and their main differences.

Differences between fast and slow MUs are shown in Figure 2. Note that this is an idealized view. Normally inside one muscle, there are all sizes of muscle fibers, and therefore, the method utilized for classification will determine the muscle fiber type detected. In an oversimplification one can only distinguish between slow and fast MUs and therefore between slow- and fast-twitch muscle fibers.

In their cross-innervation experiments, Buller et al. (1960b) cut the nerves of a muscle that was mainly slow and of a muscle that was mainly fast, and then they sutured the endings in a crossed manner. The slow muscle was now innervated with higher frequencies by the bigger motoneurons, whereas the fast muscle was activated by lower firing rates of the smaller motoneurons. Two months later both types of muscles had changed completely. The interpretation was not difficult: The type of innervation or more precisely the firing rate or *frequency* of innervation is the leading factor for the modification of a muscle fiber type.

In later experiments Pette, a German biologist, demonstrated that it was possible to produce each subtype of muscle fiber using electrical stimulation methods. The question now was, Does this work in practical training as well? To answer this question, investigating the recruitment order of MUs and the frequency phenomena in humans was necessary (see Figure 3). Under normal physiological conditions the MUs from a muscle were recruited in the order from slow to fast. A maximum voluntary contraction (MVC) always starts with the slowest MUs and ends by recruiting the fastest MUs. This is called *Henneman Principle*.

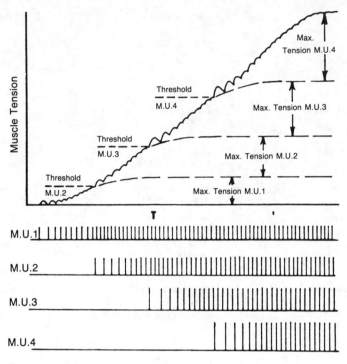

Figure 3 Recruitment principle of Henneman. (From Winter, 1979).

With respect to the force production, a second important result occurs (see Figure 4). The higher the innervation frequency or the higher the firing rate by which the muscle is activated, the greater the force production. Maximal force output caused by high firing rates is about 2 to 4 times higher than using low frequencies. This is a conceivable rationale for a complete muscle fiber not changing from slow to fast type during normal training. It would be necessary to activate a muscle maximally and with high frequency for hours, day after day. Normally an athlete works for 2 or even 3 hr a day with strength training. But the actual duration of high frequency stimuli is only 2 or 3 min. During the rest of the day innervation frequencies are mainly tonic or slow, and this is true for hours. In contrast to strength training, endurance training offers the possibility of low-frequency activation over hours, day after day, and therefore, one can easily detect changes from the fast fiber type to the slow one.

These findings are very important for a strength training:

- If you want to train the fastest MUs—remember they develop the highest forces—you must work against *high loads*, because only high loads guarantee MVC.
- To fulfill the frequency principle, the demand is to work against these high loads *as fast as possible*.

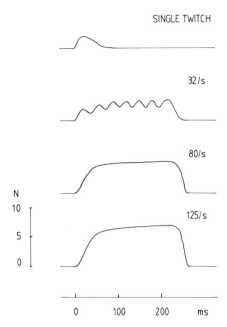

SINGLE TWITCH

32/s

80/s

N
10

5

0

125/s

0   100   200   ms

Figure 4   Frequency phenomena. (From Buller & Lewis, 1965).

Results

Still the unanswered question is, Does a strength training program of the maximal type actually lead to the most efficient increase in cross-section of the muscle? From several longitudinal and cross-sectional investigations, a representative one is presented here (Schmidtbleicher, 1985a). The aim of the study was to investigate the alterations in force-time (f-t) curves, cross-sectional area, and innervation characteristics of the triceps muscle after a 12-week training period comparing different strength training methods.

In a longitudinal study 59 male students, aged 22 to 25 years, participated in the experiment. They were divided into four homogeneous comparable groups. All training groups had four sessions weekly and practiced a concentric arm shot put movement on a special measurement device (see Figure 5).

The MAX-group (maximal MVC) carried out a training with high loads and few reps (3 × 3 × 90%, 2 × 2 × 95%, 1 × 1 × 100%, and 1 × 1 × 100% MVC + 1 kg). The P-group (power training) practiced 5 × 8 reps with 45% load of MVC. Both groups were instructed to develop their contractions as fast as possible. A third group, MR-group (maximal reps) trained 3 × 12 reps with 70% of MVC. The rest interval between the sets for the MAX- and P-groups was 5 min and 2 min for the MR-group, respectively. Pre- and posttests as well as training were executed on an

TRAINING	n	SERIES	REPS	LOAD	PAUSE
MAX -GROUP	15	3	3	90%	5 min
		2	2	95%	5 min
		1	1	100%	5 min
		1	1	100%+1 kg	
P -GROUP	15	5	7	45%	5 min
MR -GROUP	14	3	12	70%	2 min
CON -GROUP	15				
4 TRAINING SESSIONS PER WEEK FOR 12 WEEKS					

Figure 5   Training methods of the experimental groups.

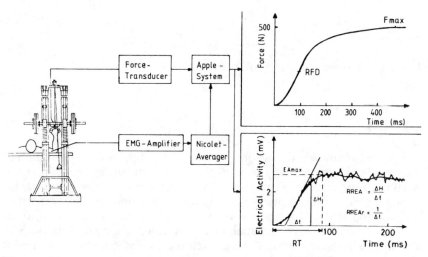

Figure 6   Measurement device (left side); isometric force-time curve (right side, upper trace); and rectified, averaged, and smoothed surface EMG of the triceps brachii.

apparatus that allowed both an isometric and a concentric shot put movement with the arm (see Figure 6).

Isometric MVC were recorded with a force-transducer in the grip, and the obtained signals were fed into a microcomputer and stored for further analysis. From 10 reps of each subject, the surface EMG of triceps brachii was recorded, rectified, and averaged (Nicolet, Model 1072), using the primary slope of the force-time curve as a trigger signal.

From the recordings, the following parameters were evaluated to describe the f-t-characteristics (see Figure 6): the maximal rate of force development (RFD) and the maximal level of isometric force (Fmax). The

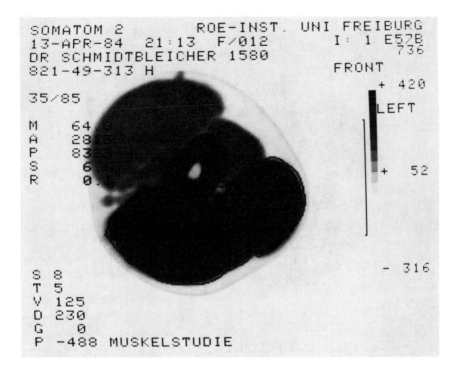

```
SOMATOM 2             ROE-INST. UNI FREIBURG
13-APR-84   21:13   F/012        I: 1 E57B
DR SCHMIDTBLEICHER 1580                  736
821-49-313 H                     FRONT
                                       + 420
35/85
                                      LEFT
M    64
A    28
P    83
S     6
R     0                           + 52


S   8
T   5                             - 316
V   125
D   230
G   0
P  -488  MUSKELSTUDIE
```

Figure 7 Computer tomogram of the right upper arm.

EMG pattern was characterized by the following parameters (Figure 6): the maximal level of electrical activity (EAmax) and the maximal rate of rise of electrical activity (RREA) and the period of time from the innervation onset until EAmax was reached (RT) (see Figure 7).

Cross-sectional area of the triceps muscle (halfway between acromion and elbow joint) was calculated by computer tomography (Siemens Somatom 2) (see Figure 8).

Analyzing the picture of the scanned upper arm, cross-sectional area of triceps brachii (AT) and the total section area (TSA) were calculated by digitizing a region of interest and using the density spectra for muscle, fat, and bone. Both parameters were compared with circumference measurements (CM).

Before the training period, all parameters showed no significant differences among the four groups as tested by a one-way ANOVA, whereas, after the training, ANOVA revealed significant differences (total section area and circumferences of muscle). Differences for all parameters except TSA and CM were significant at least at the .05 level. All modulation of the experimental groups were significant with an error probability of 5%, except TSA and CM, as tested by a paired t test.

Traditionally, hypertrophy of muscle is measured with simple anthropometric circumference measurements (CM) and, if at all, corrected for sub-

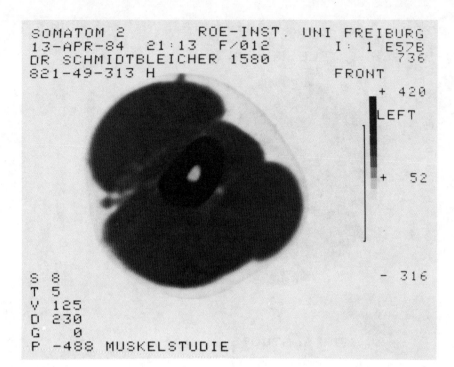

```
SOMATOM 2          ROE-INST. UNI FREIBURG
13-APR-84   21:13   F/012        I:  1 E57B
DR SCHMIDTBLEICHER 1580                 736
821-49-313 H                     FRONT
                                       + 420

                                     LEFT

                                     + 52




S  8                               - 316
T  5
V  125
D  230
G   0
P -488 MUSKELSTUDIE
```

Figure 8 Computer tomogram of the right upper arm. The white area represents the real muscle area of the triceps brachii as calculated by density spectroscopy excluding fat bone.

cutaneous fat thickness. The more precise technique of ultrasound scanning was used by Ikai and Fukunaga (1970) and Fukunaga (1976). To this author's knowledge, these are the only two longitudinal studies in humans that show an increase in the entire cross-sectional area of muscle as measured by scanning techniques. The more reliable and precise computer tomography showed that circumference measurements often led to an incorrect assessment of hypertrophy not only with respect to the effects of training methods but also for individual improvements. Moreover, increases in MVC (i.e., Fmax) may also be due to neuronal adaptation as assumed by Moritani and De Vries (1979) and shown by Haekkinen and Komi (1983). In addition to these results, the main effect of neuronal adaptation in this study consisted of significant changes of RREA (rate of rise of electrical activity) and RT (raise time), which indicated that the subjects had learned to activate their motoneuron pool in a shorter period of time (see Figures 9 and 10).

This is not true for all strength training methods, however. And this fact may explain why the published results differ from one another. The MAX- and P-group had to activate all motor units frequently. But only the MAX-group produced contractions long enough to develop a com-

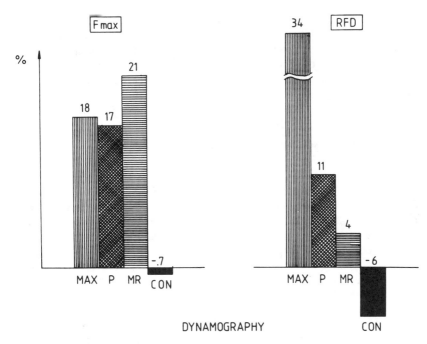

Figure 9 Improvements in maximal strength (Fmax) and in rate of force development (RFD) after 12 weeks of strength training using different strength training methods.

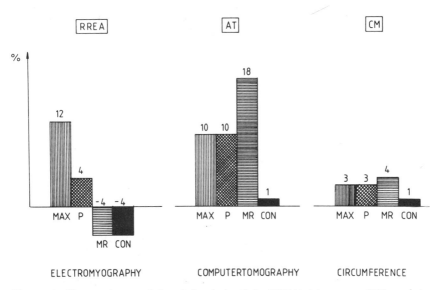

Figure 10 Changes in rate of rise of electrical activity (RREA), triceps area (AT), and circumference measurements (CM) of the upper right arm after 12 weeks of strength training using different strength training methods.

plete mechanical efficiency for the most phasic motor units (Milner-Brown, Stein, & Yemm, 1973). That would account for the high gains of the MAX-group in RREA, RT, and therefore also in RFD. More exhaustive strength training as practiced by the MR—group, on the one hand, led to a hypertrophy but, on the other hand, showed even a decrease in RREA. These results make the different theories mentioned at the beginning of the presentation conceivable.

Classification of Strength Training Methods

If one trains with high intensities (high loads and less reps), the adaptation is primarily a neuronal one. The result of this adapted innervation can be seen in a considerable improvement in rate of force development and an increase in maximal strength. Training with submaximal loads (60 to 80% of MVC) and several repetitions, on the one hand, leads to a very effective hypertrophy and therefore to a highly efficient increase in maximal strength but on the other hand, shows no neuronal adaptation, and therefore only small effects on the rate of force development. To avoid uneconomical training, adequately alternating the type of training would be interesting.

A third possibility for the amelioration of strength behavior results from a better intermuscular coordination. Improvement of strength development of this type, as opposed to the aforementioned ones is, however, *movement-specific* and therefore *not* transferable to another movement. In the final analysis this method is coordination training rather than strength training.

As we know from training practice and longitudinal research, the adaptation of muscle requires considerable time (several months to years, depending on the quality and quantity of the adaptation). On the other hand, measurable adaptation to a training stimulus directed to muscle hypertrophy can be detected after a relatively short time span. Biochemical changes appear in a few hours and lasting improvement after 2 weeks. Therefore, short-term increases of performance can be based, on one hand, on a coordinative learning effect; on the other hand, neural changes appear, which help the individual muscle to achieve greater performance capability. This is achieved by training the timing of the recruitment of motor units and by increasing the tolerance to elevated innervation frequencies (intramuscular coordination).

In a first conclusion, one can recognize that the important long-term factor responsible for muscle hypertrophy is the proliferation of contractile material in the muscle.

The first adaptations are always of an intermuscular coordinative type, and the first stabilization of training effects appears after 2 weeks (four training units per week). *Neuronal adaptations* (intramuscular type), after 6 to 8 weeks (again four training units per week), lead to few compensatory modifications. Only the hypertrophy method offers considerable improvement possibilities in strength behavior lasting over a period of several years. Experience indicates that after approximately 12 weeks of the same type of training, regardless of the type, the rate of increase drops off dramatically. Based on this knowledge, one should either use another muscle cross-section training method (as will be shown in one of the next figures) or emphasize changing to a type of training stress geared toward the neuronal system. Based on the presented results and the specific adaptations, one can organize a classification of strength training methods. (see Table 1). These methods call for short-term explosive maximal contractions against high loads, following, of course, an intensive type of warm-up (see Table 2). These methods are characterized by a large number of sets of repetitions with submaximal loads (60 to 80%). The execution of the movement is rapid to slow and ends in complete muscular failure (see Table 3).

All mixed methods not only work on the intramuscular coordination effect but also on the muscle cross-sections. For a similar length of training, the alternation of maximal strength methods and submaximal contraction methods shows better results than the mixed methods.

Beside the methods described, which deal mainly with concentric, eccentric, or isometric contractions, another group of strength training methods exists, the so-called *reactive training* methods. The aim of these training procedures is the performance of a stretch-shortening cycle (SSC) of the muscle (i.e., a combination of eccentric and concentric contractions). Stretch-shortening cycles are relatively independent motor qualities, and therefore should be trained with specific methods. First of all, one must analyze which type of SSC is necessary for the specific event. In a rough classification, one can classify two types, a short SSC and a long SSC. The main differences compared to a squat jump are shown in Figure 11.

Table 1 Methods With Maximal Contractions

Variable	Near-maximal contractions	Maximal concentric contractions	Maximal eccentric contractions	Concentric-eccentric maximal contractions
Form of work				
Concentric	X	X		X
Isometric				
Eccentric			X	X
Force development				
Explosive	X	X	X	X
Continuous				
Intensity load	90 95 97 100%	100%	ca. 150%	70-90%
Repetitions	3 1 1 1 + 1	1	5	6-8
Series	1 2 3 4 + 5	5	3	3-5
Rest interval	3-5 min	3-5 min	3 min	5 min

Note. Recommendations are according to Schmidtbleicher (1985b).

Table 2 Submaximal Contraction Methods

Variable	Standard Method I (constant load)	Standard Method II (progressively increasing load)	Bodybuilding Method I (extensive)	Bodybuilding Method II (intensive)	Isokinetic Method
Form of work					
Concentric	X	X	X	X	X
Isometric					
Eccentric					
Force development					
Explosive					
Continuous	X	X	X	X	X
Intensity load	80%	70 80 85 90%	60-70%	85-95%	e.g, 70%
Repetitions	8-10	12 10 7 5	15-20	8-5	15
Series	3-5	1 2 3 4	3-5	3-5	3
Rest interval	3-5 min	5 min	2-3 min	3-5 min	3 min

Note. To fulfill the number of repetitions described in these methods, it is necessary to call on the help of a partner for the last contractions. Recommendations are according to Schmidtbleicher (1985b).

Table 3 Mixed Methods.

Variable	Speed-strength method	Pyramid method
Form of work		
Concentric	X	X
Isometric		
Eccentric		
Force development		
Explosive	X	X
Continuous		
Intensity of load	30-50%	80 85 90 95 100 90 80
Repetitions	7	7 5 3 2 1 3 7
Series	5	1 2 3 4 5 6 7
Rest interval	3-5 min	3-5 min

Note. Recommendations are according to Schmidtbleicher (1985b).

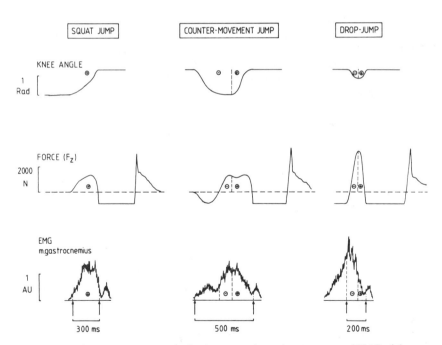

Figure 11 Differences in knee angle displacement, force-time curves, and EMG of the gastrocnemius in squat, countermovement, and drop jumps. (From Bosco, 1982).

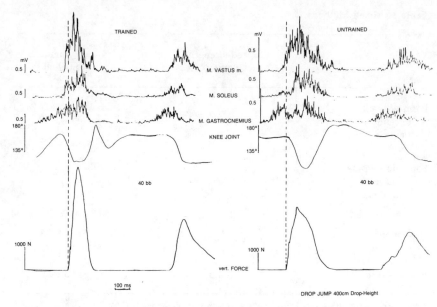

Figure 12   Differences in EMG patterns of a trained and an untrained subject performing drop jump from a height of 40 cm. Both subjects had the same body mass. (From Gollhofer, 1986).

Most important are the different innervation patterns. The role of innervation characteristics becomes evident when the EMG of trained and untrained athletes are analyzed (see Figure 12). At least three different phases occur at the innervation pattern: (a) preactivation, (b) reflectory induced phase, and (c) activation during the concentric phase.

In some of the investigated subjects we were able to detect an inhibition (see Figure 13). It was possible to determine that all reactive strength training methods aim primarily at an adaptation of the nervous system. Some of the methods which can be used for this purpose are shown in Table 4, and some examples are provided here:

- *Hopping* with both legs on the spot at either personal rhythm, with maximal frequency (i.e., maximal number of ground contacts possible), or with maximal height. In all three types, 30 reps are performed with rest intervals of 5 min between sets to allow for recovery of the nervous system. All three types can be combined in a training unit and can be done quickly and easily without apparatus.
- *Jump training.* Alternate step hopping for three sets; in each case 20 reps are performed with 5 min of rest. This is a method used for jump training. Other possibilities are "triple" or "pentajumps" for five sets of 10 reps, interspaced by 10-min rest intervals. The distance reached is used as a measure of training adaptation. Another method of reactive

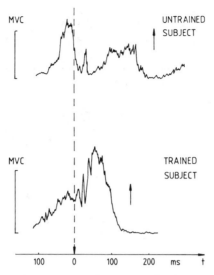

Figure 13   EMG pattern of gastrocnemius from a trained and an untrained subject performing drop jumps from 1.10 m. The amplitude of EMG is related to those of a maximum voluntary contraction (MVC). (From Schmidtbleicher and Gollhofer, 1982).

Table 4   Reactive Training Methods

Variable	Hopping single- and double-leg	Drop jumps
Form of work		
Concentric	X	X
Eccentric	X	X
Force development		
Explosive	X	X
Continuous		
Intensity load	without additional load	
Repetitions	30	15
Series	3	3-5
Rest interval	5 min	10 min

Note.   From Schmidtbleicher (1985).

jump training is used to ameliorate strength endurance: ''jump races'' over a distance of 50 m are done for three to five reps. Between reps, 5-min rests are prescribed, and between sets, 10 to 15 min intervals are indicated.

- *Depth jumping*. This, the most general method, should be practiced by high-caliber athletes only because of the injury potential. Three to five sets of 10 reps, along with rest intervals of 10 min between sets are commonly used. The height of the jumps should be set so that the athlete's heel doesn't touch the ground; if the heel touches the ground, the height is excessive. The procedure guarantees individual loading and progressive load increases. The athlete must imagine that he or she is landing on a hot plate and therefore work as quickly as possible in order to reach optimal performance. The use of cushioned landing surfaces (like mats) prevents the achievment of the desired training effect.

The use of additional loading—even relatively small weights (greater than 10% of body mass—leads to a reduction of the innervation of leg extensors and premature fatigue. These reasons, together with orthopaedic considerations, validate the concept of not using additional loads.

Conclusion

Regardless of the training method practiced, the coach as well as the athlete must precisely record the number of training units, the intensity, the number of reps, and the rest interval, so that the training goal can be precisely established. To identify only the volume of training in tons without identifying other training characteristics is meaningless. For example, a worker who lifts 2 kg, 2,000 times a day would perform 20 tons of work in a week, without any visible training adaptations—which brings one to the concept of progressive loads. During every training unit and after every training week, the maximal performance capacity must be redetermined. If this principle is not followed, training progress will soon stagnate. Another principle to be followed is the conformity of the training to the competitive movement. The range and direction of the training movement must be as similar as possible, so that the maximum transfer to the competitive movement can occur. This is valid in an increasing proportion in terms of the general goal-oriented preparation and becomes more and more important when doing specific strength training.

Another common mistake that is made is the elimination of strength training during the competitive season. This prevents the transfer of the acquired preparatory conditioning to high performance, because most of the peaking is aimed at technical preparation. During the competitive season, one should maintain the existing strength training level by performing two workouts per week. To attain the absolute high performance capacity, one should not cease strength training until 8 to 5 days before the competition.

The sophisticated use of macro- and microcycles can bring about relative peaks for "training competitions"; however, one should realize that absolute peaking can only occur about twice a year. When one increases the number of training units devoted to strength training, the athlete should elevate the proportion of "lengthening gymnastics" (stretching, etc.). Lastly one should remember that all training methods that emphasize the nervous system must be practiced in a rested state, with each contraction being executed with maximal effort and as fast as possible.

References

Bischoff, R. (1979). Tissue culture studies on the origin of myogenic cells during muscle regeneration in the rat. In A. Mauro (Ed.), *Muscle regeneration* (pp. 13-30). New York: Raven Press.

Bosco, C. (1982). Stretch-shortening cycle in skeletal muscle function. *Studies in sport, physical education and health.* Jyväskylä: University Press.

Buller, A., Eccles, C., & Eccles, R. (1960a). Differentiation of fast and slow muscles in the cat hind limb. *Journal of Physiology, 150,* 399-416.

Buller, A., Eccles, C., & Eccles, R. (1960b). Interaction between motoneurons and muscles in respect of the characteristic speeds of their responses. *Journal of Physiology, 150,* 417-439.

Buller, A., & Lewis, D. (1965). The rate of tension development in isometric tetanic contractions of mammalian fast and slow skeletal muscle. *Journal of Physiology, 176,* 337-354.

Costill, D., Coyle, E., Fink, W., Lesmes, G., & Witzmann, F. (1979). Adaptatins in skeletal muscle following strength training. *Journal of Applied Physiology, 46,* 96-99.

De Lorme, T., & Watkins, A. (1953). *Progressive resistance exercises.* New York: Appleton-Centry Crofts.

Fukunaga, T. (1976). Die absolute Muskelkraft und das Muskelkrafttraining [Absolute muscle strength and strength training]. *Sportarzt und Sportmedizine, 27,* 255-266.

Goldspink, G. (1978). Energy turnover during contraction of different types of muscles. In E. Asmussen & K. Jorgensen (Eds.), *Biomechanics VI-A* (pp. 27-39). Baltimore: University Park Press.

Gollhofer, A. (1986). *Komponenten der Schnellkraftleistung im Dehnungs-Verkürzungszyklus* [Factors influencing a stretch-shortening cycle]. Unpublished master's thesis, Freiburg.

Gordon, E. (1967). Anatomical and biomechanical adaptions of muscle to different exercises. *Journal of the American Medical Association, 201,* 755-759.

Haekkinen, K., & Komi, P. (1983). Electromyographic changes during strength training and detraining. *Medicine and Science in Sports and Exercise, 15,* 455-460.

Hettinger, T. (1968). *Isometrischen Muskeltraining. (3. Auflage)* [Isometric strength training (3rd ed.)]. Stuttgart: Thieme.

Ikai, M., & Fukunaga, T. (1970). A study on training effect on strength per unit cross-sectional area of muscle by means of ultrasonic measurements. *European Journal of Applied Physiology*, **28**, 173-180.

Jakowlew, N. (1975). Biochemische Adaptionsmechanismen der Skelettmuskeln an erhöhte Aktivität [Biochemical adaptation mechanisms in skeletal muscle to enhanced activity]. *Medizin und Sport*, **15**, 132-139.

Mauro, A. (1979). (Ed.). *Muscle regeneration*. New York: Raven Press.

Meerson, F. (1967). *Plastische Versorgung der Funktion des Organismus* [Plasticity of the functions of the organism]. Moscow: Nauka.

Meerson, F. (1973). Mechanismus der Adaption [Mechanism of the adaptation]. *Wissenschaft der UDSSR*, **7**, 425-433.

Milner-Brown, H., Stein, R., & Yemm, R. (1973). The orderly recruitment of human motor units during voluntary contractions. *Journal of Physiology*, **230**, 359-370.

Moritani, T., & De Vries, H. (1979). Neural factors versus hypertrophy in the time course of muscle strength gain. *American Journal of Physical Medicine*, **58**, 115-130.

Ontell, M. (1979). The source of ''new'' muscle fibers in neonatal muscle. In A. Mauro (Ed.), *Muscle regeneration* (pp. 137-146). New York: Raven Press.

Pette, D., Henricksson, J., & Emmerich, M. (1979). Myofibrillar protien patterns of single fibres from human muscle. *FEBS Letters*, **103**, 152-155.

Rasch, P., & Pierson, W. (1964). One position versus multiple positions in isometric exercise. *American Journal of Physical Medicine*, **43**, 10-16.

Schmidtbleicher, D. (1985a). Strength training: Part 1. Classification of methods. *Sport-Science Periodical on Research and Technology in Sports: Strength*, **W4**, 1-12.

Schmidtbleicher, D. (1985b). Strength training: Part 2. Structural analysis of motor strength qualities and its application to training. *Sports-Science Periodical on Research and Technology in Sports: Strength*, **W4**, 1-10.

Schmidtbleicher, D., & Gollhofer, A. (1982). Neuromuskuläre Untersuchungen zur Bestimmung individueller Belastungsgrößen für ein Tiefsprungtraining. [Nervomusculus research to detect individual load conditions in jump training]. *Leistungssport*, **12**, 298-307.

Winter, D.A. (1979). *Biomechanics of Human Movement*. New York: John Wiley.

Effects of Maximal Strength Training on Sprint Performance of Competitive Swimmers

Dieter Strass

Recent laboratory research has indicated that explosive type maximal strength training regimens change isometric force-time (f-t) characteristics (rate of force development, maximal force) in different forms (Bührle, 1985; Häkkinen & Komi, 1986; Komi, Karlsson, Tesch, Suominen, & Heikkinen, 1982; Schmidtbleicher, 1980, Schmidtbleicher & Bührle, 1987). These results show considerable improvements in the rate of force development with minor increases in maximal force. These different improvements in f-t characteristics are induced by specific changes in voluntary neuromuscular performance capacity. In addition to pure maximal force, which is primarily influenced by hypertrophy (Moritani & De Vries, 1979), explosive maximal force production, which is affected by neural activation (Häkkinen & Komi, 1985), is an important component of the underwater arm movement in sprint swimming.

The effects of strength training on sprint swimming performance have been investigated by Moffroid and Whipple (1970); Pipes and Wilmore (1976); Costill, Sharp, and Troup (1980); and Miyashita and Kanehisa (1983). Training methods and equipment were used in these studies that included weight training, and isometric, isotonic, and isokinetic exercises. However, very few studies have dealt with the question of whether the gains in muscular output after explosive type maximal strength training result in the improvement of sprint swimming performance (Hötke, 1985). The present pilot study, therefore, was designed to examine the effects of strength training with short-term explosive maximal dynamic contractions against high loads on the f-t characteristics and parameters of sprint swimming performance (speed, stroke frequency, stroke length) and their possible relationships.

Methods

Subjects

The experimental subjects of the study were 10 male competitive swimmers who had experience in weight training. The mean values ($\pm$ SD) for their age, height, and weight were 16.6 $\pm$ 1.2 years, 178.6 $\pm$ 7.2 cm, and 65.2 ± 9.4 kg, respectively. The control subjects consisted of 9 (7 males and 2 females) competitive swimmers who also had experience in weight training. Their anthropometric mean values (± SD) for age, height, and weight were 17.8 ± 3.9 years, 179.0 ± 7.9 cm, and 67.6 ± 9.1 kg, respectively.

Training

The strength training program of the experimental group consisted of four sessions weekly over a 6-week period. This program concentrated on training the arm extensor muscles utilizing barbells. The load on the barbell was increased every week during the training period according to one maximum repetition. The intensity of the training varied between 90 and 100% + 1 kg, and the subjects performed three reps per three sets of 90%, two reps per two sets of 95%, one rep and one set of 100%, and one rep and one set of 100% + 1 kg. The rest intervals between the series were 5 min. The subjects were instructed to develop every contraction as explosively as possible. The training program also included assisted exercises used in weight lifting for the arm flexor muscles and trunk to make training more interesting. The experimental group performed the same swimming training program after the strength training session as the control group throughout the experimental period.

Measurements

Both groups were tested on two identical occasions before and after the 6-week training period. The following pre- and post-training measurements were conducted: (a) arm strength test in the laboratory and (b) swimming tests (front crawl) of 25- and 50-m distance with maximal speeds in the swimming hall.

An apparatus of Schmidtbleicher (1980) was used to measure the isometric maximal force of the right arm (see Figure 1). After a few warm-ups and familiarization contractions, the subjects performed maximal isometric contractions against a fixed barbell with an arm position of 90° of abduction and the elbow joint kept at a right angle. All contractions were performed at the maximally produced rate of force development. Isometric maximal contractions were recorded with a force-transducer in the grip of the barbell and the obtained signals were fed into a microcomputer (Apple system) and stored for further analysis. From the recordings the following parameters were evaluated to describe the f-t characteristics: (a) maximal rate of force development (RFD) and (b) isometric maximal force level (Fmax).

From the swimming distances, the following parameters were determined: (a) mean speed ($\bar{v}$, m/s); (b) stroke frequency (MF, 1/min); and (c) stroke length (L, m). These parameters were measured by a special stopwatch—a "frequency stop watch" (Hanhart) that was calibrated for four arm cycles—and a normal stop watch. Stroke length was calculated according to the equation $\bar{v} = (L \times MF)/60$ (Reischle, 1978).

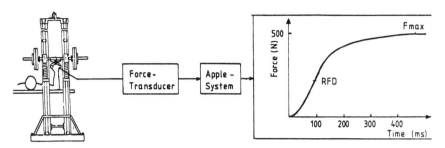

Figure 1 Left side: Test apparatus. Right side: Isometric force-time curve and the evaluated parameters for maximal force (Fmax) and maximal rate of force development (RFD).

Statistics

Means, standard deviations, and correlation coefficients were calculated by standard methods. Differences between values before and after training were tested for significance by the paired Student's t test. The level of significance was set at .05.

Results

Force-Time Characteristics

Strength training—induced changes in the f-t characteristics are presented in Figure 2. The maximal arm extension force increased from 354 ± 62 to 396 ± 61 N ($p < .01$). This corresponded to an average increase of 12.5 ± 6.8%. An increase in the values of rate of force development from 4.01 ± 0.8 to 4.96 ± 1.2 N/ms ($p < .01$) was observed, corresponding to an average increase of 24.8 ± 16.7%.

Swimming Characteristics

The examined changes in the swimming variables in both distances before and after strength training are shown in Figure 3. The mean speed in the 25-m distance improved from 1.83 ± 0.1 to 1.91 ± 0.1 m/s (4.4 ± 1.3%, $p < .001$) and in 50-m distance from 1.77 ± 0.08 to 1.81 ± 0.08 m/s (2.1 ± 0.4%, $p < .001$). In the 25-m distance the average value of stroke frequency decreased from 55.0 ± 4.0 to 53.5 ± 3.4 ($p < .05$) and in 50-m from 56.7 ± 3.2 to 54.7 ± 3.6 ($p < .05$). An increase was noted in the average values of stroke length: from 2.01 ± 0.24 to 2.16 ± 0.26 m ($p < .01$) in the 25-m and from 1.88 ± 0.10 to 2.01 ± 0.24 m ($p < .01$) 50-m distance. These values correspond to average increases of 7.0 ± 3.9% in the 25-m and 7.3 ± 4.1% in the 50-m distances. The control group showed no changes of a statistical significance in the f-t characteristics and parameters of the swimming tests between the pre- and posttraining measurements. The correlation coefficients between maximal force and

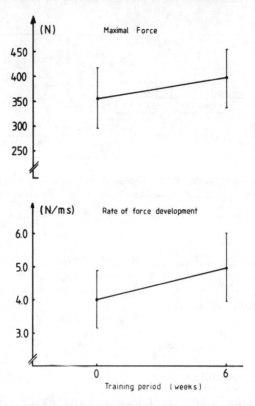

Figure 2 Means (± *SD*) of the isometric force and maximal rate of force development of the arm extensor muscles before and after 6 weeks of explosive type strength training.

parameters of swimming performance (mean speed, stroke frequency, and stroke length) in the 25- and 50-m distances, respectively, before and after strength training are shown in Table 1.

Discussion

The present strength training regimen resulted in differences of the isometric f-t characteristics. This type of strength training caused greater improvements in maximal explosive force production than in the maximal force. These findings tend to support those of Schmidtbleicher (1980; Schmidtbleicher & Bührle, 1985) and Häkkinen and Komi (1983), who have shown that improvements in explosive force production are accompanied by significant increases in the maximal rise of electrical activity of the EMG pattern. They suggested that neuromuscular adaptations with respect to firing frequency and/or in the recruitment pattern of the activated motor units may have contributed to the improvement of the explosive force development. These phenomena may also have been responsible for the present results.

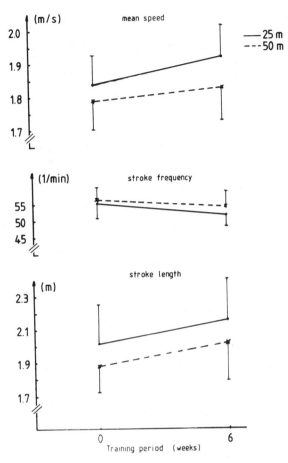

Figure 3 Means (± SD) of the mean speed, stroke frequency, and stroke length for the 25-m and 50-m distances (front crawl swimming) before and after 6 weeks of explosive type strength training.

Table 1   Correlation Coefficients Between the Maximal Force (Fmax) and Parameters of Swimming Performance in the 25- and 50-m Distance Before and After 6 Weeks of Strength Training

	Before training				After training			
Variables	$\bar{v}$	MF	L	Event	$\bar{v}$	MF	L	Event
Fmax	.64	−.33	.54	25 m	.83	−.73	.72	25 m
Fmax	.56	−.48	.62	50 m	.73	−.57	.73	50 m

Note. $\bar{v}$ = mean speed; MF = stroke frequency; L = stroke length.

Present findings show explosive type strength training induced greater improvements in the isometric f-t characteristics than in the sprint swimming performance (mean speed, stroke frequency, stroke length). Similar observations were also reported by Costill et al. (1980). Those authors found in 41 competitive swimmers, as a result of strength training by using the biokinetic swim bench, an average gain of 28% in the arm force and an enhancement in the sprint swimming performance (25 yd) of 3.6%.

The observation that f-t characteristics demonstrated greater improvements than parameters of swimming performance requires some explanations. The enhancement of rate of force development and maximal force might be a result of similar arm movements during strength training exercise and the arm exercise in the strength test. In both conditions, the triceps brachii performed largely identical movements in the force production. On the other hand, the triceps brachii are strongly involved in the front crawl arm movement, primarily in the pull and push phase (Olbrecht & Clarys, 1983; Schleihauf, 1983). However, the swimming and testing movements were different. As a result of these differences, the slight improvement in the swimming performances may have taken place during the present training.

The transfer loss would probably be smaller if dry land exercises were executed using the specific swimming movement performed in water. In reference to swimming-specific strength training, several studies (Costill et al. 1980; Pipes & Wilmore, 1976; Sharp, Troup, & Costill, 1982) demonstrated a clear superiority of the isokinetic training procedures over isotonic or isometric procedures relative to strength training for swimming. These authors pointed out that strength training with isokinetic exercises is relatively specific; that is, isokinetic apparatus allows the simulation of the swimming movement, and therefore improvements in muscle strength may affect the arm's underwater movement. However, electromyographic and kinematic analyses by Clarys (1983) and Olbrecht and Clarys (1983) have shown that the EMG pattern of the investigated muscles as well as the coordination of specific strength training exercises and performed movements (isokinetic swim bench, roller board, expander, latissimus apparatus) are substantially dissimilar to the arm movements executed while swimming. Also, Schleihauf (1983) argued that isokinetic equipment does not allow movements that simulate arm movements in front crawl swimming. Schleihauf (1983) indicated that the speed of the movements performed on isokinetic equipment at the proper stroke frequency is too low with respect to the speed of the movement during swimming.

References

Bührle, M. (1985). Dimensionen des Kraftverhaltens und ihre spezifischen Trainingsmethoden [Dimensions of strength behavior and their specific training methods]. In M. Bührle (Ed.), *Grundlagen des Maximal- und Schnellkrafttrainings. Schriftenreihe des Bundesinstituts für Sport und Sportwissenschaft* (pp. 82-111). Schorndorf: Hofmann.

Costill, D., Sharp, R., & Troup, J. (1980). Muscle strength: Contributions to sprint swimming. *Swimming World*, **21**, 29-34.

Häkkinen, K., & Komi, P.V. (1983). Changes in neuromuscular performance in voluntary and reflex contraction during strength training in man. *International Journal of Sports Medicine*, **4**, 282-288.

Häkkinen, K., & Komi, P.V. (1985). Effect of explosive type strength training on electromyographic and force production characteristics of leg extensor muscles during concentric and various stretch-shortening cycles exercises. *Scandinavian Journal of Sports Sciences*, **7**, 65-76.

Häkkinen, K., & Komi, P.V. (1986). Training-induced changes in neuromuscular performance under voluntary and reflex conditions. *European Journal of Applied Physiology*, **55**, 147-155.

Hötke, V. (1985). Empirische Untersuchung zur Effektivität von dynamischem Maximalkrafttraining bei jugendlichen Leistungsschwimmern [Empirical investigation of efficiency of dynamic maximal strength training in juvenile competitive swimmers]. *Der Schwimmtrainer*, **41-44**, 61-68.

Komi, P.V., Karlsson, J., Tesch, P., Suominen, H., & Heikkinen, E. (1982). Effects of heavy resistance and explosive type strength training methods on mechanical, functional and metabolic aspects of performance. In P.V. Komi (Ed.), *Exercise and sport biology* (pp. 90-102). Champaign, IL: Human Kinetics.

Miyashita, M., & Kanehisa, H. (1983). Effects of isokinetic, istonic and swim training on swimming performance. In A.P. Hollander, P.A. Huijing, & G. de Groot (Eds.), *Biomechanics and medicine in swimming* (pp. 329-334). Champaign, IL: Human Kinetics.

Moffroid, M.T., & Whipple, R.H. (1970). Specificity of speed exercise. *Physical Therapy*, **50**, 1692-1699.

Moritani, T., & De Vries, H. (1979). Neural factors versus hypertrophy in the course of muscle strength gain. *American Journal of Physiology and Medicine*, **58**, 115-130.

Olbrecht, J., & Clarys, J.P. (1983). EMG of specific strength training exercises for the front crawl. In A.P. Hollander, P.A. Huijing, & G. de Groot (Eds.), *Biomechanics and medicine in swimming* (pp. 136-141). Champaign, IL: Human Kinetics.

Pipes, T.V., & Wilmore, J.H. (1976). Muscular strength through isotonic and isokinetic resistance training. *Athletic Journal*, **57**, 42-45.

Reischle, K. (1978). Chronofotographische Zuglängenregistrierung bei Delphin, Rücken und Kraul [Chronofotographic registrations of stroke length of butterfly, back stroke, and front crawl]. *Beiheft zum Leistungssport*, **14**, 31-49.

Schleihauf, R.E. (1983). Specificity of strength training in swimming: A biomechanical viewpoint. In A.P. Hollander, P.A. Huijing, & G. De Groot (Eds.), *Biomechanics and medicine in swimming* (pp. 184-191). Champaign, IL: Human Kinetics.

Schmidtbleicher, D. (1980). *Maximalkraft und Bewegungsschnelligkeit* [Maximal strength and movement speed]. Bad Homburg: Limpert.

Schmidtbleicher, D., & Bührle, M. (1987). Neuronal adaptation and increase of cross-sectional area studying different strength training methods. In B. Jonsson (Ed.), *Biomechanics X-B* (pp. 615-620). Champaign, IL: Human Kinetics.

Sharp, R.L., Troup, J.P., & Costill, D.L. (1982). Relationship between power and sprint freestyle swimming. *Medicine and Science in Sports and Exercise*, **14**, 53-56.

The Brussels Swimming EMG Project

Jan Pieter Clarys

This project started in 1970, in a Dutch marine ship model test station (Figure 1) as a result of the study of fundamental and applied hydrodynamics of living human body shapes. This test station allowed for the measurement of passive drag in different positions and of active (swimming) drag. It was found contrary to the general belief that drag in a prone position 60 cm under the water surface was greater than at the water surface or swimming level and that active drag while swimming the front crawl at different velocities reached one and a half to twice the drag values of any passive drag condition (see Figure 2; Clarys, 1979; Clarys & Jiskoot, 1974; 1975; Clarys, Jiskoot, & Lewillie, 1973; Jiskoot & Clarys, 1975).

The combination of physics (hydrodynamics) and electrophysiology (EMG) may appear bizarre at first, but in reality these disciplines are highly complementary when ergonomic aspects of aquatics are considered. Hydrodynamics is concerned with drag and propulsion phenomena but because drag equals propulsion at constant velocity, propulsion is usually calculated from a drag-velocity relationship.

On the other hand, EMG deals with the direct recording of electrical potentials of the active muscles. In the case of swimming movements, it gives an expression of the dynamic involvement of specific muscles in the propulsion of the body through the water.

Figure 1 Towing carriage and drag recording in the Dutch model test station at Wageningen.

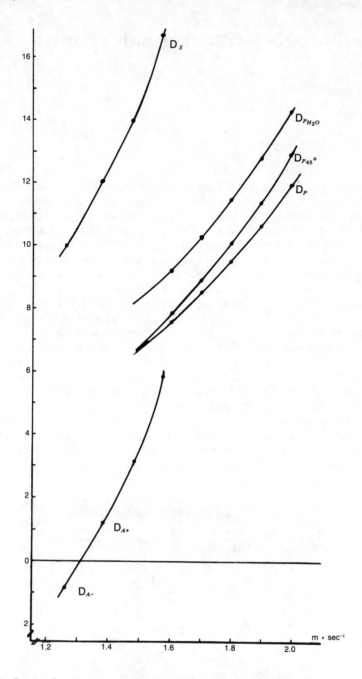

Figure 2   Passive drag in prone position (D_p); in prone position but 60 cm under the water (D_pH_2O); the directly measured "added" drag (D_A+ & D_A-) and the calculated drag while swimming the front crawl (Ds) (Clarys, 1985).

The interdisciplinary relationship between swimming propulsion (hydrodynamics) and muscular activity (electrokinesiology or EMG) becomes herewith obvious, resulting in a cinematographic, electromyographic, and resistance study of water polo and competition front crawl, of which the findings were presented in Rome in 1971 (Clarys et al., 1973). One year before the Olympic Games of Munich, it was stated that a shortening of the arm movement and an increase of accelerations overcome a higher hydrodynamic drag (Ds). Hence, drag and propulsion increase with increasing velocity, so the feedback became evident. In addition, it was electromyographically shown (in the same study) that different front crawl arm trajectories can produce identical muscular patterns but with different intensities (Figure 3). Although this finding received very little attention at the time, it was used for promoting water polo crawl as an alternative to competitive swimming training only. It has created an impulse and a direction for further development of the Brussels Swimming EMG project as illustrated in Figure 4.

Thanks to the pioneer work of Ikai, Ishii, and Miyashita (1964) and Lewillie (1967, 1968, 1973) and to the popularization of the Ikai et al. work by Counsilman (1968), the Brussels EMG project was oriented simulta-

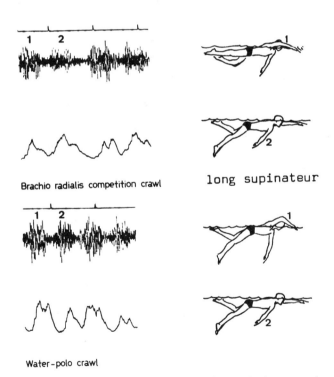

Brachio radialis competition crawl   long supinateur

Water-polo crawl

Figure 3 The raw EMG and linear envelope of muscular activity in water polo and competition front crawl.

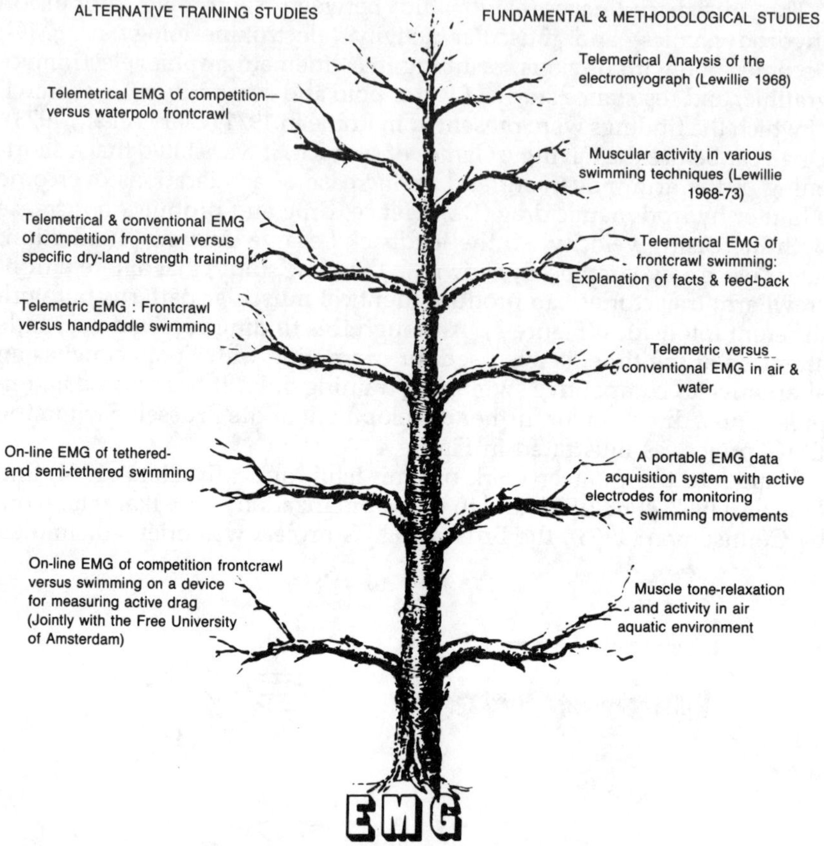

Figure 4   The fundamental methodological and applied EMG studies of the Brussels swimming EMG project.

neously into a "fundamental" methodological direction and in an "applied" direction through the investigation of alternative swimming training approaches.

Over the years, the improvements in EMG recording devices and the development of methodological approaches of both EMG data acquisition and computerized pattern analysis have proven valuable for bio-engineers, physiotherapists, sport biomechanists, electrophysiologists, and in the end for trainers, coaches, and physical education majors as well. Since the end of the 1960s (Lewillie, 1967), there has been a trend of developing miniaturized telemetric devices in order to monitor complex human movements remotely. Specifially, for kinesiological-biological purposes the telemetric devices changed from two-channel recordings (Clarys, 1985; see Figure 5; Clarys et al. 1973-1983; Lewillie, 1967, 1968, 1973) to eight-channel systems currently (Ellis, 1984; Guo & Yan, 1984). This same trend occurred in clinical EMG research at the end of the 1970s.

Apart from the obvious and numerous advantages of the telemetric measurement of muscular activity in swimming as used in the 1970s, three distinct disadvantages have been encountered under field (swimming pool) circumstances:

- Linking more than two or three transmitters in parallel is difficult because of the limited free radio wave possibilities at the moment.
- Since the beginning of the project, breaks in transmission, or atmospheric, static, or other disturbances have never been controllable.
- If a commercialized multiplexing system (actually on the market) is used (e.g., for four, six, or eight channel EMG recording), the bandspread must be increased considerably with respect to the current standards. In addition a digital multiplexer is rather costly and the record quality is not improved accordingly, probably because of amplifcation problems.

But, realizing the value of remote monitoring in kinesiological research and having the experience with two-channel telemetric EMG recordings, a totally new approach has been developed combining both the advantages of conventional and telemetric recordings (Clarys & Publie, 1987).

In order to measure muscle activity of complex isotonic and/or ballistic movements under field (e.g., dynamic swimming movements) or laboratory circumstances, different features are taken into consideration:

- The EMG data acquisition system with its electrodes should allow total kinesiological freedom to the subject or a movement without additional resistance.
- The set-up should allow adaptation to the characteristics of the field and movement circumstances, especially the synchronization system applicable not only to swimming but to skiing, archery, cycling, and so forth.
- It should allow long-term movements and movements of greater distance, and continuous measurements (up to 60 min, tape limits).
- The influences of the complex skin resistance phenomena on the signal must be omitted by means of ultra high impedance amplifiers as suggested by the Ad Hoc Committee of the International Society of Electrophysiological Kinesiology (Winter, Rau, Kadefors, Broman, & Luca, 1980).
- Six or seven muscles should be monitored simultaneously.
- The combined recording and data acquisition system should be user friendly.

Separately, all these features are not innovative because they are actually applied in existing commerical systems. However, combined into one system they are unique in sport (e.g., swimming) EMG.

To allow such a combination, we integrated a multichannel FM recorder, "active" electrodes, a regulation-amplification unit and different synchronization modes into one system with different possibilities (see Figure 5).

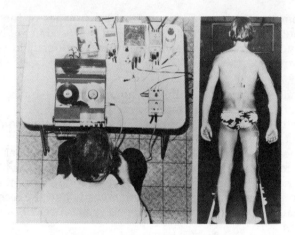

Figure 5 The two channel telemetric EMG recording system.

In most existing instrumentation, an input impedance of 10 or even 1 MΩ is common, thus the skin must be prepared until the resistance is down to less than 100 or even 10 kΩ, respectively. Of course, then the impedance between the electrodes should be measured over the whole frequency band. However, the use of a high-performance amplifier eliminates the preparation of the skin and the need to check the resistance, thus simplifying the measuring procedure (Winter et al., 1980).

Consequently to capture a noise-free EMG signal, preamplifiers in the electrodes of more than 1 GΩ were used. These operational amplifiers (OpAmp) are coupled as a voltage follower adjacent to both of the signals. A third OpAmp (as a differential amplifier) provides an asymmetrical signal with respect to the reference. A fourth noninverting coupled OpAmp provides an amplification of 20 dB and a low ohm output for branching off the electrode signal. Until recently the Brussels EMG project used metal rasp or silver, but "passive," types of electrodes. However, when combined with a series of operational amplifiers, "active" electrodes can be obtained.

A finished active electrode thus contains within a pleximolded frame, four operational amplifiers, housed in a 14-pin duel in-line (type TLO84 JFET) and six metalfilm resistances. The 2mm deep inlay of the Ag plates in the frame allows use of electrolytes and avoids skin artifacts.

These active electrodes and their pleximolded frame are coupled with a special triple conductor, containing the signal-transporting conductor, two conductors for symmetrical power supply (± 3.5 V), and shielding. The advantatge of the active electrode over the classic passive electrode is a decrease in erroneous recordings (Figure 6). This has become an important feature because it has been found that despite thorough precautions (different tapings and plastic varnish for additional electrode protection), the water does decrease the detectable electrical output of human muscle. In other words, an imaginary identical muscle contraction with

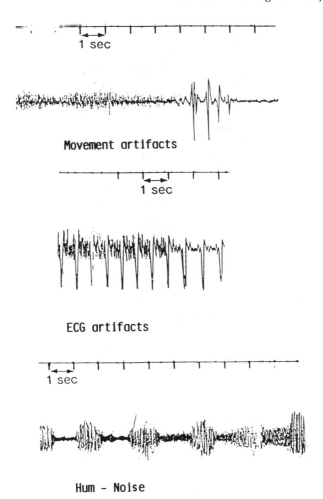

Figure 6 Erroneous EMG recordings.

identical intensity will produce more electricity in the air than in the water (Figure 4—telemetrical vs. conventional EMG in air and water; Clarys, Robeaux, & Delbeke, 1984).

The different possibilities mentioned earlier depend on the use of a portable seven-channel recorder (but still an FM recorder) and on the synchronization mode, resulting in an "on-line" EMG recording model and a "remote" EMG recording model. Both models, however, are used in combination with a six-channel portable regulation unit providing (a) the supply for the active electrodes, (b) the additional amplification, and (c) the calibration and adjustments of all six channels to the individual electrical activity.

The on-line model, manufactured for conventional EMG recording of six muscles with a Teac MR30 FM seven-channel data cassette recorder,

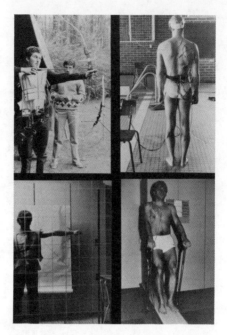

Figure 7 The on-line EMG registration and data acquistion model.

uses a six-channel, watertight portable supply and amplification unit with a fixed gain of 34 dB directly connected to six electrodes. The level adjustments are made on the recorder itself (actually used in swimming; see Figure 7).

The remote model is used for remote EMG recordings, combining an ultracompact, portable seven-channel Teac HR30 data recorder, a portable regulation unit (for supply and amplification) and six separate active electrodes, with the adjustments being made on the regulation unit (e.g., cycling and alpine skiing—see Figure 8—and in a later stage also for swimming). In both models an additional channel is used for audio memo and synchropulses.

Parallel to the methodological EMG development, the Brussels Swimming EMG Project had an informative function. It explained assumed facts, allowed for exact determination of the muscle action in the competitive front crawl, and provided normative data for comparison (the fundamental approach; Clarys et al., 1983; 1985; Figures 4 to 9).

Furthermore, in the course of the project, different alternative training methods were studied, allowing direct feedback to the coach and swimmer. The older and more recent studies are listed in chronological order on the left part of the project tree (Figure 4). Consider, for example, dryland training devices with or without "built in" accomodating resistance. This equipment is used worldwide and very popular on the market, mainly because it breaks the monotony of classical swimming

Figure 8   The remote EMG registration and data acquisition model.

training. Its popularity certainly does not result from its promoted qualities, namely increasing strength and allowing movement-specific workouts (Clarys, 1985; Olbrecht & Clarys, 1984). These combined qualities cannot be translated accordingly in corresponding muscle activity because little electromyographic similarity exists between imitation swimming movements on dry land and the front crawl movement under normal conditions. It was found that (a) there were overall time differences between dryland and "wet" arm cycle executions; (b) the muscle potential amplitdues were different in all five devices studied (expander, roller board, call craft, isokinetic swim bench, and latissimus pull; (c) most muscles showed fewer EMG peaks on dry land; (d) there were marked discrepancy scores for all comparisons (devices/muscles/functional groups/cycle phase separately); and (e) the dryland coordination creates a different pattern of movement.

In general, whenever a swimmer acts against a mechanical resistance (especially in a different environment), important pattern deviations are noted. Specific training, as described by Leeuwenhoek (1977), cannot be accomplished with dryland devices due to mechanical and environmental differences.

This observation, and our findings, coincided with the rejections of specific training on land by other authors also. Their rejections were based on sensomotoric and/or physical considerations. Absaljamon, Bashanow, Danilotschkin, and Melknow (1979) claim that the interference of unitation sensomotoric patterns on dry land damages the sensomotoric pattern that is used in water competition. However, Boicev, Damjanova, and Doksinow (1978) found no similarity between force/time to maximal force occurrence in and out of the water using isokinetics, a roller board, and call craft. They proposed to use these dryland devices in the preparatory phase of training only and not during the competitive phase.

Following the dryland exercise study, a series of different hand paddle models (Figure 10) has been investigated under training conditions in

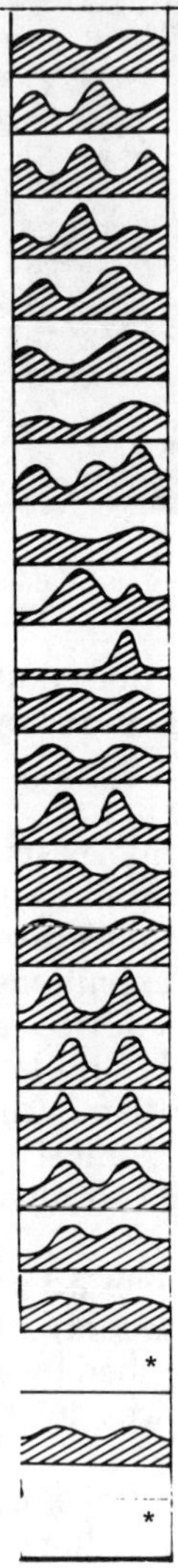

MUSCLE	MOST FREQUENT N° OF CONTRACTION AND ATTERN	% MUSCLE ACTION/ CYCLE COMPETITION SWIMMERS	% MUSCLE ACTION/ CYCLE NONCOMPE- TITION SWIMMERS
M. EXTENSOR DIGITORUM	2	30.23	38.35
M. FLEXOR CARPI ULNARIS	2'	*	43.10
M. TRICEP CAPUT LATERALE	3	38.78	28.92
M. TRICEP CAPUT LONGUM	2	39.47	35.64
M. BICEP BRACHII	2	27.00	34.61
M. DELTOIDEUS PARS ANT.	2	33.12	23.43
M. DELTOIDEUS PARS MED.	2	37.33	31.97
M. DELTOIDEUS PARS POST.	3 *	27.58	36.33
M. STERNO CLEIDO MAST.	2	25.54	21.81
M. TRAPEZIUS SINISTRA (respiration right)	2	29.91	22.57
M. TRAPEZIUS DEXTRA (respiration right)	1	24.51	29.54
M. LATTISSIMUS DORSI	2	92.34	23.66
M. PECTORALIS MAJOR (CLAV.)	2	36.75	26.10
M. PECTORALIS MAJOR (STERNO)	2	43.27	39.66
M. RECTUS ABDOMINIS (Pars superior)	2	83.13	37.86
M. RECTUS ABDOMINIS (Pars inferior)	2	91.96	48.33
M. OBLIQUUS EXT. SINISTRA	2	24.49	39.92
M. OBLIQUUS EXT. DEXTRA	2	28.64	35.84
M. GLUTAEUS MAXIMUS (pars sup.)	2	79.52	41.40
M. GLUTAEUS MAXIMUS (pars. inf)	2	122.41	31.18
M. RECTUS FEMORIS	2 *	21.61	24.57
M. SEMITENDINOSUS	2 *	18.53	36.57
M. TIBIALIS ANTERIOR	-- *	-- *	22.70
M. GASTROCNEMIUS CAP. LAT.	2 *	19.13	36.13
M. BICEP FEMORIS	-- *	-- *	32.5

* These muscles show a highly variable contraction pattern

Figure 9 Average front crawl muscle action as percentages of the relative maximal isometric contraction. Twenty-five muscle contraction patterns; number of peaks and percentage of muscle intensity for competitive and noncompetitive swimmers.

order to observe similarities and differences in muscular activity and intensity. In contrast with the dryland results, most of the models used (but not all) showed similar muscle activity, and its use under training circumstances was confirmed as specific (Bollens & Clarys, 1984). Each

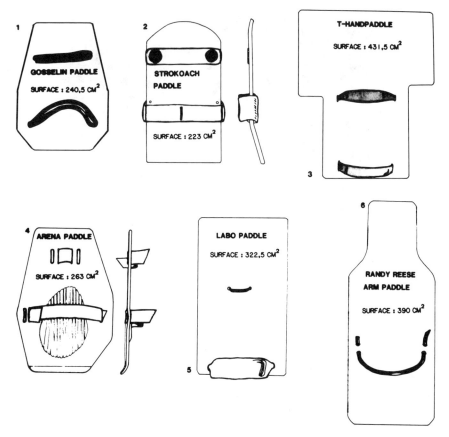

Figure 10 Hand paddle models used for an EMG study (Bollens & Clarys, 1985).

of these different studies has searched for activity or muscular similarity, beginning with the same question: Does the alternative movement (or training) correspond to free competitive swimming? Is the movement or is the training "specific"?

We agree completely with Counsilman (1978). He stated: "In developing an exercise program for swimmers, it is important to stress the specificity of these exercises. Specificity is of primary significance if maximum transfer of training effect is to occur". However, referring to our experiences in investigating so-called specific alternative training methods, one must be very careful in making sensomotoric similarity considerations and realize that there is much more than just "imitating" a movement. Today as in 1970, hydrodynamics, electrophysiology, and the psychomotor aspects of "similarity" and "specificity" are gathered again in the renewed measurement of active drag (with the MAD system) and another investigation of alternative training methods.

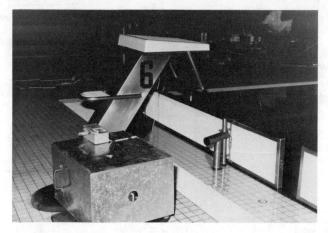

Figure 11   The fully tethered swimming device used for an EMG study.

Summary

In the 1970s and the begining of the 1980s a quadruple approach in aquatics was made, and we suggested the ergonomic links between fundamental hydrodynamics, applied dynamics of swimming, electromyographical aspects, and specific training. Within this context, an evaluation of dryland training and the use of hand paddles was made. Today the story of specific training is continuing with the study of muscular specificity during fully tethered and semitethered front crawl swimming (see Figures 11 and 12).

Details of these investigations are presented elsewhere in this volume (Bollens, Annemans, Vaes, & Clarys, 1988; Cabri, Bollens, Annemans, Publie, & Clarys, 1988); but in summary we have found that during fully tethered swimming at all studied frequencies, the muscular patterns of all investigated muscles are similar to those of free swimming. This alternative training system can be considered as specific.

During semitethered swimming at sprint velocity, the specificity of the muscular pattern is maintained up to a resistance of 10 to 12 kg. At higher resistances, the muscular action becomes nonspecific.

All researchers dealing with swimming, and hydrodynamics in particular, know that the measurement of the resistance encountered during swimming, the so-called active drag, has always been cumbersome, complex, and difficult and although different methodological approaches in the 1970s have provided corresponding results (Clarys, 1973, 1974, 1975, 1979, 1985; Di Prampero, Pendergast, Wilson, & Rennie, 1974; Holmer, 1974, 1975; Pendergast, Di Prampero, Graig, & Rennie, 1978; Rennie, Pendergast, & Di Prampero, 1975). These measurements have in common that active drag is calculated by means of extrapolation of the measured "added drag." The similarity of their independently found conclusions indicate a certain validity of the findings, but the problem of measuring active drag directly instead of indirectly remains to be solved.

Figure 12   The semitethered swimming device used for an EMG study.

tain validity of the findings, but the problem of measuring active drag directly instead of indirectly remains to be solved.

Recently, the Faculty of Physical Education (IFLO, of the Free University in Amsterdam) developed and constructed an innovative device for measuring active drag and propulsion called the MAD system, allowing for the direct measurement of forces involved in front crawl swimming (Hollander et al., 1986; Toussaint et al., 1988). Because the Department of Experimental Anatomy of the Free University in Brussels was previously involved with hydrodynamics and actually with the EMG of sport movements, a joint venture was set up between both universities to investigate the similarity between free swimming and the movements on the MAD system (Clarys et al., 1988).

The active electrodes including preamplifiers previously described are fixed on the skin at the geometrical midpoint of a contracted propulsion muscle and covered with plastic varnish. The maximal voluntary contraction is used as reference for normalization, and EMG signals are registered with an on-line system with portable amplifier on a seven-channel FM recorder (Clarys, 1985; Clarys & Publie, 1987). The swimmer pushes off aginst the grips of the MAD system with the right and left hand alternately during crawling in the indicated direction and returns the pool length swimming free at approximately the same stroke rate. Synchronization for both MAD swimming and free swimming is given verbally at each arm entry on the seventh available channel.

Again, the details of both the hydrodynamic and electromyographic approach of these studies are presented elsewhere in this volume. But in summary, muscular activity increased with increasing stroke rate in a similar manner in both free and MAD swimming.

The MAD system does not demand a different muscular use although an adaptation in movement pattern is assumed. The MAD system can be regarded as a specific measurement and/or training device. Over 16 years ago, the Brussels Swimming EMG project started in the area of hydrodynamics; obviously the ergonomic link cannot be disconnected.

References

Absaljamon, T., Bashanow, W.W., Danilotschkin, W.A., & Melkonow, A.A. (1979). Krafttrainingsapparate in der Vorbereitung von Spitzenschwimmern. Translation of Plavanje, Moscow, 1.

Boicev, K., Damjanova, R., & Doksinov, H. (1978). Vaproci na. *Fysiceskata kultura*, **1**, 672-679.

Bollens, E., & Clarys, J.P. (1984, July). *Frontcrawl training with hand paddles: A telemetric EMG investigation*. Paper presented at the 1984 Olympic Scientific Congress, Eugene, OR.

Bollens, E., Annemans, L., Vaes, W., & Clarys, J.P. (1988). Peripheral EMG comparison between semitethered and free front crawl swimming. In B.E. Ungerechts, K. Reischle, & K. Wilke (Eds.), *Swimming science V* (pp. 173-181). Champaign, IL: Human Kinetics.

Cabri, J., Bollens, E., Annemans, L., Publie, J., & Clarys, J.P. (1988). The relation of stroke frequency, force, and EMG in front crawl tethered swimming. In B.E. Ungerechts, K. Reischle, & K. Wilke (Eds.), *Swimming science V* (pp. 183-189). Champaign, IL: Human Kinetics.

Clarys, J.P. (1979). Human morphology and hydrodynamics. In J. Terauds & E.W. Bedingfield (Eds.), *Swimming III* (pp. 3-41). Baltimore: University Park Press.

Clarys, J.P. (1983). A review of EMG in swimming: Explanation of facts and/or feedback information. In A.P. Hollander, P. Huijing, & G. de Groot (Eds.), *Biomechanics and medicine in swimming* (pp. 123-135). Champaign, IL: Human Kinetics.

Clarys, J.P. (1985). Hydrodynamics and electromyography: Ergonomic aspects in aquatics. *Journal of Applied Ergonomics*, **16**(1), 11-24.

Clarys, J.P., & Jiskoot, J. (1974). Aspects de la resistance á lávancement lors de différentes positions du corp chez le nageur. *Le travail humain*, **37**(2), 323-324.

Clarys, J.P., & Jiskoot, J. (1975). Total resistance of selected body positions in the front crawl. In J.P. Clarys & L. Lewillie (Eds.), *Swimming II* (pp. 110-117). Baltimore: University Park Press.

Clarys, J.P., Jiskoot, J., & Lewillie, L. (1973). A kinematographic, electromyographic and resistance study of waterpolo and competition front crawl. In S. Cerquiglini, A. Venerando, & J. Wartenweiler (Eds.), *Biomechanics III* (pp. 446-452). Basel: Karger.

Clarys, J.P., Jiskoot, J., Rijken, H., & Brouwer, P.J. (1974). Total resistance in water and its relation to body form. In R.C. Nelson & C.A. Morehouse (Eds.), *Biomechanics IV* (pp. 187-196). Baltimore: University Park Press.

Clarys, J.P., Massez, C., Van Den Broeck, M., Piette, G., & Robeaux, R. (1983). Total telemetric surface EMG of the front crawl. In H. Matsui & K. Kobayashi (Eds.), *Biomechanics VIII-B* (pp. 951-959). Champaign, IL: Human Kinetics.

Clarys, J.P., & Publie, J. (1987). A portable EMG data acquisition system with active surface electrodes for monitoring kinesiological research. In B. Jonsson (Ed.), *Biomechanics X-A* (pp. 233-240). Champaign, IL: Human Kinetics.

Clarys, J.P., Robeaux, R., & Delbeke, G. (1984). Telemetrical versus conventional EMG in air and water. In D. Winter, R. Norman, R. Wells, K. Hayes, & A. Patla (Eds.), *Biomechanics IX* (pp. 286-294). Champaign, IL: Human Kinetics.

Clarys, J.P., Toussaint, H.M., Bollens, E., Vaes, W., Huijing, P., Groot, G. de, Hollander, A.P., & Cabri, J. (1988). Muscular specificity and intensity in swimming against a mechanical resistance. In B.E. Ungerechts, K. Reischle, & K. Wilke (Eds.), *Swimming science V* (pp. 191-199). Champaign, IL: Human Kinetics.

Counsilman, J.E. (1978). *Competitive swimming manual for coaches and swimmers*. London: Pelham Books.

Counsilman, J.E. (1968). *The science of swimming*. London: Pelham Books.

Ellis, M.I. (1984). *A new 8-channel biological telemetry system* (abstract). Liverpool Polytechnic Publications.

Guo, Q., & Yan, Q. (1964, July). *The study of muscular activity in athletes using multi-channel EMG-telemetry*. Paper presented at the 1984 Olympic Scientific Congress, Eugene, OR.

Hollander, A.P., Groot, G. de, Ingen Schenau, G.J. van, Best, H. de, Peeters, W., Meulemans, A. & Schreurs, A.W. (1986). Measurement of active drag forces during swimming. *Journal of Sport Sciences*, **4**, 21-30

Holmer, I. (1974). Physiology of swimming man. *Acta Physiologica Scandinavica* (Suppl.), **407**.

Holmer, I. (1975). Efficiency of breast stroke and freestyle swimming. In J.P. Clarys & L. Lewillie (Eds.), *Swimming II* (pp. 130-136). Baltimore: University Park Press.

Ikai, M., Ishii, K., & Miyashita, M. (1964). An electromyographical study of swimming. *Research Journal of Physical Education*, **7**, 45-54.

Jiskoot, J., & Clarys, J.P. (1975). Body resistance on and under the water surface. In J.P. Clarys & L. Lewillie (Eds.), *Swimming II* (pp. 105-109). Baltimore: University Park Press.

Lewillie, L. (1967). Analyse télémetrique de l'electromyogramme du nageur [Telemetric EMG analysis of the swimmer]. *Travail de la Société de Medicine Belege d'Education Physique et Sports, 20,* 174-177.

Lewillie, L. (1968). Telemetrical analysis of the electromyograph. In J. Wartenweiler, E. Jokl, & M. Hebbelinck (Eds.), *Biomechanics I* (pp. 147-148). Basel: Karger Verlag.

Lewillie, L. (1973). Muscular activity in swimming. In S. Cerquiglini, A. Venerando, & J. Wartenweiler (Eds.), *Biomechanics III* (pp. 440-445). Basel: Karger Verlag.

Leeuwenhoek, A.A. (1977). *Trainingsbouwstenen.* Haarlem: Uitg. de Vriesenborch.

Olbrecht, J., & Clarys, J.P. (1984). EMG of specific dry land training for the frontcrawl. In A.P. Hollander, P. Huijing, & G. de Groot (Eds.), *Biomechanics and medicine in swimming* (pp. 136-141). Champaign, IL: Human Kinetics.

Pendergast, D.R., Di Prampero, P., Graig, A., & Rennie, D.W. (1978). The influence of selected biomechanical factors on the energy cost of swimming. In B. Eriksson & B. Furber (Eds.), *Swimming medicine IV* (pp. 367-378). Baltimore: University Park Press.

Di Prampero, P.E., Pendergast, D.R., Wilson, D.W., & Rennie, D.W. (1974). Energetics of swimming man. *Journal of Applied Physiology, 37,* 1-5.

Rennie, D.W., Pendergast, D.R., & Di Prampero, P.E. (1975). Energetics of swimming in man. In J.P. Clarys & L. Lewillie (Eds.), *Swimming II* (pp. 97-104). Baltimore: University Park Press.

Toussaint, H.M., Hollander, A.P., Groot, G. de, Ingen Schenau, G.J. van, Vervoorn, K., Best, H. de, Meulemans, T., & Schreurs, W. (1988). Propelling efficiency in front crawl swimming. In B.E. Ungerechts, K. Reischle, & K. Wilke (Eds.), *Swimming science V* (pp. 45-52). Champaign, IL: Human Kinetics.

Winter, D.A., Rau, G., Kadefors, R., Broman, H., & Luca, C.J. de, (1980). *Units, terms and standards in the reporting of EMG research.* Report by the Ad Hoc Committee of the International Society of Electrophysiological Kinesiology.

Peripheral EMG Comparison Between Fully Tethered and Free Front Crawl Swimming

Erik Bollens
Lieven Annemans
Walter Vaes
Jan Pieter Clarys

Front crawl swimming has been a subject of several electromyographic (EMG) investigations. The main purpose of these studies was to make statements on muscular action in normal front crawl swimming. This resulted in normalized EMG patterns for up to 25 superficial muscles involved in front crawl swimming (Clarys, 1983; Clarys, Massez, Van Den Broeck, Piette, & Robeaux, 1983; Lewillie, 1974; Maes, Clarys, & Brouwer, 1975) and in the development of a sophisticated data-recording system (Clarys & Publie, 1987).

With this knowledge and the technical knowledge of surface EMG registration in water, EMG research in swimming focused on the specificity of some alternative training methods (i.e., comparing muscular activity in one or another test protocol with muscular activity in normal front crawl swimming). Dryland devices such as the isokinetic swim bench, roller board, expander, and call craft did not give satisfactory results. The main problem in dryland training was the elimination of the equilibrium mechanisms that are present in normal swimming (Olbrecht & Clarys, 1983). In an attempt to eliminate the influence of these mechanisms, we investigated the influence of six different types of hand paddles on the muscular activity during swimming the front crawl. This study showed that hand paddle swimming is muscle-specific with normal front crawl swimming although not unconditionally the same (Bollens & Clarys, 1984).

Although tethered swimming, another alternative swimming method, has been the subject of a number of scientific studies, none of these investigations were concerned with the muscular specificity aspects of this training method (Cureton, 1930; Mosterd & Jongbloed, 1964; Van Manen & Rijken, 1975; Zatsiorsky & Safarian, 1972).

The present study dealt with verifying similarities or differences in muscular activity between normal (free) front crawl swimming and fully tethered swimming.

Methods and Materials

The activity of five superficial muscles was simultaneously registered by means of active surface electrodes on a Teac MR 30 data recorder. Three propulsive muscles of the arm were investigated: (a) triceps, caput longus, (b) pectoralis major, pars sternocostalis, and (c) latissimus dorsi; and two propulsive muscles of the lower limb: (a) rectus femoris and (b) gastrocnemius, caput laterale.

The selection criterion for the male subjects was a swimming time of 59.0 s or less for 100-m front crawl swimming. Thirteen subjects with a mean best time of 56.9 s were tested.

In order to swim fully tethered, the subject was fitted with a waist belt with wires running to a wooden dowel (as in Costill, 1966; Goldfuss & Nelson, 1971; Meade, 1976) that was attached to a dynamometer. A water-resistant headphone with a remote tape recorder, on which several different stroke frequencies were recorded, was used to keep the stroke frequency constant. Three stroke frequencies were simulated: 100%, determined by swimming at a sprint velocity; and 85 and 70%, calculated from the measured frequency at 100% velocity. These pacings were previously reproduced by a metronome and recorded on tape and afterward transmitted to the swimmer through watertight headphones.

At the beginning of an arm cycle (i.e., when the left hand hit the water surface), synchronization of EMG data with the actual swimming movement was performed by adding a disturbance signal on the seventh amplitude-modulated channel of the data recorder. After calibrating the dynamometer and recording the relative maximal voluntary contraction (RMVC) as a reference myopotential (i.e., 100%) (Clarys, 1983), subjects were asked to swim first two trials of 20 m at full speed (without being tethered). The stroke frequency of 100% was determined by the mean time per arm cycle performed during five consecutive arm cycles. The remote tape recorder was switched on with the corresponding pace of 100%. This tape was followed by the calculated pace of 85 and 70%, respectively. For these three stroke frequencies, EMG was registered for normal (free) swimming.

The same order of performances was then performed by the subject while fully tethered on the dynamometer. By placing tension on the rope connected to the dynamometer, the swimmer evoked readings on the dynamometer. These values were registered on the seventh channel of the data recorder.

Results and Discussion

The results from the dynamometer showed that as stroke frequency decreased, the force exerted on the dynamometer also decreased. Details are discussed in Cabri, Annemans, Clarys, Bollens, & Publie (1988).

The linear envelope of the raw EMG signal was normalized according to Bollens and Clarys (1984). The integration of the normalized linear

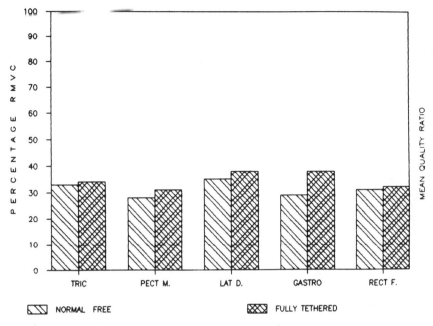

Figure 1   Average muscular activity (in percentage of RMVC) for all stroke frequencies.

envelope was considered as a measure of the intensity of the muscular contraction.

Comparing the average intensities (see Figure 1), it was found by means of a two-way ANOVA that except for the latissimus dorsi (10% level), none of the tested muscles during fully tethered swimming induced a significantly higher muscular activity compared with normal free swimming. Nevertheless, there was a clear tendency toward greater intensities of muscular contraction in all the EMG diagrams during fully tethered swimming and for every stroke frequency.

The quality of the EMG data (i.e., whether an EMG diagram in tethered swimming was similar or not to the EMG diagram in normal free swimming) was analyzed according to the criteria described in Bollens and Clarys (1984). For this study, these criteria have been described in terms of amplitude, timing, and a combination of both.

If the EMG diagram of the normal free swimming at a given pace is used as a basic reference, one can express the difference in the test modality (tethered swimming) with this reference by a scale from 0 (no difference at all) to 12 (completely different). In an attempt to quantify the quality of a normalized EMG diagram, 12 quality ratios are defined in Table 1.

Analyzing the results in this way, the following average quality ratios were found: Figure 2 shows that as stroke rate decreased, differences between normal and fully tethered swimming also decreased for the arm

Table 1   Different Criteria on Which the Discussion Is Based

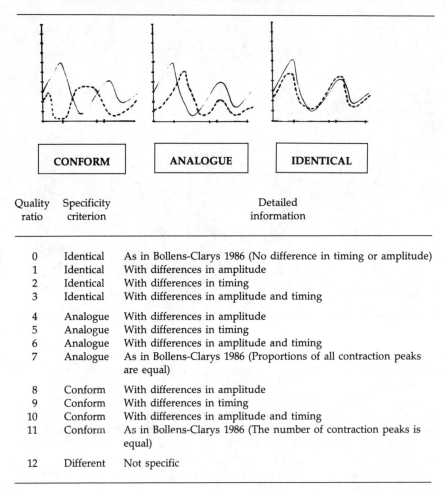

Quality ratio	Specificity criterion	Detailed information
0	Identical	As in Bollens-Clarys 1986 (No difference in timing or amplitude)
1	Identical	With differences in amplitude
2	Identical	With differences in timing
3	Identical	With differences in amplitude and timing
4	Analogue	With differences in amplitude
5	Analogue	With differences in timing
6	Analogue	With differences in amplitude and timing
7	Analogue	As in Bollens-Clarys 1986 (Proportions of all contraction peaks are equal)
8	Conform	With differences in amplitude
9	Conform	With differences in timing
10	Conform	With differences in amplitude and timing
11	Conform	As in Bollens-Clarys 1986 (The number of contraction peaks is equal)
12	Different	Not specific

and shoulder muscles. The opposite was true for the leg musculature. Details of this reverse tendency are discussed in a following section of this chapter.

As a first impression it can be seen that in general, for the distribution of the quality ratios, there was a disparity of quality ratios 9, 10, and 11 (see Figure 3). A pronounced peak for quality ratio 12 indicated the percentage of totally deviating EMG diagrams. This was especially the case for the leg muscles. Except for the totally different EMG diagrams, the remaining ones were qualitatively better, meaning more similar, according to the "conform" criteria in Bollens and Clarys (1984). If one focuses on the arm muscles only, one may notice that the quality of the

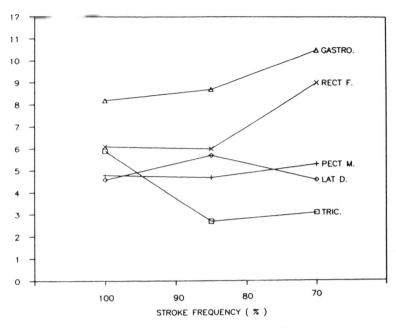

Figure 2 Influence of the stroke frequency on the mean quality ratio.

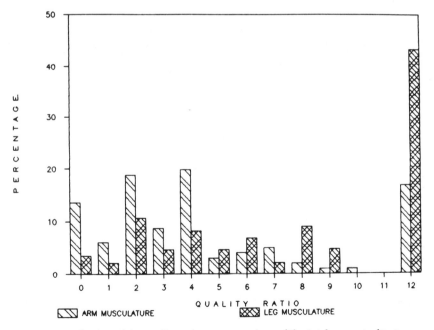

Figure 3 Distribution of the quality ratio as a percentage of the total amount of test cases for the differences between normal and fully tethered swimming.

EMG diagrams of fully tethered swimming, compared with normal free swimming, show similarity at quality levels that are at least analog (quality ratio < 8).

A second general observation is that the quality ratios 2, 4, and 6 are overrepresented.

In the following section, the specificity of the fully tethered swimming is discussed. Considering the classifications in Table 1, EMG diagrams resulting from fully tethered swimming are considered specific with normal free swimming if the quality ratio of the difference is equal to or less than 11.

For the quality of swimming at maximal stroke rate, the arm muscular action in fully tethered swimming at 100% was very specific. The leg musculature, however, shows larger differences (see Table 2). If these figures are compared with the quality differences in normal free swimming at 100 and 85% (see Figure 4), these differences are not significant. In general, the fully tethered swimming did not produce greater deviations in the muscular contraction pattern than the effect of normal free swimming at a pace of 85% compared with 100%. Therefore, it can be concluded that fully tethered swimming at a stroke frequency of a 100% is a specific training method with muscle activity similar to normal swimming.

In the fully tethered swimming at a pace of 85%, in comparison with the results of the maximal stroke frequency, quality of arm muscle EMG pattern tended to increase and leg muscle to decrease. This is also illustrated in Figure 2. One can conclude for this stroke frequency (85%) that arm muscular activity is specific (but not identical) and even more specific than in swimming at 100%. Leg musculature, on the contrary, shows totally different EMG diagrams in 42% of the cases.

For the comparison between fully tethered swimming and normal free swimming at a 70% stroke frequency, the quality of the EMG diagrams shows the same tendency as when comparing maximal stroke frequency with the 85% level. The quality of the leg musculature activity becomes worse. A total of 69% of the EMG diagrams were totally different. Thus,

Table 2 Average Quality Ratio and Percentage of Totally Different EMG Diagram Versus Stroke Frequency

Muscle stroke frequency	Arm muscles		Leg muscles	
	X	%	X	%
100%	5.9	21	7.3	31
85%	4.4	13	7.4	42
70%	4.3	13	9.8	69

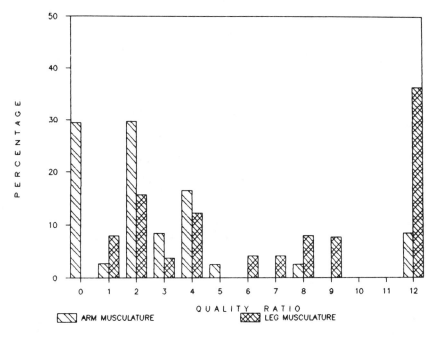

Figure 4   Distribution of the quality ratio as a percentage of the total amount of test cases for the differences between normal swimming at 100% and 85% stroke frequency.

only 31% of the contraction patterns were similar, but even then the similarity was at a lower level of specificity (conform, analog). Arm action, on the other hand, was getting better qualitatively.

Finally, it can be concluded that fully tethered swimming is similar to normal free swimming. However, this statement is only true for the tested arm musculature, where a decrease in the stroke rate induces an increase in the quality of the reproduced EMG diagrams. The tested leg muscles, on the contrary, show an inverse tendency, with percentages of totally different EMG diagrams of 31% at a stroke frequency of 100% and going up to 69% at the 70% stroke frequency. It is difficult to conclude that the tested leg muscles show similar EMG patterns in fully tethered swimming compared with normal free swimming. However, the fact is that even in normal free swimming, the influence of stroke frequency on the quality of the EMG diagram is considerable (see Figure 2).

Acknowledgments

The authors wish to thank Nationale Loterij Belgie for its financial support.

References

Bollens, E., & Clarys, J.P. (1984, July). *Front crawl training with hand paddles: A telemetric EMG investigation.* Paper presented at the 1984 Olympic Scientific Congress, Eugene, OR.

Cabri, J.M.H., Annemans, L., Clarys, J.P., Bollens, E., & Publie, J. (1988). The relation of stroke frequency, force, and EMG in front crawl tethered swimming. In B.E. Ungerechts, K. Reischle, & K. Wilke (Eds.), *Swimming science V* (pp. 183-189). Champaign, IL: Human Kinetics.

Clarys, J.P. (1983). A review of EMG in swimming: Explanation of facts and/or feedback information. In A.P. Hollander, P. Huijing, & G. de Groot (Eds.), *Biomechanics and medicine in swimming* (pp. 123-135). Champaign, IL: Human Kinetics.

Clarys, J.P., Massez, C., Van Den Broeck, M., Piette, G., & Robeaux, R. (1983). Total telemetric surface EMG of the front crawl. In H. Matsui & K. Kobayashi (Eds.), *Biomechanics VIII-B* (pp. 951-959). Champaign, IL: Human Kinetics.

Clarys, J.P., & Publie, J. (1987). A portable EMG data acquisition system with active surface electrodes for monitoring kinesiological research. In B. Jonsson (Ed.), *Biomechanics X-A* (pp. 233-240). Champaign, IL: Human Kinetics.

Costill, D.L. (1966). Use of a swimming ergometer in physiological research. *Research Quarterly, 37,* 564-567.

Cureton, T.K. (1930). Mechanics and kinesiology of swimming. *Research Quarterly, 1,* 87-121.

Goldfuss, A.G., & Nelson, R.C. (1971). A temporal and force analysis of the crawl stroke during tethered swimming. In L. Lewillie, & J.P. Clarys (Eds.), *Proceedings of the 1st Symposium on Biomechanics in Swimming* (pp. 129-142). Bruxelles: Presse Universitaire de Bruxelles.

Lewillie, L. (1974). Telemetry of electromyographic and electrogoniometric signals in swimming. In R.C. Nelson & C.A. Morehouse (Eds.), *Biomechanics IV* (pp. 203-207). Baltimore: University Park Press.

Maes, L., Clarys, J.P., & Brouwer, P.J. (1975). Electromyograph for the evaluation of handicapped swimmers. In J.P. Clarys & L. Lewillie (Eds.), *Swimming II* (pp. 268-275). Baltimore: University Park Press.

Meade, T.A., Jr. (1976). A new approach and method of weight training for swimmers. *Swimming Technique, 13,* 66-70

Mosterd, W.L., & Jongbloed, J. (1964). Analysis of the stroke of highly trained swimmers. *Arbeitsphyiologie, 20,* 288-293.

Olbrecht, J., & Clarys, J.P. (1983). EMG of specific strength training exercises for the frontcrawl. In A.P. Hollander, P. Huijing, & G. de Groot (Eds.), *Biomechanics and medicine in swimming* (pp. 136-141). Champaign, IL: Human Kinetics.

Van Manen, J.D., & Rijken, H. (1975). Dynamic measurement techniques on swimming bodies at the Netherlands ship model basin. In J.P. Clarys & L. Lewillie (Eds.), *Swimming II* (pp. 70-79). Baltimore: University Park Press.

Zatsiorsky, V.M. & Safarian, I.G. (1972). Untersuchung von Faktoren zur bestimmungden maximalen Geschwindigkeit in Freistilschwimmen [Investigation of factors determining maximal speed in freestyle swimming]. *Theorie und Praxis Körper Kultur, 8*, 695-709.

The Relation of Stroke Frequency, Force, and EMG in Front Crawl Tethered Swimming

Jan M.H. Cabri
Lieven Annemans,
Jan Pieter Clarys
Erik Bollens
Jan Publie

Tethered swimming has been widely used, not only for training purposes but also in many different research areas (i.e., biomechanics, hydrodynamics, physiology, etc.). In the past 20 years, this method has been used as an alternative "wet" strength training method, particularly because some of the dryland training devices could not be considered as "specific to swimming" (Clarys, 1985; Olbrecht & Clarys, 1983) although they pretend to be so. With the knowledge that fully tethered swimming induces electromyographic (EMG) patterns similar to free swimming and thus may be considered specific to swimming (Bollens, Annemans, Clarys, & Vaes, 1988; Roberts, 1977) the main purpose of this study was to investigate the relationships between different stroke rates (during front crawl on a fully tethered swimming device), the forces developed, and the normalized EMG of the main propulsive arm and leg muscles using (a) raw EMG, (b)integrated EMG, and (c) linear envelope (Winter, Rau, Kadefors, Broman, & Luca, 1980).

The relationship between intensity of muscle activity and actual force is described by the integrated electromyography/force ratio (IEMG/IF), for it is an expression of the efficiency of electrical activity (De Vries, 1968). Moreover, Viitasalo (1984) stated that this ratio provides a fairly good representation of the relationship between muscle activity and force on the one hand, and contraction velocity on the other. He concluded that from a certain amount of IEMG activity (neural input), slow (isometric) contractions may produce much higher forces in comparison with high velocity (explosive type) contractions (as in jumping). The purposes of this investigation, therefore, were to investigate the (a) influence of different stroke frequencies on the forces developed by the swimmer, (b) influence of different stroke frequencies on the IEMG/IF ratio or the relationship between stroke rate and muscular efficiency, and (c) relationship between the normalized EMG patterns and the normalized force amplitudes.

Material and Methods

Thirteen male top swimmers were selected to perform the fully tethered swimming tests as part of the Brussels Swimming EMG Project. The investigated muscles were the triceps brachii (long head), pectoralis major, flexor carpi ulnaris, latissimus dorsi, rectus femoris, and gastrocnemius (lateral head).

The EMG recordings (Figure 1) were obtained using an on-line recording device with portable amplifer and active electrodes, as described by Clarys and Publie (1987). After preparing the skin, the six active surface electrodes were fixed at the geometric midpoint of the muscle belly and connected to the amplifier and the seven-channel high frequency Teac MR30 recorder. The "swim dynamometer" (Figure 2) was fixed to the side of the swimming pool and was connected to the swimmer by means of a belt. The force output of the dynamometer was registered simultaneously with the electrical activity of the six muscles and synchronized with the swimming movement. To control the individual stroke frequencies at 100, 85, and 70%, respectively, the following procedure was used. First, each swimmer was asked to perform a 15-m free swimming sprint, during which the 100% stroke frequency was measured. After calculation of the 85 and 70% stroke frequency of that individual, a metronome was used to reproduce these different rhythms on tape. With minor amplification, these signals were retransmitted to the subject by means of a water-tight headphone (Figure 3). In this manner, the stroke rates were specific to each swimmer.

The following tests were performed and analyzed:

- Stroke rate at 100%, with recordings of arms and legs simultaneously
- Stroke rate at 85%, with recordings of arms and legs simultaneously

Figure 1   Fully tethered front crawl swimming. The swim dynamometer was fixed on the border of the pool. The electromyogrpahic signals of the muscles investigated were transmitted via the multi-channel cable to the recorder.

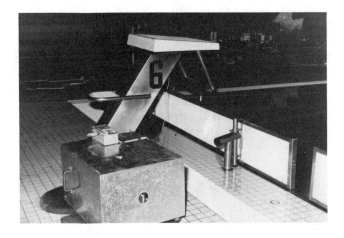

Figure 2   The swim dynamometer fixed to the side of the pool.

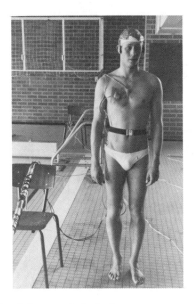

Figure 3   Subject with headphone and electrodes.

- Stroke rate at 75%, with recordings of arms and legs simultaneously
- Stroke rate at 100%, with recordings of the leg muscles only
- Stroke rate at 100%, with recordings of the arm muscles only

The linear envelopes of the raw EMG were normalized in reference to the maximal voluntary isometric contraction (MVIC) and were plotted and integrated via a Kontron IBAS I computer system (Clarys, 1988).

The force data obtained with the swim dynamometer were also normalized according to a similar procedure. After calibration of the dynamometer by means of known weights, the force patterns were standardized based on a weight of 20 kg (100%). The integration was also done on the Kontron IBAS I computer. The absolute mean forces were normalized using the following equation: % force × 20/100.

In summary, the subject swam at a controlled stroke frequency against a resistance (force) that was registered simultaneously with the EMG muscular activity. These three different variables were submitted to a two-way ANOVA, a Student's t test, and a correlation matrix.

Results and Discussion

The influence of stroke frequency on force is shown in Figure 4. As expected, the stroke frequency had a positive influence on the forces exerted by the swimmer during the front crawl movement. The mean forces increased as the stroke frequencies increased from 70, 85, to 100% ($p \leqslant$

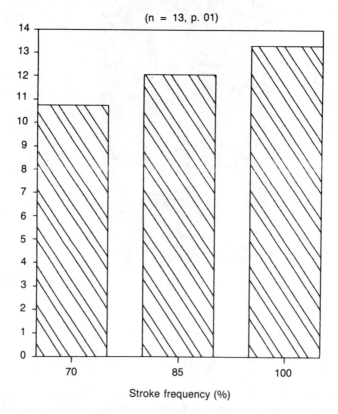

Figure 4   Force plotted against stroke frequency.

.01), respectively. These findings confirm previous investigations (Adams, Martin, Yeater, & Gilson, 1984; Martin, Yeater, & White, 1981) that reported higher stroke frequencies imply higher forces.

The influence of stroke frequency on efficiency of electrical activity (the IEMG/IF ratio) is displayed in Table 1, including the relationship between muscle intensity and force. The pectoralis and rectus femoris show a significant increase in intensity/force ratio with increasing stroke frequencies. This would imply a decreasing efficiency, as described by Viitasalo (1984). Hence, the lower stroke frequency (70%) seems to be more efficient in force production (Figure 5), probably because more time is taken to perform and finish a full stroke. But the fact that higher stroke fre-

Table 1   Muscle Intensity (IEMG), Force (IF), and Muscle Intensity Versus Force of the Investigated Muscle (n = 12)

Muscle	Stroke frequency					
	100%		85%		70%	
	M	SD	M	SD	M	SD
Triceps brachii (caput longum)						
Muscle intensity**	40.80	9.26	35.13	8.23	31.03	7.35
Force	13.30	1.54	12.06	1.56	10.75	1.34
Correlation	− .409		− .472		− .396	
Intensity vs. force	2.910	1.312	2.777	1.280	2.750	1.302
Pectoralis major (pars sternocostalis)						
Muscle intensity**	37.53	14.35	32.18	8.13	25.93	7.71
Force	13.30	1.54	12.06	1.56	10.75	1.34
Correlation	− .249		.272		− .396	
Intensity vs. force	2.884	1.378	2.492	1.031	2.240	0.928
Latissimus dorsi						
Muscle intensity**	42.96	10.98	35.64	8.28	31.21	8.44
Force	13.30	1.54	12.06	1.56	10.75	1.34
Correlation	.054		.021		.280	
Intensity vs. force	3.027	1.293	2.779	1.166	2.700	1.094
Gastrocnemius (caput laterale)						
Muscle intensity*	41.91	22.43	32.29	19.91	39.66	20.82
Force	13.30	1.54	12.06	1.56	10.75	1.34
Correlation	− .148		− .109		− .241	
Intensity vs.force**	2.988	1.966	2.561	1.982	3.533	2.394
Rectus femoris						
Muscle intensity**	39.47	10.07	33.02	12.98	26.44	9.704
Force	13.30	1.54	12.06	1.56	10.75	1.34
Correlation	− .108		− .234		.046	
Intensity vs. force	2.786	1.186	2.602	1.432	2.230	1.116

*$p \leqslant .05$; **$p \leqslant .01$.

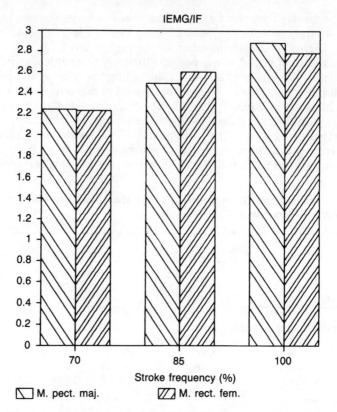

Figure 5 Muscle intensity versus force ratio (IEMG/IF) of pectoralis major (pect. maj.) and rectus femoris (rect. fem.) at the investigated stroke frequencies.

quencies overcome a higher drag (Clarys, Jiskoot, & Lewillie, 1973) implies that for the different velocities studied here, a performance advantage is obtained in both short- and long-distance events.

Although higher stroke frequencies result in higher muscle intensities, no significant correlation was found between IEMG and the force developed for any muscle investigated at any stroke frequency. However, except for the gastrocnemius, muscle activity and force patterns had a tendency to increase with increased stroke frequencies, during which the forces increased significantly. But, at the same time, these findings indicate a decrease in the efficiency of electrical activity, which may be due to a nonlinear increase in the EMG (rather than to the force).

The differences found between the EMG activities of these three stroke rates can be explained by the fact that in fast contraction velocites (as in the 100% stroke frequency), fast-twitch muscle fibers make a greater contribution to force production (Thorstensson, 1976). Also, the action potential amplitudes of fast-twitch units and their firing frequency have been shown to be greater than those of the slow-twitch units (Viitasalo, 1984).

These findings imply that with increased force, more muscle activity (intensity) is needed to produce the force at a higher contraction velocity (stroke frequency). This suggests the efficacy of the strength training effect using high stroke frequency training of different durations.

References

Adams, T.A., Martin, R.B., Yeater, R.A., & Gilson, K.A. (1983). Tethered force and velocity relationships. *Swimming Technique*, **20**(3), 21-26.

Bollens, E., Annemans, L., Clarys, J.P., & Vaes, W. (1988). Peripheral EMG comparison between fully tethered and free front crawl swimming. In B. Ungerechts, K. Reischle, & K. Wilke (Eds.), *Swimming science V* (pp. 173-181). Champaign, IL: Human Kinetics.

Clarys, J.P. (1985). Hydrodynamics and eletromyography: Ergonomic aspects in aquatics. *Journal of Applied Ergonomics*, **16**(1), 11-24.

Clarys, J.P. (1988). The Brussels swimming EMG project. In B.E. Ungerechts, K. Reischle, & K. Wilke (Eds.), *Swimming science V* (pp. 157-172). Champaign, IL: Human Kinetics.

Clarys, J.P., Jiskoot, J., & Lewillie, L. (1973). A kinematical, electromyographical, and resistance study of water polo and competition front crawl. In S. Cerquiglini, A. Venerando, & J. Wartenweiler (Eds.), *Biomechanics III* (pp. 446-452). Basel: S. Karger.

Clarys, J.P., & Publie, J. (1987). A portable EMG data acquisition system with active surface electrodes for monitoring kinesiological research. In B. Jonsson (Ed.), *Biomechanics X-A* (pp. 233-240). Champaign, IL: Human Kinetics.

De Vries, H.A. (1968). Efficiency of electrical activity as a physiologic measure of the functional state of muscle tissue. *American Journal of Physical Medicine*, **47**(1), 10-22.

Martin, R.B., Yeater, R.A., & White, M.K. (1981). A simple analytical model for the crawl stroke. *Journal of Biomechanics*, **14**, 539-548.

Olbrecht, J., & Clarys, J.P. (1983). EMG of specific strength training exercises for the front crawl. In A.P. Hollander, P. Huijing, & G. de Groot (Eds.), *Biomechanics and medicine in swimming* (pp. 136-141). Champaign, IL: Human Kinetics.

Roberts, J.B. (1977). New approach and method of specific isokinetic training for swimmers. *Swimming Technique*, **14**, 38-39.

Thorstensson, A. (1978). Muscle strength, fibre types and enzyme activities in man. *Acta Physiologica Scandinavica* (Suppl. 443), 7-15.

Viitasalo, J.T. (1984). Electromechanical behavior of the knee extensor musculature in maximal isometric and concentric contractions and in jumping. *Electromyographical and Clinical Neurophysiology*, **24**, 293-303.

Winter, D.A., Rau, G., Kadefors, R., Broman, H., & Luca, C. de. (1980). *Units, terms and standards in the reporting of EMG research*. Report by the Ad Hoc Committee of the International Society of Electrophysiological Kinesiology (ISEK).

Muscular Specificity and Intensity in Swimming Against a Mechanical Resistance—Surface EMG in MAD and Free Swimming

Jan Pieter Clarys
Huub M. Toussaint
Erik Bollens
Walter Vaes
Peter A. Huijing
Gert de Groot
A. Peter Hollander
Brigitte De Witte
Jan Cabri

The measurement of active drag using a MAD system provides a new approach to hydrodynamic analysis of the front crawl movement. The MAD system allows swimming force recordings in a natural environment—water—and assumes that the turbulent flow around the moving body is the same in both MAD and free swimming. Even if these flows are different, the Reynolds number (R) range of the human body ($6.6 \times 10^5 < R < 3.9 \times 10^6$; see Figure 1) gives no indication whatsoever that the turbulence, and therefore total drag, could be altered or eventually reduced (Clarys, 1985). However, an adaptation of the swimmer's arm movements to the MAD system does occur, for the push-off is made against a fixed point. Evidence for this statement was collected from 9 subjects swimming similarly (slow and fast), both on the MAD system and freely, with underwater light trace photography including an acceleration indicator (through a stable multivibrator). Movement patterns of the foot (lamp at malleolus externus), the shoulder (lamp at acromion), and the hand (lamp at digitus minimus) were recorded and compared per individual. The movement patterns of feet and shoulder showed little or no differences. However, the hand movement pattern in all subjects was very much influenced and changed by the MAD system. Discrepancies occur in a steeper input-gliding phase, a missing S-shaped movement, and a nonexistent pull-push trajectory (Figure 2).

In order to study differences in muscular activity due to the movement adaptation on the MAD system, EMGs were recorded for a group of 17

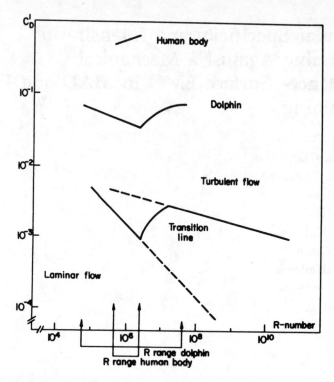

Figure 1 The laminar and turbulent flows including Reynold number range for dolphins and humans in relation to the drag coefficient C_D (Clarys, 1985).

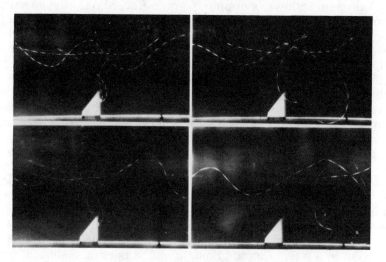

Figure 2 Light traces of foot, shoulder, and hand trajectories under the water surface in MAD swimming (left) and free front crawl swimming (right) and slow (top) and sprint (bottom) velocities.

Table 1 Stroke Frequencies per Second for the 10 MAD Lengths and 3 Free Swimming Lengths

Style	1	2	3	4	Length 5	6	7	8	9	10
MAD	0.4950	0.4098	0.4756	0.5128	0.5998	0.5165	0.4807	0.5707	0.5656	0.6097
Free[a]	0.4608	0.6042	0.7911							

[a]Free length 1 was slow; 2, submaximal; and 3, sprint pace.

well-trained swimmers, during both free and MAD swimming. An on-line seven-channel FM data recording system, with active electrodes and portable amplification unit was used (Clarys & Publie, 1987) for the purpose.

Using the raw EMG and corresponding linear envelope, a total of 4,460 data points were analyzed for the pectoralis major, the triceps brachii, the flexor digitorum superficialis, and the latissimus dorsi.

Procedures

The subjects were asked to swim 10 pool lengths (25 m) on the MAD system at arbitrarily increasing velocities (from very slow to sprint) and 3 pool lengths free swimming: (a) very slow, (b) submaximal or 80% of sprint, and (c) full 100% sprint. Simultaneous on-line EMG recordings during 10 ($\pm$ 2) arm cycles per chosen velocity (or pool length) allowed the calculation of the stroke frequency for the different velocities investigated (Table 1). Also, the qualitative analysis of activity reproducibility, arm cycle time, and both qualitative and quantitative pattern analysis were possible.

The reproducibility of the muscular activity and the comparison of arm cycle time were verified using the linear evelopes of all the data obtained; whereas for the muscular pattern analysis including the amplitude and number of contraction peaks, both MAD and free swimming mucles activity were compared for differences (or similarities) at corresponding stroke frequencies only. As illustrated in Table 1, the consecutive arm cycles of slow free swimming (Lap 1) were compared with the EMG data of the MAD Trial 3. The EMG of submaximal free swimming (Lap 2) was compared with the 5th MAD trial, and free swimming (Lap 3) sprint was compared with the MAD 10th or sprint trial.

It needs to be emphasized that at 100% full sprint over a short distance, the free swimming had a significantly higher stroke frequency, which might partially explain the movement pattern difference found in the light traces (Figure 2) and some of the hydrodynamic differences found during MAD recordings (Toussaint et al., 1988).

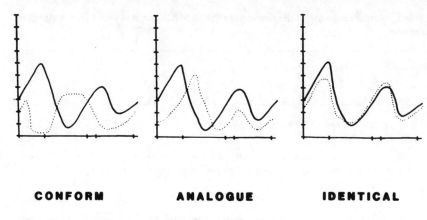

CONFORM   **ANALOGUE**   **IDENTICAL**

Figure 3   Three criteria for EMG pattern similarity.

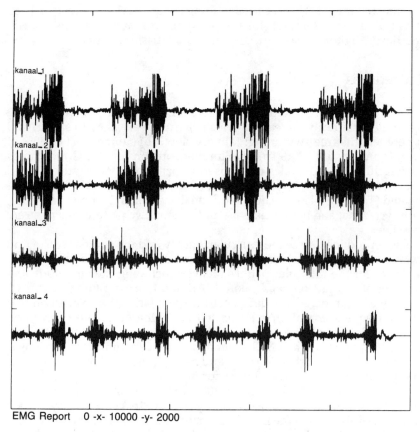

Figure 4   Repetition constancy and reproducibility of different arm cycles and different muscles.

The EMG recordings were normalized for both time and amplitude (MVC) using a Kontron-IBAS I computer system to determine EMG pattern and intensity differences or similarities.

The transformations of the linear envelope or normalized EMG diagrams were then compared according to three criteria of form similitude (Figure 3; Bollens & Clarys, 1984). If none of these criteria occurred, the EMG pattern or muscular activity was considered as different. The muscular intensities exerted during the test situations were compared using the integrated EMG values (IEMG) of the normalized linear envelopes (or EMG diagrams).

Results and Discussion

Figure 4 shows a series of arm cycles and corresponding contractions. This illustrative example was found for all muscles and all subjects at all velocities measured. It gave a very distinct indication of both a high repetition constancy and a high reproducibility of the EMG activity recordings in free swimming as well as in swimming on the MAD device. However, the EMG repetition constancy and reproducibility of front crawl (free) swimming is a well-established fact (Clarys 1983, 1985; Clarys, Jiskoot, & Lewillie; 1973; Ikai, Ishii, & Miyashita, 1964; Lewillie, 1968, 1974) but is now produced in a similar manner by pusing off from a series of push-off pads attached to a horizontal rod mounted 0.8 m below the water surface.

Examples of identical, analogue, conform, and totally different observations are shown in Figure 5. Figure 6 shows the percentages of specific and nonspecific (different) EMG pattern observations.

By comparing the graphic forms of the normalized diagrams, arm cycle by arm cycle, within the three velocities (slow, submaximal, sprint) and using the form criteria shown in Figure 3, it has been found that an overall majority of analogue and identical patterns together constitute 83.8% of the compared observations. A total of 9% were found to be conform patterns, and only 7.2% of the normalized diagrams were found to be totally different.

With respect to the biomechanical differences between the execution of the MAD movement and free swimming (Figure 2), such a high level of muscular specificity is remarkable. Earlier "specificity" studies showed no muscle similarities (e.g., free swimming vs. dry land exercises; Olbrecht & Clarys, 1983) or at least a majority of conform observations (e.g., free swimming vs. hand paddle swimming (Bollens & Clarys, 1984).

In addition of the 7.2% "different" observations, all occurred in the EMG patterns of the flexor digitorum superficialis, confirming the high interindividual variability and suggesting that different individual actions of the hand and forearm exist against a mechanical resistance such as the MAD push-off pads. A similar situation was found not only in previous swimming EMG studies (Clarys & Olbrecht, 1983) but in other sports also (Clarys et al., 1986).

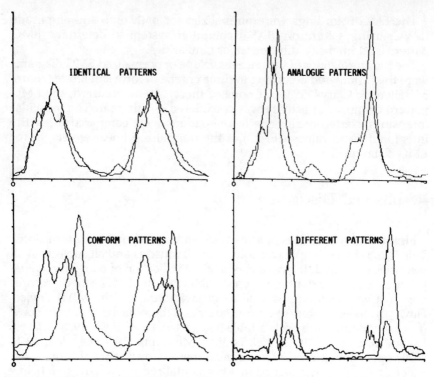

Figure 5 Examples of similarities and difference in EMG patterns (normalized linear envelope) of MAD and free swimming.

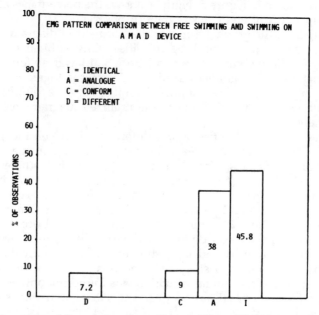

Figure 6 Percentage of the number of specific and different EMG pattern observations.

Because of the variability of the flexor digitorum superficialis (and presumably of all forearm muscles in this type of movement), the evaluation of muscular intensity is based on the shoulder girdle muscles only. Table 2 focuses on the IEMG intensity results for the slow submaximal-sprint velocities separately but for all muscle together, and Table 3 lists the IEMG intensities for all muscles and all velocities together.

Neither at slow, submaximal, nor sprint velocity were significant differences in muscular intensity found between free and MAD swimming (Table 2). But within both free and MAD swimming the muscular intensity exerted at low stroke frequencies did differ significantly with the intensity at sprint rhythm, but this again confirms known facts where free front crawl swimming is concerned. When the muscular intensities of all muscles were averaged for all velocities measured again, no significant difference was found between the investigated swimming techniques (Table 3). Similary, for each separate muscle and the average over all velocities, again no significant difference was found.

However, even if no statistical differences in muscular activity were found, there was a distinct tendency in MAD swimming to show absolute

Table 2   Normalized Intensity at Slow, Submaximal, and Sprint Velocities (Average IEMG, All Muscles)

Velocity	M	SD	M difference
Slow			
Free	11.51	0.83	4.57
MAD	16.09	4.13	
Submaximal			
Free	18.69	2.80	4.55
MAD	23.24	4.89	
Sprint			
Free	26.92	7.94	1.44
MAD	28.36	8.20	
Free slow × sprint			12.27*
MAD slow × sprint			15.40

*$p = .005$.

Table 3   Normalized Muscle Intensities Averaged for All Subjects, Muscles, and Velocities

Technique	M	SD
Free	18.41	10.00
MAD	21.49	10.47

$p = .005$ (not significantly different); mean difference = 3.08.

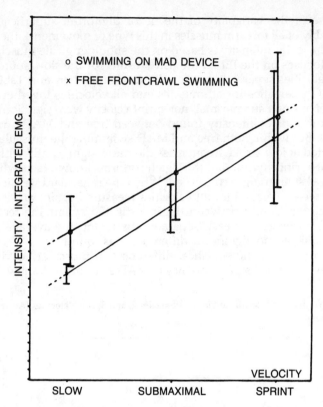

Figure 7 Mean and standard deviation of all intensities (IEMG muscles + subjects) during free swimming and swimming on the MAD device at three increasing velocities.

higher muscular work considering the total amount of comparative observations (see Figure 7).

Conclusions

These comparative experiments have shown that there is a very high degree of muscular pattern and intensity similarity in both free swimming and swimming against a mechanical resistance (MAD swimming), even though the kinesiological aspects of the movement trajectory were proven different beforehand. MAD swimming does not employ different muscles although the adaptation of the arm movement is present.

Expert trainers sometimes use different sources of information and different (theoretical) interpretations of what is and what can be specific-alternative training. Therefore, it should be emphasized that the "dry-land" training against mechanical resistances are nonspecific. Herewith it can be confirmed that "swimming" training against mechanical resistances (in quasi, the MAD system) is to be regarded as a specific training device and similarly as a specific measurement tool.

Rcfcrences

Bollens, E., & Clarys, J.P. (1984, July). *Frontcrawl training with hand paddles: A telemetric EMG investigation.* Paper presented at the 1984 Olympic Scientific Congress, Eugene, OR.

Clarys, J.P. (1983). A review of EMG in swimming: Explanation of facts and/or feedback information. In A.P. Hollander, P. Huijing, & G. de Groot (Eds.), *Biomechanics and medicine in swimming* (pp. 123-135). Champaign, IL: Human Kinetics.

Clarys, J.P. (1985). Hydrodynamics and electromyography: Ergonomic aspects in aquatics. *Journal of Applied Ergonomics, 16*(1), 11-24.

Clarys, J.P., Bollens, E., Sleeckx, R., Vermeiren, M., Taeymans, J., & Publie, J. (1985). *Muscular EMG control in Olympic archery.* Paper presented at the International Archery Seminar of Olympic Solidarity, Crest Hotel, Antwerp, Belgium.

Clarys, J.P., Jiskoot, J., & Lewillie, L. (1973). A kinematographic, electromyographic and resistance study of waterpolo and competition frontcrawl. In S. Cerquiglini, A. Venerando, & J. Wartenweiler (Eds.), *Biomechanics III* (pp. 446-452). Basel: Karger.

Clarys, J.P., & Olbrecht, J. (1983). Peripheral control of complex swimming movements using telemetric and conventional electromyography. In H. Rieder, K. Bös, N. Mechling, & K. Reischle (Eds.), *Motorik- und Bewegungsforschung* [Motor and movement research], (pp. 111-116). Schorndorf: Karl Hofmann. (Schriftenreihe des Bundesinstituts für Sportwissenschaft, Band 50).

Clarys, J.P., & Publie, J. (1987). A portable EMG data acquisition system with active surface electrodes for monitoring kinesiological research. In B. Jonsson (Ed.), *Biomechanics X-A* (pp. 233-240). Champaign, IL: Human Kinetics.

Ikai, M., Ishii, K., & Miyashita, M. (1964). An electromyographical study of swimming. *Research Journal of Physical Education, 7*, 45-54.

Lewillie, L. (1968). Telemetrical analysis using the electromyograph. In J. Wartenweiler, E. Jokl, & M. Hebbelinck (Eds.), *Biomechanics I* (pp. 147-148). Basel: Karger.

Lewille, L. (1974). Telemetry of electromyographic and electrogoniometric signals in swimming. In R.C. Nelson & C.A. Morehouse (Eds.), *Biomechanics IV* (pp. 203-207). Baltimore: University Park Press.

Olbrecht, J., & Clarys, J.P. (1983). EMG of specific dry land training for the frontcrawl. In A.P. Hollander, P. Huijing, & G. de Groot (Eds.), *Biomechanics and medicine in swimming* (pp. 136-141). Champaign, IL: Human Kinetics.

Toussaint, H.M., Hollander, A.P., Groot, G. de, Ingen Schenau, G. J. van, Vervoorn, K., Best, H. de, Meulemans, A., & Schreurs, W. (1988). Propelling efficiency in front crawl swimming. In B.E. Ungerechts, K. Reischle, & K. Wilke (Eds.), *Swimming science V* (pp. 45-52). Champaign, IL: Human Kinetics.

A Telemetric System for the Analysis of Six Muscle Activities in Swimming

Annie H. Rouard
Georges Quezel-Ambrunaz
Roger P. Billat

In competitive swimming, oxygen uptake, drag, and lift all increase with swimming speed. These modifications can produce and/or result from changes in muscular activity. Thus, one might wonder whether muscular contractions and synchronizations also increase in relation to an increase of swimming speed.

In order to answer the above questions, equipment for electromyography measurements was required. There was no standard apparatus for this kind of measurement on the market, and a review of electronics journals such as the Institute of Electronical Electrical Engineers (*IEEE*) and of publications on electromyography in sports showed that telemetric systems have not been widely used and often limited to a few channels (Clarys & Olbrecht, 1982; Lewillie, 1974; Piette & Clarys, 1979). So, the first step was to conceive and refine a specific apparatus.

To accomplish this, researchers, engineers, technicians, and trainers decided three criteria:

- Object of study: Our goal was to collect simultaneously the electrical activities of six muscles that could be visualized directly by the subject utilizing a display system.
- Subject disturbance: The system should not be too cumbersome or too difficult to attach. It should also be light.
- Water-proofing: The apparatus must be waterproof, unbreakable, and reliable.

The result was a six-channel telemetric system. We opted for surface electromyography, which is more adaptable to global studies on sportsmen and better accepted by subjects (O'Connell & Gardner, 1963; Spirings, Charles, & Mendryks, 1977). The apparatus was different from others. Its characteristics, the determiniation of validity, and the results are outlined in the following sections.

Instrumentation

The system was composed of four parts: sensors, amplifier, a summation and broadcasting device, and a receiving and demodulating device.

Sensors

The sensors were Beckman-type electrodes, 11 mm in diameter. In silver-chloride (Ag-Cl) down silver (Ag), they provided better stability and favored ionic conduction (Grubbs & Worley, 1983). Standard placements (Winter, Rau, Kadefors, Broman, & Luca, 1980; Zipp, 1982) cannot always be employed to moving subjects; the muscle slips under the skin and thus the electrodes lose their activity. Clarys' (1985) suggestion was used for electrode placement, which utilizes the geometric center of muscle in a maximal isometric contraction. At this point, two electrodes were fixed vertically with a 20-mm distance between them. The skin was first rasped, rubbed, and cleaned with an alcohol-acetone-ether mix. Electrodes were fixed with Blenderm covered with Nobecutane and Elastoplast to increase water tightness and solidity. The most important characteristic of the sensors was the use of one reference for each muscle studied. Fixed outside the muscle, this electrically neutral point formed a ground. On the other hand, the elimination of a common reference permitted a reduction in the wire length and therefore minimized artifacts. This reference could be compared to using an instrumentation amplifier, for it amplified the difference between the two electrodes and the ground.

Amplifier

The gain of the specially developed differential amplifier was 1000. It also had a very high input impedance and a good common rejection mode (Basmajian, Clifford, McLeod, & Nunnaly, 1975) and was housed in a little resin-molded metallic box fixed on the muscle being studied with Elastoplast.

Its originality was in the fact that it had a shunt to a red light-emitting diode (LED). On each little box the lighting point of the LED could be fine-tuned with adjustable resistors. Thus, in the course of movements the LEDs lit up when muscular activity overran their lighting point, and during tests the muscular synchronizations could be visualized. Then, the amplified EMG signals were transmitted to a summation and transmitting device.

Summation and Transmitting Device

The summation and transmitting device was housed in a 12 × 7 × 4-cm case, fixed to the swimmer's back with a belt. The amplified EMG signals were transmitted to a voltage-to-frequency converter by a capacitive link to eliminate direct current due to electrode polarization. Each signal was coded with a subcarrier frequency higher than the muscle frequency (15 to 500 Hz). Two kHz intervals between each subcarrier frequency gave a better interband rejection. After summation, the resultant modulated a radio frequency transmitter (RF) that had a frequency of 72 MHz. Its power was 200 MW and its size minimized to 6 × 3 × 1.5 cm. This frequency permitted the use of a half-meter flexible plastic antenna (Lawrence, 1972). This system was not multiplexed and had the advantage of being able to transmit simultaneously the information from six muscles. Another advantage was the power supply of two 9-V cells contained in the instrument box attached to the back of the subject. They ensured a two-hr experiment without interruption. Furthermore, the subject was galvanometrically insulated.

Receiving Device

The receiving device, which was on the side of the pool, was set at 72.455 MHz. It had a sensitivity of 2 V, which could be decreased to minimize disturbances resulting from collateral transmitters. It had a maximal range of 800 m. Power was supplied by a 5-V external source. Actual size was reduced to 4 × 4 × 1.5 cm. This system was combined with kinematical data so that the EMGs could be interpreted with the corresponding movements of the swimmer.

Method

To associate EMGs with swimming movements, underwater video films (25 fps) were taken using a camera driven at the swimmer's speed on rails along the pool. To synchronize EMGs with the video, the summed signals were stored on one of the videotape recorder sound tracks, whose band pass was 12 kHz. On the second sound track, synchronizing signals were recorded (Elliot & Blanksby, 1979). Lighted LEDs could also be used to synchronize electromyograms and movements.

Treatment of Data

The treatment of data involved the calculation of linear and angular velocities, respectively, of the pelvis and the arm, for five subsections of all the strokes (Van Tilborgh, Colman, & Persyn, 1985). For EMGs, the summed signal was first demodulated. Then six high-rejection rate bandpass filters allowed channel separation. Each subcarrier frequency modulated by EMG signals was transmitted to a frequency-to-voltage converter centered on the subcarrier frequency. Through elimination of direct current by a filter, only alternating current corresponding to EMG signals was obtained. Then, an analogue-to-digital converter digitized the EMG signals, which were stored in six different files in an IBM personal computer. Signals were quantified with a specific program. Actual data are still in the process of being gathered. Multivariate and longitidinal data will be analyzed in accordance with the Longi method (Pontier & Pernin, 1985).

References

Basmajian, J.V., Clifford, H.C, McLeod, W.D., & Nunnally, H.N. (1975). *Computers in electromyography*. London: Butterworths.

Clarys, J.P. (1985). Hydrodynamics and electromyography: Ergonomics aspects in aquatics. *Journal of Applied Ergonomics*, **16**(1), 11-24.

Clarys, J.P., & Olbrecht, J. (1982). Peripheral control of complex swimming movements using telemetric and conventional electromyography. In H. Rieder, K. Bös, N. Mechling, & K. Reischle (Eds.), *Motorik- und Bewegungsforschung* [Motor and movement research] (pp. 111-116). Schorndorf: Karl Hofmann. (Schriftenreihe des Bundesinstituts für Sportwissenschaft, Band 50).

Elliot, B.C., & Blanksby, B.A. (1979). The synchronization of muscle activity and body segment movement during a running cycle. *Medicine and Science in Sports*, **11**(4), 322-327.

Grubbs, D.S., & Worley, D.S. (1983). New technique for reducing the impedance of silver-silver chloride electrodes. *Medical & Biological Engineering & Computing*, **21**, 232-234.

Lawrence, O.R. (1972). *Electronique: Principes et applications* [Electronics: Principles and applications]. New York: McGraw Hill.

Lewillie, L. (1974). Telemetry of electromyographic and electrogoniometric signals in swimming. In R.C. Nelson & C.A. Morehouse (Eds.), *Biomechanics IV* (pp. 203-207). Baltimore: University Park Press.

O'Connell, A.L., & Gardner, E.B. (1963). The use of electromyography in kinesiological research. *Research Quarterly*, **34**, 166-184.

Piette, G., & Clarys, J.P. (1979). Telemetric EMG of the front crawl movement. In J. Terauds & E.W. Bedingfield (Eds.), *Swimming III* (pp. 153-159). Baltimore: University Park Press.

Pontier, J., & Pernin, M.O. (1985). Multivariate and longitudinal data on growing children solved by LONGI. *Proceedings of the 3rd International Symposium on Data Analysis*.

Spirings, E., Charles, D., & Mendryks, S. (1977). An EMG measurement system for moving subjects. *Canadian Journal of Applied Sport Science*, **2**, 149-151.

Van Tilborgh, L., Colman, V., & Persyn, U. (1985). Instruction assistée par micro-ordinateur en natation [Micro-ordinator-assisted training in swimming]. *Journées d'Automne de l'A.C.A.P.S.*

Winter, D.A., Rau, G., Kadefors, R., Broman, H., Luca, C.J. de. (1980). *Units, terms and standards in the reporting of EMG research*. Report by the

Ad Hoc Committee of the International Society of Electrophysiological Kinesiology.

Zipp, P. (1982). Recommendations for the standardization of lead positions in surface electromyography. *European Journal of Applied Physiology, 50,* 55-70.

PART V

TRAINING AND PHYSIOLOGY

The Application of Energy Metabolism to Swimming Training

Ernest W. Maglischo

The purpose of this article is to present a plan for training all of the energy systems involved in swimming races. The process of energy metabolism is summarized in the first section. The second section details the three major forms of training that can be used to imporve these energy systems. It also includes some suggestions for needed research.

Summary of Energy Metabolism

Swimming from one end of the pool to the other is made possible by the contraction of muscles. These muscles need energy in order for that contraction to occur. The energy used to generate contraction is supplied by the breakdown of adenosine triphosphate (ATP), a chemical that is stored in all muscle cells. It must constantly be replaced by creatine phosphate (CP) and glycogen, two additonal chemicals that are stored in the muscles.

ATP and CP are collectively known as the high energy phosphates. They provide most of the energy for "getting races out fast" in the first 25 to 50 m. *Anaerobic metabolism*, or the breakdown of glycogen to lactic acid, is the next most rapid source of ATP replacement. There is, however, some loss in swimming speed because of the additional reactions required to replace ATP through this process. The most serious problem associated with anaerobic metabolism is that severe fatigue results from the accumulation of lactic acid. When lactic acid accumulates in muscle, pH declines, resulting in a loss of cordination and speed.

The least rapid source of energy release results from the breakdown of glycogen to carbon dioxide and water and is known as *aerobic metabolism*. This is the most economical energy source because more molecules of ATP can be replaced and because lactic acid does not accumulate so rapidly when aerobic metabolism plays a major role in ATP replacement.

The Three Forms of Training

Based on the previous summary of energy metabolism, there are three forms of training that all swimmers should use to train the three energy systems that were described:

1. Aerobic training: This form of training improves the processes involved in the aerobic release of energy. It is important for swimming faster through the middle of races.
2. Anaerobic training: This form of training improves the anaerobic release of energy so that swimmers can sprint faster in the last 50 m of races.
3. Speed training: This form enhances the release of energy from the high energy phosphates. It is an important form of training for improving the ability to get races out faster.

These forms of training are described in the next section. The discussion will center on (a) suggestions for constructing effective repeat sets and (b) some possible avenues for research.

Aerobic Training

As indicated previously, the purpose of aerobic training is to improve the ability of athletes to swim faster without a large accumulation of lactic acid.

Recent research indicates that the aerobic-anaerobic threshold concept forms the basis for the most effective training of aerobic metabolism (Hollmann et al., 1981; Madsen & Olbrecht, 1984). Mader, Heck, and Hollmann (1976) are credited with introducing the concept to the Western world. It has since been modified by Skinner and McLellan (1980) and others.

The anaerobic threshold corresponds to the maximum speed that an athlete can maintain aerobically. The aerobic threshold corresponds to the minimum training speed that will encourage an improvement in aerobic endurance. It has been suggested that athletes will improve their aerobic endurance faster with less risk of overtraining if they train at speeds somewhere between these two thresholds. Athletes should also train above the anaerobic threshold occasionally in order to stimulate the rate of aerobic improvement.

The aerobic and anaerobic thresholds are measured by taking blood samples following repeated practice swims at different speeds and then analyzing these samples for lactic acid content. The aerobic threshold is analagous to speeds that produce a blood lactic acid of content of 2 mM/l (see Figure 1). For most athletes, the anaerobic threshold relates to speeds that produce a blood lactic acid content of approximately 4 mM/l (see Figure 1).

Three Types of Aerobic Training

In accordance with the aerobic-anaerobic threshold concept, the three types of aerobic training that swimmers need are (a) developmental, (b) maintenance, and (c) overload.

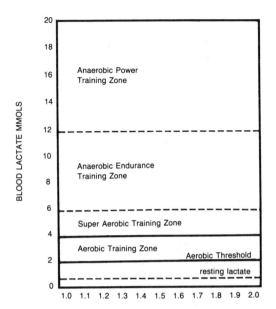

Figure 1 Zones for training based on blood lactate concentrations.

Developmental aerobic training. This type of training corresponds to speeds that will produce blood lactic acid concentrations that are between 3 and 4 mM/l. These speeds, because they are as fast as athletes can swim aerobically, will result in the most rapid improvement of the aerobic metabolic processes. Surprisingly, faster speeds have been found to be less effective for this purpose (Hollmann et al., 1981; Madsen & Olbrecht, 1984). This may be because they cause a rapid accumulation of lactic acid. Lactic acid accumulation reduces the total mileage that a swimmer can tolerate and inhibits adaptations of aerobic metabolism. It is suggested that 50% of a swimmer's aerobic yardage should be completed at these speeds.

Any repeat distance can be used for this purpose. Distances of 400 m and longer are recommended, however, because long repeat distances may encourage greater adaptations of the aerobic metabolic sources. The sets should be 3,000 m in length or longer for senior swimmers. For younger or less skilled swimmers a good guideline is that the set should require a minimum of 30 min to complete. Rest periods should be short, 5 to 30 s in length. Athletes should swim at the fastest possible average speed that can be maintained for the entire set.

If these guidelines are followed, blood testing should not be necessary. Motivated athletes should be forced to swim at speeds at or just below the anaerobic threshold because they will not be able to maintain an even pace for a set of this length if they swim faster than threshold pace. Heart rates and subjective feelings of effort can be used if additional guidelines are desired. Heart rates should be 150 to 180 bpm, and swimming efforts should correspond to 7 or 8 on a scale based on a maximum effort of 10. These guidelines are summarized in Table 1.

Maintenance aerobic training. This type of training is used on days when athletes need to reduce their effort and to provide an opportunity for tissue repair, energy replacement, and restoration of homeostasis. On these days, it is important to swim at or just above the aerobic threshold so that training adaptations are not lost. Approximately 25% of a swimmer's aerobic distance should be completed at these speeds.

Any repeat distance can be used for this type of training. The sets should, once again, be a minimum of 3,000 m in length for senior swimmers or should require at least 30 min to complete. Rest periods should be short (5 to 30 s), and efforts should be moderate. Heart rates of 130 to 150 bpm probably indicate the proper speed. Perceived efforts in the 6 to 7 range are also good indicators of the proper training speed (see Table 1). Repeat speeds should be approximately 3 s/100 m slower than speeds achieved in developmental aerobic sets.

Overload aerobic training. Occasionally, swimming just above the anaerobic threshold is important, that is, at speeds that produce blood lactic acid concentrations between 5 and 6 mM/l. This type of training is analogous to a maximum aerobic effort. It provides a stimulus that may cause aerobic capacity to improve at a more rapid rate. It is, however, a very stressful type of training because large amounts of lactic acid are produced in the muscles and because the rate of glycogen depletion is considerably increased. Therefore, it must be used sparingly, perhaps every third or fourth aerobic training session. Accordingly, approximately 25% of a swimmer's aerobic distance should be completed at these speeds.

As with the previous two types of training, any repeat distance will suffice for this purpose. However, distances of 100 to 400 m are recommended. Repeat sets should be 1,000 to 2,000 m in length, or they should require 15 to 20 min for completion. Rest periods should be slightly longer than those used in the previous two types of training described in order to maintain faster average speeds. Intervals of 30 s to 1 min should be adequate. Repeat speeds should be approximately 3 s faster than those achieved in developmental aerobic sets. Heart rates should be near maximum by the end of the set, and athletes should feel that they are swimming in the 8 to 9 effort range (see Table 1).

Suggestions for Research

It should be mentioned that there are several critics of the aerobic-anaerobic threshold concept of aerobic training. Some coaches and researchers who subscribe to the "swim at race pace" theory of training specificity believe that the speeds suggested earlier are too slow for effective improvement of aerobic endurance. Certain researchers doubt the existence of aerobic and anaerobic thresholds (Brooks, 1985), whereas

Table 1 Guidelines for Training

Forms of training	Blood lactate (mM/l)	Speed (% of max)	Heart rate (bpm)	Perceived effort (10 = max)	Set length	Rest
Aerobic						
Maintenance	2	65-75	130-150	6-7	> 30 min	5-30 s
Developmental	3-4	70-90	150-180	7-8	> 30 min	5-30 s
Overload	5-6	80-95	180-200	8-9	15-20 min	30-60 s
Anaerobic						
Anaerobic endurance	6-12	85-95	maximum	9-10	600-1,000 m	15-60 s
Anaerobic power	12-20	95-100	maximum	9-10	300-600 m	5-15 min
Speed	na	97-100	na	10	300-600 m	1-5 min

na = not applicable.

others doubt that blood lactate accurately reflects the metabolism occurring in exercising muscles (Green, Hughson, Orr, & Ranney, 1983).

Several questions have arisen about this training procedure that require research, including the following:

- Is performance improved most by swimming long sets at speeds between the aerobic and anaerobic thresholds, or would athletes be better advised to train for shorter periods of time at race speed?
- Would it be better for athletes to train at their individual aerobic and anaerobic thresholds rather than some arbitrary concentration such as 4 mM/l?
- Is endurance improved best without overtraining when athletes swim at speeds that produce blood lactate concentrations between 2 and 3 mM/l, or should they train at speeds that produce concentrations between 3 and 4 mM/l?

Anaerobic Training

The purpose of anaerobic training is to improve a swimmer's ability to sprint faster at the end of races when muscle pH is dropping to levels that cause severe pain, a loss of muscular power, and reduced coordination. This purpose is accomplished in two ways: (a) by improving the buffering capacity of muscles and (b) by increasing the rate of lactic acid production.

If swimmers can produce lactic acid faster and in greater quantities and yet buffer it more efficiently, they will be able to sprint longer and faster at the end of races. Increases in lactate production result primarily from improvements in the enzyme systems involved (Baldwin, Winder, Terjung, & Holloszy, 1972; Gollnick, Armstrong, Saubert, Piehl, & Saltin, 1972; Saubert, Armstrong, Shepherd, & Gollnick, 1973; Staudte, Exner, & Pette, 1973).

Another important aspect of anaerobic training might be termed psychological, that is, an improvement in pain tolerance. When athletes are subjected to the pain of lactate accumulation they become capable of swimming faster without giving in to that pain.

Based on the previous discussion, two types of training should improve anaerobic endurance: anaerobic endurance training and anaerobic power training.

Anaerobic Endurance Training

The purpose of anaerobic endurance training is to improve the rate of lactic acid production so that swimmers can sprint faster at the end of races. Athletes should swim fast repeats with short rest intervals. This will stimulate the muscles to produce lactic acid at a fast rate several times in a training session.

Repeat distances of 50 to 200 m are recommended for this purpose. They produce the highest rate of lactate accumulation. Sets should be 15 s to 1 min in length. Speeds should be 85 to 95% of race speed and heart rates should be near maximum. Perceived efforts should be in the 8 to 10 range (see Table 1).

Combining this form of training with repeats designed to improve the athlete's sense of pace is often wise. In this case, the repeats should be swum at present or desired race speeds using the shortest possible rest interval. Broken swims are ideal for this purpose. Repeat distances should be half of the race distance or less to allow race speeds to be maintained.

Anaerobic Power Training

This type of training improves muscle buffering capacity. In this case they should swim very fast repeats with long rest intervals. By doing so near maximum levels of lactic acid are reached in the muscles. The muscles, in turn, adapt so that they improve their ability to tolerate the pain of lactate accumulation.

Repeat distances of 50 to 200 m are recommended here for the same reason given in the previous section. Sets should be 300 to 600 m in length. Rest periods should be long (5-15 min) so that muscle lactate concentrations can be reduced sufficiently to allow fast speeds and greater need for buffering on succeeding swims. Swimming at half-speed during the rest interval will hasten the recovery process (Belcastro & Bonen, 1975). Speeds should be 95 to 100% of race speed. Heart rates should, of course, be near maximum. Perceived efforts should be in the 9 to 10 range (see Table 1).

Suggestions for Research

Regarding anaerobic training, some of the important questions that remain to be answered include the following:

- How many days per week and how many weeks per season can a swimmer engage in anaerobic training without becoming overtrained?
- What are the optimum repeat distances, set lengths, speeds, and rest intervals for anaerobic endurance and anaerobic power training?
- Will swimming underdistance anaerobic repeats at race speeds reduce muscle lactate accumulation and/or the decline of muscle pH during races more effectively than they can be reduced by aerobic training?

Speed Training

The purpose of speed training is to improve a swimmer's maximum speed so that he or she can take races out faster. The recommended repeat distances are between 10 and 50 m. Speeds should be as fast as possible; faster than race speed is recommended. Rest intervals should be 1 to 5 min in length to allow the swimmer time for nearly complete recovery (see Table 1). If adequate recovery time is not allowed, lactic acid will accumulate and the repeat speeds will slow down.

This will defeat the purpose of sprint sets. Discomfort should be mild during these sets. Sensations of pain are an indication that lactic acid is accumulating. Heart rates are not valid indicators of training efforts because of the short repeat distances. Athletes should swim their major stroke(s) in these repeats, because the training adaptations they seek will only occur in muscle fibers that have been exercised. Therefore, the only way they can be certain of training the same fibers they will use in races is to swim their major stroke(s) in training (Saltin et al., 1976).

Variations on Speed Training

Power training on land may help to improve sprinting speed (Costill, Sharp, & Troup, 1980). Swimming short sprints against resistance supplied by surgical tubing, drag suits, and so forth may also be an effective way to increase stroking power. This form of training has been termed *sprint-resisted*. While stroke mechanics deteriorate somewhat when swimming against resistance, this form of training mimics the actual stroke closer than any other form of resistance training (Maglischo, Maglischo, Zier, & Santos, 1985).

Another innovation in speed training is to use devices that help swimmers sprint faster than they can sprint unassisted. This form of training is termed *sprint-assisted*. Swim fins and swimming with the "snap-back" of surgical tubing are two methods that have been tried. They produce a type of overload that cannot be achieved in any other manner; that is, they allow swimmers to swim faster than they can unassisted. Swimmers change their stroke mechanics somewhat when engaging in sprint-assisted training (Maglischo et al., 1985). However, if used sparingly, the benefits of sprint-assisted training should outweigh this disadvantage.

Suggestions for Research

The following are some questions regarding sprint training that need further research.

- Can strength or power that is developed on land in nonspecific (i.e., weight training) exercises or in specific stroke-simulative resistance exercises (i.e., swim benches) be used to improve speed in the water?
- Is sprint-assisted or sprint-resisted training the superior method for improving sprint speed?
- What are the optimum repeat distances, numbers of repeats, speeds, and rest intervals for improving sprinting speed?

References

Baldwin, K., Winder, W., Terjung, R., & Holloszy, J. (1972). Glycolytic capacity of red, white and intermediate muscle: Adaptive response to running. *Medicine and Science in Sports and Exercise, 4*, 50.

Balcastro, A.N., & Bonen, A. (1975). Lactic acid removal rates during controlled and uncontrolled recovery after exercise. *Journal of Applied Physiology, 39*(6), 932-936.

Brooks, G.A. (1985). Anaerobic threshold: Review of the concept and directions for future research. *Medicine and Science in Sports and Exercise, 17*(1), 23-31.

Costill, D.L., Sharp, R., & Troup, J. (1980). Muscle strength: Contributions to sprint swimming. *Swimming World, 21*, 29-34.

Green, H.J., Hughson, R.L., Orr, G.W., & Ranney, D.A. (1983). Anaerobic threshold, blood lactate, and muscle metabolites in progressive exercise. *Journal of Applied Physiology, 54*(4), 1032-1038.

Gollnick, P., Armstrong, R., Saubert, C., Piehl, K., & Saltin, B. (1972). Enzyme activity and fiber composition in skeletal muscle of untrained and trained men. *Journal of Applied Physiology, 33*(3), 312-319.

Hollmann, W., Rost, R., Liesen, H., Dufaux, B., Heck, B., & Mader, A. (1981). Assessment of different forms of physical activity with respect to preventive and rehabilitative cardiology. *International Journal of Sports Medicine, 2*, 67-80.

Mader, A., Heck, H., & Hollmann, W. (1976). Evaluation of lactic acid anaerobic energy contribution by determination of postexercise lactic acid concentration of ear capillary blood in middle-distance runners and swimmers. In F. Landry & W. Orban (Eds.), *The International Congress of Physical Activity Sciences: Vol 4. Exercise physiology* (pp. 187-199). Miami: Symposia Specialists.

Madsen, O., & Olbrecht, J. (1984). Specifics of aerobic training. In B. Ousley (Ed.), *American Swimming Coaches Association 1983 World Clinic yearbook* (pp. 15-29). Ft. Lauderdale, FL: American Swimming Coaches Association.

Maglischo, E.W., Maglischo, C.W., Zier, D.J., & Santos, T.R. (1985). The effect of sprint-assisted and sprint-resisted swimming on stroke mechanics. *Journal of Swimming Research, 1*(2), 27-33.

Saltin, B., Nazar, K., Costill, D.L., Stein, E., Jansson, E., Essen, B., & Gollnick, P.D. (1976). The nature of the training response: peripheral and central adaptations to one-legged exercise. *Acta Physiologica Scandanavica, 96*, 289-305.

Saubert, C., Armstrong, R., Shepherd, R., & Gollnick, P.D. (1973). Anaerobic enzyme adaptation to sprint training in rats. *Pflügers Archiv, 341*, 305-312.

Skinner, J.S., & McLellan, T.H. (1980). The transition from aerobic to anaerobic metabolism. *Research Quarterly*, **14**, 234-248.

Staudte, H., Exner, G., & Pette, D. (1973). Effect of short-term high intensity (sprint) training on some contractile and metabolic characteristics of fast and slow muscle of the rat. *Pflügers Archiv*, **344**, 159-168.

Aerobic Economy and Competitive Performance of U.S. Elite Swimmers

Peter J. Van Handel
Andrea Katz
James R. Morrow
John P. Troup
Jack T. Daniels
Patrick W. Bradley

The sport of swimming presents a unique challange to the measurement of energy cost. Although tethered swimming has provided information on the maximal physiological status of athletes (Bonen, Wilson, Yarkony, & Belcastro 1980; Costill, 1966; Costill et al., 1985), Magel and Faulkner (1967) found that in trained swimmers tethered values were significantly less than those obtained in free swimming. There is also some question as to the reliability and validity of extrapolation techniques (Costill et al., 1985; Leger, Seliger, & Brassud, 1980). In a homogenous group of runners, $\dot{V}O_2$max was also a poor discriminator of competitive success (Conley & Krackenbull, 1980; Costill, Branam, Eddy, & Sparks, 1971; Foster, Costill, Daniels, & Fink, 1978; Pollock, Jackson, & Pate, 1980; Sjodin, & Svedenhag, 1985). Other variables such as the fractional utilization of maximal aerobic capacity (Costill, Thomason, & Roberts, 1973; Sjodin & Svedenhag, 1985) or the economy of effort (Daniels, 1974; Daniels, Krahenbuhl, Foster, Gilbert, & Daniels, 1977; McMiken & Daniels, 1976; Pollock et al., 1980; Powers, Dodd, Deason, Byrd, & McKnight, 1983) may be at least as important for competitive success.

This chapter describes a method for determining oxygen cost in free swimming and quantifies aerobic economy of submaximal swimming and its relationship to competitive efforts of world-class swimmers.

General Protocols

Subjects in this study were 19 male and 18 female competitive swimmers, accounting for 53 top three places at the 1985 United States Nationals, 18 American and two world records, and 10 Olympic medals in 1984.

Expired air was obtained during untethered free swimming by a modification of the Douglas bag method utilizing a specially designed collection device (Daniels, 1971). The athlete wore a headpiece containing the inspiratory/expiratory valve-snorkle system, allowing the expired air to be serially ported into meteorlogical balloons. Fractions of expired oxygen and carbon dioxide were measured on calibrated electronic analyzers and volume by a portable dry gas meter calibrated to Tissot values. Based upon previous studies (Di Prampero, Pendergast, Wilson, & Rennie, 1974), the drag effects of the breathing apparatus were assumed to be similar in magnitude to that of the head turning that occurs in the natural overarm crawl (Counsilman, 1968), so the oxygen cost values were not corrected for this effect. Collections were made during the last minute of each of three evenly split 400-m freestyle swims. This distance was chosen to ensure that physiological variables were steady state and representative of the speed of swimming. Swim velocity (v = m/s) was calculated from the average of the 50-m splits. A fourth 400-m swim was split progressively faster to achieve maximal oxygen consumption ($\dot{V}O_2max$) during the last 100 to 150 m. All swims were from a push start in a 50-m pool and with an open turn prior to the last length, during which the expired air samples were collected while walking along with the swimmer. The average v ranged from 1.11 m/s (6:00 for 400 m) for the slowest individual submaximal swim to 1.60 m/s (4:10 for 400 m) for the fastest maximal effort. Postswim heart rates were obtained by radio telemetry and blood lactic acid from semiautomated polarographic analyses of finger puncture samples (Van Handel, Troup, & Bradley, 1986).

All statistical analyses were completed using $SPSS_x$ (1983), including regression of $\dot{V}O_2$, heart rate, and lactate on v and single and multiple stepwise regression of these variables with 400-m freestyle competition times. Post hoc tests set an alpha level of .05 for statistical significance.

Economy or efficiency of effort was described in terms of $\dot{V}O_2max$ at a given v. A common regression line was determined by regression $\dot{V}O_2$ on v across all subjects at all vs. Thus, a predicted $\dot{V}O_2$ cost was obtained for only v. If a swimmer's actual $\dot{V}O_2$ was below that of the predicted oxygen cost, the swimmer was deemed economical or efficient because the actual oxygen cost for that v was less than that predicted (typical oxygen consumption at that v). Those with oxygen consumption above the regression line were deemed uneconomical in terms of oxygen consumption for the v. For each subject, actual minus predicted $\dot{V}O_2$ was calculated across all trials to estimate total economy. Those with high negative values were typically below the regression line for all vs (economical). Those with high positive numbers were typically above the regression line for all vs (uneconomical). The general equation for this statistical analysis was

$$(y1 - \hat{y}1) + (y2 - \hat{y}2) + (y3 - \hat{y}3) + ...(yn - \hat{y}n)$$

where $y1, y2, y3 ...yn$ = ml 02 • kg • min^{-1} and

$\hat{y}1, \hat{y}2, \hat{y}3 ... \hat{y}n$ = a + bx; x = $v1, v2, v3 ... vn$.

Results and Discussion

Figure 1 illustrates the regressions of O_2 demand with free swimming and presents mean $\dot{V}O_2$max data. The latter were considerably higher than those previously obtained on swimmers, perhaps due to differences in the competitive level of the group and/or the testing methodologies employed. Either swimmers of this caliber have not been tested, or values were not obtained in free swimming (Bonen et al., 1980; Costill, 1966; Costill et al., 1985; Di Prampero et al., 1974; Holmer, 1972, 1978; Levoie, Leger, Leone, & Provencher, 1985; Leger et al., 1980; Magel & Faulkner, 1967; Montpetit, Leger, Lavoie, & Cazorla, 1981; Swaine & Reilly, 1983). Magel and Faulkner (1967), for example, found that for trained swimmers, tethered values were significantly less than those obtained in free swimming. Other studies examined club or university athletes or studied effects of training upon unskilled swimmers.

Average velocities of 1.2, 1.4, and 1.6 m/s are equivalent to 5:33, 4:45, and 4:10 for a 400-m swim. Statistical analysis of slope and intercept indicated no significant differences between men and women (Figure 1). The common regression of $\dot{V}O_2$ (ml/kg • min^{-1}) on v is also presented ($r = .876; p < .02$). Earlier studies on elite runners or cyclists have demonstrated that at comparable work intensities there were no sex differences in relative O_2 cost (Baldwin et al., 1986; Katz, Puhl, Bradley, & Van Handel, 1986; Pate, Barnes, & Miler, 1985). The present data extend these observations to swimmers as well, though it should be noted that because the males were significantly heavier than the female swimmers, gross oxygen costs (l/min) were significantly different between the sexes.

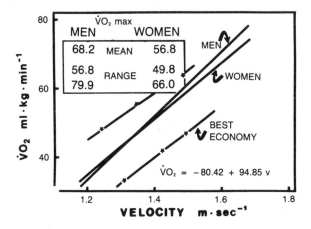

Figure 1 Energy cost of untethered swimming for elite male and female athletes. Relative O_2 costs were similar for men and women, although individual cost curves varied considerably above or below the group regression by approximately 10 ml O_2/kg. The range, $\dot{V}O_2$max, and common regression of submaximal $\dot{V}O_2$ on velocity are also given.

Because $\dot{V}O_2$maxes were also significantly different between sexes (Figure 1) while the relative submaximal cost curves were equivalent, the women, therefore, had to swim at a significantly greater percentage of aerobic capacity for any given v. At 1.4 m/s, for example, costs were roughly 77 and 91% of group maximums for men and women, respectively. Similar observations have been made on less accomplished swimmers (Costill et al., 1985) and for runners at various levels of competitive success (Baldwin et al., 1986; Daniels, 1974; Daniels et al., 1977), suggesting that both $\dot{V}O_2$max and fractional utilization are important discriminating variables for sex differences in athletes competing in common events.

Individual oxygen cost curves ranged approximately 10 ml O_2/kg on either side of the regression. The "best" and "worst" individual curves are also shown in Figure 1. McArdle, Glaser, and Magel (1971) also found that in a group of well-trained swimmers, individual energy costs varied widely.

The present economy curves (Figure 1) and calculated estimates of efficiency (ml O_2/m) were considerably lower than those reported in earlier studies of free swimming at slower velocities and utilizing less competitively successful athletes (Costill et al., 1985; Di Prampero et al., 1974; Lavoie et al., 1985) indicating that not only do elite-level swimmers have higher $\dot{V}O_2$maxes but they are also more efficient. Costill et al. (1985) found that although competitive and recreational swimmers had similar $\dot{V}O_2$maxes and the intercept of $\dot{V}O_2$ on v were the same, slopes were different. Efficiency values of approximately 50 ml O_2 and 40 ml O_2 at velocites of 1.2 m/s were obtained for trained collegiate male and female swimmers, respectively. At 85% $\dot{V}O_2$max, values were about 1.0 ml O_2 higher and more than 75 ml O_2 for recreational swimmers. Oxygen cost per meter for the elite males and females in the present study yielded values of approximately 36 and 28 ml O_2/m at 1.2 m/s and roughly 49 and 34 ml O_2 at 85% $\dot{V}O_2$max. Holmer (1972) also found that trained swimmers had much lower oxygen cost curves than nonswimmers, and Karpovich and Millman (1944) indicated that unskilled swimmers expend 2 to 5 times as much energy as skilled swimmers. Clearly, the elite athletes studied in this project not only had high aerobic capacities but also were very efficient at any swim velocity. These differences may be due, in part, to the fact that efficiency of swimming increases as speed increases (Di Prampero et al., 1974) and that at slow speeds kicking requires a proportionally greater oxygen uptake but contributes little to propulsion (Adrian, 1966; Karpovich, 1935).

The submaximal oxygen demand to run at a specific speed has also been found to vary widely among subjects (Costill et al., 1973; Daniels, 1974; McMiken & Daniels, 1976; Sjodin & Svedenhag, 1985). Recent studies on a homogenous group of elite distance runners (Bradley, Daniels, Baldwin, Scardina, & Morrow, 1986) suggested that athletes with relatively low maximal aerobic capacities also tended to be economical. Good economy may compensate for low maximal capacity, allowing the athlete to compete favorably. On the other hand, although economy has been found to account for a significant amount of variation in running performance among subjects with similar $\dot{V}O_2$maxes and can distinguish between good and elite runners (Conley & Krackenbull, 1980), for homogeneous groups, no significant relationship can be found between a measure of performance and economy (Bradley et al., 1986; Davies & Thompson, 1979). For all subjects ($N = 37$) in the present study, there was a weak negative though significant relationship between $\dot{V}O_2$max and economy ($r = .314$, $p < .04$; Fig 3 upper panel) indicating that individuals with lower $\dot{V}O_2$max values tended to be more economical in swimming energy cost.

A total of 16 swimmers in this study (10 males, 6 females) raced over 400-m distances within 1 week of the physiological testing. A highly significant relationship existed between $\dot{V}O_2$max and competition time (Figure 2; $r = .616$, $p < .005$), although only 38% of the variance in performance could be explained by $\dot{V}O_2$max. Males have both higher aerobic maximums and faster swim times (see Figure 1; Costill et al., 1985; Holmer, 1972; Lavoie, Taylor, & Montpetit, 1981). Therefore, the overall wide range of values for the two variables generates a spurious significant relationship. Similar statistical effects occur when highly trained, moderately trained, and sedentary subjects are included describing a heterogeneous population. If males and females are considered separately, no relationship existed between performance and $\dot{V}O_2$max. These data are also presented in Figure 2. The lengths of the horizontal and vertical bars represent the ranges found for each variable and group.

Blood lactic acid and heart rates were also obtained after each submaximal and the maximal effort. Individual blood lactate economy curves were calculated as described for oxygen demand. Because the females were at a higher percentage of maximal aerobic capacity than the males for any given absolute value of v, it might be expected that they would have displayed a relatively greater heart rate and blood lactic acid response. This was the case although tests for group differences on slope and intercept of these curves were nonsignificant. Maximal heart rates and the peak blood lactates were 202 bpm and 7.2 mM and 202 bpm and 5.3 mM for the males and females, respectively.

Submaximal oxygen and lactic acid economy and maximal $\dot{V}O_2$, heart rate, and blood lactic acid values were used in single and step-wise multi-

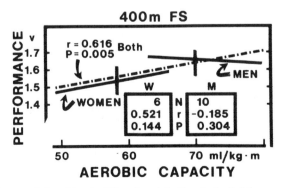

Figure 2 $\dot{V}O_2$max relationships to 400-m freestyle time (velocity) for men, women, and the total group. A significant relationship only existed when men and women were combined.

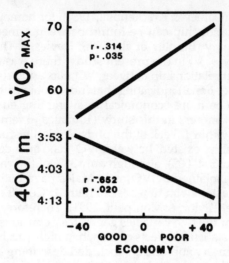

Figure 3 Economy of submaximal swimming (i.e., location of the O_2 cost curve relative to the group regression) related to both $\dot{V}O_2$max and 400-m freestyle competition time. Generally, better economy compensated for lower maximal capacity; economy was the best single predictor of swim time.

ple linear regression analysis to assess the relationships to swimming performance. The best single predictor of competition time was economy ($r = -.652$; $p < .020$; see Figure 3, lower panel). The coefficient of determination did not increase significantly with the addition of other variables, including $\dot{V}O_2$max, HLa economy, and HLamax. That a measure of economy better describes performance capacity for a homogeneous population of swimmers may be due to the fact that swimming efficiency is more dependent on skill and training than is running efficiency and that the range of individual efficiency or economy values for swimming are more variable due to factors such as stroke mechanics, body density, size, and shape, which can vary greatly in individuals. In any case, the data imply that having both a high $\dot{V}O_2$max and good economy is a prerequisite for success in swimming.

Acknowledgments

Support for this program was provided by an Elite Athlete Program Grant to U.S. Swimming and the Sports Sciences Division of the U.S. Olympic Committee.

References

Adrian, M.J., Singh, M., & Karpovich, P.V. (1966). Energy cost of leg kick, arm stroke, and whole crawl stroke. *Journal of Applied Physiology*, **21**, 1763-1766.

Baldwin, C., Bradley, P., Daniels, J., Daniels, N., Katz, A., & Morrow, J. (1986). Comparison of submaximal oxygen cost of running between elite male and female distance runners. *Medicine and Science in Sports and Exercise*, **18** (Suppl.), S37.

Bonen, A., Wilson, B.A., Yarkony, M., & Belcastro, A.N. (1980). Maximal oxygen uptake during free, tethered and flume swimming. *Journal of Applied Physiology*, **48**, 232-235.

Bradley, P., Daniels, J., Baldwin, C., Scardina, N., & Morrow, J. (1986). Running economy: Quantification and relationship with physiological determinants of performance. *Medicine and Science in Sports and Exercise*, **18** (Suppl.), S37.

Conley, D.L., & Krahenbuhl, G.S. (1980). Running economy and distance running performance of highly trained athletes. *Medicine and Science in Sports and Exericise*, **12**, 357-360.

Costill, D.L. (1966). Use of a swimming ergometer in physiological research. *Research Quarterly*, **37**, 564-567.

Costill, D.L., Branam, G., Eddy, D., & Sparks, K. (1971). Determinants of marathon running success. *Internationale Zeitschrift für Angewandte Physiologie*, **29**, 249-254.

Costill, D.L., Kovaleski, J., Porter, D., Kirwan, J., Fielding, R. & King, D. (1985). Energy expenditure during front crawl swimming: Predicting success in middle-distance events. *International Journal of Sports Medicine*, **6**, 266-270.

Costill, D.L., Thomason, H., & Roberts, E. (1973). Fractional utilization of the aerobic capacity during distance running. *Medicine and Science in Sports*, **5**, 248-252.

Counsilman, J.E. (1968). *The science of swimming*. Englewood Cliffs, NJ: Prentice-Hall.

Daniels, J. (1971). Portable respiratory gas collection equipment. *Journal of Applied Physiology*, **31**, 164-167.

Daniels, J. (1974). Physiological charcteristics of champion male athletes. *Research Quarterly*, **45**, 342-348.

Daniels, J., Krackenbull, G., Foster, C., Gilbert, J., & Daniels, S. (1977). Aerobic responses of female distance runners to submaximal and maximal exercise. *Annals New York Academy of Science*, **301**, 726-733.

Davies, C.T.M., & Thompson, M.W. (1979). Aerobic performance of female and male marathon and ultramarathon athletes. *European Journal of Applied Physiology*, **41**, 233-245.

Di Prampero, P.E., Pendergast, D.R., Wilson, D.W., & Rennie, D.W. (1974). Energetics of swimming in man. *Journal of Applied Physiology*, **7**, 1-5.

Foster, C., Costill, D.L., Daniels, J.T., & Fink, W.J. (1978). Skeletal muscle enzyme activity, fiber composition and $\dot{V}O_2$max in relation to distance running performance. *European Journal of Applied Physiology*, **39**, 73-80.

Holmer, I. (1972). Oxyten uptake during swimming in man. *Journal of Applied Physiology*, **33**, 502-509.

Holmer, I. (1978). Physiological adjustments to swimming. *Geneeskunde Sport*, **11**, 22-26.

Karpovich, P.V. (1935). Analysis of the propelling force in the crawl stroke. *Research Quarterly*, **6**, 49-58.

Karpovitch, P.V., & Millman, N. (1944). Energy expenditure in swimming. *American Journal of Physiology*, **142**, 140-144.

Katz, A., Puhl, J., Bradley, P.W., & Van Handle, P.J. (1986). Lack of coincidence between heart rate and blood lactic acid deflections from linearity during ergometer cycling. *Medicine and Science in Sports and Exercise*, **18** (Suppl), S82.

Lavoie, J.M., Leger, L.A., Leone, M., & Provencher, P.J. (1985). A maximal multistage swim test to determine the functional and maximal aerobic power of competitive swimmers. *Journal of Swimming Research*, **1**, 17-22.

Lavoie, J.M., Taylor, A.W., & Montpetit, R.R. (1981). Physiological effects of training in elite swimmers as measured by a free swimming test. *Journal of Sports Medicine*, **21**, 38-42.

Leger, L.A., Seliger, V, & Brassud, L. (1980). Backward extrapolation of VO_2max values from the O_2 recovery curve. *Medicine and Science in Sports and Exercise*, **12**, 24-27.

Magel, J.R., & Faulkner, J.A. (1967). Maximum oxygen uptake of college swimmers. *Journal of Applied Physiology*, **22**, 924-928.

McMiken, D.F., & Daniels, J.T. (1976). Aerobic requirements of maximum aerobic power in treadmill and track running. *Medicine and Science in Sports*, **8**, 14-17.

Montpetit, R.R., Leger, L.A., Lavoie, J., & Cazorla, M. (1981). VO_2 peak during free swimming using the backward extrapolation of the O_2 recovery curve. *European Journal of Applied Physiology*, **47**, 385-391.

Pate, R.R., Barnes, C., & Miler, W. (1985). A physiological comparison of performance matched female and male distance runners. *Research Quarterly for Exercise and Sport*, **56**, 245-250.

Pollock, M.L., Jackson, A.S., & Pate, R.R. (1980). Discriminant analysis of physiological differences between good and elite distance runners. *Research Quarterly for Exercise and Sport*, **51**, 521-532.

Powers, S.K., Dodd, S., Deason, R., Byrd, R., & McKnight, T. (1983). Ventilatory threshold, running economy and distance running performance of trained athletes. *Research Quarterly for Exercise and Sport*, **54**, 179-182.

Sjodin, B., & Svedenhag, J. (1985). Applied physiology of marathon running. *Journal of Sports Medicine*, **2**, 83-99.

SPSS, Inc. (1983). *SPSSx users guide*. Chicago: McGraw-Hill.

Swaine, I., & Reilly, T. (1983). The freely chosen swimming stroke rate in a maximal swim and on a biokinetic swimbench. *Medicine and Science in Sports and Exercise,* **15**, 370-375.

Van Handel, P.J., Troup, J.P., & Bradley, P.W. (1986). *A method for obtaining and analyzing lactic acid in micro samples of whole blood.* Manuscript submitted for publication.

Energy Expenditure During Front Crawl Swimming: A Comparison Between Males and Females

Richard M. Montpetit
Georges Cazorla
Jean-Marc Lavoie

Previous studies (Montpetit, Lavoie, Cazorla, 1983; Pendergast, Di Prampero, Craig, Wilson, & Rennie, 1977) have shown differences in the oxygen demand of swimming the front crawl (liters of O_2/min) between males and females. These observations, however, were made from unmatched groups in regard to both ability level and body size. In this study the oxygen costs of swimming the front crawl were compared in male and female competitive swimmers who were selected to form equivalent groups as far as body mass and swimming experience were concerned, but at the same time a large range existed in these parameters.

Procedure

Subjects

The subjects consisted of 38 males and 38 females. They were selected on the basis of swimming experience (minimum 3 years) and body weight.

Table 1 Physical Characteristics of Subjects

Characteristic	Males $n = 38$	Females $n = 38$
Age range (years)	11–22	11–18
Mean age (years)	14.9	14.1
Height range (cm)	140–184	138–180
Mean height (cm)	165.4	163.1
Body weight range (kg)	33.5–80.5	31.0–80.5
Mean weight (kg)	54.1	53.8

A summary of their physical characteristics is given in Table 1. All subjects trained regularly: the older ones, an average of 10 sessions per week, the younger ones at least 5 sessions per week. The majority of the subjects were familiar with the testing apparatus and procedures as they had been tested at a swim training camp the previous year.

Methods

All swimming experiments were performed in a 50-m pool in which the water temperature was 26 to 27 °C. Oxygen consumption ($\dot{V}O_2$) was measured by the Douglas bag technique, using the gas collection equipment described by Montpetit, Léger, Lavoie, and Cazorla (1981). After a warm-up of 1,000 m then a rest of 5 min, the subjects completed three submaximal swims, 4 min in duration with 5-min rest between swims. Most measurements were made at 1.0, 1.1, and 1.2 m $\cdot$ s^{-1}. A few observations at higher speeds, up to 1.25 m $\cdot$ s^{-1}, were also made. Serial, 45-s gas collections were made over the last 1.5 min of each 4-min swim. The values obtained for individual swimmers indicated that they were all in steady state for the two collections at each speed. The mean of the two collections were used to calculate the oxygen demand. The subjects were paced by light pacers; however, the precise swimming speed was calculated by using a stopwatch to measure the time needed to swim the middle 40-m portion of the 50-m pool length.

Gas samples were passed through a drying tube and analyzed for O_2 and CO_2 with the Beckman E-2 and LB-1 analyzers, respectively. These gas analyzers were calibrated at the beginning of each test, using standards previously analyzed with a Gallenkamp-Lloyd volumetric analyzer. Volumes of expired gas were measured with a calibrated Tissot spirometer.

Statistical Analysis

The $\dot{V}O_2$ values were used to compute linear regression equations by the method of least squares. Swimming speed was the independent variable, and $\dot{V}O_2$ was the dependent variable. The comparison of the $\dot{V}O_2$ at three velocities for males versus females was carried out using a two-way analysis of variance with repeated measures.

Results

In both males and females, steady state $\dot{V}O_2$ increased linearly with swimming velocity. No significant sex difference was observed for the slopes of these relationships. An analysis of variance for repeated measures on the $\dot{V}O_2$ values for the two groups on the three trials (velocities) indicated no significant group effect, a significant trials effect (velocities), and no significant Groups × Trials interaction, which indicates the groups were not differentially affected by the increase in velocity. These results justified the pooling of the data. The relationship between velocity and oxygen demand of the combined groups was described by this equation (r = .86, SEE = 0.275):

$$\dot{V}O_2 \ (l \bullet min^{-1}) = 3.75 \times velocity \ (m \bullet s^{-1}) - 1.71$$

To assess the contribution of speed and body weight to the oxygen demand prediction, a multiple regression equation was calculated (see Figure 1). The multiple regression for the whole group was the following:

$$\hat{Y} = 3.65 \ v + .02 \ W - 2.545$$

where $\hat{Y}$ is $\dot{V}O_2$ in $l \bullet min^{-1}$; v is velocity in $m \bullet s^{-1}$; W is body weight in kilograms. The resulting multiple correlation was .86, which accounted for about 74% of the variance in the criterion variable, with a standard error of estimate of 0.22. The remaining variance is likely due to technical and other factors. In a practical sense, at an equal aerobic energy expenditure rate, an 80-kg person could swim at 1.1 $m \bullet s^{-1}$, whereas a 60-kg swimmer could reach speeds of 1.19 $m \bullet s^{-1}$. All other factors being equal, such a difference (0.09 $m \bullet s^{-1}$) would amount to approximately 30 s over a distance of 400 m.

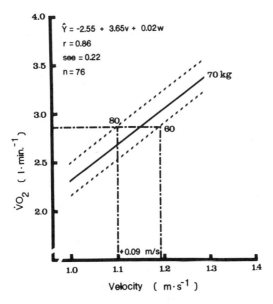

Figure 1 The relationship between steady state oxygen uptake and swimming velocity for a given body weight.

Discussion

The present results, with respect to the absence of differences in the O_2 demand of front crawl swimming between males and females, is not in agreement with data obtained by Pendergast et al. (1977) and Costill et al. (1985). This can be attributed in part to the fact that these studies have not controlled for body size. Moreover, the groups studied by these authors were not equated by swimming experience, and the comparisons were made incidentally.

Pendergast et al. (1977) found women to have a significantly lower O_2 cost than men, even after correction for surface area. Careful scrutiny of their results (Table 1, p. 476) reveals that they did not have enough evidence to substantiate their claim that women swim more economically than men. Only four males and five females were tested at a velocity (1.15 m • s^{-1}) that is comparable to ours (1.2 m • s^{-1}). Given the considerable interindividual variations reported by these authors, it would seem that the chance of extreme values affecting the computed means would be high. At lower velocities (0.8 to 0.9 m • s^{-1}), they reported for the swimmers (it was not clear whether these swimmers were competitive or recreational) a cost of 26.1 and 26.2 l of O_2 km^{-1} •m^2 surface area for men and women, respectively. At even lower velocities (0.60 to 075 m • s^{-1}) a comparison with the data of the present study would seem unrealistic because good swimmers aren't able to swim at such slow speeds—they paddle.

Costill et al. (1985) reported a 24.7% greater oxygen cost of swimming at a common velocity of 1.2 m • s^{-1}, for males as compared to females. Although the authors found energy costs to be affected by lean body weight and by the product of velocity and distance per stroke (an index of swimming ability), they did not report the size of their subjects, nor if they had equal swimming experience, when comparing the two groups.

Swimming energetics is governed not only by body size but also by morphological and technical factors. In this study, we controlled for both size and swimming experience. We can assume that the swimmers were, in a general sense, morphologically quite similar. Technical ability was taken into account only indirectly by equating years of competitive swimming experience.

Although the body weight is that supported in water, it is still good representation of size, as noted by the high corrleation with surface area (r = .93) and weight in air (r = .88). The high correlation between weight in air and weight in water is attributed to the homogeneity of the groups with respect to percentage body fat. The importance of body weight among competitive swimmers of comparable experience is suggested by Figure 2. The relationship between weight and the O_2 demand at a velocity of 1.0 m • s^{-1} is shown. The coefficient of determination (R^2) for the data indicates that within this cluster of swimmers, 40% of the variation observed in O^2 cost can be explained by the variation in body weight.

Regardless of sex, the concept of a linear relationship between velocity and $\dot{V}O_2$ seems to hold for submaximal swimming over the range of ve-

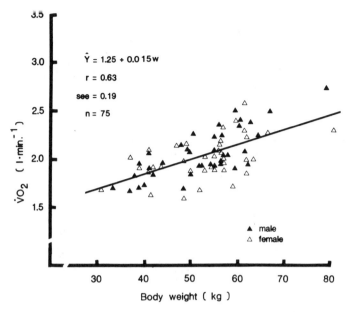

Figure 2   The relationship between steady state oxygen uptake at a swimming velocity of 1.0 m • s^{-1} and body weight in 75 swimmers (males and females).

locities studied (1.0 to 1.25 m • s^{-1}). This agrees with previously reported studies (Holmer, 1974; LePere & Porter, 1975; Montpetit et al., 1983).

The question can be asked, How well does the general multiple regression equation compare with the observed oxygen consumption for individuals in other studies? Table 2 displays the percentage deviations from the values calculated from the general equation and the observed individual values published by different authors. At a speed ranging from 1.0 to 1.2 m • s^{-1}, the calculations for the regression fall within 10% of the observed values.

In terms of swimming economy, as noted from the oxygen cost per distance swam, at a common velocity of 1.2 m • s^{-1} the female swimmers consumed 39.0 l • km^{-1} of O_2, whereas their male counterparts used 40.7 l • km^{-1}. This amounts to a difference of 4.2%, which, however, is not statistically significant. Costill et al. (1985) reported values of 40.5 l • km^{-1} and 50.5 l • km^{-1} for female and male swimmers, repectively, at this same velocity. As previously mentioned, the size and experience levels of the subjects in the two groups were not reported.

Conclusion

In conclusion, there is no difference due to sex in the oxygen demand of front crawl swimming when body size and swimming experience are taken into account. Despite this equality in O_2 cost, considerable inter-

Table 2   Difference Between Calculated O_2 Demand From Multiple Regression and Observed Values From Various Studies

Reference	Sex	Velocity m · s^{-1}	N	Observed $\dot{V}O_2$ (l · min)	Calculated $\dot{V}O_2$ from regression	Difference %
Pugh et al., 1960	F	1.10	1[a]	2.62	2.57	− 2.0
Holmer, 1972	M	1.00	1[a]	2.42	2.50	+ 3.2
Holmer, 1974	F	1.20	1[a]	2.80	3.10	+ 9.7
Pendergast, 1977	F	1.15	5	2.80	2.70	− 3.7
Montpetit, 1983	M	1.20	24	3.27	2.94	− 10.0
Montpetit, 1983	F	1.20	17	2.71	2.76	− 1.8
Chatard, Padilla, Cazorla, & Lacour, 1985	M	1.10	42	2.86	2.60	− 9.0

[a]Values for one individual, male (M) or female (F) as indicated, because of limited N at that velocity.

individual variabllltly persists when taken together (males and females) or separately. This can be attributed to technical proficiency and/or other factors. Body size as represented by mass in this study explains 40% of the total variance in the O_2 demand of front crawl swimming. The performance difference in aerobic events (i.e., 400 to 800-m crawl and 400 individual-medley) between males and females is principally due to muscular and metabolic power ($\dot{V}O_2max$).

References

Chatard, J.-C., Padilla, S., Cazorla, G., & Lacour, J.R. (1985). Influence of body height, weight, hydrodstatic lift and training on the energy cost of the front crawl. *The New Zealand Journal of Sports Medicine*, **13**, 82-84.

Costill, D.L., Kovaleski, J., Porter, D., Kirwan, J., Fielding, R., & King, D. (1985). Energy expenditure during front crawl swimming: Predicting success in middle-distance events. *International Journal of Sports Medicine*, **6**, 266-270.

Holmer, I. (1972). Oxygen uptake during swimming in man. *Journal of Applied Physiology*, **33**, 502-509.

Holmer, I. (1974). Physiology of swimming man. *Acta Physiologica Scandinavica*, **407**, (Suppl.) 1-53.

LePere, C.B., & Porter, G.H. (1975). Cardiovascular and metabolic response of skilled and recreational swimmers during running and swimming. In A.W. Taylor (Ed.), *Application of science and medicine to sport*. Springfield, IL: Charles C Thomas.

Montpetit, R.R., Léger, L.A., Lavoie, J.-M., & Cazorla, G. (1981). $\dot{V}O_2$ peak during free swimming using the backward extrapolation of the O_2 recovery curve. *European Journal of Applied Physiology*, **47**, 385-391.

Montpetit, R.R., Lavoie, J.-M., & Cazorla, G. (1983). Aerobic energy cost of swimming the front crawl at high velocity in international class and adolescent swimmers. In A.P. Hollander, P.A. Huijing, & G. de Groot (Eds.), *Biomechanics and medicine in swimming* (pp. 228-234). Champaign, IL: Human Kinetics.

Pendergast, D.R., Di Prampero, P.E., Craig, A.B., Jr., Wilson, D.R., & Rennie, D.W. (1977). Quantitative analysis of the front crawl in men and women. *Journal of Applied Physiology*, **43**, 475-479.

Pugh, L.G.C.E., Edholm, O.G., Fox, R.H., Wolf, H.S., Hervey, G.R., Hammond, W.H., Tanner, J.M., & Whitehouse, R.H. (1960). A physiological study of channel swimming. *Clinical Science*, **19**, 257-273.

Relevance of the Adrenocortical Hormone Aldosterone to Long-Distance Swimming

Werner Skipka

Earlier investigations have demonstrated that injection of the mineralocorticoid hormone aldosterone increases the oxygen uptake during submaximal and maximal exercise on a cycle ergometer (Skipka & Schöning, 1981). Experiments by Bedrak and Samoiloff (1967) demonstrating a higher activity of muscular oxidative enzymes after aldosterone injection and by Wong and Walsh (1971), who observed an increased oxygen uptake of rat diaphrams caused by aldosterone, indicate that the augmented oxygen uptake after aldosterone application is due to an augmented aerobic metabolic rate of muscles. The present study was designed to investigate whether the aldosterone-induced increase of the arobic metabolism leads to an improvement of performance capacity of long-distance swimmers.

Methods

Ten experienced male swimmers (20 to 29 years of age) were each assigned to two experimental treatments. In the aldosterone experiments, the synthetic mineralocorticoid Aldocorten (0.5 mg) was injected subcutaneously 5 and 3 hr before swimming the 800-m crawl under competitive conditions, whereas in the control experiments a placebo was applied (1 ml of 0.9% solution of NaCl). Half of the subjects performed control experiments 7 days before the aldosterone experiments, the other half vice versa.

The swimming times were recorded every 100-m interval. Heart rates were monitored continuously by telemetry during swimming and during the first 10 min of the recovery period. Blood of the hyperemized ear lobe was taken for acid-base measurements at the following times: immediately before the first injection; 5 min before starting swimming; and 1, 4, and 10 min after swimming. Significance was tested by use of the paired Students t test.

Results

During control experiments, the swimming times for the 800-m crawl were 10:37.5 min $\pm$ 11.5 s. In the experiments with aldosterone injections,

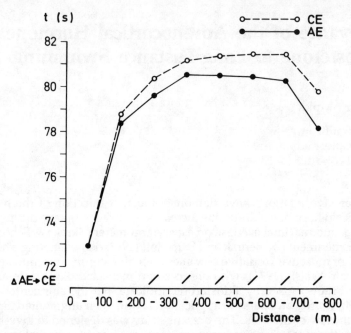

Figure 1 Mean values of the front crawl swimming times (t) for each 100 m over the distance of 800 m, during control experiments (CE) and after aldosterone injection (AE). Significant differences between CE and AE are indicated by a slash (/) ($p < .05$).

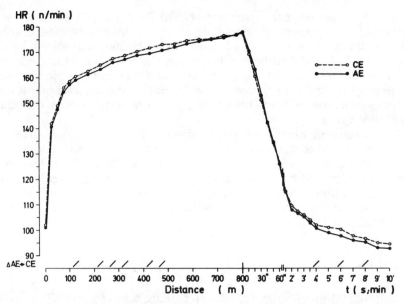

Figure 2 Mean values of heart rate (HR) before (0 m), during (25 to 800 m), and after (10 s to 10 min) swimming exercise. Abbreviations and symbols as in Figure 1.

the subjects swam significantly faster over the last 600 m (see Figure 1). This resulted in a significant decrease in the total time of 6.5 $\pm$ 2.1 s (p < .01).

Despite the fact that swimmers with aldosterone treatment were faster over distances exceeding 200 m, they displayed significant (p < .025) diminished elevations in heart rate up to the 500-m distance (see Figure 2). During the recovery period, a more pronounced decrement of heart rate was observed after the aldosterone injection. This difference was statistically significant from the 4th to the 8th min. Acid base values before as well as after swimming did not differ significantly between the two experimental conditions. The maximal acidosis for both groups was measured 1 min after termination of swimming. Mean acid-base values in control and aldosterone groups, respectively, were as follows: lactate 9.77 and 9.97 mmol/l; pH 7.231 and 7.223; base excess − 12.2 and − 12.6 mmol/l.

Discussion

The results might be attributed to an influence of aldosterone on the aerobic metabolism. This seems mostly to be caused by an aldosterone-induced increase of the activity of oxidative enzymes observed in skeleton muscles (Bedrak & Samoiloff, 1967) as well as in rat kidneys and toad bladders (Kirsten, Kirsten, Leaf, & Sharp, 1968; Liu, Liew, & Gornall, 1972). In addition, a 200% increase in the density of cristae mitochondriales after aldosterone injection was found (Pfaller, Fischer, Strieder, Wurnig, & Deetjen, 1974). Furthermore, an increase of fatty acid oxidation by aldosterone induced an enhanced oxygen uptake (Kirsten et al., 1977).

Former investigations with stepwise increased exercise on a cycle ergometer revealed that aldosterone induced an elevation of oxygen uptake by 7.7% and of exercise capacity by 3% (Skipka & Schöning, 1981). The determination of power in the present study by the product of an individual constant (k) and the cube of the swimming velocity (v^3) (Karpovich & Pestrecov, 1939) displays an increase of 3.1% and matches well with former results.

The importance of the hormone aldosterone on the oxygen uptake during exercise is supported by two other studies. In experiments by Schramm, Skipka, and Stegemann (1983) with a constant, defined exercise intensity, an increase in oxygen consumption of 6.9% was demonstrated. Sundsfjord, Strømme, and Aakvaag (1975) suppressed the plasma aldosterone concentration by about 30%, which resulted in a decrement of 5% in oxygen uptake during a cycle ergometer experiment.

An elevated activity of oxidative enzymes as well as an augmented fatty acid oxidation induce a pronounced turnover in the tricarboxylic acid cycle. Therefore, the production of lactic acid will be reduced. Considering the investigations of Thimm, Carvalho, Babka, and Meier zu Verl (1984), who described the dominant influence of lactic acid on regulation of heart rate, the slightly delayed increase in heart rate during swimming might express a delayed production of lactic acid under aldosterone conditions (see Figure 2). Such a reduction of the anaerobic metabolic rate caused by an augmented oxygen uptake was demonstrated by the experiments of Schramm et al. (1983), in which aldosterone induced a less marked acidosis.

Figure 1 reveals that the differences in swimming velocities between aldosterone and control experiments tend to increase with an increase in swimming distance. The difference in energy expenditure should be supplied in the final phase by a more pronounced anaerobic metabolic rate in the aldosterone experiments. This would lead to the similar acid-base values combined with an equivalent heart rate. The reduced and similar heart rates, respectively, during higher performances after aldosterone application should produce an increased oxygen extraction from the blood. In cycle ergometer experiments, indications for such an increase could be presented only for the range below endurance capacity (Skipka & Schöning, 1981). An inotropic action (stronger contraction) of aldosterone on the heart (Tanz, 1962) must be considered.

Conclusion

It seems evident that maximal anaerobic capacity is not influenced by aldosterone because acid-base values in the present investigations, in which the subjects reached their maximal exercise capacity, did not differ significantly between aldosterone and control experiments. In all probability the increase in performance capacity observed during the aldosterone experiments was caused by an increase in aerobic metabolism; meanwhile, the anaerobic part of energy supply remained unchanged.

The investigation indicated that aldosterone delays the process of fatigue, leading to an improvement in performance capacity. Consequently, the timing and intensity of the warm-up period, relevant for an endogenous augmentation of plasma aldosterone level (Skipka, Böning, Deck, & Schenk, 1978; Sundsfjord et al., 1975) has to be considered more carefully. With respect to the findings of Karrasch and Müller (1951), the faster decrease in the heart rate after the end of swimming might express an accelerated regeneration by aldosterone. The relevance of such an effect is obvious for repeated competitions over short periods of time.

References

Bedrak, E., & Samoiloff, V. (1967). Comparative effects of aldosterone and heat acclimatization on oxidative enzymes in rat tissue. *Canadian Journal of Physiology and Pharmacology, 45*, 717-722.

Karpovich, V., & Pestrecov, K. (1939). Mechanical work and efficiency in swimming crawl and back strokes. *Arbeitsphysiologie, 10*, 504-514.

Karrasch, K., & Müller, E.A. (1951). Das Verhalten der Pulsfrequenz in der Erholungsperiode nach körperlicher Arbeit. *Arbeitsphysiologie, 14*, 369-382.

Kirsten, E., Kirsten, R., Leaf, A., & Sharp, G.W.G. (1968). Increased activity of enzymes of the tricarboxylic acid cycle in response to aldosterone in the toad bladder. *Pflügers Archiv, 300,* 213-225.

Kirsten, R., Nelson, K., Rüschendorf, U., Seger, W., Scholz, T., & Kirsten, E. (1977). Effects of aldosterone on lipid metabolism and renal oxygen consumption in the rat. *Pflügers Archiv, 368,* 189-194.

Liu, D.R., Liew, C.C., & Gornall, A.G. (1972). Effects of aldosterone on mitochondrial enzymes and cytochromes of rat tissues. *Canadian Journal of Biochemistry, 50,* 1219-1225.

Pfaller, W., Fischer, W.M., Strieder, N., Wurnig, H., & Deetjen, P. (1974). Morphologic changes of cortical nephron cells in potassium-adapted rats. *Laboratory Investigation, 31,* 678-684.

Schramm, U., Skipka, W., & Stegemann, J. (1983). Altered relationship between aerobic and anaerobic metabolic rate induced by aldosterone during short-term exercise. *International Journal of Sports Medicine, 4,* 57.

Skipka, W., Böning, D., Deck, K.A., & Schenk, U. (1978). Aldosterone excretion and renal function during and after 2 hour physical exercise. *Pflügers Archiv, 373,* R57.

Skipka, W., & Schöning, L. (1981). Increased aerobic metabolic rate during physical exercise after aldosterone application. In F. Obal & G. Benedek (Eds.), *Advances in physiological sciences: Vol. 18. Environmental physiology,* (pp. 273-277). Budapest: Akadémiai Kiadó.

Sundsfjord, J.A., Strømme, S.B., & Aakvaag, A. (1975). Plasma aldosterone (PA), plasma renin activity (PRA) and cortisol (PF) during exercise. In H. Howald & J.R. Poortmans (Eds.), *Metabolic adaptation to prolonged physical exercise* (pp. 308-314). Basel: Birkhäuser.

Tanz, R.D. (1962). Studies on the inotropic action of aldosterone on isolated cardiac tissue preparations; including the effects of pH, ouabain and SC-8109. *Journal of Pharmacology and Experimental Therapy, 135,* 71-78.

Thimm, F., Carvalho, M., Babka, M., & Meier zu Verl, E. (1984). Reflex increase in heart rate induced by perfusing the hind leg of the rat with solutions containing lactic acid. *Pflügers Archiv, 400,* 286-293.

Wong, S.C., & Walsh, E.O. (1971). Effects of morphine on the hormonal control of metabolism. *Biochemical Pharmacology, 20,* 417-421.

Hematological and Biochemical Indices During the Tapering Period of Competitive Swimmers

Yoshiharu Yamamoto
Yoshiteru Mutoh
Mitsumasa Miyashita

The term *tapering* is used to express the decrease in work level that the competitive swimmer undergoes during practice in order to rest and prepare for a good performance. It is believed that there is no phase of the coach's program of which he or she is less sure than the taper (Counsilman, 1977).

During the intensive training period with repeated continuous exercise bouts, swimmers are likely to suffer various physiological stresses such as a decrease in blood hemoglobin concentration (Hb) due to the destruction of red blood cells (Yoshimura, 1970; Yoshimura et al., 1980) and an increase in serum creatine phosphokinase (CPK) activity (Enzyme Commission [E.C] 2.7.3.2) Berg & Haralambie, 1978; Haralambie & Senser, 1980; Riley, Pyke, Roberts, & England, 1975; Sanders & Bloor, 1975) due to the deformities or altered permeability of tissue cell membranes (Highman & Altland, 1963). Previous studies concerning tapering reported that there were conistent increases in Hb (Burke, Falsetti, Feld, Patton, & Kennedy, 1981; Rushall & Busch, 1980) and decreases in CPK (Burke, Falsetti, Feld, Patton, & Kennedy, 1982), which indicated the recovery phenomenon from the previously mentioned physiological stresses.

However, it is unknown whether only Hb and CPK, among the many blood constituents, show unique changes during tapering periods. Also unexamined is the number of days necessary to complete these changes in blood chemistry.

The purpose of this study was to select some blood constituents that show unique changes during the tapering period and to observe the time course of the changes in detail.

Methods

Subjects

The subjects were 20 national class collegiate and 8 high school swimmers. The collegiate swimmers participated in Study 1 and the high school

244 Yamamoto, Mutoh, and Miyashita

Table 1 Age, Height, and Weight of the Subjects

Trait	Study 1	Study 2
Age (years)	19.9 ± 1.0	17.1 ± 0.8
Height (cm)	176.5 ± 4.9	170.3 ± 5.3
Weight (kg)	71.0 ± 5.1	64.3 ± 4.8

Note. All values are reported as mean ± *SD*.

swimmers in Study 2, which will be described later. Table 1 shows the mean age, height, and weight of the subjects in both studies. Prior to the experiment, each subject consented to participate by signing a written consent form after being informed of the purpose and the risks therein.

Experimental Designs

Study 1 was conducted to select some blood constituents that show unique changes primarily during the tapering period. Mean workout distance (MWD; m/day) of a certain training period was calculated by dividing total distance by the number of days of the training period; i.e., swimming distance was averaged over training and nontraining days. Interindividual differences of MWD were not more than 200 m/day. Figure 1A represents the seasonal variation in MWD of the collegiate swimmers in Study 1. MWD increased gradually from late March and reached nearly 10,000 m/day from May 26 to July 15 (the intensive training period). Tapering was then performed for the important meets held during early August and early September. Resting venous blood samples from the antecubital vein were taken in the early morning prior to breakfast eight times from March 23 through August 29.

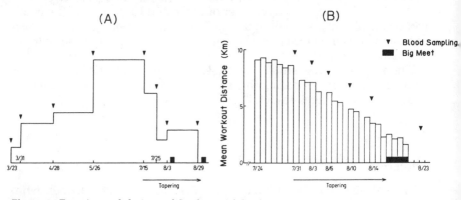

Figure 1 Experimental designs of Study 1 and Study 2.

Study 2 was conducted to examine the time course of the changes of blood constituents. In Study 2, MWD was calculated day by day and is shown in Figure 1B. The tapering began on July 31st and lasted about 2 weeks until an important meet was held from August 17 to 21. During the tapering period, MWD decreased almost linearly until the meet. Venous samples were taken five times (once every 3 to 4 days) during the tapering period and once after the meet in a similar fashion to Study 1.

In both studies, subjects continued weight training until immediately before the meets.

Analyses

Venous blood samples in Study 1 were offered for the analyses of white blood cell counts (WBC), Hb, hematocrit (Hct), serum glutamic oxalacetic transaminase (GOT) activity (E.C.2.6.1.1), serum glutamic pyruvic transaminase (GPT) activity (E.C.2.6.1.2) and CPK. WBC, Hb, and Hct were analyzed using a Coulter Model-S blood counter. GOT, GPT, and CPK were analyzed enzymatically with a Hitachi 736-60M-2 automatic analyzer.

In Study 2, only Hb, Hct, GPT and CPK were analyzed based on the results of Study 1, which are described later.

In both studies, a paired t test was conducted for each successive sampling in order to show intraindividual differences.

Results

Table 2 shows t values of intraindividual changes in blood constituents during the intensive training period (May 26 to July 15) and the tapering

Table 2   The t Values of Intraindividual Changes in Blood Constituents During Intensive Training and Tapering

Constituent	Intensive training	Tapering		
	5/26–7/15	7/15–7/25	7/26–8/3	8/3–8/29
WBC	4.49**	1.36	0.63	1.41
Hb	4.42**	0.05	1.07	3.40**
Hct	5.36**	1.05	1.57	2.80**
GOT	0.30	0.51	1.02	0.39
GPT	3.97**	5.82**	1.36	0.39
CPK	4.93**	2.49**	1.80*	2.75**

Note.   WBC = white blood cell count; Hb = blood hemoglobin concentration; Hct = hermatocrit; GOT = serum glutamic oxalacetic transaminase; GPT = serum glutemic pyruvic transaminase; CPK = serum creatine phosphokinase.

$*p < .05$. $**p < .01$.

246   Yamamoto, Mutoh, and Miyashita

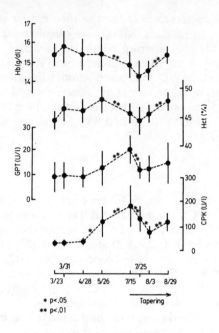

Figure 2   The changes in Hb, Hct, GPT, and CPK in Study 1. See text for abbreviations. Vertical bars express *SD*.

period (July 16 to August 29) in Study 1. During the intensive training period, significant ($p < .01$) intraindividual changes were observed in all blood constituents, except GOT. Among these blood constituents, Hb, Hct, GPT, and CPK showed significant ($p < .01$; $p < .05$ for CPK from July 26 to August 3) intraindividual changes during at least one interval during the tapering period.

Figure 2 shows the changes in Hb, Hct, GPT, and CPK in Study 1. Hb and Hct decreased significantly ($p < .01$) during the intensive training period and increased significantly ($p < .01$) in the late tapering period (August 4 to 29). GPT increased significantly ($p < .01$) during the intensive training period and decreased significantly ($p < .01$) during the early tapering period (July 16 to 25). CPK also increased significantly ($p < .01$) during the intensive training period and decreased significantly ($p < .01$) during the early tapering period, followed by consistent significant ($p < .05$) decreases during the middle tapering period (July 26 to August 3). Then CPK rose slightly but significantly ($p < .01$) during the late tapering period as MWD increased slightly.

Figure 3 shows the changes in Hb, Hct, GPT, and CPK in Study 2. Immediately after the onset of the tapering, GPT and CPK decreased significantly ($p < .01$) in 4 days. Until the 7th day of tapering, Hb and Hct rose and CPK fell significantly ($p < .01$); however, GPT increased significantly ($p < .01$) after a significant decrease during the first 4 days of the

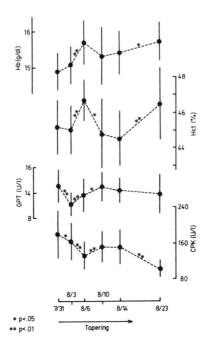

Figure 3 The changes in Hb, Hct, GPT, and CPK in Study 2. See text for abbreviations.

tapering period. There were then relatively small changes in Hb, GPT, and CPK until the end of the 2-week tapering period while Hct showed large and significant ($p < .05$) decreases. During the 10 days following the tapering period, Hb and Hct increased significantly ($p < .01$ and $p < .05$, respectively), and CPK decreased significantly.

Discussion

The results of Study 1 showed that among the several blood constituents studied, Hb, Hct, GPT, and CPK had significant intraindividual changes during both the intensive training period and the tapering period.

It has been shown that there is a tendency of Hb to decrease in athletes during an intensive training period. Yoshimura (1970) called this phenomenon "sports anemia." Yoshimura et al. (1980) stated that this is due to the increased erythrocyte membrane instability caused by elevated levels of circulating catecholamines, osmotic stress from venous acidosis, and the increased movement of erythrocytes. Both Hct and Hb decreased significantly during the intensive training period in Study 1, indicating a strong possibility of enhanced hemolysis.

Sports anemia is followed by accelerated hematopoiesis, thus initiating polyglobulia when athletes take an adequate rest (Yoshimura, 1970).

Good positive correlations between Hb and maximal oxygen uptake ($\dot{V}O_2$max) have been reported (Ekblom et al., 1972, 1976). Kanstrup and Ekblom (1984) reported that lowering Hb by plasma volume expansion did not lead to a lowered $\dot{V}O_2$max, whereas hypovolemic anemia (blood withdrawal) led to lowering the $\dot{V}O_2$max. They concluded that one of the main determinants of $\dot{V}O_2$max was the total amount of hemoglobin rather than Hb. As decreases in Hb during the intensive training period were possibly due to hemolysis, one of the important physiological phenomona of tapering lies in the recovery of the total amount of hemoglobin and hence increased $\dot{V}O_2$max.

Several blood enzymes—CPK (Berg & Haralambie, 1978; Haralambie & Senser, 1980; Hunter & Critz, 1971; Riley et al., 1975; Sanders and Bloor, 1975), GOT (Hunter & Critz, 1971; Riley et al., 1975), adenylate kinase (E.C.2.7.4.3) (Riley et al., 1975; Sanders & Bloor, 1975), lactate dehydrogenase (E.C.1.1.1.27) (Hunter & Critz, 1971; Riley et al., 1975), and hexose phosphate isomerase (E.C.1.1.1.49) (Berg & Haralambie, 1978; Haralambie & Senser, 1980)—have been reported to increase after continuous exercise bouts. Increased blood levels of these cellular enzymes are attributed to the deformities or altered permeability of tissue cell membranes (Highman & Altland, 1963). In Study 1, GPT and CPK increased significantly during the intensive training period and decreased during the tapering period. Hunter and Critz (1971) reported that resting levels of CPK decreased after 10 weeks of moderate cycle training (30 min/day, 3 times/week) and stated that the increased amount of ATP available might assist in maintaining the integrity of the cellular membrane and thus reduce the efflux of enzymes associated with exercise. The decreased levels of GPT and CPK during the tapering period might be attributed to the same mechanism indicated by Hunter and Critz (1971), but additional studies are needed to confirm this hypothesis.

In study 2, the time course of the changes in four blood constituents were observed during the tapering period, which showed unique variations from Study 1. Except the measurements from August 23 until after the meet, Hb and Hct showed the highest values and CPK showed the lowest, on the average, at the 7th day of the tapering period. However, GPT did not show these tendencies during the tapering period and changed somewhat randomly. Costill (1985) reported that during 4 weeks of detraining in competitive swimmers who had preliminary training, muscle glycogen content was not maintained above the levels of a preliminary untrained group for more than 1 week of detraining. In light of this result and the results of Study 2, it can be said that tapering done similary to Study 2 will be of no value if the duration of the tapering period exceeds 7 days, because only the effect of the detraining will be significant.

In Study 1 and Study 2, the most sensitive index of physiological stress during the intensive training period and the tapering period was CPK. There was a significant ($p < .01$) correlation between CPK and MWD ($r = .64$); however, no significant ($p > .05$) correlation between Hb, Hct, GPT, and MWD was observed, indicating that these blood constituents were less sensitive to physiological stress.

In conclusion, during the tapering period of competitive swimmers, Hb, Hct, and CPK showed systematic changes, but CPK was the most sensilive index of physiological stress. These changes could be attained within a significantly short period of time (about 7 days) if MWD decreases linearly, as was done in Study 2.

References

Berg, A., & Haralambie, G. (1978). Changes in serum creatine kinase and hexose phosphate isomerase activity with exercise duration. *European Journal of Applied Physiology*, **39**, 191-201.

Burke, E.R., Falsetti, H.L., Feld, R.D., Patton, G.S., & Kennedy, C.C. (November 1981–January 1982). Blood testing to determine overtraining in swimmers. *Swimming Technique*, pp. 29-32.

Burke, E.R., Falsetti, H.L., Feld, R.D., Patton, G.S., & Kennedy, C.C. (1982). Creatine kinase levels in competitive swimmers during a season of training. *Scandinavian Journal of Sports Science*, **4**(1), 1-4.

Costill, D.L. (1985). The 1985 C.H. McCloy Research Lecture: Practical problems in exercise physiology research. *Research Quarterly of Exercise and Sports*, **56**(4), 378-384.

Counsilman, J.E. (1977). *Competitive swimming manual for coaches and swimmers*. Bloomington, IN: Author.

Haralambie, G., & Senser, L. (1980). Metabolic changes in man during long-distance swimming. *European Journal of Applied Physiology*, **43**, 115-125.

Highman, B., & Altland, J.D. (1963). Effect of exercise and training on serum enzyme and tissue changes in rats. *American Journal of Physiology*, **205**(1), 162-166.

Hunter, J.B., & Critz, J.B. (1971). Effect of training on plasma enzyme levels in man. *Journal of Applied Physiology*, **31**(1), 20-23.

Kanstrup, I, & Ekblom, B. (1984). Blood volume and hemoglobin concentration as determinants of maximal aerobic power. *Medicine and Science in Sports and Exercise*, **16**(3), 256-262.

Riley, W.J., Pyke, F.S., Roberts, A.D., & England, J.F. (1975). The effect of long-distance running on some biochemical variables. *Clinical Chimische Acta*, **65**, 83-89.

Rushall, B.S., & Busch, J.D., (1980). Hematological responses to training in elite swimmers. *Canadian Journal of Applied Sports Science*, **5**, 164-169.

Sanders, T.M., & Bloor, C.M. (1975). Effect of repeated endurance exercise on serum enzyme activities in well-conditioned males. *Medicine and Science in Sports*, **7**(1), 44-47.

Yoshimura, H. (1970). Anemia during physical training (sports anemia). *Nutrition Reviews*, **28**(10), 251-253.

Yoshimura, H., Inove, T., Yamada, T., & Shiraki, K. (1980). Anemia during hard physical training (sports anemia) and its causal mechanism with special reference to protein nutrition. *World Review of Nutrition and Dietetics*, **35**, 1-86.

Metabolic and Cardiac Responses of Swimmers, Modern Pentathletes, and Water Polo Players During Freestyle Swimming to a Maximum

Georges Cazorla
Richard R. Montpetit

Man's physiological response to swimming has, as a whole, been studied in detail (Dixon & Faulkner, 1971; Holmer, 1974; McArdle, Glaser & Magel, 1971), but the majority of these studies have only been conducted on competitive and recreational swimmers. Water polo players and pentathletes also compete in the aquatic medium. Water polo players do not race as such, but they must swim in short, rapid bursts and must stay afloat for long periods of time. Their training involves considerable lower limb activity. Pentathletes participate in a 300-m race as part of their five-event competitive program. They train both on land (running to compete in the 4,000-m race) and in water. The metabolic and circulatory responses during swimming of water polo players and pentathletes may be expected to be different from that of swimmers.

Reported here are results of studies carried out to compare the oxygen demand and cardiac responses during freestyle (crawl) swimming at increasing velocities (0.9 to 1.5 m $\cdot$ s^{-1}) in pantathletes, water polo players, and swimmers. Also included is the relative importance of $\dot{V}O_2$max and swimming economy (the steady state oxygen demand for a standardized swimming speed) for the prediction of the 300-m performance in swimmers and pentathletes.

Procedures

Subjects

Eight national water polo players, 14 international pentathletes, and 19 international swimmers who had been continuously training for a minimum of 3 years prior to their participation in this investigation served as subjects. Their respective training programs continued throughout the duration of the project. A summary of the physical characteristics of the subjects is given in Table 1.

Table 1 Physical Characteristics of Subject

Sport	Age (years)	Height (cm)	Weight (kg)	$\dot{V}O_2$max free swimming ($l \cdot min^{-1}$)	($ml \cdot kg^{-1}min^{-1}$)	Body fat (%)
Water polo ($n = 8$)	20.8±2.5	177.4±3.5	74.3±6.0	4.48±0.29	60.8±3.0	12.1±3.9
Pentathlon ($n = 14$)	21.9±4.4	178.0±5.5	70.7±5.3	4.20±0.58	59.4±5.5	10.0±2.2
Swimming ($n = 19$)	20.7±3.0	182.6±4.8	74.7±5.3	4.51±0.41	60.3±4.3	11.8±2.1

Methods

All swimming experiments were conducted in a 50-m pool in which the water temperature was 26 to 26.5 °C.

The subjects were instructed to warm up during 5 min of swimming and then to swim 200-m distances as speeds (v) increasing 0.1 m · s^{-1} every 200 m until unable to maintain the pace imposed by pacer lights. The starting speed was 0.9 m · s^{-1}. The true swimming speed maintained at each work load was measured over 40 m within two points 5 m from each end of the pool in order to eliminate the influence of the turns and glide on the mean speed. Oxygen uptake was measured using open circuit spirometry. The expired gases were collected during the last minute at each level, in a rubber bag that moved along the side of the pool on a trolley. Exhaustion ($\dot{V}O_2$max) was reached within four to eight levels of swimming. Heart rate (HR) was monitored continuously using a battery-operated electrocardiography (Fukuda ME-CARDISUNY 501 C Electro-cardiograph). Performance data were obtained during a 300-m swimming race performed by both the pentathletes and swimmers during the same week as the testing.

The relationship between competitive racing time and $\dot{V}O_2$max, submaximal $\dot{V}O_2$ at 1.1 m · s^{-1}, HR max at 1.1 m · s^{-1}, and velocity at $\dot{V}O_2$max was evaluated using multiple regression. The variable that produced the highest zero-order correlation with performance was entered first, then the others. An analysis of covariance was used to test for differences in slopes as well as among groups. In addition, an analysis of trend was performed to provide information about the form of the oxygen uptake/velocity relationships. This involved a curve-fitting procedure using orthogonal polynomials up to the cubic degree. Between-group differences for $\dot{V}O_2$max, HR max, $\dot{V}O_2$submax at 1.1 m · s^{-1}, and so forth were assessed using a one-way ANOVA, with a Scheffé Test as a post hoc procedure. All reference to statistically significant results are based on the .05 level of significance.

Results

The subjects in this study exhibited a tight cluster of body sizes. The mean $\dot{V}O_2$max and relative fat were also similar. The swimmers' HR max, however, was significantly lower than that of the pentathletes and water polo players. Similarly, swimming velocity at $\dot{V}O_2$max was significantly higher for the swimmers (1.39 m • s⁻¹) than for the pentathletes (1.24 m • s⁻¹) or the water polo players (1.20 m • s⁻¹).

The relationship between the oxygen demand of submaximal swimming and velocity was linear in all groups (v ranged for 0.9 to 1.5 m • s⁻¹). An analysis of covariance revealed equality of slopes but showed a significant difference in the y-intercepts of the three lines (Figure 1). Within the range of velocities measured, the mean $\dot{V}O_2$submax of the swimmers was significantly lower than that of the water polo players but not different from the pentathletes. At a common velocity of 1.1 m • s⁻¹, the cost per distance swim ($\dot{V}O_2$/d) was 55.4 ± 4.0 l • km⁻¹ for the swimmers, 61.7 ± 8.0 l • km⁻¹ for the pentathletes, and 67.2 ± 8.0 l • km⁻¹ for the water polo players.

The heart rate/swimming velocity relationship was linear up to 185 bpm for all subjects. At a common velocity of 1.1 m • s⁻¹, the mean HR was 137.4 ± 70.6 bpm for the swimmers, 170.3 ± 21.0 bpm for the water polo players, and 172.7 ± 19.8 bpm for the pentathletes.

The correlations between the metabolic and cardiac data and performance for the pentathletes and swimmers are presented in Table 2.

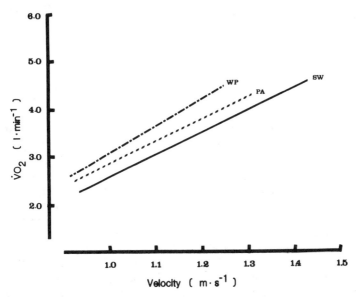

Figure 1 The relationship between steady state oxygen uptake and swimming velocity (crawl) for water polo players (WP), pentatheltes (PA), and swimmers (SW).

Table 2   Simple and Multiple Correlations of Metabolic and Cardiac Variables With Performance (Swim Speed for 300 m in m • s^{-1})

Variables	r	R	R^2	SEE	Regression equation
Pentathletes					
$\dot{V}O_2$max	.77	.77	.60	0.056	$P = 0.91 + 0.113\ (\dot{V}O_2max)$
$\dot{V}O_2^{1.1}$	− .33	.96	.92	0.026	$P = 1.21 + 0.135\ (\dot{V}O_2max) - 0.12\ (\dot{V}O_2^{1.1})$
%HR max	− .94	.97	.93	0.023	$P = 1.64 - 0.005\ (\%HR\ max) + 0.04\ (\dot{V}O_2max)$
Swimmers					
$\dot{V}O_2$max	.80	.80	.64	0.028	$P = 1.25 + 0.077\ (\dot{V}O_2max)$
$\dot{V}O_2^{1.1}$	− .20	.86	.75	0.025	$P = 1.34 + 0.083\ (\dot{V}O_2max) - 0.036\ (\dot{V}O_2^{1.1})$
%HR max	− .69	.87	.76	0.025	$P = 1.46 + 0.06\ (\dot{V}O_2max) - 0.002\ (\%HR\ max)$

Note.   SEE = standard error of the estimates; $\dot{V}O_2$max = $\dot{V}O_2$max (l • min^{-1}); $\dot{V}O_2^{1.1}$ = Oxygen uptake at $v = 1.1$ m • s^{-1}; %HR max = percentage heart rate max at $v = 1.1$ m • s^{-1}.

$\dot{V}O_2$max was generally well correlated with performance in both groups. Percentage heart rate max at a given velocity (1.1 m • s^{-1}) was very highly correlated with performance in the pentathletes but moderately correlated with performance in the swimmers. The relationship between performance in a 300-m race and the aerobic requirements of a standardized swimming pace (1.1 m • s^{-1}) was low but statistically significant. Regression equations for predicting performance from the above variables are also presented in Table 2.

Discussion

The results of the present study contrasted with some previous observations (Di Prampero, Graig, Wilson, & Rennie, 1977; Holmer, 1974) in that $\dot{V}O_2$max of skilled swimmers is higher than that of less proficient swimmers when both are tested in freestyle swimming. On the other hand, Costill et al. (1985) have reported just as in the present study that there are no significant differences in $\dot{V}O_2$max of freestyle swimming between competitive and recreational swimmers. However, the swimming velocities at which $\dot{V}O_2$max were attained were significantly different, a fact that indicates marked differences in technique and proficiency. In the present study, this level of proficiency between groups was based on race results, which was dissimilar to the specificity of the exercise but did not appear to influence the $\dot{V}O_2$max attained during aquatic work. It appears that the application of effective stroke technique is very important if one is to attain high swimming velocities. This is reflected in the swimming economy, as noted from the oxygen demand at a common velocity. The swimmers used 16 and 24% less oxygen than the pentathletes and water polo players, respectively.

Furthermore, the swimmers' higher proficiency in the front crawl had its effect on the metabolic and cardiac responses. This was at least partially attributable to the 25% volume of training in the aquatic medium done by the swimmers. This, in turn, was most probably related to the greater endurance level of the upper arm musculature specifically solicited in swimming. Of interest was the low submaximal heart (Δ20%) at a common velocity of 1.1 m • s^{-1} noted in the swimmers as compared to the other groups. In addition, maximal HR of the swimmers was significantly lower (M = 194 bpm) and the water polo players (M = 190 bpm). Assuming a similar maximum cardiac output (based on equal $\dot{V}O_2$max) as suggested by Faulkner, Heigenhauser, and Schork (1977), the estimated stroke volume of the swimmers would be higher than the other two groups. This was most probably the result of an endurance training effect due to the large volume and intensity of training that is common with swimmers (8,000 to 12,000 m/day for this group).

The more recent investigations that have studied the oxygen demand/ swimming velocity relationship have found that relationship to be essentially linear (Costill et al., 1985; Montpetit, Lavoie, & Cazorla, 1983). For all groups in the present study, oxygen uptake increased in a linear fashion with swimming velocity throughout the range of velocities investigated. The authors who have alluded to a curvilinear relationship (Di Prampero, Pendergast, Wilson, & Rennie, 1974; Pendergast et al., 1977) have included in their calculations of the oxygen requirements both aerobic and anaerobic energy sources, a procedure found to be questionable (Brooks & Fahey, 1984).

Despite the similarity of $\dot{V}O_2$max for the pentathletes and swimmers, the performances of the two groups, as noted during the 300-m swim, were notably different. Swimming economy appears to be a major factor responsible for these differences. The differences in swimming economy between the two groups were of the order of 20% in favor of the swimmers. When looking at the subjects individually the subject with the best performance had the highest $\dot{V}O_2$max but also the lowest $\dot{V}O_2$submax at a given velocity. This is in accord with the concept developed by Di Prampero et al. (1974) in which swimming velocity was shown to be a function of metabolic power ($\dot{V}O_2$max) and universally related to the cost per distance swim: $v = E/c$ where E = maximal aerobic energy expended and C the oxygen cost per given distance.

Within-group comparisons showed a fairly high correlation between performance and $\dot{V}O_2$max for the pentathletes (r = .77) and for the swimmers (r = .80). These values were of the same order as those reported by Costill et al. (1985) for 37 competitive swimmers (males and females). With a more homogeneous group of swimmers, the correlation would undoubtedly be lower as is suggested by studies done with runners (Conley & Krahenbuhl, 1980; Foster, 1983.

Although $\dot{V}O_2$max and performance are moderately correlated, accurately predicting performance for any of the groups is not adequate. The standard error of predicting the performance was of the order of 7 s for 300 m. The inclusion of swimming economy in the equation improves the predictive power for both groups. The correlation increased to .96 for the pentathletes and to .86 for the swimmers, and the standard error for predicting the performance was reduced to 3.0 s for both groups. When % HR max at 1.1 m • s^{-1} and $\dot{V}O_2$max were used as predictor variables, the correlation reached .97 but the standard error of the estimate remained the same.

Although the best predictor variables were the same for the two groups, their beta weights were different, indicating that the same factors influenced to a different degree the performance of the pentathletes and swimmers and that the data should not be pooled. The regression equations form two distinct lines. This fact was also demonstrated by Costill et al. (1985).

In terms of defining overall potential for competitive middle-distance swimming, $\dot{V}O_2$max represents a remarkably powerful tool. Knowledge of $\dot{V}O_2$max alone may explain 60% or more of the variation in performance and should certainly help coaches gain insight regarding overall potential. The determination of $\dot{V}O_2$max swimming can now be easily measured by the technique first used by Cazorla, Montpetit, Prokop, and Cervetti (1982), the validity and reliability of which was collaborated by Lavoie, Léger, Montpetit, and Chabot (1983) and more recently by Costill et al. (1985). The inclusion of submaximal measures (i.e., swimming, %HR max at a given velocity) allows one to explain an even greater portion (approximately 80%) of the variation in performance. These factors are easily measured and thus are important to include in a periodic evaluation program for athletes who compete in the aquatic medium.

References

Brooks, G.A., & Fahey, D. (1984). *Human physiology*. New York: John Wiley and Sons.

Cazorla, G., Montpetit, R., Prokop, P., & Cervetti, J.P. (1982). De l'évaluation des nageurs de haut niveau á la détection des jeunes talents [Evaluation of top-level swimmers through the detection of young talent]. *Document INSEP*, 185-208.

Conley, D.L., & Krahenbuhl, G.S. (1980). Running economy and distance running performance of highly trained athletes. *Medicine and Science in Sports and Exercise, 12*, 357-360.

Costill, D.L., Kovaliski, J., Porter, D., Kirvan, J., Fielding, R., & King D. (1985). Energy expenditure during front crawl swimming: Predicting success in middle-distance events. *International Journal of Sports Medicine, 6*, 266-270.

Di Prampero, P.E., Pendergast, D.R., Wilson, D.R., & Rennie, D.W. (1974). Energetics of swimming in man. *Journal of Applied Physiology, 37*, 1-5.

Dixon, R.W., & Faulkner, J.A. (1971). The cardiac output–oxygen uptake relationship of men during maximum effort running and swimming. *Journal of Applied Physiology, 30*, 653-656.

Faulkner, J.A., Heigenhauser, G.F., & Schork, A. (1977). The cardiac output–oxygen uptake relationship of men during graded bicycle ergometry. *Medicine and Science in Sports*, **9**, 148-154.

Foster, C. (1983). $\dot{V}O_2$max and training indices as determinants of competitive running performance. *Journal of Sport Sciences*, **1**, 13-22.

Holmer, I. (1974). Physiology of swimming man. *Acta Physiologica Scandinavica* (Suppl. 407), 1-53.

Lavoie, J.-M., Léger, L., Montpetit, R., & Chabot, S. (1983). Backward extrapolation of $\dot{V}O_2$ from the O_2 recovery curve after a voluntary maximal 400-m swim. In A.P. Hollander, P.A. Huijing, & G. de Groot (Eds.), *Biomechanics and medicine in swimming* (pp. 222-227). Champaign, IL: Human Kinetics.

McArdle, W.D., Glaser, R.M., & Magel, J.R. (1971). Metabolic and circulatory response during free swimming and treadmill walking. *Journal of Applied Physiology*, **30**, 733-738.

Montpetit, R.R., Lavoie, J.-M., & Cazorla, G. (1983). Aerobic energy cost of swimming the front crawl at high velocity in international class and adolescent swimmers. In A.P. Hollander, P.A. Huijing, & G. de Groot (Eds.), *Biomechanics and medicine in swimming* (pp. 228-234). Champaign, IL: Human Kinetics.

Pendergast, D.R., Di Prampero, P.E., Graig, A.B., Wilson, D.R., & Rennie, D.W. (1977). Quantitative analysis of the front crawl in men and women. *Journal of Applied Physiology*, **43**, 475-479.

PART VI

LACTATE PRODUCTION AND PERFORMANCE

The Relationship of Lactic Acid to Long-Distance Swimming and the 2 × 400-m "2-Speed Test" and the Implications for Adjusting Training Intensities

Jan Olbrecht
Alois Mader
Ørjen Madsen
Heinrich Liesen
Wilder Hollmann

The concentration of lactic acid has been used not only to control the sport-specific performance capacity of athletes (Keul, Kindermann, & Simon, 1978; Madsen, 1982; Margaria, 1976; Saltin, 1973; Stegmann & Kindermann, 1982) but also to determine the optimal training intensity (Föhrenbach, Mader, & Hollmann, 1981; Keul et al., 1979; Liesen, Mader, Heck, & Hollmann, 1977; Mader, Madsen, & Hollmann, 1980; Madsen & Olbrecht, 1983). Not everyone, however, can make use of this method. Therefore, an attempt was made to find an alternative method—a type of test, without any lactate measurements, that could be used to adapt individual training intensities to the endurance capacity of each athlete.

The present study compared the relationship between swimming speed and lactic acid accumulation during the 2 × 400-m "2-speed test" (Mader et al., 1980) and during 30 and 60 min of continuous swimming. In accordance with the changes in the relationship between lactate and speed in prolonged and interval-type exercises (Olbrecht, Madsen, Mader, Liesen, & Hollmann, 1985), a range of intensities was established for different types of endurance training for the tested athletes.

Materials and Methods

A total of 39 female and 49 male German competitive swimmers participated in this study. The test program, composed of six tests, was carried out during 9 days. A 2 × 400 m "2-speed test", with the first 400 m swum at submaximal speed (85 to 90% of the best 400-m time) and the second 400 m swum at maximal speed after a 20-min rest, was administered at the beginning and end of the experiment. This test was used (a) to determine the individual swimming speed at a lactic acid

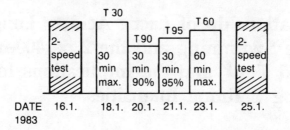

DATE 16.1.   18.1. 20.1. 21.1. 23.1.   25.1.
1983

Figure 1 Sequence of the different continuous swimming tests. A 2 × 400-m "2-speed test" was included before and after the test period to control the endurance capacity during the whole test period.

concentration of 4 mmol/l (= V4) in order to obtain a reference for the endurance performance capacity of the athlete; and (b) to consider changes in this performance capacity during the experimental period. The second test consisted of swimming 30 min at maximal but constant speed (= V30 max). This test was then followed by two 30-min tests at 90 and 95% of V30 max and by a 60-min test again at maximal speed (Figure 1).

Before each test and at the 1st, 3rd, 5th, and 7th min after the exercise, 20 μl blood was taken from the earlobe to determine enzymatically the lactic acid concentration. Statistical differences were checked with the Neuman-Keuls Test (Sachs, 1978).

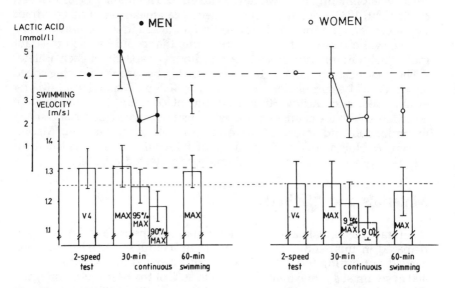

Figure 2 Swimming speed and lactic acid concentration (mean ± SD) of the 30- and 60-min continuous swimming tests, related to the swimming speed at 4 mmol/l (V4) determined by a 2 × 400-m "2-speed test."

Results

During the 30-min maximal test, the female and male swimmers achieved an average swimming speed (V30max) of 1.25 ± 0.08 and 1.32 ± 0.08 m/s, respectively (Figure 2). For the female swimmers no significant ($p < .05$) difference was found between V30max and V4 (= 1.25 ± 0.08 m/s). For the male swimmers, on the other hand, a small but statistically significant ($p < .05$) difference (V4 = 1.30 ± 0.08 m/s) was present.

The lactic acid concentration after the exercise was of 3.95 ± 1.33 mmol/l for the females and of 4.96 ± 1.67 mmol/l for the males. After 30 min of swimming at 95% of V30max, a significantly lower maximal lactate concentration was apparent in comparison to the lactic level after swimming at maximal speed. A further reduction in the swimming speed to 90% did not yield a statistical difference in the lactate concentrations in comparison to the swim test at 95% of the maximal swimming speed.

Both the females and the males achieved a nonsignificant difference in the average swimming speeds between V4 and the 60-min maximal test. The average lactic acid concentration, on the other hand, remained considerably less than 4 mmol/l for the females (2.44 ± 0.81 mmol/l) as well as for the males (3.01 ± 0.60 mmol/l).

We found for females and males a high significant correlation between V4 and the maximal swimming speed during the 30- and 60-min swims ($r = .94$ and $.97$ respectively).

The correlation between the postexercise maximal lactic acid concentrations and the average swimming speeds of individuals in the 30- and 60-min maximal tests, expressed as a percentage of V4, proved to be highly significant for the male swimmers ($r = .78$ and $.68$ for the 30- and 60-min tests, respectively). For the female swimmers on the other hand, a significant correlation was not found in the 60-min maximal test between the lactic acid concentration after the swim and swimming velocity.

Discussion

A primary problem in endurance sports is to determine the specific performance capacity of athletes and to establish an intensity for endurance training in accordance with individual performance capacities. The determination of this perfomance capacity has until now been achieved by the determination of the individual relationship between swimming speed and lactate.

In swimming, one usually uses two test procedures: the 2-speed test and a one-step 400-m submaximal test. Both test procedures measure the specific swimming endurance. The 2-speed test allows predictions to be made about the present performance capacity in competition. Based on our other studies that describe the individual changes in the relation between lactate and swimming speed for different interval training programs (Olbrecht et al. 1985; unpublished data), these test results also allowed us to predict the most convenient individual swimming speed to improve aerobic capacity. It was noticed that subjects with high lactic acid concentrations after the second run of the 2-speed test also had the highest lactate concentrations after the 30-min maximal test ($r = .70$ and $.60$ for females and males, respectively). For the 30-min maximal test, a highly significant ($p < .001$) negative correlation was found for the male swimmers ($r = -.58$) and a significant ($p < .01$) negative correlation ($r = -.44$) for the female swimmers between V4 and the maximal lactate concentrations after the continuous swim test. Between V4 and V30max, expressed in percentage V4, a highly significant negative correlation ($r = -.81$) was also found for the male subjects.

The disadvantage of lactate test procedure for training is the price of the instrumentation and the materials. The important objective of the present study was to examine the usefulness of another test procedure in swimming as a diagnostic instrument (to determine the specific performance capacity) and to monitor training.

The high correspondence between the average swimming speed to a lactic acid concentration of 4 mmol/l that was determined in a 2 × 400-m 2-speed test (= V4) and the average swimming speed in a 30-min maximal test led to the expectation that this continuous test makes it possible to estimate the individual 4mmol/l speed (V4) without having to measure lactic acid. In the 30-min maximal test V4 correlated negatively with the postexercise lactic acid concentration as well as with the percentage of V4 that was present after the maximal test. That meant that the higher the swimming aerobic performance capacity was, measured at V4, the lower the lactate concentration after the maximal 30-min test. Besides, the percentage of V4 that could be utilized during the maximal test was lower. The V30max must therefore first be converted before one can precisely determine the most suitable individual V4. This can be calculated by the following formula:

$$\text{Females: V4} = 0.93254 \times \text{V30max} + 0.9609$$

$$\text{Males: V4} = 1.1842 \times \text{V30max} - 0.25309$$

In the 30-min swims a highly significant correlation, in a speed range of 95 to 105% of V4, was found between the lactic acid concentration and the swimming speed in percentage V4. That implied that in this speed range the metabolic load can be determined in accordance with the purpose of aerobic training.

Conclusion

All these findings were utilized in a computer program to evaluate the performance capacities and to predict performances in competition and the intensity levels for endurance training. To obtain the information about endurance training, one needs time and lactate from a 1 × 400-m or a 2 × 400-m swim or time and distance of a 30-min test. The coach receives a report (see Table 1) of the calculated swimming times for classic endurance

Table 1 Diagnosis Report of Performance Capacity and Recommended Training of a Male Sprinter

	Test Results	
S.P.	Test date: 12.10.85	Pool length = 50 m

Test : 2-distance test 2 × 100 m Freestyle

	Swim 1	Swim 2
Time (s)	1:02.19	0:55.90
Velocity (m/s)	1.608	1.789
Max. Lactate (Mm)	4.5	12.8

Diagnosis About the Tested Distance (100 m)[a]

	Linear			Exponential	
Lactate	Speed	Time	Speed	Time	Lactate
2	1.553	1:04.38	1.526	1:05.52	2
4	1.596	1:02.62	1.593	1:02.75	4
6	1.640	1:00.95	1.646	1:00.71	6
8	1.684	0:59.37	1.693	0:59.05	8
10	1.727	0:57.87	1.735	0:57.62	10
12	1.771	0:56.45	1.774	0:56.36	12

Diagnosis About the Tested Distance (400 m)

	Linear			Exponential	
Lactate	Speed	Time	Speed	Time	Lactate
2	1.355	4:55.19	1.339	4:58.57	2
4	1.388	4:48.04	1.391	4:47.37	4
6	1.422	4:41.22	1.433	4:39.05	6
8	1.455	4:34.72	1.469	4:32.30	8

Diagnosis About the Training
Intensity and Swim Speed Scale for Endurance Training

		Extensive → → → → → → → → → → → Intensive			
Set	Rest	La2	La3	La4	La5
100 m	10 s	1:10.7	1:10.1	1:08.1	1:06.6
	30 s	1:09.2	1:08.3	1:06.4	1:04.8
200 m	10 s	2:24.8	2:22.5	2:19.8	2:16.5
	30 s	2:23.0	2:20.9	2:16.7	2:14.6
400 m	10 s	4:53.9	4:50.9	4:45.1	4:39.6
	30 s	4:52.7	4:46.6	4:41.5	4:36.1
Continuous swim					
20-45 min[b]		1:15.6	1:13.6	1:11.7	1:09.9

Note. The diagnosis is based on the objective of a male sprinter to swim a 100-m competition in 53.1 s. A 2 × 100-m "2-speed test" provides information about the possibility to

(Cont.)

Table 1 (Cont.)

yield the time and the kind of training needed to succeed. A 30-min test (2,500 m in 30:30.2 min) was added to estimate swimming times (intensities) for different classic endurance exercises to remain in a range of 2 to 5 mmol/l postexercise lactate.

[a]To swim 0:53.10 in competition, 17.1 mmol/l must be reached. The swimmer stands statistically no chances (58.99%) of realizing the expected performance. We advise endurance training until 1.75 m/s (or 0:57.08) is reached by 4.0 mmol/l. [b]Time/100 m

training programs in a range from 2 to 5 mmol/l postexercise lactate. Using this table, he or she can very objectively control the load during a training program.

References

Föhrenbach, R., Mader, A., & Hollmann, W. (1981). Umfang und Intensität im Dauerlauftraining von Mittelstreckenläuferinnen des DLV und Massnahmen zur individuellen Trainings- und Wettkampfoptimierung [Amount and intensity of long distance runs of female middle distance runners of the DLV and measures to optimize training and competition performances]. *Leistungssport*, **11**, 458-472.

Keul, J., Kindermann, W., & Simon, G. (1978). Die aerobe und anaerobe Kapazität als Grundlage für die Leistungsdiagnostik [Aerobic and anaerobic capacity as the basis for performance diagnosis]. *Leistungssport*, **8**, 23-32.

Keul, J., Simon, G., Berg, A., Dickhutt, H.H., Goerttler, J., & Kobel, R. (1979). Bestimmung der individuellen anaeroben Schwelle zur Leistungsbewertung und Trainingsgestaltung [Estimation of the individual anaerobic threshold to the performance capacity and to set up the training]. *Deutsches Zeitschrift für Sportmedizin*, **7**, 212-216.

Liesen, H., Mader, A., Heck, H., & Hollmann, W. (1977). Die Ausdauerleistungsfähigkeit bei verschiedenen Sportarten unter besonderer Berücksichtigung des Metabolismus: Zur Ermittlung der optimalen Belastungsintensität im Training [The endurance capacity in different sports with regard to the metabolism: The estimation of the optimal training intensity]. *Leistungssport*, **7** (Suppl.), 63-79.

Mader, A., Madsen, Ø., & Hollmann, W. (1980). Zur Beurteilung der laktaziden Energiebereitstellung für Trainings- und Wettkampfleistungen im Schwimmen [The evaluation of the anaerobic energy supply with regard to the performances in training and competition in swimming]. *Leistungssport*, **10**, 263-279, 408-418.

Madsen, Ø. (1982). *Untersuchungen über Einflussgrössen auf Parameter des Energie-stoffwechsels beim freien Kraulschwimmen* [The influences on the parameters of the energy supply during free-style swimming]. Unpublished doctoral dissertation, Der Deutsche Sporthochschule, Köln.

Madsen, Ø., & Olbrecht, J. (1983). Specifics of aerobic training. In R.M. Ousley (Ed.), *Annual of the American Swimming Coaches Association* (pp. 15-33). Fort Lauderdale, FL: ASCA Press.

Olbrecht, J., Madsen, Ø., Mader, A., Liesen, H., & Hollmann, W. (1985). Relationship between swimming velocity and lactic concentration during continuous and intermittent training exercises. *International Journal of Sports Medicine, 6*, 74-77.

Margaria, R. (1976). *Biomechanics and energetics of muscular exercise.* Oxford: Clarendon Press.

Sachs, L. (1978). *Angewandte Statistik* [Applied statistics]. Berlin: Springer.

Saltin, B. (1973). Metabolic fundamental in exercise. *Medicine and Science in Sports, 5*, 137.

Stegmann, H., & Kindermann, W. (1982). Comparison of prolonged exercise tests at the individual anaerobic threshold of 4 mmol/l lactate. *International Journal of Sports Medicine, 3*, 105-110.

Stegmann, H., Kindermann, W., & Schnabel, A. (1981). Lactate kinetics and individual anaerobic threshold. *International Journal of Sports Medicine, 2*, 160-165.

Oxygen Consumption and Blood Lactic Acid Response to Training and Taper

Peter J. Van Handel
Andrea Katz
John P. Troup
Jack T. Daniels
Patrick W. Bradley

Detraining or *taper* is commonly practiced in preparation for competition, but it may result in significant reductions in aerobic capacity and endurance in running (Hickson, Foster, Pollock, Galassi, & Rich, 1985) and muscle force and power in swimming (Neufer, Costill, Fielding, Flynn, & Kirwan, 1986). The purpose of this study was to monitor energetics during intense training and taper in highly trained swimmers in preparation for U.S. national competitions.

Methods

Subjects were college-aged swimmers (5 men, 4 women), including 3 medal-winners at the 1984 Olympic Games in Los Angeles. Testing was conducted at three time periods during the competitive season: (a) immediately preceding the U.S. long-course season; (b) at the start of taper for the U.S. Long-Course Nationals; and (c) at the end of this taper, less than 1 week prior to the U.S. National competition. This represented approximately 60 days of highly intense long-course training and 20 days of taper. Peak training volume reached 10,000 to 12,000 m/day split into two sessions and conducted 5 days/week. One workout was held on each of the remaining 2 days/week. Training volume during taper dropped to 2,000 to 3,000 m/day with reductions in both frequency and duration of workouts. Intensity was maintained and increased with faster splits and shorter rest intervals.

Measurements included sumaximal and maximal energy cost of unrestricted (untethered) freestyle swimming. Expired air was obtained by a modification of the Douglas Bag method utilizing a specially designed headpiece containing a snorkle and inspiratory/expiratory valve system (Daniels, 1971; Van Handel, Katz, Troup, Daniels, & Bradley, 1988). Fractions of expired oxygen and carbon dioxide were measured by previously calibrated polarographic and infrared electronic analyzers. Expired gas volumes were measured by a portable dry gas meter calibrated to known Tissot volumes. Collections were made during the last minute of each of three evenly split, 400-m steady state freestyle swims. Each was approximately 5 s/100 m faster than the previous effort and was initiated after approximately a 6-min inactive recovery. A fourth 400-m swim was paced with descending 50-m splits so that maximal oxygen uptake ($\dot{V}O_2$max) was attained during the last 100 to 150 m. Swims were from a push start in a 50-m pool and with an open turn the last length. Each individual submaximal $\dot{V}O_2$ versus velocity (v) curve was statistically analyzed by computer to describe the location of the data points relative to the group regression (Bradley, Daniels, Baldwin, Scardina, & Morrow, 1986). This is described as *economy of effort*.

Immediate postswim heart rates were obtained by carotid palpation and/or radio telemetry. Blood lactic acid (HLa) concentration was measured from whole blood samples obtained from finger punctures (Van Handel, Troup, & Bradley, 1986) and assayed by polarographic techniques. The blood samples were obtained immediately after submaximal exercise and 2-min postmaximal swim. HLa profiles were also established for each athlete on a separate day of testing. Freestyle 200-m repeats at approximately 70, 80, and 90% effort were performed with inactive rest intervals of 2-min duration. Blood samples were obtained immediately after each repeat and at 3, 10, and 15 min during inactive recovery.

Regression techniques were used to describe the relationship between $\dot{V}O_2$ and HLa on v. Repeated measures one-way ANOVA was used to test for time effects on variables in response to training and taper. For post hoc tests, an alpha level of .05 was accepted for statistical significance.

Results and Discussion

Table 1 presents the maximal test values achieved for $\dot{V}O_2$, heart rate, and HLa. $\dot{V}O_2$max increased ($r = .917$, $p \leqslant .05$) from the start of long-course training to the beginning of taper. This increase (61.5 to 65.4 ml O_2/kg • min^{-1}) was due to an absolute improvement in aerobic capacity as body weights were unchanged. There were no additional changes in these variables measured at the conclusion of the taper period. The absolute and percentage gains in $\dot{V}O_2$max were comparable to those achieved by less skilled swimmers with lower initial maximal capacities (Lavoie, Taylor, & Montpetit, 1981; Magel et al., 1974), and the values were greater than those obtained on other collegiate or elite swimmers (Costill et al. 1985; Holmer, 1972; Lavoie et al., 1981; Lavoie, Léger, Leone, & Provencher, 1985; Magel et al., 1974; Magel & Faulkner, 1967).

Submaximal $\dot{V}O_2$ versus v curves (i.e., economy) were similar for all test sessions (Figure 1), indicating that energy cost of swimming was unaffected by the training-taper sequence. Comparison of these curves to other estimates of swimming efficiency or economy indicated that the present athletes were considerably more economical than other swimmers at comparable velocities (Di Prampero, Pendergast, Wilson, & Rennie, 1974; Costill et al., 1985; Holmer, 1972; Lavoie et al., 1985). Be-

Table 1 Maximal Values Obtained During Pretraining and Pre- and Posttaper[a]

Period	Weight (kg)	$\dot{V}O_2$[b] (ml · kg · min⁻¹)	Heart rate (bpm)	HLa (mM)	400 m[c] (min:s)
Pre-long course	69.7	61.5	192	7.3	4:28
training	57.3–80.9	49.3–77.1	180–199	5.1–10.2	4:12–4:44
Pretaper	69.0	65.4[d]	198[d]	6.9	4:23
	56.9–80.1	51.1–79.9	190–204	5.4–9.0	4:07–4:41
Posttaper	68.2	66.6[d]	193	7.5	4:24
	58.4–78.1	4.92–80.3	182–199	5.7–9.0	4:06–4:45

[a]$n = 9$; values are group mean and the range. [b]$\dot{V}O_2$max increased with training but was not affected by 20 days of taper. [c]Time swum during the $\dot{V}O_2$max test; push start, open turns last 100 m. [d]Significantly different than pre-long-course; $p < .05$.

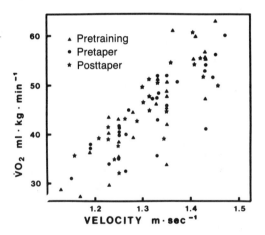

Figure 1 Submaximal oxygen costs for 400-m freestyle swims. Regressions calculated for each test session were unaffected by training or taper, suggesting that economy of effort was similar.

cause VO_2max had increased and remained elevated for the final two test sessions, any given v was attained at a lower fractional utilization of aerobic capacity.

Figure 2 presents the HLa values obtained after each series of 200-m repeat swims. Anaysis of regression data demonstrated a significant difference in the intercept of HLa on v from the first to the second test session (start of training to the beginning of taper), that is, a curve shift to the right so that any given lactate level was attained at a faster v. Neither the slopes of these regression lines nor the recovery lactate curves were affected by training or taper. From the beginning to the end of taper (Test

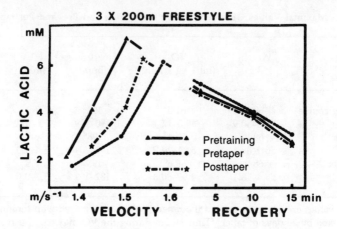

Figure 2   Blood lactic acid values obtained after 200-m freestyle swims at 70, 80, and 90% maximal effort and in recovery. A right-shift occurred with training, possibly related to the increase in $\dot{V}O_2$max. The left shift with detraining was not associated with a decrease in total body aerobic capacity.

Sessions 2 and 3), there was a nonsignificant curve shift back to the left. A given HLa value was achieved at a slower v. Again, recovery curves were unaffected.

The initial right-shift in the lactate profile could be explained, in part, by the concurrent increase in $\dot{V}O_2$max (Table 1). Any given work intensity was accomplished at a lower fractional utilization of the aerobic capacity. At 1.4 m/s, for example, energy costs were 85 and 80% of $\dot{V}O_2$max for pretraining and pretaper test sessions. The HLa curve shift back to the left at the end of the taper, however, cannot be explained by a concurrent loss of total body aerobic capacity as $\dot{V}O_2$max remained significantly elevated.

Neufer et al. (1986) recently studied detraining effects in college-aged swimmers. Athletes were assigned to three groups for a taper period of 4 weeks: (a) 3,000 yd/session, three/week; (b) 3,000 yd/session, one/week; and (c) no activity. Whereas arm strength was unaffected by taper, power measured in a tethered swim was significantly reduced and blood lactic acid after standard swims increased in inverse proportion to the amount of weekly training. $\dot{V}O_2$max also decreased for the no activity and one session/week groups.

The current data and Neufer's observations support the work by Hickson et al. (1985) on factors associated with maintenance of aerobic power and short-term (5-min) endurance during detraining, suggesting that intensity is much more critical than either frequency or duration factors. Thus, the present data indicate that the backward, left-shift in HLa curves with detraining/taper was not due to a loss of total body aerobic capacity. Rather this left shift may be related to loss of muscular power (Neufer et al., 1986), the altered lactate responses reflecting a relatively greater anaerobic demand because of reduced force production per unit muscle mass.

Studies on the muscle's capacity to develop force and to do work with fatigue and intense training are limited (Jacobs, 1981; Sherman et al., 1984). Costill, King, Thomas, and Hargreaves (1985) reported unpublished observations that during periods of intense swim training strength and power decreased significantly. Jacobs (1981) found a markedly reduced capacity to generate force and produce work when muscle gycogen was depleted. Both the proportional utilization and rate of glycogen use increase as exercise intensity increases (Bergstrom & Hultman, 1972; Karlsson, 1980; Saltin & Karlsson, 1971), and recovery of muscle glycogen stores may be incomplete with inadequate rest and/or low carbohydrate intake. More recently, Sherman et al. (1984) found significant decreases in muscle peak torque and work for a postmarathon run. Recovery was not complete after 7 days, and moderate exercise did not help the recovery process. Thus, highly intense training in taper maintains aerobic power but perhaps at the expense of chronic substrate depletion, fatigue, and subsequently reduced ability to generate force and power.

Two important points need to be considered in this regard. First, although strength and power are generally related to success in sprint swimming (Costill, Sharp, & Troup, 1980; Miyashita & Kanehisa, 1979; Sharp, Troup, & Costill, 1982), percentage gains in performance do not match those in power. Yancher, Larsen, and Baer (1983) suggest that the relationship is a fifth-exponential curve; that is, rather large increases in power result in only small increases in velocity. More importantly, for individuals who are already using force/stroke efficiently or who have high power-to-displacement ratios, velocity increases may not occur by increasing power.

Second, a degree of interaction is likely among intensity of workouts, duration of taper, and alterations in the energetics of swimming. Costill et al. (1985) found that with 14 days of taper muscle power increased significantly with essentially no change in blood lactic acid or acid/base status to standard swims. In contrast, they also found that with 4 weeks of taper, there was a significant decrease in $\dot{V}O_2$max, muscle power, and altered lactic acid kinetics. The extent of these changes were, in part, dependent upon the quantity of work performed during taper (Neufer et al., 1986).

As aerobic capacity is unrelated to swim performance in elite, homogenous groups (Van Handel et al., 1987) and intense training is associated with reduced force and power and low energy stores, it may be more beneficial to further optimize effects of taper by also reducing intensity of daily training. This is not so much to increase capacity for power production above normal levels as to allow for adequate rest and recovery.

Acknowledgments

This study was supported by an Elite Athlete Program Grant to U.S. Swimming and Sports Sciences Division for the U.S. Olympic Committee.

References

Bergstrom, J., & Hultman, E. (1972). Nutrition and physical performance. *Journal of the American Medical Association, 221,* 999-1006.

Bradley, P.W., Daniels, J.T., Baldwin, C., Scardina, N., & Morrow, J. (1986). Running economy: Quantification and relationship with physiological determinants of performance. *Medicine and Science in Sports and Exercise, 18* (Suppl.), S37.

Costill, D.L., King, D.S., Thomas, R., & Hargreaves, M. (1985). Effects of reduced training on muscular power in swimmers. *The Physician and Sportsmedicine, 13,* 94-101.

Costill, D.L., Kovaleski, J., Porter, D., Kirwan, J., Fielding, R., & King, D. (1985). Energy expenditure during front crawl swimming: Predicting success in middle-distance events. *International Journal of Sports Medicine, 6,* 266-270.

Costill, D.L., Sharp, R., & Troup, J.P. (1980). Muscle strength: Contributions to sprint swimming. *Swimming World, 21,* 29-34.

Daniels, J. (1971). Portable respiratory gas collection equipment. *Journal of Applied Physiology, 31,* 164-167.

Di Prampero, P.E., Pendergast, D.R., Wilson, D.W., & Rennie, D.W. (1974). Energetics of swimming in man. *Journal of Applied Physiology, 37,* 1-5.

Hickson, R.C., Foster, C., Pollock, M.L., Galassi, T.M., & Rich, S. (1985). Reduced training intensities and loss of aerobic power, endurance and cardiac growth. *Journal of Applied Physiology: Respiratory, Environmental & Exercise Physiology, 58,* 492-499.

Holmer, I. (1972). Oxygen uptake during swimming in man. *Journal of Applied Physiology, 33,* 502-509.

Jacobs, I. (1981). Lactate, muscle glycogen and exercise performance in man. *Acta Physiologica Scandinavica* (Suppl. 495), 1-35.

Karlsson, J. (1980). Localized muscular fatigue: Role of muscle metabolism and substrate depletion. In R.S. Hutton & D.S. Miller (Eds.), *Exercise and sports science reviews* (Vol. 7, pp. 1-42). Philadelphia: Franklin Institute.

Lavoie, J., Taylor, A.W., & Montpetit, R.R. (1981). Physiological effects of training in elite swimmers as measured by a free swimming test. *Journal of Sports Medicine, 21,* 38-42.

Lavoie, J., Léger, L.A., Leone, M., & Provencher, P.J. (1985). A maximal multistage swim test to determine the functional and maximal aerobic power of competitive swimmers. *Journal of Swimming Research, 1,* 17-22.

Magel, J.R., & Faulkner, J.A. (1967). Maximum oxygen uptakes of college swimmers. *Journal of Applied Physiology, 22,* 929-938.

Magel, J.R., Foglia, G.F., McArdle, W.D., Gutin, B., Pechar, G.S., & Katch, F.I. (1974). Specificity of swim training on maximum oxygen uptake. *Journal of Applied Physiology, 38,* 151-155.

Miyashita, M., & Kanehisa, H. (1979). Dynamic peak torque related to age, sex and performance. *Research Quarterly*, **50**, 249-255.

Neufer, P.D., Costill, D.L., Fielding, R.A., Flynn, M.G., & Kirwan, J.P. (1986). Effect of reduced training on muscular strength and endurance in competitive male swimmers. *Medicine and Science in Sports and Exercise*, **18**, (Suppl.), S77.

Saltin, B., & Karlsson, J. (1971). Muscle glycogen utilization during work of different intensities. In B. Saltin & B. Pernow (Eds.), *Muscle metabolism during exercise* (pp. 288-299). New York: Plenum Press.

Sharp, R.L., Troup, J.P., & Costill, D.L. (1982). Relationship between power and sprint freestyle swimming. *Medicine and Science in Sports and Exercise*, **14**, 53-56.

Sherman, W.M., Armstrong, L.E., Murray, T.M., Hagerman, F.C., Costill, D.L., Staron, R.C., & Ivy, J.L. (1984). Effect of a 42.2 km footrace and subsequent rest or exercise on muscular strength and work capacity. *Journal of Applied Physiology: Respiratory, Environmental & Exercise Physiology*, **57**, 1668-1673.

Van Handel, P.J., Katz, A., Troup, J.P., Daniels, J.T., & Bradley, P.W. (1988). Aerobic economy and competitive swim performance of U.S. elite swimmers. In B.E. Ungerechts, K. Wilke, & K. Reischle (Eds.), *Swimming science V* (pp. 219-227). Champaign, IL: Human Kinetics.

Van Handel, P.J., Troup, J.P., & Bradley, P.W. *A method for obtaining and analyzing lactic acid in micro samples of whole blood*. Manuscript submitted for publication.

Yancher, R., Larsen, O., & Baer, C. (1983, February–April). Power and velocity relationships in swimming. *Swimming Technique*, pp. 16-18.

Postcompetition Blood Lactate Concentration in Highly Ranked Australian Swimmers

Richard D. Telford
Allan G. Hahn
Edward A. Catchpole
Anthony R. Parker
William F. Sweetenham

Over the past decade, considerable emphasis has been placed on blood lactic acid measurement during submaximal and maximal training swims as an aid to the design of training programs. The earlier work of Mader, Heck, and Hollman (1976) was applied to swimming by such researchers as Sharp, Vitelli, Costill, and Thomas (1984) and Maglischo, Maglischo, Smith, Bishop, and Horland (1984). A review article of these applications has recently been published (Heck et al., 1985).

Sawka, Knowlton, Miles, and Critz (1979), who reported on blood lactate values obtained in collegiate swimmers, pointed out that very little information has been published on the maximal levels of blood lactate accumulation during competition. The purpose of the current investigation was to measure postcompetition blood lactate levels from some of Australia's best swimmers. More specifically, the purposes were to determine (a) the postcompetition maximal blood lactate concentrations (MBLA) obtained during heats and finals; (b) the values attained by more and less accomplished swimmers; and (c) MBLA values of male and female competitors during 25- and 50-m pool competitions in successive weeks.

Methods

The subjects were 23 male and 13 female swimmers selected for training at the Australian Institute of Sport because of high national rankings in at least one event. The male swimmers had a mean (standard error) age of 19.6 (0.46) years and an average height of 182.9 (1.57) cm. Their mean weight was 77.2 (1.65) kg. For the females the corresponding measures were 19.4 (0.49) years, 174.8 (1.56) cm, and 65.8 (1.81) kg.

The MBLA was obtained after events in two meets 1 week apart following 4 months of winter preparation. These meets were highlights of the training season, especially the first, which was the Australian National 25-m championship. The second meet, in the 50-m pool, was also considered a season highlight and included international swimmers. The swimmers aimed to achieve personal best performances in both meets. During each meet the swimmers competed in heats in the morning and finals in the afternoon or evening, with an interval of 5 to 10 hr between races. At the end of each race, the swimmers left the pool, walked approximately 25-m, and remained seated as blood samples were drawn. The samples were obtained from an earlobe at approximately 2, 4, and 6 min following the race. Where levels showed a continued rise over the first 6 minutes of recovery, further samples were taken until maximal levels were obtained. The highest value obtained from these samples was taken as the MBLA. The blood was collected in capillary tubes prepared with fluoride, nitrite, and heparin, and the actual lactate analyses were carried out within minutes of collection using an Analox automated lactate analyser (Analox Instruments Ltd., Paddington, London, England). This instrument functions by measuring the oxygen change when oxidase enzymes react with lactate under controlled semianaerobic conditions. The accuracy of the machine was maintained by regular calibration with standard lactate solutions.

Statistical Methods and Results

In all, 192 individual swims in heats and finals were used in the analysis. These were distances ranging from 50 to 1,500 m (but mostly 100 m and 200 m) and consisting of freestyle, backstroke, breaststroke, butterfly, and individual medley events. Possible differences in lactate levels due to the varying distances were allowed for in the statistical analysis but no account was taken of the different strokes. Analysis was by the statistical package GLIM (Numerical Algorithms Group, Oxford, U.K.).

The effect of MBLA of the 25- and 50-m lengths was determined by fitting the model

$$\text{MBLA} = \text{SEX} + \text{SEX.PERSON} + \text{DISTANCE} + \text{MEET} \qquad (1)$$

(using the notation of GLIM) to the 100 individual swims in heats and finals. The SEX factor allowed for the difference in MBLA between males and females, and SEX.PERSON allowed for differences in variation among the swimmers according to sex. The DISTANCE factor measured dependence of MBLA on the distance of the event and was significant at the .01 level, with highest levels of MBLA for the 100-, 200-, and 400-m events, less (by about 2 mM/l) for the 1,500-m event, and least (by another 2 mM/l) for the 50-m event.

More suprisingly, the MEET factor, representing the difference in MBLA levels in the 25- and 50-m lengths, was significant at the .001 level, with the estimated average increase in MBLA for males and females from 25- to 50-m lengths being 3.8 mM/l with a standard error of 0.6 mM/l. The average values of MBLA for the two different lengths are shown separately for males and females in Table 1. (The estimated difference is not exactly

Table 1 Absolute Values of MBLA (Means and Standard Errors in mmol/l) and Significance of the Effects of Meet and Sex

| | 25-m pool meet | | | 50-m pool meet | | | Significance of differences due to meet |
	n	Mean	SE	n	Mean	SE	
Final							
Males	32	8.23	0.45	25	11.70	0.65	$p < .001$
Females	23	7.76	0.48	20	12.22	0.66	$p < .001$
Heat							
Males	35	7.57	0.32	30	11.09	0.58	$p < .001$
Females	18	5.77	0.37	9	9.87	1.04	$p < .001$

Note. No significance of differences due to sex were found except for 25-m heats, $p < .01$.

equal to the difference in average values, due to the nonorthogonal design of the experiment.)

None of the interaction terms that could be fitted to Equation 1 were significant, showing that the effect of MEET was reasonably constant over males and females (see Table 1) and over the various distances.

Differences in absolute MBLA levels between males and females were estimated from the model

$$MBLA = SEX + MEET + SEX.MEET \qquad (2)$$

which was fitted separately for each distance in the heats and again in the finals, and pooled over all distances in the heats and in the finals. In the heats the females achieved significantly lower MBLA than the males (estimated difference 2.1 mM/l, standard error 0.7 mM/l, $p < .01$), and this effect was fairly uniform over distances. But in the finals there was virtually no difference in MBLA levels achieved by males and females (estimated difference 0.1 mM/l, $p > .05$).

To estimate the increase in MBLA from heat to final, only swimmers who competed in the heat and final were used and the difference in MBLA (ΔMBLA = MBLA [final] − MBLA [heat]) was estimated from the model

$$\Delta MBLA = SEX + SEX.PERSON + MEET + DISTANCE \qquad (3)$$

There was a significant overall increase in MBLA from heat to final, although the size of this increase varied greatly between males and females and also between the 25- and 50-m lengths. The results are shown in Table 2.

To compare MBLA levels between highly accomplished and less accomplished swimmers, the model

$$MBLA = SEX + SEX.PERSON + MEET + PLACE \qquad (4)$$

Table 2 Mean and Standard Errors (in mmol/l) of the Differences in MBLA Obtained in Heats and Finals

	ΔMBLA[a]		Significance of difference
	Mean	SE	
25-m pool meet			
Males	0.69	0.52	NS
Females	2.24	0.61	$p < .001$
Combined	1.27	0.41	$p < .01$
50-m pool meet			
Males	1.35	0.82	NS
Females	2.64	1.60	NS
Combined	1.72	0.75	$p < .05$
25- and 50-m pool meets combined			
Males	0.68	0.47	NS
Females	2.41	0.61	$p < .001$
Combined	1.28	0.38	$p < .001$

Note. NS = not significant. [a]ΔMBLA = MBLA (final) − MBLA (heat).

Table 3 Differences in MBLA (Means and Standard Errors in mmol/l) Obtained by the Final Place-Getters and Non-Place-Getters

	Mean	SE	Significance of difference
MBLA in final (Place-getters − non-place-getters)	1.33	0.66	$p < .05$
ΔMBLA[a] (Place-getters − non-place-getters)	3.0	1.1	$p < .01$

[a]ΔMBLA = MBLA (final) − MBLA (heat).

was fitted to the finals data only. The term PLACE distinguished between place-getters (in the first four) and non-place-getters. A similar model for ΔMBLA was also fitted to compare the increase in MBLA from heat to final achieved by the place-getters as compared with non-place-getters. As shown in Table 3, the place-getters achieved slightly higher MBLA in the finals than the non-place-getters but more significantly showed a much greater increase in MBLA from heat to final.

Discussion

The measurement of lactate concentrations in the blood of athletes must be interpreted with caution. Certainly increased production of lactic acid by muscle is indicative of greater anaerobic energy output. However, variable rates of introduction and removal of lactic acid to and from the blood, according to individual physiology and variable race pace patterns as well as individually varying blood volumes, prevent the simple interpretation that a higher blood lactate level means greater anaerobic metabolism. Nevertheless, it is reasonable to assume that a greater MBLA for a given individual in a given event indicates an increase in anaerobic energy production, especially if the race pace is faster. It follows that the finding of similar MBLA in male and female swimmers across the range of events investigated cannot be interpreted as equivalent anaerobic contribution in males and females.

On the other hand, blood lactates are of considerable value in designing the level of training stress, as exemplified by the work of Mader et al. (1976). The results outlined in Table 1 suggest that during training, when simulated racing efforts are required, males and females should be expected to develop similar MBLA values. Worthy of consideration, however, is that a single maximal noncompetitive effort may not elicit the same time nor MBLA as competition (Sawka et al., 1979). On the other hand, maximal repetition, 100-m swimming may ultimately produce higher MBLA values than will a single competitive effort (Telford and Hahn, 1984).

The finals resulted in significantly higher MBLA values than did the heats, the difference being 1.3 mM/l or approximately 12%. In the heats the swimmers did have to produce fast times in order to make the finals, hence explaining the relatively higher MBLA levels in the latter races. Although the statistical analysis is not shown separately, the figures in Table 3 indicate that the better swimmers were able to swim their heats to finish with a lower MBLA than the non-place-getters. This suggests that they performed their heats more aerobically. Even partial depletion of glycogen stores may compromise maximal physical exertion (Hultman & Bergström 1973), and even short duration strenuous exercise may lead to reduction of the working muscles' glycogen supply (Gollnick et al., 1973). As shown by Gollnick, Piehl, Karlsson, and Saltin (1975), selective depletion of glycogen from fast-twitch muscle fibers may occur with brief high-intensity efforts. Less accomplished swimmers, then, may possibly have an added disadvantage in that their anaerobically more taxing heat might have a greater tendency to hinder their performance in the ensuing final even after an interval of several hours. Of course this disadvantage may also apply to any swimmer who happens to swim in a very fast heat.

It is interesting that MBLA values recorded after the finals in the 50-m pool were higher than those recorded for similar events in the 25-m pool. Sawka, Knowlton, Miles, and Critz (1979) found that increased motivation increased lactic acid accumulation and reduced the time taken for maximal effort over a certain distance. Although 25- and 50-m pool swim times are difficult to compare, motivation was unlikely to have influenced these results because, if anything, more importance was placed by coaches and swimmers on the National 25-m pool events, where lower lactates were recorded. Another possibility for the differences in MBLA at the two meets was that the lactate determinations themselves were systematically biased from one week to the other. This, too, was unlikely as the same machine, enzyme batch, and calibration techniques were used, with swimmers' blood samples being taken after similar postswim intervals.

Two futher explanations seem more plausible. One is that the first competition together with the extra week of relatively easy training (i.e., taper period) could have brought about changes to the lactate production and/or removal processes. Increased MBLA during periods of reduced training has been noted previously (Telford, Gilbert, Tumilty, Woolston, & Sweetenham, 1984). Whether changes in MBLA result from an extension of an already substantial taper period is questionable. The other explanation relates to the length of the pool. It is well established that 25-m pool competitions produce faster times than those held in a 50-m pool. This is presumably related to the doubled frequency of turns in the 25-m pool enabling the legs to contribute more effectively to the propulsion. The analysis given in this article strongly suggests that MBLA levels after competition are influenced by the length of the pool. If this is so, then the correspondingly more frequent period of relative inactivity of the arms and shoulders during the turn and glide may be the factor influencing the lactate metabolism and/or clearance. A dependence of lactate level on pool length would have significant implications for coaches, who would have to be careful to apply the principle of training specificity to their training venue as well as to the events and individuals. More systematic study of the influence of pool length on MBLA is therefore needed.

To summarize, conclusions derived from this study are as follows:

1. MBLA is greater in finals than other heats.
2. The first four place-getters achieved slightly higher MBLA values than non-place-getters, and the place-getters also showed a much greater increase in MBLA from heat to final.
3. Males and females achieved similar MBLA values.
4. Racing in the 50-m pool appeared to elicit higher MBLA values than in the 25-m pool.

Acknowledgments

Thanks are extended to Mr. D.M. Tumilty, Ms. J. Barnes, and Mr. M. Lancaster—all from the Sports Science Laboratory at the Australian Institute of Sport—for their technical assistance in the collection of blood samples. Thanks are also extended to Mr. B. Rhodes from the Phillip Institute of Technology, Bundoora, Victoria, for his preparation of the data

file for computer statistical analysis and to Ms. R. Power for word processing. Finally, gratitude is expressed to the Australian Meat and Livestock
Cooperation and Vitaglow Pty. Ltd. for their supporting roles.

References

Gollnick, P.D., Armstrong, R.B., Saubert, C.W., Sembrowich, W.L.,
Shephard, R.E., & Saltin, B. (1973). Glycogen depletion patterns in
human skeletal muscle during prolonged work. *Pflügers Archiv*, **344**,
1-12.

Gollnick, P.D., Piehl, K., Karlsson, J., & Saltin, B. (1975). Glycogen depletion patterns in human skeletal muscle fibers after varying types and
intensities of exercise. In H. Howald & J.R. Poortmans (Eds.), *Metabolic adaptations to prolonged physical exercise* (pp. 416-421). Basel: Birkäuser.

Heck, H., Mader, A., Hess, G., Mücke, S., Müller, R., & Hollmann, W.
(1985). Justification of the 4 mmol/l lactate threshold. *International Journal
of Sports Medicine*, **6**, 117-130.

Hermansen, L., Hultman, E., & Saltin, B. (1967). Muscle glycogen during
prolonged exercise. *Acta Physiologica Scandinavica*, **71**, 129-139.

Hultman, E., & Bergström, J. (1973). Local energy supplying substrates as
limiting factors in different types of leg muscle work in normal man. In J.
Keul (Ed.), *Limiting factors of physical performance* (pp. 113-124). Stuttgart: Georg Thieme Verlag.

Mader, A., Heck, H., & Hollman, W. (1976). Evaluation of lactic acid
anaerobic energy contribution by determination of post-exercise lactic
acid concentration of ear capillary blood in middle distance runners and
swimmers. In F. Landing & W. Orban (Eds.), *Exercise physiology* (Vol.
4, pp. 187-199). Miami: Symposia Specialists.

Maglischo, E.W., Maglischo, C.M., Smith, R.E., Bishop, R.A., & Horland,
P.N. (1984). Determining the proper training speeds for swimmers. *Journal of Swimming Research*, **1**, 32-38.

Sawka, M.N., Knowlton, R.G., Miles, D.S., & Critz, J.B. (1979). Post competition blood lactate concentrations in collegiate swimmers. *European
Journal of Applied Physiology*, **41**, 93-99.

Sharp, R.L., Vitelli, C.A., Costill, D.L., & Thomas, R. (1984). Comparison
between blood lactate and heart rate profiles during a season of competitive swim training. *Journal of Swimming Research*, **1**, 17-20.

Telford, R.D., Gilbert, P., Tumilty, D.M., Woolston, M., & Sweetenham,
W. (1984). *Laboratory measures of well performed male and female swimmers
and comparison of two different training programs.* Unpublished manuscript.

Telford, R.D., & Hahn, A.G. (1984). [Blood lactate accumulation during
repeated maximal effort 100 metre swims]. Unpublished raw data.

Interaction Between Aerobic/Anaerobic Loading and Biomechanical Performance in Freestyle Swimming

Kari L. Keskinen
Paavo V. Komi

The mean velocity of freestyle swimming ($\overline{V}$) is equal to the product of the stroke rate (SR) and the stroke length (SL). SR refers to one complete cycle of one arm in a given unit of time. The duration of a stroke cycle depends on the angular velocity of rotational movement of the arm around the shoulder joint and on the distance that the most distal part of the upper extremity travels through the water and the air during stroking. SL is the distance that the swimmer moves forward during one complete stroke cycle of one arm. It depends on the horizontal components of drag and lift forces on segments of a swimmer and therefore on the swimmer's muscular power output (Grimston & Hay, 1986; Hay, 1978; Miller, 1975).

In general, SR and SL are negatively related to each other, and the combination of these two variables is highly individualized. Although the interdependence of SR and SL is very high, several factors may influence their interrelationships. Among them are anthropometric characteristics, which have been shown to influence SR and more importantly SL (Clarys, Jiskoot, Rijken, & Brouwer, 1974; DeGaray, Levine, & Carter, 1974; Grimston & Hay, 1986; Reischle, 1978). The swimming velocity may also have different reflections on SR and SL depending on the individual's performance capacity in water and swimming skill. The increase in $\overline{V}$ has been found to be more strongly related to an increase in SR than to a decrease in SL, and SL demonstrates considerable intra- and interindividual variability. However, a hypothesis has been proposed that SR cannot be increased beyond the optimal level without a loss in $\overline{V}$ (Craig & Pendergast, 1979; East, 1970). Furthermore, the swimmers with different swimming performances have much greater variability in SL than in SR in competitive swimming (Craig & Pendergast, 1979; Craig, Skehan, Pawelczyk, & Boomer, 1985; East, 1970; Hay & Guimares, 1983; Letzelter & Freitag, 1982).

These observations have led to the assumption that the complex interrelationship among SR, SL, and $\overline{V}$ may reflect individual swimming efficiency as well as overall metabolism (Costill et al., 1985). The present study was therefore designed to evaluate $\overline{V}$ of freestyle swimming utilizing the

SR and *SL* in three different intensity levels in aerobic/anaerobic loading situations.

Methods

The subjects were 11 male competitive swimmers of medium-high to top national level in Finland. Table 1 describes their physical and performance characteristics.

A 50-m indoor swimming pool was used to arrange the different aerobic/ anaerobic loading situations of freestyle swimming. The swimming consisted of a set of 10 to 14 × 100-m swims with the velocity increased progressively starting very slowly (approximately 25 s + best 100-m freestyle time) up to exhaustion (Gullstrand & Holmer, 1980). The swimmers were instructed to employ an even pace in their trials and to increase the velocity by about 1.5 s after each of the 100-m swims.

In order to define the different levels of aerobic/anaerobic metabolism, 50 μl of blood was taken from the hyperemisized earlobes for the analyses of blood lactate concentration (BLa) before starting the swimming trials, during the first minute after the cessation of each of the 100-m swims and 3, 5, 7, and 9 min after the last 100-m swim. The lactate concentration was analyzed by using an enzymatic method of Biochemica Boehringer (Boehringer Mannheim, 1979). Times for each of the 100-m swims and for 10 to 15 stroke cycles per 50 m of stroking were measured manually for calculation of mean $\overline{V}$ and *SR*. Mean *SL* was obtained by dividing $\overline{V}$ by *SR*.

Three different intensity levels were derived based on the blood lactate concentrations: (a) low intensity (BLa at its basal level), (b) medium intensity (BLa < 8 mmol × l^{-1}), and (c) high intensity (BLa > 8 mmol × l^{-1}. The threshold to determine the change from the basic BLa level was set at $\Delta 0.5$ mmol. The values greater than this threshold level therefore belonged to the higher intensity categories.

The statistical analyses consisted of means and standard deviations for all measured variables, and the regression analyses were conducted between *SR*, *SL*, $\overline{V}$ and BLa for all measurements and separately in the three different intensity levels.

Table 1 The Physical and Performance Characteristics of the Subjects ($N = 11$)

Value	Age (years)	Height (cm)	Weight (kg)	Fat (%)[a]	100-m record (s)	200-m record (min)	400-m record (min)
M	19.5	182.7	71.6	11.1	56.0	2:01.0	4:20.7
SD	3.5	6.5	6.0	1.4	2.3	4.3	8.5
Range	16.0–25.0	175.0–198.5	61.1–82.5	8.7–13.3	52.9–59.5	1:55.7–2:08.4	4:05.8–4:32.5

[a]Estimated from skinfolds according to Durnin and Rahaman (1967).

Results

The data were analyzed so that the relationships among the different variables could be examined for all of the data and separately for the three intensity levels.

Total Sample

Figure 1 presents the relationships among the selected variables. The plots demonstrate significant parabolic relationships in all cases. However, the scatter of points varied between comparisons, and it was especially large in SL versus $\overline{V}$ comparison. A very close relationship and with a smaller scatter of points existed between SR and $\overline{V}$ and also between SR and SL. Blood lactate increased continuously with the increase in swimming velocity. When blood lactate was compared with SR and SL, it demonstrated opposite responses in the two relationships.

Intensity Levels

Because the intensity levels as used in the present study have been employed in the training of swimmers, it was of interest to examine how the relationships as presented for the total data also applied in the various aerobic/anaerobic intensities.

SR was best related to $\overline{V}$ when the values were taken from the medium-intensity swims (Figure 2). The same was true for SR versus blood lactate, and this relationship was significant only for the medium-intensity exercises (Figure 3).

SL showed greater variability at all velocities (see Figure 1). The intensity level comparison showed that SL and BLa had a positive ($p < .01$) relationship at the low-intensity swims, negative ($p < .01$) at medium intensity, but no significant relation at high-intensity swims (Figure 4). Blood lactate, which in the total sample (see Figure 1E) increased quadratically with an increase in swimming velocity, had the strongest linear relationship with $\overline{V}$ at medium intensity, and no significant relationship at high intensity (Figure 5). As expected SR and SL had a significant negative ($p < .001$) relationship at all intensity levels. However, SL and $\overline{V}$ demonstrated no significant relationship at the three intensity levels.

Figure 6 summarizes the significant relationships both for the total sample (Figure 6A) and separately for the three intensity levels (Figures 6B, C, D).

Discussion

The present data agreed with several studies (Craig & Pendergast, 1979; Craig et al., 1985; East, 1970; Letzelter & Freitag, 1982, 1983) in total sample interrelationships among $\overline{V}$, SR, and SL (see Figure 6A). $\overline{V}$ increased with

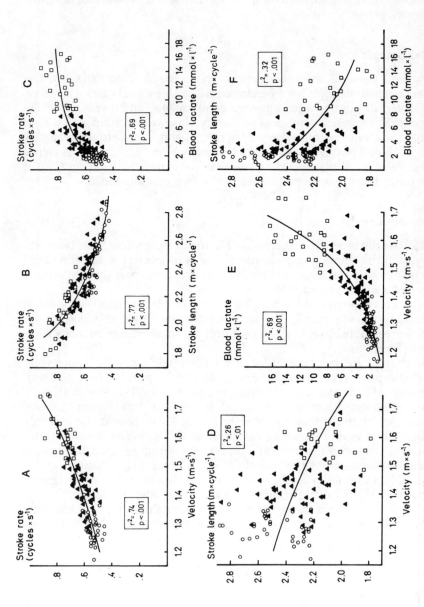

Figure 1 Individual plots of the different measured values. Symbols: 0 = low intensity swimming; ▲ = medium intensity swimming; □ = high intensity swimming.

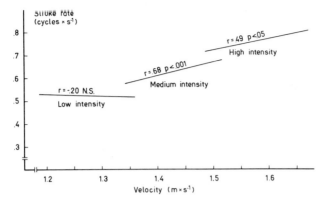

Figure 2   Relationship between stroke rate and swimming velocity as analyzed separately for the three intensity levels.

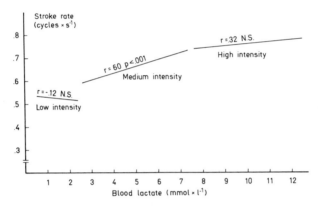

Figure 3   Relationship between stroke rate and blood lactate concentration as analyzed separately for the three intensity levels.

increasing SR, whereas SL decreased. When examining the different levels of aerobic/anaerobic intensities, the interrelationships among these parameters changed markedly. The medium-intensity swimming was almost identical to the total data except for the lack of negative correlation between $\overline{V}$ and SL (see Figures 6A and C). This emphasized the large range of interindividual variability as seen in SL (see Figure 1D). SL was, on the average, longest at the low-intensity swims, and it correlated positively with BLa, which in turn had a posititive correlation with $\overline{V}$ (see Figure 6B). SL and $\overline{V}$ had a positive correlation ($r = .29$) with each other although it was not statistically significant. This nonsignificant relationship may, however, be used to strengthen the possibility of a hypothesis that in low-intensity swimming the increases in $\overline{V}$ are caused mainly by lengthening of SL while SR is only slightly increased (see Figure 4). The long SL

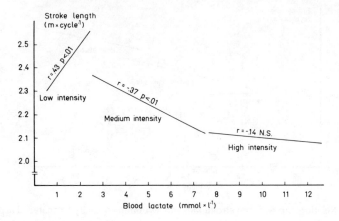

Figure 4   Relationship between stroke length and blood lactate concentration as analyzed separately for the three intensity levels.

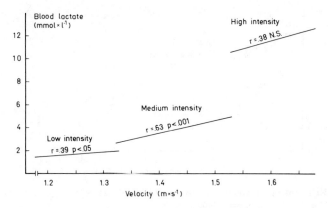

Figure 5   Relationship between blood lactate concentration and swimming velocity as analyzed separately for the three intensity levels.

in low-intensity swimming may partly be due to longer gliding phases within the stroke cycles as compared to medium-intensity swimming. It may also be due to metabolically easy aerobic swimming intensity. According to Gullstrand and Holmer (1980), swimming velocities in the present low-intensity 100-m swims were mainly aerobic, with effective elimination of BLa. When swimming intensity increased over 0.5 mmol $\times$ l^{-1} from the basal level, *SL* started to decrease (Figures 1F and 6B, C), which might be a result of muscle fatigue during the aerobic/anaerobic transition. Whether the reduction in SL was caused by local muscle fatigue or by increasing metabolic acidosis itself or both cannot be concluded from the present data. The high-intensity swimming differed from the low-intensity swims so that there was a significant correlation between $\bar{V}$ and

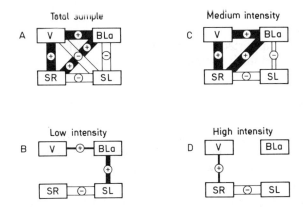

Figure 6   A schematic description of the intercorrelations between $\bar{V}$, BLa, SR, and SL. The thickness of the lines describes the strength of the positive and negative correlations (either filled or open, respectively).

SR but no correlations between $\bar{V}$ and BLa, SR and BLa, and SL and BLa (see Figure 6). This may demonstrate great variability among swimmers in swimming efficiency and in lactate production during the present type of progressive set of 100-m swims. This notion agrees with Craig et al. (1985), who stated that the best performers in the 1984 U.S.A. Olympic Swimming Trials increased their SR more than a group of slower swimmers. They also reported longer SL in the best swimmers compared to their inferior counterparts, and more importantly they demonstrated that the increase in competitive swimming velocities during an 8-year period from 1976 to 1984 was mainly due to increased SL (Craig & Pendergast, 1979; Craig et al., 1985).

When a selected intensity level is used as training mode the relationships between the variables do not necessarily conform with the overall relationships. The present result suggested that during low-intensity training it is beneficial to practice the lengthening of SL in order to develop local muscle endurance capacity. In medium-intensity swimming it is important to try to resist the decrease in SL while increasing SR in order to develop greater mechanical swimming economy and therefore muscular power output.

Costill et al. (1985) pointed out the importance of swimming with the fewest number of stroke cycles at a given velocity (Costill et al., 1985). In high-intensity swimming $\bar{V}$ may be increased by increasing the SR. Furthermore, if the suggestion is true that an optimal level of SR during competitive swimming exists (e.g., Craig & Pendergast, 1979; East, 1970; Hay, 1978) then the swimmer should use this "optimum" SR in his or her training. At low- and medium-intensity training, the lower SR with longer SL may be desirable. These suggestions point out that the interrelationships between SR and SL should be considered in swimming training. However, the final question of how these relationships change when the conditioning progresses remains unanswered.

Acknowledgments

This study was supported by grants from the Finnish Central Sports Federation and the Finnish Swimming Association.

References

Boehringer Mannheim: Test-Fibel. (1979). *Enzymatische Bestimmung von Lactat im Plasma, Blut und Liquor.* Mannheim: Author.

Clarys, J.P., Jiskoot, J., Rijken, H., & Brouwer, P.J. (1974). Total resistance in water and its relation to body form. In R.C. Nelson & C.A. Morehouse (Eds.), *Biomechanics IV* (pp. 187-196). Baltimore: University Park Press.

Costill, D.L., Kovaleski, J., Porter, D., Kirwan, J., Fielding, R., & King, D. (1985). Energy expenditure during front crawl swimming: Predicting success in middle-distance events. *International Journal of Sports Medicine,* **6**, 266-270.

Craig, A.B., Jr., & Pendergast, D.R. (1979). Relationships of stroke rate, distance per stroke, and velocity in competive swimming. *Medicine and Science in Sport,* **11**, 278-283.

Craig, A.B., Jr., Skehan, P.L., Pawelczyk, J.A., & Boomer, W.L. (1985). Velocity, stroke rate, and distance per stroke during elite swimming competition. *Medicine and Science in Sports and Exercise,* **17**, 625-634.

DeGaray, A., Levine, L., & Carter, J. (Eds.). (1974). *Genetic and anthropological studies of Olympic athletes.* New York: Academic Press.

Durnin, J., & Rahaman, M. (1967). The assessment of the amount of fat in the human body from the measurements of skinfold thickness. *British Journal of Nutrition,* **21**, 681-689.

East, D.J. (1970). An analysis of stroke frequency, stroke length and performance. *New Zealand Journal of Health, Physical Education and Recreation,* **3**, 16-27.

Grimston, S.K., & Hay, J.G. (1986). Relationships among anthropometric and stroking characteristics of college swimmers. *Medicine and Science in Sports and Exercise,* **18**, 60-68.

Gullstrand, L., & Holmer, I. (1980). Fysiologiska tester av landslagssimmare: Anaerob energileverans-mätningen av blodmjölksyra [The psychological tests for the national team level swimmers: Measurement of anaerobic energy metabolism by blood lactate]. *Simsport,* **3**, 15-17.

Hay, J.G. (1978). Swimming. In J. Hay (Ed.), *The biomechanics of sport techniques* (pp. 337-381). Englewood Cliffs, NJ: Prentice-Hall.

Hay, J.G., & Guimares, A.C.S. (1983, August–October). A quantitative look at swimming biomechanics. *Swimming Technique,* pp. 11-17.

Letzelter, H., & Freitag, W. (1982). Geschwindigkeits- und Zugverhalten im 200-m-Freistilschwimmen von Männern und Frauen der europäischen Spitzenklasse [Speed and stroke characteristics in the 200-m freestyle swimming of top-level European men and women]. *Leistungssport, 12,* 442-452.

Letzelter, H., & Freitag, W. (1983). Stroke length and stroke frequency, variations in men's and women's 100-m freestyle swimming. In A.P. Hollander, P.A. Huijing, & G. de Groot (Eds.), *Biomechanics and medicine in swimming* (pp. 315-322). Champaign, IL: Human Kinetics.

Miller, D.I. (1975). Biomechanics of swimming. In J.H. Wilmore & J.F. Keogh (Eds.), *Exercise and sport sciences reviews* (Vol. 3, pp. 219-248). Orlando, FL: Academic Press.

Reischle, K. (1978). Chronofotographische Zuglängen-registrierung bei Delphin, Rücken und Kraul [Chronophotographic stroke length recordings of the dolphin, backstroke and crawl]. *Beiheft zum Leistungssport, 14,* 31-49.

Relationship of Blood Lactate Accumulation to Stroke Rate and Distance per Stroke in Top Female Swimmers

Michael Weiss
Klaus Reischle
Niels Bouws
Gerrit Simon
Helmut Weicker

Swimming velocity (v) is the function of stroke rate ($\dot{S}$) and distance per stroke (d/S). As shown by Craig and Pendergast (1979) stroke rate is a nonlinear function of v: When $\dot{S}$ is increased above the optimal point, v decreases. The reason for this nonlinear function between $\dot{S}$ and v is a shortening of d/S.

Energy demand (E) in swimming depends on efficiency (eff.), body drag (d_b), and v; therefore E is a function of $\dot{S}$ and d/S. The total energy delivery is the sum of aerobic metabolism ($\dot{V}O_2$) and anaerobic metabolism (glycolysis leading to lactate production and the breakdown of phosphates, especially creatin phosphate [CP]). When swimming longer than 20 s under steady state conditions, CP is constant. At low speeds, lactate produced can be eliminated and blood lactate remains constant, but at high speeds above 70 or 80% $\dot{V}O_2$max, blood lactate accumulates (anaerobic threshold onset of blood lactate accumulation [OBLA]) as a function of $\dot{S}$ and d/S. Furthermore, efficiency during constant work depends on frequency in all cyclic movements. This has been shown for bicycle ergometers (Stegemann, Ulmer, & Heinrich, 1968), rowing (Raatz & Krause, 1977), and running (Cavanagh & Williams, 1982) as well as in swimming (Kipke, 1978; Swaine & Reilly, 1983). The aim of the present study was to evaluate the dependence of blood lactate accumulation on $\dot{S}$ and d/S during different swimming velocities and distances in female high-skilled swimmers.

Methods

A total of 43 German female swimmers of the first and second German National Team and the National Junior Team were studied. Experimental design, swimming time per 300 m, and in 100-m submaximal swims and measurements are given in Figure 1. The swimmers underwent a step test, swimming 300 m with constant velocity. After a pause of 30 s for

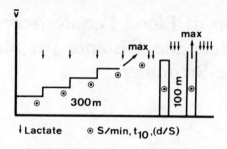

	300 m		100 m subm
FREE:	4min:45sec	-15sec per step	1min:09sec
BACK:	5 :14	-15	1 :16
BREAST:	5 :30	-15	1 :25
BUTTERFLY:	- - - - - - - - - - - - -		1 :13

Figure 1 Design and measurements of the study.

taking blood lactate from the subject's hyperemized earlobe, the velocity
was increased step by step until a constant speed could not be maintained.
After a recovery period of at least 2 hr, they swam 100 m submaximal
with a given constant velocity and 20 min later 100 m with maximal velocity. After each 100-m swim, blood was taken up to 10 min. Lactate
was determined enzymatically by a commerical micromethod (Lactate Kit
Testomar, Fa. Behring)

When swimming 300 m, between 230 and 240 m or 270 and 280 m, time
per 10m (t_{10}) was measured and $\dot{S}$ determined by a stopwatch for four
complete arm cycles and expressed in S/min. During the 100-m swims,
the same measurements were done between 70 and 80 m. From those
measurements d/S was calculated:

$$v = \dot{S} \times \frac{d}{S} \qquad v = \frac{10\ m}{t_{10}\ s} \qquad \dot{S} = \frac{\dot{S}}{60\ s}$$

$$\frac{d}{\dot{S}} = \frac{v}{\dot{S}} = \frac{10\ m \times 60\ s}{t_{10}\ s \times \dot{S}} = \frac{600}{t_{10} \times \dot{S}}\ m$$

Further measurements were taken of maximal force on the biokinetic
swim bench (Biokinetic Instruments) and anthropometric data (height,
weight, lean body mass, arm length) to determine if d/S was more influenced by force, anthropometric data, or physical condition.

Results

Mean values of lactate and S/min from the aerobic 300-m test of 5 breaststroke, 4 backstroke, and 34 freestyle swimmers are shown in Figure 2.
Lactate shows the typical exponential increase with increasing velocity
in all stroke patterns. Higher velocity could be reached by the best swim-

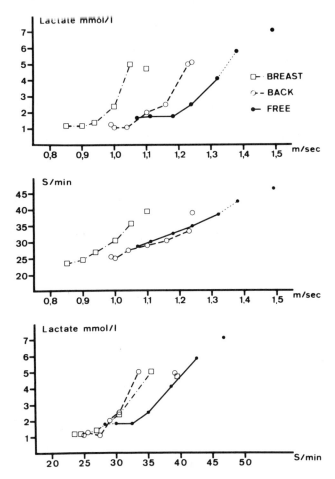

Figure 2   Mean values of lactate and stroke rate (S/min) related to velocity and relationship of lactate to stroke rate in three different stroke patterns during the 300-m test.

mers with lower increase in lactate as might be expected from the mean values of all swimmers. Those points are not connected with lines to the other mean values. Lactate curves of different stroke patterns are clearly different. S/min in relation to speed shows an exponential function in breaststroke but a nearly linear one in swimming backstroke or front crawl. The relationship of S/min to velocity in the latter two stroke patterns is nearly the same, whereas the exponential relation of lactate to S/min was nearly the same in breaststroke and backstroke.

Mean values and standard deviations of lactate, S/min and d/S in relation to velocity are given in Figure 3 for freestyle swimming and Figure 4 for breaststroke. These two figures show the results of the 300-m test and the two 100-m tests each connected with lines. Where lines are broken, not all the females swam this step. Among the 34 swimmers were short-

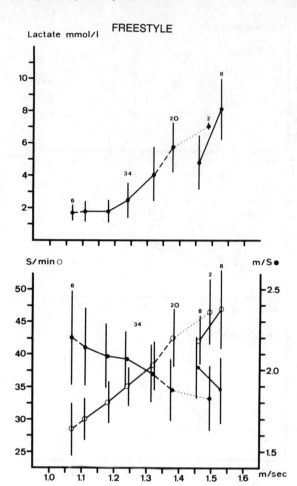

Figure 3   Mean values and standard deviations for lactate, stroke rate (S/min), and distance per stroke (m/S) related to velocity in the 300-m test and 100-m submaximal and maximal freestyle swims.

and long-distance freestyle swimmers, butterfly swimmers, and some breaststrokers and backstrokers. Therefore, the standard deviation was very high. In the 300-m step test (Figure 3), six of the girls started at a velocity of 1.07 m/s and 34 at 1.11 m/s. All of them could maintain 1.32 m/s; 20 reached the step 1.38; and the 2 best, 1.49. Blood lactate values increased at around 1.24 m/s, and a more pronounced increase was noted above this velocity. Stroke rate at the second step was 30 S/min and d/S was 2.14 m. Frequency increased in a near linear manner, and only a low decrease of d/S occurred up to 1.24 m/s. At higher velocities both variables changed more rapidly at the point where the blood lactate increased. In the 2 best swimmers, the decrease of d/S was less pronounced and

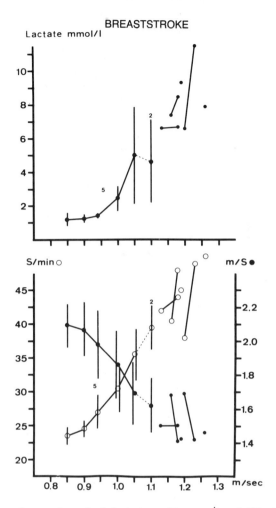

Figure 4 Mean values and standard deviations of lactate, $\dot{S}$, and d/S related to velocity in the 300-m test swimming the breaststroke and individual values during the submaximal and maximal 100-m swims.

there was a lesser increase in lactate. During the 100-m submaximal swim, d/S in relation to v was greater and $\dot{S}$ was lower compared to the last steps of the 300-m swim.

Results from the five breaststrokers (Figure 4) were comparable. The decrease in d/S and increase in $\dot{S}$ were very small and within the standard deviation when increased from 0.85 to 0.90 m/s (Steps 1 and 2). After this, they increased nearly linearly up to 1.0 m/s, as long as there was no increase of blood lactate above 2.45 mmol/l. The 2 best swimmers were able to increase stroke frequency and velocity without a further increase in lactate. Figure 4 shows the individual results of the 100-m test on the

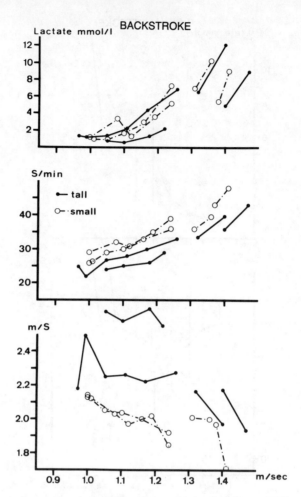

Figure 5 Individual curves of lactate, $\overset{\bullet}{S}$, d/S, related to velocity in the 300-m swim test and submaximal and maximal 100-m swims for the backstroke swimmers.

right because not all were swimming the submaximal 100 m. One swimmer showed no decrease of d/S when swimming near maximal.

Figure 5 shows individual curves of 4 women swimming the backstroke. At comparable velocity, d/S was longer and $\overset{\bullet}{S}$ slower in the 2 tall women. A decrease in d/S yielded more individual differences than in other stroke patterns. One of the subjects could maintain a long d/S during the 300-m test and a strong linear relationship of $\overset{\bullet}{S}$ to v despite the increasing blood lactate values. However during the submaximal 100-m test at nearly the same lactate levels, d/S was shorter and a rapid decrease took place during the maximal 100 m swim. One of the shorter females was able to maintain a long d/S in the maximal 100-m swim.

When compared together, the different stroke patterns showed differences in the relationships of d/S to v. Swimming very slowly, d/S was the longest in the backstroke and shortest in the breaststroke. With increasing v, the decrease was more pronounced in the breaststroke, except during the second step, and there was less of a decrement in the back crawl. Some individuals were able to maintain long d/S up to high velocities, but a decrease took place in all cases when blood lactate reached high levels. When related to body or arm length or to lean body mass, no systematic changes of results occurred despite a smaller standard deviation. Analysis of linear correlations showed only a few and no systematic correlations between biomechanical parameters and blood lactate, possibly because they seem to be exponential functions. From the figures, one can observe a change of the relationship around the anaerobic threshold.

The rapid increase in lactate took place at a frequency of 28 S/min in the breaststroke and backstroke and at 32 S/min in the front crawl, whereas the relationships of S/min to v in the front and back crawl were very similar (see Figure 2 bottom and middle panel). Maximal pulling force measured on the biokinetic swim bench correlated positively with d/S and v when swimming at maximal speed and inversely with S. No systematic correlations were found with lactate throughout all stroke patterns.

Discussion

The test protocol used in this study was designed for determination of aerobic and anaerobic capacity of swimmers (Simon, Thiesmann, Frohberger, & Clasing, 1983). By measuring stroke rate and calculating distance per stroke, an attempt was made to evaluate the influence of a swimmer's biomechanical behavior on aerobic and anaerobic energy requirements. Influence of stroke rate on oxygen consumption and lactate accumulation ere expected for three reasons: (a) swimming velocity depends on stroke rate, (b) efficiency and body drag depend on velocity, and (c) efficiency of all cyclic movements depends on frequency of movement.

Optimal efficiency in cycling was reported at a frequency of around 50 rpm (Stegemann et al., 1968); in rowing at about 30 pulls/min with a decrease above 34 pulls/min (Raatz & Krause, 1977); and maximal power output on a swim bench between 40 and 45 pulls/min (Thronton & Flavell, 1979). Maximal oxygen uptake on the swim bench at 45 pulls/min correlated with maximal v during swimming (Swaine & Reilly, 1983). When S increases above optimal levels, swimming velocity decreases (Craig & Pendergast, 1979). McArdle, Glaser, & Magel (1979) found a nearly linear relationship between S and v and oxygen consumption and therefore between S and $\dot{V}O_2$. To the contrary, Kipke, (1978) reported a decrease in $\dot{V}O_2$ when S decreased and when swimming at high velocities, with a high S, a decrease of $\dot{V}O_2$, but a more pronounced and higher lactate production. The present results show that blood lactate accumulation related to S parallels the exponential relationship of lactate to velocity but with a shift to the left in backstroke swimmers. Up to the anaerobic threshold the increase of S was related to v in a linear manner and d/S decreased in nearly the same manner. With the onset of blood lactate accumulation, the stroke was shortened and swimmers required a higher stroke frequency.

When swimming very slowly or slowly, the shortening of d/S was less than swimming at a medium or fast velocity. This was more pronounced in the breaststroke and less pronounced in the back crawl compared to freestyle swimming. One explanation may be that in this study the role of the leg kick was not considered but it is known that combining arm and leg work leads to elevation of blood lactate levels despite working with the same power output. Therefore, it cannot be determined if the elevation of S was the main reason for blood lactate accumulation, especially if comparing the stroke frequency in this study with the values for the most economical stroke rates from the literature. On the other hand, because of the sharp decrease of d/S when lactate levels were high, it was assumed that muscular fatigue during anaerobic work led to a breakdown of the optimal swimming technique. Therefore, aerobic capacity seemed to play an important role in maintaining the optimal technique when swimming at high velocities with high S.

This conclusion came from some individual curves and from the behavior of the best 2 swimmers, who reached higher velocites in the 300-m test shown in Figure 3 and whose d/S could be better maintained compared to the rest of the swimmers. Few swimmers were able to maintain a long d/S despite elevated blood lactate (for example, see Figure 5). It can be concluded that lactate tolerance or anaerobic capacity also plays an important role in maintaining optimal swimming technique. Lack of correlation between power output on swim bench and performance in the 300-m test or d/S indicated that there exists different types of swimmers: sprinters whose performances depend on maximal force (Sharp, Troup, & Costill, 1982) and anaerobic capacity, therefore maintaining a long d/S; and others who can maintain higher S because of better aerobic capacity and, therefore, lower lactate levels at higher speeds.

Acknowledgments

We thank K. Hehl for her helpful assistance.

References

Cavanagh, P.R., & Williams, K.R. (1982). The effect of stride length variation on oxygen uptake during distance running. *Medicine and Science in Sports and Exercise*, **14**, 30-35.

Craig, A.B., & Pendergast, D.R. (1979). Relationships of stroke rate, distance per stroke, and velocity in competitive swimming. *Medicine and Science in Sports*, **11**, 278-283.

Kipke, L. (1978). Dynamics of oxygen intake during step-by-step loading in a swimming flume. In B. Eriksson and B. Furberg (Eds.), *Swimming medicine IV* (pp. 137-142). Baltimore: University Park Press.

McArdle, W.D., Glaser, R.N., & Magel, J.R. (1971). Metabolic and cardio-respiratory response during free swimming and treadmill walking. *Journal of Applied Physiology*, **30**, 733-738.

Raatz, D., & Krause, R. (1977). Vergleichende Untersuchungen am Ruder-ergometer zur Bestimmung der optimalen Schlagzahl [Examination on a rowing ergometer for determination of optimal stroke frequency]. *Sportarzt und Sportmedizin*, **28**, 238-242.

Sharp, R.L., Troup, J.P., & Costill, D.L. (1982). Relationship between power and sprint freestyle swimming. *Medicine and Science in Sports and Exercise*, **14**, 53-56.

Simon, G., Thiesmann, M., Frohberger, U., & Clasing, D. (1983). Ergometrie im Wasser—Eine neue Form der Leistungsdiagnostik bei Schwimmern [Ergometry in water—A new form of training diagnosis in swimming]. *Deutsche Zeitschrift für Sportmedizin*, **34**, 5-14.

Stegemann, J., Ulmer, H.-V., & Heinrich, K.-W. (1968). Die Beziehung zwischen Kraft und Kraftempfinden als Ursache für die Wahl energetisch ungünstiger Tretfrequenzen beim Radsport [The relation between force and perception of force as a reason for choosing energetically inefficient cranking frequencies in competitive cycling]. *Internationale Zeitschrift für angewandte Physiologie und einschließlich Arbeitsphysiologie*, **25**, 224-234.

Swaine, I., & Reilly, T. (1983). The freely chosen swimming stroke rate in a maximal swim and on a biokinetic swim bench. *Medicine and Science in Sports*, **15**, 370-375.

Thornton, N., & Flavell, E.R. (1979). Power peak training. *Swimming Technique*, **16**(2), 44-47.

Assessment of Anaerobic Capacity in Swimmers by a Two-Phase Laboratory and Field Test

Adalbert Szögy

Physical work capacity has an important influence on sports performances, especially in the cyclic sports. Therefore, the diagnosis and prognosis of the aerobic and the anaerobic capacity represent useful criteria for counseling in the training process.

The anaerobic capacity also influences performances in swimming, especially in the short-distance events. The term *anaerobic capacity*, with its components maximum anaerobic power and anaerobic stamina, can be defined as the aptitude to exert short-time maximum work loads under oxygen-deficit conditions. This is influenced by physical qualities (speed, strength, and coordination); morphological factors (muscle mass and percentage of fast-twitch fibers); functional factors (impulse transmission speed, the influence of the biofeedback of proprioceptors, and the utilization of elastic energy); and metabolic factors (alactacid energy reserves, glycolytic rate, and acidosis tolerance). These facors are trainable to different degrees from highly to hardly at all (Szögy, 1985).

Opposite to the aerobic capacity, in evaluation of anaerobic capacity there is no tendency for standardization and therefore a variety of methods exists for evaluation (Bar-Or, Dotan, & Inbar, 1977; Georgescu, 1969; Kindermann & Schnabel, 1980; Margaria, 1966; Simon & Thiesmann, 1985; Szögy & Cherebetiu, 1974). At the Institute for Sportsmedicine in Frankfurt, a method was developed for the evaluation of the anaerobic capacity based on the following conditions (Szögy, 1985):

- The subject must be able to influence the magnitude of the workload.
- The performance shall be measurable in physical units.
- It shall permit the evaluation of anaerobic power and stamina.
- Next to the diagnosis of the anaerobic capacity, it shall also permit a prognosis by the evaluation of remaining energy reserves.
- It should be applicable in the laboratory and also under specific field conditions.

Subjects and Methods

The investigation was performed employing 20 mediocre freestyle swimmers and one top swimmer (world and Olympic champion) chosen as an optimal model. The mean age of the 20 swimmers was 18.3 years and of the top swimmer, 20 years.

The anaerobic capacity was determined in the laboratory by a two-phase test. A Universal ergometer (Mijnhardt, Odijk) was used as a bicycle and hand grip ergometer. In the speed-dependent range of this ergometer, the work load increases parabolically with the revolutions per minute (rpm). It is equipped with a switch that permits one to choose for 100-rpm work loads of 200, 400, 600, 800, or 1,000 W. During this test, the 600-W range was used, with offers for male subjects a well-balanced relationship between strength and speed demands. The ergometer is equipped with a direct reading instrument for the total work performed.

The purpose of the bicycle ergometer test in a sitting position was the assessment of the anaerobic capacity of the legs. With the hand grip ergometer test in standing position, the anaerobic capacity of the arms was determined. The bicycle and the hand grip ergometric test were carried out on two different days.

The first phase of the test, used for the determination of the maximum anaerobic power, demanded a maximum work load for 15 s produced by a maxium rpm at the given work load. Every 5 s the total work performed in watt-seconds was noted. The purpose of the 15-s work load was to guarantee a certain lactate production that was to be used for the evaluation of the alactacid energy reserves. Therefore, blood lactate was determined from the hyperemized earlobe before and 3, 6, and 9 min after the test. A lactate analyzer (model 640, Kontron, Eching) was used for these analyses. From the highest lactate value after the test, the resting value was subtracted to obtain the Δ-lactate. The highest 5-s watt value was utilized as the value for the diagnosis of the maximum anaerobic power.

After a recovery period of 1 hr, the second phase of the test was performed. The purpose of this phase was the assessment of the anaerobic stamina. Therefore, the subject had to reproduce, if possible, the work load of the first phase and continue it for 45 s. The attained watt-seconds were divided by 45 for the calculation of the mean watt value for the second phase. This was the value used for the diagnosis of anaerobic stamina. Blood lactate was determined before and after the work load.

For the prognosis of maximum anaerobic power the alactacid quotient was calculated, expressed as the relationship between the total work performed and the lactate production both work load phases (from Szögy, Böhmer, Ambrus, & Brune, 1984):

$$\text{Alactacid quotient} = \frac{\text{\% total work performed (watt-seconds) 15 s/45 s}}{\text{\% } \Delta\text{-lactate (mmol/l) \qquad 15s/45s}}$$

The higher the quotient, the higher was the estimate of the alactacid energy reserve in ATP and PC. For the prognosis of the anaerobic stamina, the highest absolute value of lactate following the second phase was used. The lower the value, the higher was the estimated reserve of acidosis tolerance.

The two phases of the swimming field test were carried out on a third day using a 25-m swimming pool. The subjects swam freestyle. In the first phase of the test for the assessment of the maximum anaerobic power, the subjects swam with maximum speed over 50 m. The time was taken as well over 25 and 50 m. Maximum anaerobic power was considered as the higher velocity in meters per second over 25 m. Before and after the test, blood lactate was determined. In the second phase of the swimming test, a 100-m distance was swum with maximum speed. Anaerobic stamina was considered as the mean velocity in meters per second. Blood lactate was again determined. The prognosis of the two components of the anaerobic capacity was evaluated by the same methods as used in the laboratory tests. The only difference was that the total work performed in the alactacid quotient was in this case expressed as meters per second multiplied by the distance instead of watt-seconds.

Results and Discussion

There was no significant correlation among bicycle ergometry, hand grip ergometry, and swimming. This can be explained through the use of different activated muscle groups and different kinds of work loads. Nevertheless, graphically it was still evident that there was a similarity between the development of the values from bicycle ergometry and hand grip

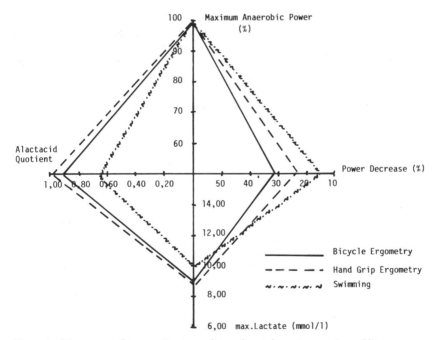

Figure 1 Mean anaerobic capacity in mediocre freestyle swimmers (n = 20).

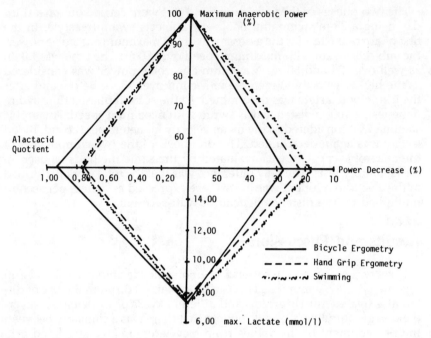

Figure 2 Individual anaerobic capacity in a top swimmer.

ergometry and the concomitant difference in the swimming variables in the mediocre swimmers. (see Figure 1). contrary to this finding, the top swimmer showed a similarity between hand grip ergometry and swimming parameters but a difference in the bicycle ergometer parameters (see Figure 2). This second observation seems logical, because in freestyle swimming the arms provide the most important propulsive force.

The analysis of the different values in three tests shows evidence of higher values in favor of the top swimmer (see Table 1). The differences were between 10 and 35%. The greatest differences were found in the hand grip ergometry. This confirms the graphic findings and leads to the recommendation that the examined mediocre swimmers must give priority to improving their anaerobic arm-working capacity.

The top swimmer also showed deficits, especially concerning the higher power decrease between maximum power and anaerobic stamina in swimming. The relatively lower anaerobic work capacity of his legs in comparison with the arms indicated that he should give priority to improving his anaerobic leg work capacity. In bicycle ergometry and swimming he possessed higher energy reserves than the mediocre swimmers. However, these methods alone are not sufficient for improvement of swimming performances. They must be integrated with an improvement in the biomechanical efficiency of the swimming techniques.

Table 1 Age and Anthropometric and Anaerobic Capacity Values in Freestyle Swimmers

Variable	Mediocre swimmers ($n = 20$) ($M \pm s$)		Top swimmer (TS)	Difference in favor of TS (%)
Age (years)	18.3	± 0.9	20	—
Height (cm)	178.4	± 5.2	201	—
Weight (kg)	70.7	± 8.6	86.0	—
Bicycle ergometry				
Watt 5s	798.0	± 105.00	960.0	+ 20.3
Watt 45s	544.5	± 65.10	693.0	+ 27.3
Power decrease (%)	31.4	± 5.80	27.8	+ 12.9
Alactacid quotient	0.92	± 0.33	0.94	+ 2.2
Max. lactate	8.98	± 1.29	7.07	+ 27.0
Handgrip ergometry				
Watt 5s	517.0	± 106.10	640.0	+ 23.8
Watt 45s	390.5	± 67.20	527.0	+ 35.0
Power decrease (%)	23.7	± 7.60	17.6	+ 34.7
Alactacid quotient	0.98	± 0.39	0.77	− 27.3
Max. lactate	8.79	± 2.18	7.55	+ 16.4
Swimming				
25 m (m/s)	1.81	± 0.09	2.14	+ 18.2
100 m (m/s)	1.60	± 0.09	1.76	+ 10.0
Power decrease (%)	11.7	± 2.80	17.70	− 51.3
Alactacid quotient	0.66	± 0.05	0.77	+ 16.7
Max. lactate	9.94	± 1.22	7.03	+ 41.4

References

Bar-Or, O., Dotan, R., & Inbar, O. (1977). A 30-s all-out ergometric test— Its reliability and validity for anaerobic capacity (abstract). *Israel Journal of Medical Sciences*, **13**, 326-327.

Georgescu, M. (1969). Eine Methode zur Messung der Leistungsfähigkeit und einiger Parameter der Motorik bei harten und kurzdauernded Belastungen [A method for determination of the physical work capacity and some motorial values during hard and short term work loading]. *Sportarzt und Sportmedizin*, **20**, 25-31, 61-67.

Kindermann, W., & Schnabel, A. (1980). Möglichkeiten der aeroben und anaeroben Leistungsdiagnostik unter Laborbedingungen [Possibilities of the diagnosis of the aerobic and anaerobic capacity in laboratory conditions]. In Schmidt & Meyer (Eds.), *Internationales Symposium: Neue Aspekte in der Leistungsmedizin, Graz* (pp. 19-33), Würzburg.

Margaria, R. (1966). Assessment of physical activity in oxidative and anaerobic maximal exercise. *Internationale Zeitschrift für angewandte Physiologie*, **22**, 115-124.

Simon, G., & Thiesmann, M. (1985, September). *Assessment of the anaerobic capacity in swimmers*. Paper presented at the International Congress: Importance in Training Physiology and Clinical Importance of Anaerobic Capacity, St. Johann, Tyrolia.

Szögy, A. (1985, September). *Contributions concerning the anaerobic power testing in athletes*. Paper presented at the International Congress: Importance in Training Physiology and Clinical Importance of Anaerobic Capacity, St. Johann, Tyrolia.

Szögy, A., & Cherebetiu, G. (1974). Minutentest auf dem Fahrradergometer zur Bestimmung der anaeroben Kapazität [A 1-min bicycle ergometer test for determination of anaerobic capacity]. *European Journal of Applied Physiology, 33*, 171-176.

Szögy, A., Böhmer, D., Ambrus, P., & Brune, S. (1984). Zur Bestimmung der anaeroben Kapazität bei Radrennfahrern [Anaerobic capacity in cyclists]. *Deutsche Zeitschrift für Sportmedizin, 35*, 153-160.

Postcompetition Blood Lactate Measurements and Swimming Performance: Illustrated by Data From a 400-m Olympic Record Holder

Jean-Claude Chatard
Michel Paulin
Jean-Rene Lacour

One of the most important problems in swimming competition is to know whether the swimmers' efforts are maximal or not, essential information for coaches and swimmers. To answer this question in other sports, one measure utilized has been the postcompetition blood lactate concentration (L). Keul, Kindermann, and Simon (1978) showed that in running, a maximal exercise was characterized by an L higher than 20 mM. Swimming is a rather different sport because it concerns a larger muscle mass. Specific references to swimming are thus needed to establish the relationship between L and performance level. Sawka, Knowlton, Miles, and Critz (1979) began to investigate L in freestyle swims over distances of 50 to 1,000 yd and in the 200-yd individual medley, butterfly, breast-, and backstrokes. The aim of the present study was to systematically document the maximal concentration of blood lactate (L max) measured at the end of competitions over 50 to 1,500 m in all the strokes. Among the same swimmers, some comparisons were made between different distances and strokes in order to investigate the possible effects of motivation and specific training programs. The L results measured on Thomas Fahrner (TF) during the 1983-84 Olympic season were used as an individual illustration of the general trends derived from these data.

Subjects and Methods

A total of 766 measurements were performed on 134 (51 female and 83 male) competitive swimmers from March 1983 to March 1986. These swimmers were between 12 and 32 years old. Among them 44 (37 male and 7 female) swam at a regional level, 59 (26 male and 33 female) at a national level, and 31 (20 male and 11 female) at an international level of competition.

Two blood samples were taken at the finger extremity after the 1st and 3rd minutes following the competition. Lactate concentrations were measured by the elctroenzymatic method (Racine, Kleuk & Kochsieck, 1975) with a lactate analyzer LA 640 (Roche Bioelectronique Kontron) using the method of Geyssant, Dormois, Barthèlemy, and Lacour (1985). This technique uses microsamples (20 μl) that can be stored for at least 2 weeks at room temperature before measuring without affecting the results. Out of these two samples, the highest measured concentration was considered L max.

The results presented take into account only the best performances and the associated L max of each swimmer. However, the best performance frequency in conjunction with L max was sought. The influence of L max and age on the performance level was determined for the 100-m freestyle swim because of the large number (60) of swimmers. Among the swimmers who competed in several swims during the same month, the highest L max values were then compared.

Results

Overall Results

The mean L max and mean times of performance are summarized in Figure 1 and Table 1. The highest L maxes were observed in the 400-m individual medley event, the lowest in the 50-, 800-, and 1,500-m freestyle events. The 200-m swims induced consistently higher L max than 100-m swims. The differences were not consistent between the 200-m and the 400-m swims the L max values measured among 60 (26 female and 34 male) swimmers in the 100-m freestyle event were related to performance ($r = .45$) and to age ($r = .59$). Performance and age were also related ($r = .63$).

Intraindividual Performance L max Relationships

Among the swimmers whose L max was measured at least 5 times in 3 years, the highest L max occurred with the best performance in 42 out

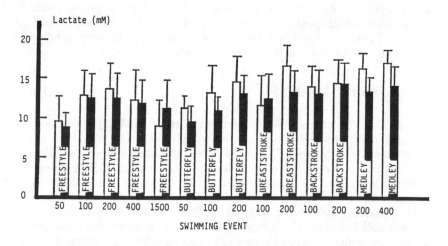

Figure 1   Mean L max for competitive swimming events.

Table 1 Means (M), Standard Deviations (SD) and Extreme Values (EV) of the Swimmers' Performances (min and s)

Event[a]	M	SD	EV	n
50-m freestyle	26.7	1.9	24.5–30.1	6
	29.6	1.7	27.1–32.2	7
100-m freestyle	58.4	5.4	1:10.0–50.1	34
	1:02.8	3.6	1:10.9–56.6	26
200-m freestyle	2:07.9	11.6	2:30.7–1:48.4	30
	2:17.1	11.0	2:37.1–2:04.3	15
400-m freestyle	4:27.6	27.1	5:30.5–3:48.4	20
	4:34.4	8.2	4:46.2–4:22.5	12
1,500-m freestyle[b]	17:48.3	1:33.2	21:17.2–15:26.7	25
800-m freestyle[c]	9:36.5	31.1	8.45–10:14.8	11
50-m butterfly	28.7	2.6	31.9–25.7	4
	32.0	1.0	33.1–31.3	4
100-m butterfly	1:07.2	9.3	1:20.3–56.3	14
	1.11.8	4.5	1:20.5–1:05.9	9
200-m butterfly	2:18.3	11.0	2:39.0–2:05.5	12
	2:30.8	11.1	2:54.6–2:20.5	7
100-m backstroke	1:10.2	8.2	1:24.0–58.4	19
	1:18.5	6.1	1:21.9–1:06.6	10
200-m backstroke	2:20.5	17.3	2:50.2–2:02	13
	2:24.0	9.5	2:34.0–2:15.5	3
100-m breaststroke	1:14.8	6.7	1:25.2–1:04.4	14
	1:21.0	6.8	1:31.0–1:10.3	7
200-m breaststroke	2:36.3	14.3	2:57.0–2:13.1	12
	2:53.5	6.0	2:58.0–2:44.9	4
200-m medley	2:16.7	12.5	2:34.4–2:06.0	9
	2:34.3	7.0	2:45.0–2:27.9	5
400-m medley	4:46.7	5.4	4:52.7–4:36.5	7
	5:18.3	14.8	5:37.0–5:03.8	6

[a]First values are for male swimmers, Second values are for female swimmers; [b]male swimmer only; [c]female swimmer only.

of 50 swims (84%). Among others, this occurred in only 63 out of 92 swims (68%). The highest L max values were obtained most frequently in the 400-m individual medley, 8 times out of 9, when compared to the 200-m individual medley and 11 times out of 11 when compared to the 400-m freestyle. This frequency was 14 out of 17 when comparing the 400-m freestyle to the 100-m freestyle event. But it occurred only 15 times out of 25 when comparing the 400-m freestyle to the 200-m freestyle event. The L max level of 13 swimmers who competed 5 times or more in a 1-month period, were compared in two distance swims, the 100-versus 200-m or 200- versus 400-m. In 12 out of 13 swimmers L max was consistently higher in one event as contrasted to the other. In 62 swimmers studied during a month period in two different events, 16 swimmers had their best L max in the event of the shortest distance. According to international notation, the performances were better (690 ± 110 points versus

630 ± 110 points) 15 times out of 16. The morning trials and afternoon finals were studied on 42 swimmers in 96 swims. During 72 swims (23 swimmers) the best performances were associated with the highest L max. On the other hand, 24 times (19 swimmers) in the afternoon the better performances occured with a lower L max.

Results for TF

The TF L max results are summarized in Table 2. In the winter of 1983-84 the highest L max was measured in the 400-m (17.6 mM), although the highest value in the 200-m event was very close (17.3 mM). On the contrary, in the 100-m event the L max was the lowest value (12.8 mM). In the 400-m event, the best performance was associated with the highest L max but not in the 200-m event. The highest L maxes were measured with the highest levels of motivation (in the qualifying trials of the 200-m European championship and in the 400-m challenge swim against Vladimar Salnikov, the world record holder). In the spring of 1984 L max for all three distances were on the average lower than those obtained during the winter (15.4 ± 2 vs 13.4 ± 1.1 mM).

Discussion

The relationship between the highest L max and the best peformance is one of the main features of this study. The significance is that when a swimmer completes a performance, best or not, associated with an L max lower than usual he or she can expect a better performance later. This better performance will be associated with a better L max, or even a higher value. However, these results should be viewed with caution when consideration is given to the differences between the morning and afternoon L max. The circadian rhythms (Winget, De Moshia, & Holley,

Table 2   Performances and the Corresponding L max of Thomas Fahrner During the 1983-84 Season

Distance	December	February	March	June	Olympic Games
100-m	—	:51	—	:52	—
L max	—	12.8	—	12	—
200-m	1:48.8	1:48.4	1:52.1	1:50.5	1:49.6
L max	17.3	15	13.1	14.8	?
400-m	3:54.3	3:48.4	3:55.7	3:52.8	3:50.8
L max	14.4	17.6	13.1	14.2	?

Note. Times given in minutes and seconds, L max in mM. Winter swims were done in a 25-m pool and spring swims in a 50-m pool.

1985) may explain why best performances are sometimes associated with lower L max. Some L variations could be related to eating or to preceding exercises (Karlsson & Jacobs, 1982). The values of L max, in relation to the distance swam, agree with the results of Sawka et al. (1979). But these authors did not study the 400-m individual medley. In the present study both the 400-m and 200-m distances induced the highest values.

The second main finding in this study was that, whatever the distance, the highest lactate was associated with the specialized distance of the swimmer. In the 100-m swims the higher values of L max might be related to genetical predisposition. Costill (1978) showed that sprint swimmers have 60 to 65% fast-twitch fibers. They can thus produce more lactate. In the 1,500-m swim the training alone is responsible for this phenomenon. TF's example illustrates this point of view. In March 1986, in the 100-yd event, a 17.2 mM L max was measured, although he had never before exceeded 13 mM. TF had never practiced muscular weight training before 1984, whereas since 1984 this type of training has formed a large part of his preparation. On the other hand, in the 500 yd event L max is only 14.9 mM. All these facts are in agreement with his training, which has been less intensive in the longer distances. This is consistent with Houston, Wilson, Green, Thomson, and Ranney (1981) who showed that a highly intensive training program increases the L max values and performances more than a moderate training program.

In summary, the postcompetition measurements of L max allow one to determine if the exercise was maximal, in order to supplement the somewhat subjective feelings of the swimmers. Also, they allow one to determine the distances and the strokes for which the swimmers have concentrated their training or for which they may be better suited.

References

Costill, D.L. (1978). Adaptations in skeletal muscle during training for sprint and endurance swimming. In B. Eriksson & B. Furberg (Eds.), *Swimming medicine IV* (pp. 233-248). Baltimore: University Park Press.

Geyssant, A., Dormois, D., Barthèlemy, J.C., & Lacour, J.R. (1985). Lactate tate determination with the lactate analyser LA 640: A critical study. *Scandinavian Journal of Clinical Laboratory Investigations, 45,* 145-149.

Houston, M.E., Wilson, D.M., Green, H.J., Thomson, J.A., & Ranney, D.A. (1981). Physiological and muscle enzyme adaptations to two different intensities of swim training. *European Journal of Applied Physiology, 46,* 283-291.

Karlsson, J., & Jacobs, I. (1982). Onset of blood lactate accumulation during muscular exercise as a threshold concept. *International Journal of Sports Medicine, 3,* 190-201.

Keul, J., Kindermann, W., & Simon, G. (1978). La transition aérobie-anaérobie lors de la pratique de certains sports. In J.R. Lacour (Ed.), *Energétique et sports de compétition* (pp. 37-67). 42100 Saint-Etienne-France.

Racine, P., Kleuk, H., & Kochsieck, K. (1975). Rapid lactate determination with an eletrochemical enzymatic sensor: Clinical usability and comparative measurements. *Journal of Clinical Chemistry and Clinical Biochemistry*, **13**, 533-539.

Sawka, M.N., Knowlton, R.G., Miles, D.S., & Critz, J.B. (1979). Post competition blood lactate concentrations in collegiate swimmers. *European Journal of Applied Physiology*, **41**, 93-99.

Winget, C., De Moshia, C., & Holley, D.C. (1985). Circadian rhythms and athletic performance. *Medicine and Science in Sports and Exercise*, **17**, 498-516.

PART VII

MEDICAL ASPECTS

The Activity of Trunk Muscles in Paraplegic Patients After Breaststroke Initiation

Brigitte De Witte
Rita Loyens
René Robeaux
Jan P. Clarys

Sport activities permit paraplegics to maintain the physical efficiency level that was obtained during medical rehabilitation, and they are the best way to improve efficiency because they allow a proper effort dosage (Pachalski & Mekarski, 1980). Swimming for the physically handicapped creates some problems, because differences in physical abilities depend upon individual handicaps, but swimming is an activity that lends itself to the disabled (Guttman, 1965; Trussell, 1971). Earlier research (Duffield, 1973; Nicol, Schmidt-Hansberg, & McMillan, 1979; Paeth, 1984; Vis, 1971, 1975) showed the positive therapeutical effects for the handicapped of training in water.

In the evolution of teaching swimming techniques, consideration must be given to the various needs and abilities of the handicapped so that they can control the movement of the asymmetrical body shapes (e.g., the Halliwick method). In this regard, no two individuals are alike. Many studies have been undertaken to gather information or to explain the teaching techniques in swimming with the handicapped. Persyn, Surmont, Wouters, and De Mayer (1975) stated that the individual solution for adequate movement in water is as variable as the possible differences in handicaps; therefore, it is difficult to develop norms.

Some researchers recommend the use of a specific swimming technique for supporting or strengthening certain muscle groups. Very few of these recommendations are based on scientific experiences (Duffield, 1973; Lorenzen, 1970; Vis, 1971). Besides this, the experimental investigations on the function of muscles during swimming, especially the breaststroke, are limited to the able-bodied. Electromyography (EMG) of the breaststroke has been studied by Ikai, Ishii, and Miyashita (1964, 14 muscles); Lewillie (1971, 3 muscles; 1974; 2 muscles); Tokuyama, Okamoto, and Kumamoto (1976, 14 muscles); Yoshizawa, Tokuyama, Okamoto, and Kumamoto (1976, 16 muscles); and by Yoshizawa, Okamoto, Kumamoto, Tokuyama, and Oka (1978; 16 muscles). Maes, Clarys, and Brouwer (1975) related the EMG results of five muscles during the breaststroke to the ''normal'' and disabled swimmer. Persyn et al. (1975) concluded that the physically handicapped swimmer at the "Special Olympic" level often fails to receive adequate training from swimming experts. Considering the poor swimming technique among the best swimmers, the situation is probably much worse for the remaining handicapped persons. In order to set up a basic teaching program on swimming technique for paraplegics, instruction in the breaststroke was initiated for 4 patients with different levels of spinal cord injury. Based on the literature that the breaststroke is an effective way to develop back and shoulder muscles and the importance of these muscle groups for the paraplegic's general efficiency exercises, the participation level of trunk muscles during breaststroke was studied using telemetric EMG in the second phase of this study.

Methods and Procedures

The subjects were paraplegic patients (3 males and 1 female) with different handicaps: (a) 1 patient had a seventh thoracic vertebra level of spinal cord injury (T7) with spasticity and abdominal muscle strains and had never swum at all; (b) the 2nd paraplegic with poor spasticity and a tenth thoracic vertebra level of injury (T10) did not swim after his accident; (c) the 3rd subject with flaccid paralysis and a first lumbar vertebra level of injury (L1) had swum two times since his handicap; (d) the last female patient with a first sacral vertebra level of injury (S1) and flaccid paralysis had not swum since her accident, either. Moreover, the last 3 subjects were poor swimmers before their accident, which explained a certain lack of interest in swimming. All of them had achieved a satisfactory condition during the last stage of the rehabilitation and had good control of the bladder/bowel functions.

In the first phase, an initial program based on the literature was used. The method utilized incorporated the following principles: (a) mental and physical adjustments in water, according to Hirst and Müchaelis (1972) and Nicol et al. (1979); (b) floating without any artifical appliance, as suggested by Lorenzen (1970), Paeth (1984), and Bleasdale (1975); and (c) propulsion, as described by Lorenzen and by Bleasdale. The first principle included an appreciation of the differencs in the elements—land versus water—and the encouragement to use any newly developed ability without mental or physical assistance. The ability to maintain a posture in water— and the skill to regain a balanced position from the supine float to the downwards float by use of the arms was taught as the next step of the initial phase of the program. In the propulsion phase, the backstroke, i.e., the back crawl, was proposed as the most efficient stroke for these handicapped individuals. As an early exercise, the subject was taught to do double-arm overhead movements before starting the alternating arm movements. Once this technique was successful, they were considered able to be taught the breaststroke according to their individual handicaps and without any appliance.

For the EMG study during the breaststroke, a telemetric recording system with transmitter and receiver was used. The electrical activities of three trunk muscles were recorded on a two-channel UHER recorder

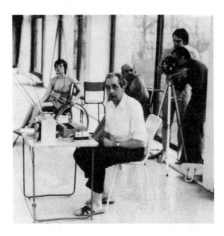

Figure 1   Test setup for the telemetric EMG (receiver, recorder, and 16-mm camera).

and transferred to a minograph 81 (Elema-Schönander, Sweden) ink-writer. This test apparatus and its different characteristics have been described previously by Lewillie (1968, 1973) and improved by Clarys, Jiskoot, and Lewillie (1973) and Clarys, Massez, Van Den Broeck, Piette, & Robeaux (1983). The electromogyrams and breaststroke movements were synchronized with a 16-mm cinematography, by means of voltmeters and a flashing light placed in the visual field of the camera and connected to the magnetic tape recorder (Figure 1). Each flash of the light created a signal mark on the EMG recordings. A supplementary output on the amplifier provided the connection for the voltmeters. This technique permitted the muscle participation to be defined exactly within the total breaststroke movement.

The following muscles were selected according to the criteria used in the Brussels EMG and swimming project described by Maes et al. (1975): the trapezius, latissimus dorsi, and rectus abdominis. The trapezius was used as the control muscle. The electrodes were little rasps, 5 × 5 mm. The reference electrode (ground) was larger and was fixed on the sternal manubrium. The subjects swam 15-m widths at arbitrarily 75% of their maxium efforts.

One of the problems in data recording was the inability to measure the maximal voluntary contraction (MVC) of each muscle tested in these paraplegics sitting in a wheelchair. The basic concept of measuring MVC in the field is to express the activity in percentages of maxium. Besides, this method allows for quantification of results and effective comparison of the recordings from different subjects and from different muscles. For the comparison of quantitative data in this study, all dynamic contraction values were expressed as a percentage of the highest amplitude of the individual control muscle (Winter, Rau, Kadefors, Broman, & Luca, 1980) (i.e., low, average, and high muscular activity). Analysis of the EMG patterns in relation to the movement patterns and to the time of one complete arm cycle were made and were compared with data of able-bodied individuals from Ikai et al. (1964), Tokuyama et al. (1976), and Yoshizawa et al. (1976).

Results and Discussion

After the breaststroke initiation, all 4 paraplegic patients could swim without any appliances or assistance. In the water, the subjects experienced that their limbs were lighter. Taking into account their lower limbs were in a passive capacity, they had difficulty in learning active floating or the "arrow" made by the hands in different positions. Compared with the breaststroke, the backstroke with a double-arm overhead movement was the most efficient stroke, considering the better movement and breathing purposes. When arms circled alternately, the tendency to roll the body along its longitudinal axis became more pronounced the higher the level of spinal cord injury. This confirmed the observations of Paeth (1984) and Bleasdale (1975). During the breaststroke, the same tendency was observed for the swimmer with the highest level of spinal cord lesion. Therefore, he was asked to keep looking forward and to minimize head movement.

At the beginning of the breaststroke instruction, all 4 paraplegics tended to place the head in a submerged position in the water. The subject with the lowest level of injury (i.e., S1), solved the problem by contracting the back muscles. In the course of time, this paraplegic felt more comfortable with the breaststroke than with the backstroke. The EMG patterns confirmed that all 4 paraplegics could swim the breaststroke correctly with the arms alone. However, compared with the able-bodied, an irregularity of the arm trajectory was present. Thereby, the movements of the arms were less complete. We believe, according to Persyn et al. (1975), that if one has an efficient movement of the upper extremities, then the flexibility and shape (streamline) of the lower extremities are more important than their strength. One major difference was found from the cinematographical analyses of the paraplegic swimmers. During the breaststroke, the recovery phase was missing or was less pronounced. As indicated by Guttmann (1965) and Trussel (1971), we also found that the higher the level of spinal cord injury was, the more difficult were the swimming movements. Because the subject with the highest level of spinal cord injury (i.e., T7) and with the most severe spasticity could not remain in a prone position, the sinking of the lower limbs caused a break in the streamlined features of the body. This position could be corrected by modifying the arm movements. To our astonishment, the paraplegic with the T10 injury began to swim even before a state of equilibrum of the body in water was taught. For the one with the L1 lesion and who swam two times since his accident, the first two points of the initial program could have been omitted. After the teaching program, he decided in favor of the breaststroke because it afforded him a better view over the pool.

When swimming in water of 31 °C, none of the 4 paraplegics experienced difficulty with muscle spasms. This confirmed the assumptions of Paeth (1984). But because of this water temperature, they had to put up with the inconvenience of greater fatigue, as compared with the EMG patterns in water temperature of 28 °C.

As for Subject 1 with the highest level (T7) of spinal cord injury, the EMG patterns of the trapezius and latissimus dorsi showed important irregularities (Figure 2). In addition, these patterns were not reproducible. It was observed that this subject swam with very irregular arm movements. The results revealed that the musclar activities of trapezius were

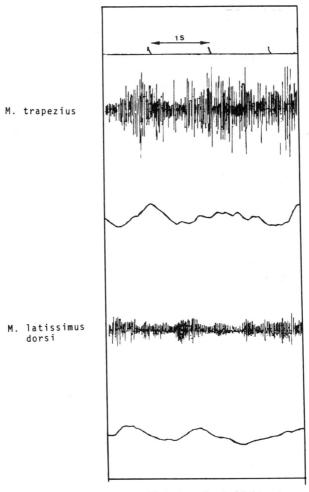

Figure 2   EMG pattern of the trapezius and latissimus dorsi of Subject 1, a paraplegic with a T7 level of spinal cord injury.

more important but also more irregular than the latissimus dorsi. As the duration and form of contractions of both muscles were very variable, the comparison with the results of Ikai et al. (1964) remained impossible. By comparing the EMG patterns of the rectus abdominis with the trapezius, very poor discharges of the rectus abdominis were found. Referring to Tokuyama et al. (1976) and Yoshizawa et al. (1976), the disappearance of activity of the rectus abdominis indicated that the pelvis was not well stabilized. This might explain the difficulties the subject experienced in keeping his body parallel to the water surface. Again remarkable irregularities were observed in the entire EMG pattern of the recuts abdominis. In able-bodied swimmers who use their legs as well, the peak patterns of the rectus abdominis and trapezius were similar, whereas in this case they were very rare or nonexistent.

The 2nd patient (i.e., paraplegic with T10 level of injury) showed more regular activites for the trapezius and latassimus dorsi muscles. The patterns were reproducible. The EMG diagrams also confirmed that this patient swam with more regular arm movements as compared to Subject 1. As for the trapezius, the start and end of contraction were very visible (Figure 3, B to E). In addition, regular frequencies were found. The latissimus dorsi contraction was very similar to the control muscle for the whole duration of the EMG pattern, including the frequencies and amplitudes (Figure 3). Although there were clear similarities between the peak patterns of the trapezius and latissimus dorsi in this paraplegic, these results, however, were in contrast with the able-bodied swimmers, because the peaks of the trapezius did not coincide with those of the latissimus dorsi in the study of Ikai et al. (1964). For the EMG patterns of the trapezius and rectus abdominis, the amplitude and frequency of contraction were more regular than those of the 1st subject. Compared with the control muscle, the rectus abdominis worked in a smaller degree, but regular contractions with peaks were clear (Figure 4). The durations of contractions of the rectus abdominis were also shorter and started later than the control muscle. A relation between the peak patterns of both muscles could be demonstrated in this case; therefore, this finding was similar to the results described by Ikai et al. (1964).

In Subject 3 (L1) the discharges of the trapezius were more regular in comparison with those of the 1st subject, though they showed more irregularities than those of the 2nd one. In the contraction patterns, peaks were unclear, and besides additional discharges between two contractions were observed (Figure 5A). An irregular frequency pattern was seen for the latissimus dorsi, whereas for the control muscle the irregularities were more pronounced in the amplitudes of the contractions (Figure 5 A and B). Both muscles, but especially the latissimus dorsi, showed a double-peaked EMG pattern. As for the EMG activity of the latissimus dorsi during the whole duration of contraction, similarities with the trapezius were difficult to demonstrate. During some cycles of the swimming movements, additional discharges of the latissimus dorsi were found, resulting in a four-contraction peak pattern of the latissimus dorsi with a two-contraction peak pattern of the control muscle (Figure 5A). Moreover, the contraction peaks of the latissimus dorsi occurred between

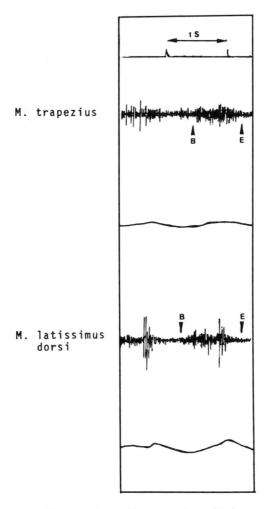

Figure 3   EMG pattern of the trapezius and latissimus dorsi of Subject 2, a paraplegic with a T10 level of spinal cord injury. B = beginning of contraction; E = end of contraction.

two contraction peaks, coinciding as well with one contraction peak of the trapezius. In this regard, the EMG patterns of both muscles showed differences with the results of the able-bodied swimmers. Important irregular discharges (i.e., frequency and amplitude) in the EMG pattern of the rectus abdominis were observed, compared with the second patient studied. But referring to the first paraplegic, less irregularity was found, especially in the frequency patterns. In comparison with the trapezius, the discharges of the rectus abdominis were very poor, including unclear contraction peaks. Besides, very few of these peaks coincided with those of the control muscle. The similarities with the results of Ikai et al. (1964) thus were difficult to demonstrate.

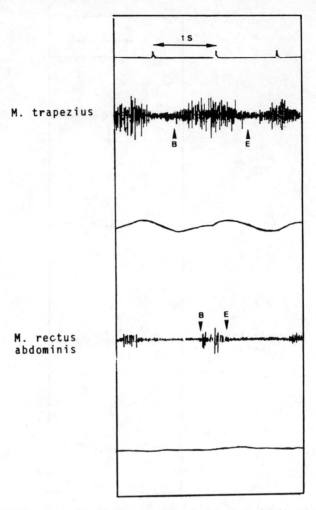

Figure 4 EMG pattern of the trapezius and rectus abdominis of Subject 2, a paraplegic with a T10 level of spinal cord injury. B = beginning of contraction; E = end of contraction.

The last subject (S1 injury) demonstrated important activities and remarkable regularities (i.e, frequency, amplitude, and duration of contraction) in the EMG pattern of the trapezius (Figure 6 A and B). The whole duration of contration was clear; however, additional discharges were found. The activites of the latissimus dorsi were less regular and had smaller durations of contraction in comparison with the control muscle (Figure 6B). The contractions of the latissimus dorsi that coincided with those of the trapezius had a smaller amplitude (Figure 6 A and B). In regards to the EMG patterns of both muscles that confirmed the regular arm movements and took into account that more muscles could partici-

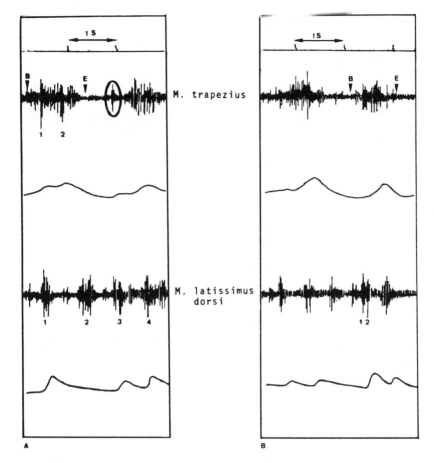

Figure 5   EMG pattern of the trapezius and latissimus dorsi of Subject 3, a paraplegic with an L1 level of spinal cord injury. B = beginning of contraction; E = end of contraction).

pate during swimming movements, there was a strong tendency for these results to duplicate those of normal swimmers. Comparing two contractions of the control muscle, discharges between them were also found in the EMG pattern of the latissimus dorsi (Figure 6 A and B). These additional activities for both muscles were also observed by Ikai et al. (1964). As for the rectus abdominis, the contractions were irregular, as well as the frequency and the amplitude (Figure 7). Compared with the control muscle, the rectus abdominis worked to a much lesser degree. More additional contractions were observed in comparison with the trapezius and the latissimus dorsi. Again, the similarities with the EMG diagrams of the trapezius and rectus abdominis as described by Ikai et al. (1964) were very poor.

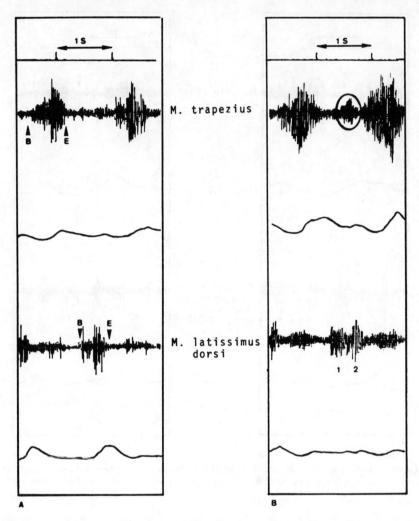

Figure 6   EMG pattern of the trapezius and latissimus dorsi of Subject 4, a paraplegic with an S1 level of spinal cord injury. B = beginning of contraction; E = end of contraction.

Conclusions

The assumptions of Trussell (1971) and Bleasdale (1975) that the paraplegic will be able to swim prone or supine were confirmed, because of all four patients could swim the backstroke and the breaststroke as well. However, after the initial breaststroke instruction, we believe that the position of the body in the water was affected by the level of spinal cord injury on the one hand and by the occurrence of muscle spasms on the other hand. The EMG patterns also confirmed differences and irregularities in the arm trajectory in comparison with the normal swimmers.

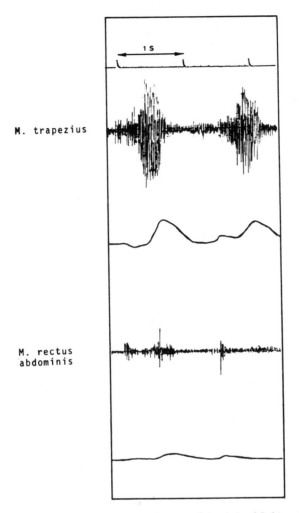

Figure 7 EMG pattern of the trapezius and rectus abdominis of Subject 4, a paraplegic with an S1 level of spinal cord injury.

As for the EMG activities of the trapezius and latissimus dorsi as described by Ikai et al. (1964), the most similar patterns were observed in the patient with the lowest level of spinal cord injury. For the trapezius and recuts abdominis, similarity between able-bodied swimmers and these paraplegics during the breaststroke was poor, because the same relationship between contraction peaks was only found in one subject, whereas the EMG patterns remained irregular in the 3 other patients. In accordance to Tokuyama et al. (1976) and Yoshizawa et al. (1976), who also reported little activity of the rectus abdominis during the breaststroke in unskilled swimmers, these results support the idea that the pelvis was not well stabilized in these paraplegics. Despite the limitations in this study with paraplegics, the assumption can be made that the higher the level of spinal cord injury is, the more difficult the breaststroke becomes, and also that the general EMG patterns of the muscles studied are influenced by the proficiency of the breaststroke technique.

References

Bleasdale, N. (1975). Swimming and the paraplegic. *Paraplegia, 13,* 124-127.

Clarys, J.P., Jiskoot, J., & Lewillie, L. (1973). A kinematographical, electro-myographical and resistance study of water polo and competition front crawl. In S. Cerquiglini, A. Venerando, & J. Wartenweiler (Eds.), *Biomechanics III* (pp. 446-452). Basel: Karger Verlag.

Clarys, J.P., Massez, C., Van Den Broeck, M., Piette, G., & Robeaux, R. (1983). Total telemetric EMG of the front crawl. In H. Matsui & K. Kobayashi (Eds.), *Biomechanics VIII-B* (pp. 951-957). Champaign, IL: Human Kinetics.

Duffield, M.H. (Ed.). (1973). *Exercise in water.* London: Baillière, Tindall and Cassell.

Guttman, S.L. (1965). Reflections on sport for the physcially handicapped. *Physiotherapy, 51,* 252-253.

Hirst, C., & Müchaelis, E. (Eds.). (1972). *Development activites for children in special education.* Columbus, OH: C.E. Merrill.

Ikai, M., Ishii, K., & Miyashita, M. (1964). An electromyographical study of swimming. *Research Journal of Physical Education, 7,* 47-54.

Lewillie, L. (1968). Telemetrical analysis of the electromyograph. In J. Wartenweiler, E. Jokl, & M. Hebbelinck (Eds.), *Biomechanics I* (pp. 147-149). Basel: Karger Verlag.

Lewillie, L. (1971). Quantitative comparison of the electromyograph of the swimmer. In L. Lewillie & J.P. Clarys (Eds.), *Swimming I* (pp. 155-159). Brussels: Université Libre de Bruxelles.

Lewillie, L. (1973). Muscular activity in swimming. In S. Cerquiglini, A. Venerando, & J. Wartenweiler (Eds.), *Biomechanics III* (pp. 440-445). Basel: Karger Verlag.

Lewillie, L. (1974). Telemetry of electromyographic and electrogoniometric signals in swimming. In R.C. Nelson & C.A. Morehouse (Eds.), *Biomechanics IV* (pp. 203-207). Baltimore: University Park Press.

Lorenzen, H. (1970). *Behinderte Schwimmen* [Handicapped swimming]. Wuppertal: H. Putty Verlag.

Maes, L., Clarys, J.P., & Brouwer, P.J. (1975). Electromyography for the evaluation of handicapped swimmers. In J.P. Clarys & L. Lewillie (Eds.), *Swimming II* (pp. 268-275). Baltimore: University Park Press.

Nicol, K., Schmidt-Hansberg, H., & McMillan, J. (1979). Biomechanical principles applied to the Halliwick method of teaching swimming to phyoically handicapped individuals. In J. Terauds & E.W. Bedingfield (Eds.), *Swimming III* (pp. 173-181). Baltimore: University Park Press.

Paeth, B. (1984). Schwimmtherapie 'Halliwick-Methode' nach James McMillan bei erwachsenen Patienten mit neurologischen Erkrankungen [The Halliwick method of swimming therapy, according to James McMillan, in adult patients with neurological diseases]. *Krankengymnastik, 36*, 100-112.

Pachalski, A., & Mekarski, T. (1980). Effect of swimming on increasing of cardiorespiratory capacity in paraplegics. *Paraplegia, 18*, 190-196.

Persyn, U., Surmont, E., Wouters, L., & De Mayer, J. (1975). Analysis of techniques used by swimmers in the Para-Olympic Games. In J.P. Clarys & L. Lewillie (Eds.), *Swimming II* (pp. 276-281). Baltimore: University Park Press.

Tokuyama, H., Okamoto, T., & Kumamoto, M. (1976). Electromyographic study of swimming in infants and children. In P.V. Komi (Ed.), *Biomechanics V-B* (pp. 215-221). Baltimore: University Park Press.

Trussell, E.C. (1971). *Guidelines for teaching the disabled to swim*. Dudley: Netherton Printers.

Vis, W.P.M. (1975). Special swimming instruction for multiple handicapped. In J.P. Clarys & L. Lewillie (Eds.), *Swimming II* (pp. 263-267). Baltimore: Univeristy Park Press.

Vis, W.P.M. (1971). *Zwemmen als therapie* [Swimming as therapy]. Rotterdam: Leminscaat.

Winter, D.A., Rau, G., Kadefors, R., Broman, H., & Luca, C.J. de (1980). *Units, terms and standards in reporting of EMG research* (Report by the Ad-Hoc Committee of the International Society of Electrophysiological Kinesiology) Waterloo, Canada: ISEK Publication.

Yoshizawa, M., Okamoto, T., Kumamoto, M., Tokuyama, H., & Oka, H. (1978). Electromyographic study of two styles in breaststroke as performed by top swimmers. In E. Asmussen & K. Jorgensen (Eds.), *Biomechanics VI-B* (pp. 126-131). Baltimore: University Park Press.

Yoshizawa, M., Tokuyama, H., Okamoto, T., & Kumamoto, M. (1976). Electromyographic study of the breaststroke. In P.V. Komi (Ed.), *Biomechanics V-B* (pp. 222-229). Baltimore: University Park Press.

Chronic Injuries of Elite Competitive Swimmers, Divers, Water Polo Players, and Synchronized Swimmers

Yoshiteru Mutoh
Miwako Takamoto
Mitsumasa Miyashita

The recent reduction in swimming times and the improvements in swimming performances have paralleled better training techniques, more accessible swimming facilities, and the increase in swimming coaches. Regular specialized training begins at young ages and continues throughout the entire period of growth of aquatic sport athletes. These advances have led to an increased chronic strain on the elite athlete's musculoskeletal system, which has in turn led to an increase in the incidence of chronic injuries. Literature concerning the chronic injuries of competitive swimmers, such as swimmer's shoulder and/or breaststroker's knee have been cited (Kennedy, Hawkins, & Krissoff, 1978); however, few reports on chronic injuries of divers, water polo players, and synchronized swimmers are available.

This study was designed to determine the incidence and the pattern of chronic injuries among elite comptitive aquatic athletes.

Methods

The subjects consisted of 66 Japanese elite aquatic athletes: 19 competitive swimmers, 10 divers, 13 water polo players who participated in the Universiade Games in Kobe in 1985, and 24 national-caliber synchronized swimmers including 8 members of the 1985 national championship team. All subjects completed a questionnaire including questions concerning their training periods and experiences with chronic injuries. Competitive swimmers, divers, and water polo players were administered the questionnaire during the Universiade Games, and the synchronized swimmers completed the questionnaire during a midseason physical and medical examination.

Results

Table 1 shows the sex, age, and years of specialized training for each group of subjects. All athletes clearly were capable of participating in international compeitition and had completed at least 8 years of specialized training. Injuries totalled 125: competitive swimmers, 37 injuries; divers, 30 injuries; water polo players, 27 injuries; and synchronized swimmers, 31 injuries. All the competitive swimmers and divers, 92% of the water polo players, and 79% of the synchronized swimmers—averaging 91% of all the athletes—indicated they had experienced chronic injuries (Table 2). The incidence of chronic injuries was surprisingly high for 60% of all subjects who responded had chronic injuries at the time. Many of these athletes competed while suffering some type of injury. An average of 85% of those who experienced chronic injuries were receiving medical treatment. This indicated that the chronic injuries experienced were serious enough that the athletes had to obtain medical attention and advice from physicians.

Frequency by site of the chronic injury among the competitive swimmers was as follows: low back (37.1%), shoulder (31.4%), knee (20.0%), and ankle (5.7%). Among the divers, the injuries of the low back (27.6%), wrist (24.1%), shoulder (20.7%), and neck (10.3%) accounted for over 80% of the total injuries. The water polo players had 37.0% low back, 25.9%

Table 1   Age, Sex, and Year of Training of Subjects

Event	Male	Female	Total	Age (years)	Years trained
Competitive swimming	9	10	19	19.6 ± 1.5[a]	8.5 ± 2.6
Diving	5	5	10	20.0 ± 1.2	8.0 ± 3.1
Water polo	13	—	13	22.3 ± 2.0	8.5 ± 1.5
Synchronized swimming	—	24	24	17.9 ± 2.1	7.9 ± 2.1

[a]Average ± SD

Table 2   Experience and Treatment of Chronic Injuries

Event	Experienced previously	Experiencing during study	Medical treatment
Competitive swimming	19/19 (100%)	11/19 (57.9%)	16/19 (84.2%)
Diving	10/10 (100%)	9/10 (90%)	10/10 (100%)
Water polo	12/13 (92.3%)	11/13 (84.6%)	11/12 (92.3%)
Synchronized swimming	10/24 (79.2%)	8/24 (33.3%)	14/19 (73.7%)
Total	60/66 (90.9%)	39/66 (59.7%)	51/60 (85%)

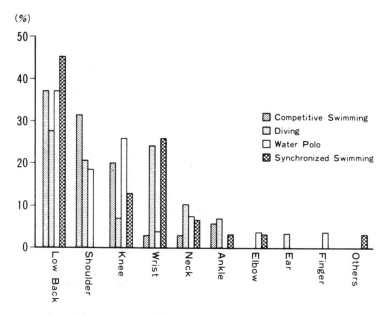

Figure 1 The incidence by site of the chronic injury among the competitive swimmers, divers, water polo players, and synchronized swimmers.

knee, 18.5% shoulder, and 7.4% neck injuries. The majority of injuries of the synchronized swimmers consisted of 45.2% low back, 25.8% wrist, 12.9% knee, and 6.5% neck (see Figure 1).

Low back injuries were the most common among the athletes in the four groups, especially synchronized swimmers. Shoulder injuries were also common among these athletes except for the synchronized swimmers. Knee injuries were more frequently experienced by water polo players and competitive swimmers than by the athletes in the other two categories. Wrist injuries were common, secondary to low back injuries among synchronized swimmers and divers. However, divers were the most susceptible to neck injuries of the four athletic groups. Ankle injuries were seen at the rate of 3 to 7% among the athletes except for water polo players. Elbow injuries accounted for approximately 3% of the injuries of water polo players and synchronized swimmers. Ear and finger injuries were only noted in divers and water polo players, respectively.

Thus, these results indicated that there is a specific site pattern of chronic injuries experienced by elite aquatic athletes in these events.

Discussion

In 1984, synchronized swimming was approved as an official event for the Olympic Games in Los Angeles. Hence, the four events of competitive swimming, diving, water polo, and synchronized swimming are all now included in the Olympic Games. In order to be successful in one of these events, specialized training must be imposed on the growing athlete for a long period of time.

These elite aquatic athletes participating in the present study, for example, completed at least 8 years of specialized training beginning at approximately age 10. Researchers have noted that long-term specialized athletic training leads to repetitive microtrauma to the immature musculoskeletal system, resulting in overuse injuries among young athletes (Kozar & Lord, 1983).

Rovere and Nichols (1985) revealed that there was a significant relationship between frequent knee pain with increasing age and increasing years of competitive swimming. This study showed that approximately 90% of elite aquatic athletes experienced some type of chronic injury, and approximately 60% competed with an injury during mid-season.

A specific injury pattern was apparent to each of the four aquatic events with low back injuries being the most common injury of the elite athlete in each event. Richardson, Jobe, and Collins (1980) referred to shoulder pain as the most common orthopedic problem in competitive swimming, and almost 50% of the swimmers examined by Dominguez (1980) complained of shoulder pain. On the other hand, Mutoh (1983) stated that low back injury comprised 33% of the 51 clinical cases of injuries of Japanese swimmers. The reason why low back injuries were more numerous than shoulder injuries in the present study may be, first of all, that most Japanese swimmers are "kickers," for whom maximal forward thrust comes from the power of the kick rather than the arm pull. Second, dryland training in any of the events, including abdominal muscle strengthening exercises and/or flexibility exercises of the back and lower extremities, are insufficient.

Wrist and neck injuries are characteristic among divers. These injuries might be caused by the repetitive impact upon entry into the water from heights. Among the water polo players, knee injuries due to the frequency of the eggbeater kick and injuries of the upper extremities associated with the throwing action were prevalent. Average release velocity was estimated at nearly 20 m/s; therefore, water polo players undoubtedly subject their shoulder and upper extremities to considerable stress (Whiting, Poffer, Finerman, Griegor, & Malatis 1985). Synchronized swimmers were susceptable to injuries of the wrist and elbow. The forearm is constantly working to perform sculling movements to maintain various body positions. Nagano and Ohata (1983) presented a stress fracture case of the ulna in an elite synchronized swimmer. Repetitive muscle contractions around the elbow and wrist may promote chronic injuries. Thus, the prevention and/or early detection of chronic injuries in elite aquatic sport athletes should be stressed, keeping in mind the specific injuries characteristic to each event.

References

Dominguez, R.H. (1980). Shoulder pain in swimmers. *The Physician and Sportsmedicine*, **8**, 37-48.

Kennedy, J.C., Hawkins, R., & Krissoff, W.B. (1978). Orthopaedic manifestations of swimming. *The American Journal of Sports Medicine,* **6,** 309-322.

Kozar, B., & Lord, R.M. (1983). Overuse injury in the young athlete: Reasons for concern. *The Physician and Sportsmedicine,* **7,** 116-122.

Mutoh, Y. (1983). Mechanism and prevention of swimming injury [in Japanese]. *Japanese Journal of Sports Science,* **2,** 527-544.

Nagano, T., & Ohata, N. (1983). Stress fracture of the ulna in a synchronized swimmer [in Japanese]. *The Journal of Eastern Japanese Society of Sports Medicine,* **4,** 163-166

Richardson, A.B., Jobe, F.W., & Collins, H.R. (1980). The shoulder in competitive swimming. *The American Journal of Sports Medicine,* **8,** 159-163.

Rovere, G.D., & Nichols, A.W. (1985). Frequency, associated factors, and treatment of breaststroker's knee in competitive swimmers. *The American Journal of Sports Medicine,* **13,** 99-104.

Whiting, W.C., Puffer, J.C., Finerman, G.A., Gregor, R.J., & Maletis, G.B. (1985). Three-dimensional cinematographic analysis of water polo throwing in elite performers. *The American Journal of Sports Medicine,* **13,** 95-98.

PART VIII

EVALUATION AND EDUCATION

Computerized Evaluation and Advice in Swimming

Ulrik Persyn
Luc Van Tilborgh
Daniel Daly
Veronique Colman
Dirk J. Vijfvinkel
Dirk Verhetsel

In most Western countries, government support cannot be expected for extensive evaluations of large numbers of elite swimmers in a laboratory. For this reason, research in the Leuven Evaluation Center for Swimmers has been directed toward the development of a user-friendly system, allowing an expert to make rapid diagnoses and to provide advice at poolside. Attention is given to simple observation and measuring instrumentation as well as to personal computer (PC) software. The PC allows hydromechanical, kinanthropometric, physiological, and other data to be used for the evaluation of swimmers and for the education of swimming consultants.

In order to select information relevant to performance, a review was made of effective instruction for correcting the movement and/or improving physical characteristics, and thus resulting in enhanced swimming performances. Diverse categories of relevant information have been collected in the Evaluation Center on 600 elite swimmers (10 to 22 years old) from various countries.

Use of a Diagnosis Profile and a Movement Protocol

The information selected for advice is presented in Figure 1 (for a breaststroke specialist) on a diagnosis profile (A) and a movement protocol (B), containing:

- *Identification*, information is corrected for sex and biological age (estimated from skeletal age (Beunen, 1972). For ethical reasons biological age is not specified.
- *Training background*, in the water and on dry land (collected in a questionnaire).
- *Physical characteristics*, including body build, flexibility, and strength (Vervaecke & Persyn, 1982) along with aerobic and anaerobic capacity (Mader & Hollman, 1978), measured using specific tests.

341

- *Hydrodynamic information*, such as drag, buoyancy, and propulsion (measured on-line with specific instrumentation) (Persyn, 1984; Van Tilborgh, Daly, & Persyn, 1983).
- *Swimming performance*, in the global stroke and in pulling and kicking, collected from federation statistics and with tests (Daly, Van Tilborgh, & Persyn, 1984).
- *Movement parameters*, such as angles of body segments and timing of phases (digitized on film or videotape).

For certain groups and cases, medical (Renson, Lysens, Persyn, & Ostyn, 1982-1983) and psychological (Vanden Auweele, 1982-1983) examinations were also made.

Automation: From Measurement and Observation to Advice and Prediction

The Profile and Movement Protocol

Evaluations may take place in any pool, using mobile test instrumentation, as well as in the laboratory. In the mobile situation, no time-consuming and expensive estimation of the skeletal age and testing of the aerobic and anaerobic capacity, nor medical and psychological examintions, are conducted. However, one should try to obtain this information from local laboratories.

Even in the mobile situation, the diagnosis profile can be ready immediately following the testing, measuring, and videorecording, if the questionnaire concerning training background and swimming performances is available beforehand. The testing of the physical and hydrodynamic characteristics can be made on-line, allowing the results to be sent directly to a PC. Corrections for sex and age and calculations of indices are made automatically (e.g., ht^2/wt ratio; see Figure 1, no. 10), masculinity (no. 11), and endomorphy (no. 12).

The completion of the movement protocol from a videorecording has also been computerized; however, digitizing takes about 15 min per stroke. Both the profile and the protocol can be printed out immediately.

Automated Advice

Even with a clear diagnosis profile and movement protocol, individualized instruction remains complex. Therefore, the advice has been computerized as well: Instructions are displayed in animations and graphs, and a hard copy is made and printed on the profile and the protocol.

The session with swimmer and coach can start 30 min after the testing is completed, and normally it takes 30 min per individual. This allows two strokes to be digitized, as is most frequently requested by the coaches.

For individualized assistance, not only observation and measurement data are required but also some options, which have not been clearly determined by research results, must be taken.

As an example, individual instruction for strength training and technique drills and integrated advice was proposed for the breaststroke swimmer, as seen in Figure 1. The water training program, which was already controlled by coaches, will not be stressed here.

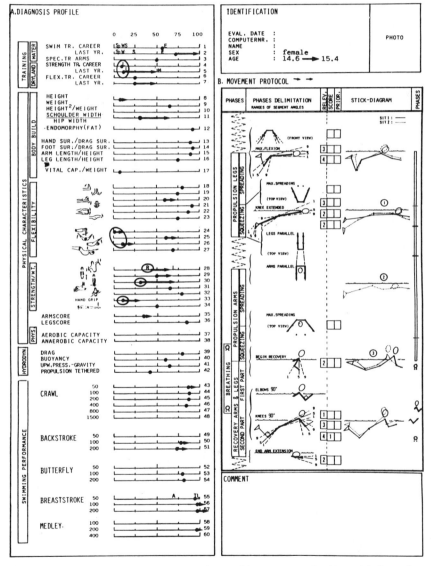

Figure 1 Diagnosis profile and movement protocol for a computerized breaststroke evaluation. A detailed explanation for using the scoring form is available from the author on request.

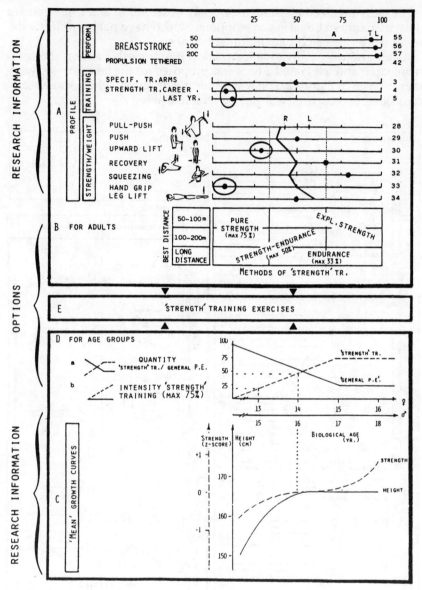

Figure 2 Research information and options used in computerized individual advice for strength training.

Advice for Strength Training

Figure 2 shows some research information and options used to provide appropriate strength training in this swimmer's first evaluation session. The following reasoning is currently being implemented in a PC program.

Research information.   In A, profile information is specified for:

- swimming performances for varying distances (no. 55 to 57)—top performances in 100- and 200-m breaststroke, slightly weaker in 50-m, and relatively poor in pulling speed (no. 55a);
- propulsion in pulling, while tethered swimming (no. 42)—poor for her level;
- specific arm training, only pulling in swimming (no. 3)—limited for her level;
- background in dry land and strength training (no. 4 to 5)—very limited;
- individual isometric strength scores (no. 28 to 34). The mean score for the 20% best breaststroke swimmers investigated (European top level) is plotted by the broken line (Persyn & Vervaecke, 1984)—most of her scores were satisfactory.

In C, an overview is given of mean growth curves for both height and strength within the population investigated (cross-sectional) (Van Tilborgh, Daly, Vervaecke, & Persyn, 1984). Biological age, as well as sex, must also be taken into account.

Options.   When dealing with an adult swimmer, in B appropriate methods of strength training (percentage of maximum intensity and number of repetitions, as specified in Figure 1) are presented: explosive strength, pure strength, strength-endurance, and endurance. The proposed training method is directly based on (a) the diverse strength scores, seen in the profile (in A, vertically above), and (b) the best swimming distance: 50- to 100-m, 100 to 200-m, or long distance (horizontally).

When dealing with an age-group swimmer, in D careful individual options must be taken in accordance with the growth curves (C) and (a) for the relationship between the quantity of strength training and general physical education, and (b) for the intensity of strength training.

Finally, in E, appropriate exercises are proposed, in accordance with the available equipment.

If the breaststroke specialist in question were biologically mature (16 years), she could for the most part train strength-endurance (B, central square); her best distance is 100- to 200-m and most of her strength scores are in the central sector of A.

Her biological as well as chronological age was, however, only 14 years, and she had done only a very little amount of strength training. She was advised to spend 1 hr a day on dryland training—50% in general P.E. and 50% on strength training—but to limit this to 50% of the maximum intensity, even for poor strength scores (see Figure 2D). Fifty percent intensity was thus suggested for training the weak hand grip (no. 33). For the other specific muscle groups, maximum 33% or endurance training was recommended. To improve pull-push strength (no. 28) on the weak side, she was advised to practice swimming turns on this side as well.

Advice for Swimming Technique

In the first evaluation session, the swimmer demonstrated the current breaststroke technique with a fairly horizontal spreading and squeezing of the legs (see Figure 1B, 1, full lines). It was decided to try the new-look, undulating technique (Van Tilborgh, Willems, & Persyn, 1988). In a next evaluation session, 9 months later, this trial appeared to be successful: Her best time at 200 m improved 7 s. This dolphin-like technique, depicted by the dotted line, allows the whole body to undulate close to the surface through one narrow sinusoidal pipe and to propel with the hands and the feet in relatively still water. This technique is characterized by:

- a downward spreading and extension of the legs accompanied by a downward extension of the arms, resulting in a piking body position with the hips close to the surface;
- an upward spreading of the arms accompanied by an upward raising of the legs, resulting in an undulated body position, cambering in the chest; and
- an active squeezing of the arms and the first part of the arm recovery (close to the surface) accompanied by an active raising of the lower legs and a contraction of the lower back muscles, resulting in an elevated body position and again allowing the hips to be kept close to the surface.

Integrated Advice

To obtain the first characteristic of this undulating technique, piking, there was no physical limitation. For the second characteristic, the upward spreading of the arms, the shoulder upward extension flexibility was too limited, even in the second evaluation session (see Figure 1, no. 26, indicated by the arrow). For the third characteristic, the active squeezing of the arms, the weak links—hand grip and latissimus strength—had been sufficiently trained after the first session (no. 33 and 30).

One can expect that, as this girl gets older, she will need more time to study and have less time to swim. She should then place more emphasis on her 50- to 100-m performances and, as a result, she will need to train her explosive strength (see Figure 2B). At this stage the resultant impulses in each movement phase will be calculated from 16-mm film analysis, using a personal computer (PC) model of the body adapted from Hanavan (Van Tilborgh et al., 1987). PC graphics animations can then be used to illustrate simulated movements.

Automated Performance Estimation

From body build, flexibility, and strength characteristics, an estimation of the theoretical swimming performances can be made. This performance calculation may be used for the purpose of detection of errors but is mainly applied in a diagnostic way.

The mean error of estimation is around 3%. If the real performance is significantly poorer than the estimated performance, computerized video analysis is required. If the poor performance cannot be explained by faulty style, a more time-consuming control procedure must be undertaken, including a 16-mm film analysis and medical and psychological examinations. When a swimmer performs as well as (or even better than) estimated and appears thus to have found the best stroke pattern, additional examinations are not required. One should be very careful in giving new advice, except for the weak physical characteristics.

These performance estimations are based upon three conceptual scores: a trunk score (for streamline or drag) and an arm and a leg score (for propulsion), see Figure 1, 35 to 36. For the arm score, for example, diverse measurements are combined in one formula: the arm length and the surface of the forearm and hand, along with strength in the shoulder girdle and hand, and flexibility in the shoulder girdle. Two swimmers with different scores can achieve the same swimming speed. The current statistical procedures (multiple regressions) are applied to this biomechanical concept (Daly, Persyn, Van Tilborgh, & Riemaker, 1988).

Thanks to the PC measuring physical characteristics, calculating and printing out the conceptual scores and the performance scores takes about 10 min per individual.

Automated Performance Prediction

Predicting performance for the long term is much more risky than estimating the performance of which one presently should be capable. The development of swimming performances not only depends on the quality of an evaluation but also on the quality of the guidance.

The swimmer discussed here was intensively guided. Therefore, an attempt was made to predict her performance improvement, which was checked 9 months later. With an increase of dryland training (see Figure 1A, 5, and 7, indicated with arrows), an improvement in flexibility and strength should result (see Figure 1A, 24 to 26; 28 to 30, 33) and consequently an improvement in swimming performances (43 to 60) was expected.

In this case, the performance improvements were larger than estimated from improvements in physical characteristics. This was explained by the change in technique from a horizontal leg squeezing to the undulating technique, which was not considered in the multiple regressions (see Figure 1B).

Conclusion

With predictions one needs to remain extremely careful, especially in countries where very few research consultants are working in swimming clubs. From the experience gained in the evaluation of 600 swimmers, it has become increasingly clear that feedback is only effective when a swimming expert is working frequently and directly with coaches and swimmers.

Furthermore, the evaluation procedure can only be applied effectively when the Swimming Federation and Olympic Committee, on the one hand, and institutes of physical education, on the other hand, coordinate their efforts. For measuring, testing, videorecording, and PC data processing most physical education institutes have the required specialists and equipment to use the software described here.

Acknowledgments

Coworkers in computer implementation were D. Riemaker, C. Verbrugge, and T. Vermeersch.

References

Beunen, G. (1972). *Skeletale maturiteiten en "Physical Fitness"* [Skeletal maturity and physical fitness]. Unpublished doctoral dissertation, Catholic University, Leuven, Belgium.

Daly, D., Persyn, U., Van Tilborgh, L., & Riemaker, D. (1988). Estimation of sprint performance in breaststroke from body characteristics. In B.E. Ungerechts, K. Reischle, & K. Wilke (Eds.), *Swimming science V* (pp. 101-107). Champaign, IL: Human Kinetics.

Daly, D., Van Tilborgh, L., & Persyn, U. (1984, July). *Prediction of the appropriate pattern in crawl swimming in women*. Paper presented at the 1984 Olympic Scientific Congress, Eugene, OR.

Mader, A., & Hollman, W. (1978). Evaluation of lactic acid anaerobic energy contribution by determination of postexercise lactic acid concentration of ear capillary blood in middle-distance runners and swimmers. In F. Landry & W.A.R. Orban (Eds.), *Exercise physiology* (pp. 187-200). Miami: Symposia Specialists.

Persyn, U. (1984, November). *Computer aided evaluation: Report*. Paper presented at the Olympic Solidarity Seminar, Leuven, Belgium.

Persyn, U., & Vervaecke, H. (1984). Droogtraining voor zwemmers [Dryland training for swimmers]. In V. Stijnen & A. Claessens (Eds.), *Physical fitness: Een multidisciplinaire benadering—Hermes (Leuven)*, **17**, 255-264.

Renson, L., Lysens, R., Persyn, U., & Ostyn, M. (1982-1983). De incidentie van overbelastingsletsels bij zwemmers [The occurrence of overuse injuries in swimmers]. *Werken van de Vlaamse Vereniging voor Sportgeneeskunde en Sportwetenschappen*, **32**, 115-122.

Van Tilborgh, L., Daly, D., & Persyn, U. (1983). The influence of some somatic factors on passive drag, gravity and buoyancy forces in competitive swimmers. In A.P. Hollander, P.A. Huijing, & G. de Groot (Eds.), *Biomechanics and medicine in swimming* (pp. 207-214). Champaign, IL: Human Kinetics.

Van Tilborgh, L., Daly, D., Vervaecke, H., & Persyn, U. (1984). The evolution of some crawl performance determinant factors in women competitive swimmers. In J. Borms, R. Hauspie, A. Sand, C. Susanne, & M. Hebbelinck (Eds.), *Human growth and development* (pp. 525-534). New York: Plenum Press.

Van Tilborgh, L., Willems, E.J., & Persyn, U. (1988). Estimation of breaststroke propulsion and resistance resultant impulses from film analysis. In B.E. Ungerechts, K. Reischle, & K. Wilke (Eds.), *Swimming science V* (pp. 67-71). Champaign, IL: Human Kinetics.

Vanden Auweele, Y. (1982-1983). Psychische overbelasting bij jonge zwemen atletiek beloftes [Psychgological stress in promising young swimmers and track and field athletes]. *Werken van de Vlaamse Vereniging voor Sportgeneeskunde en Sportwetenschappen.* **32**, 123-140.

Vervaecke, H., & Persyn, U. (1981). Some differences between men and women in various factors which determine swimming performances. In J. Borms, M. Hebbelinck, & A. Venerando (Eds.), *The woman athlete: Medicine and sport* (Vol. 15, 150-156). Basel: Karger.

A Biomechanical Analysis of the 1984 U.S. Olympic Freestyle Distance Swimmers

Cheryl W. Maglischo
Ernest W. Maglischo
Joseph Higgins
Richard Hinrichs
David Luedtke
Robert E. Schleihauf
Anne Thayer

The propulsive efficiency of competitive swimmers has been a matter of considerable interest for many decades (Alley, 1952; Plagenhoff, 1971; Barthels & Adrian, 1974; Schleihauf, 1978; Schleihauf et al., 1985). In 1974, Schleihauf introduced a method for estimating the instantaneous propulsive force that is generated by swimmers as they stroke down the pool. This method is based on using vector analysis to solve for the resultant and propulsive forces when the velocity, direction, and angle of attack of the hand and arm are known.

Schleihauf's method was used to study the propulsive effectiveness of selected members of the 1984 U.S Olympic Swimming Team while they attended a pre-games training camp in Mission Viejo, California during July 1984. The project was funded by United States Swimming with the permission of the athletes and coaching staff. The Sports Medicine Committee of United States Swimming selected the authors to conduct the investigation. The purpose of this paper was to present the results from the distance freestyle swimmers.

Methods and Procedures

Six distance freestylers were filmed, 3 women and 3 men. Each athlete was asked to push off of the wall and swim 25 m at his or her Olympic qualifying pace. Times were recorded to ensure that the paces were correct, and the swimmers were asked to repeat the swims when the paces were slower or faster than the respective race paces. This procedure was followed for each event in which the swimmer qualified.

The locations of certain body parts were marked with shiny black tape or small battery-operated lights. The points marked were the tip of the middle finger, the bases of the index and little fingers, and the wrist.

Two 16-mm LoCam cameras were used in the filming process. They were placed in watertight Plexiglas housings and lowered into the pool in fixed positions so that the athletes swam through the field of view. One camera was placed on the bottom of the pool to record underneath views. The other was placed at the end of the pool approximately 30 cm underwater to record front views. The cameras were activated simultaneously by a common switch. They were operating at 66 fps.

After the film was processed, it was digitized using a Numonics digitizer and an Eiki 16-mm projector. Every frame was digitized for one complete underwater arm stroke of both the right and left arms.

The digitized information was then analyzed by means of a computer program that had been written by Schleihauf. This program calculated stroke patterns from front, side, and underneath views. These patterns were determined from the paths traced by the middle fingers of the swimmers' hands. Hand velocities were also calculated from movements of the middle finger. The three markings on the fingers and the marking on the wrist were used to calculate the angle of attack of the hand. This information was combined with directional and velocity computations to determine the total force produced by the swimmer's arms stroke and that portion of the force that was propulsive.

Results

An analysis of the data revealed four distinct propulsive phases during the underwater arm stroke. These phases are illustrated by a female subject's left arm stroke in Figure 1. That figure depicts stroke patterns

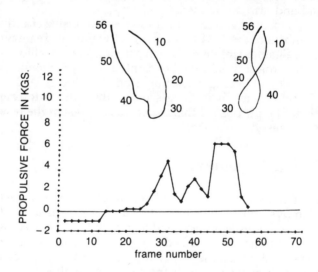

Figure 1 Stroke patterns and propulsive forces for a female distance freestyle swimmer of the 1984 U.S. Olympic Swimming Team. A side view stroke pattern is shown on the right. The stroke pattern on the left is drawn from a front view.

drawn from both front and side views. The side view is on the left and the front view is on the right. The front view is drawn as a mirror image so that the reader can trace the movements by following the pattern with his or her left hand. A line graph of the propulsive force produced during the arm stroke is also shown.

The stroke patterns indicate that all stroking movements were three-dimensional in nature. For example, it can be seen from the side view that between Frames 10 and 20, the swimmer in Figure 1 was moving her hand downward and forward. The front view reveals that her hand was also traveling somewhat outward during this same period.

Descriptions of the four propulsive phases follow. Although the three-dimensional nature of each phase will be described the term used to identify each phase will be based on the predominant direction that the hand is moving.

1. *Downsweep.* This phase took place between Frames 20 and 30 in Figure 1. It began midway through the long downward sweep after entry, when the swimmer's hand also began traveling outward and backward. It ended when the swimmer's hand began sweeping inward.
2. *Insweep.* This phase occurred between Frames 30 and 40. It began as the hand swept inward under the body and ended when the swimmer began a sweeping outward motion.
3. *Outsweep.* This phase was present between Frames 40 and 50 in Figure 1. It began when the swimmer's hand swept outward from underneath her body and ended when her hand was moving in a primarily upward direction toward the surface. The swimmer in Figure 1 tended to blend this portion of the arm stroke with the final phase, the upsweep, such that they became one continuous motion. Although her hand was sweeping outward somewhat, the predominant direction of motion was upward and backward. Other subjects in this study had a much more distinct outward sweep during this phase. The stroke patterns of one such subject are depicted in Figure 2. Notice that, between Frames 42 and 56, his hand was moving outward much more than it moved upward and backward.

   Two of the 6 subjects in this study used a style similar to the one depicted in Figure 1 on both their right and left armstrokes. One swimmer used the style shown in Figure 2 exclusively. The remaining subjects used a combination of these two styles. That is, they tended to combine the outsweep and upsweep into one motion during either the right or left arm stroke while using a very distinct outward sweep during the opposite arm stroke.
4. *Upsweep.* This particular phase of the arm stroke took place between Frames 40 and 50 in Figure 1 and between Frames 60 and 70 in Figure 2. It began when the hand was moving upward, backward, and slightly outward and ended when the motion of the hand became upward and forward.

It is interesting that each of the distance swimmers in this study was able to generate large propulsive peaks (3 kg or more), during only one

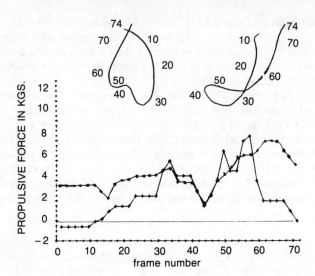

Figure 2   Stroke patterns and propulsive forces for a male distance freestyler from the 1984 U.S. Olympic Swimming Team.

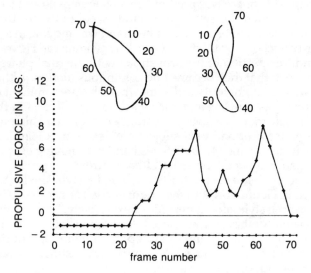

Figure 3   Stroke patterns and propulsive forces for a male distance freestyler. This swimmer generated most of his propulsion when he was stroking in directions that were primarily vertical.

or two of the four sweeping movements. The swimmer in Figure 1 had a propulsive peak near the end of her downsweep and another during the upsweep. The swimmer in Figure 2 achieved his propulsive peaks during the insweep and outsweep.

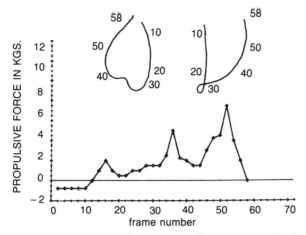

Figure 4 Stroke patterns and propulsive forces for a female distance freestyler. This swimmer also generated most of her propulsive force during vertical stroking movements.

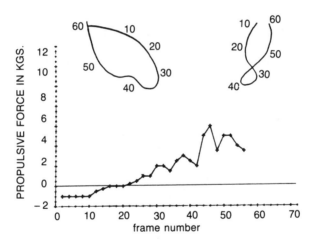

Figure 5 Stroke patterns and propulsive forces for a female distance freestyler. This swimmer generated most of her propulsion during the upsweep.

The right arm stroke patterns and propulsive force data for the 4 remaining athletes are shown in Figures 3, 4, 5, and 6. The male swimmer in Figure 3 achieved his major propulsive peaks during the downsweep (Frames 30 to 40) and upsweep (Frames 54 to 64). The female swimmer in Figure 4 achieved her major propulsive peaks during the outsweep (Frames 30 to 40) and the upsweep (Frames 40 to 50). The female swimmer in Figure 5 attained only one major propulsive peak between Frames 40-50 in a combined outsweep-upsweep motion. The male swimmer in Figure 6 also achieved only one major propulsive peak, and it occurred during the insweep between Frames 30 and 42.

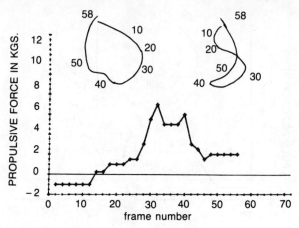

Figure 6   Stroke patterns and propulsive forces for a male distance freestyler. This swimmer had one major propulsive peak, during the insweep.

Another interesting aspect was that the subjects tended to favor either lateral or vertical stroking motions. Those swimmers who gained most of their propulsion when their hands were moving in primarily vertical directions, that is, during the downsweep and/or the upsweep portions of their arm stroke, were not very effective when they were sweeping their hands in lateral directions. Conversely, the laterally oriented swimmers were not very effective when they were sweeping their hands vertically.

This tendency to favor either lateral or vertical stroking motions is illustrated by the swimmers in Figures 1 through 6. Notice the small propulsive peak during the insweep (Frames 36 to 40) for the vertically oriented swimmer in Figure 1. This swimmer minimized the inward sweep so that she was able to move on to the more productive upsweep portion of her arm stroke. The vertically oriented male swimmer in Figure 3 showed a similar pattern between Frames 46 and 50 when he swept his hand inward. The vertically oriented female swimmer in Figure 5 also used a minimal insweep between Frames 30 and 40 so she could get the combined out and upsweep portion where she was most effective.

The laterally oriented swimmers in Figures 2 and 6 were only minimally effective during the vertical portions of their arm strokes. For the swimmer in Figure 2, the downsweep occurred between Frames 20 and 30, whereas the upsweep was taking place between Frames 60 and 70. The downsweep and upsweep occurred between Frames 20 and 30 and between Frames 50 and 56, respectively, for the swimmer in Figure 6.

Discussion

Why did the distance swimmers in this study utilize only one or two propulsive phases of their arm stroke when four were available to them?

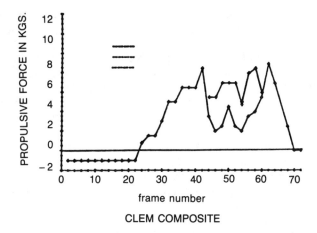

CLEM COMPOSITE

Figure 7 Propulsive forces for a hypothetical swimmer created by combining the most propulsive stroke phases of the 3 male distance freestylers studied.

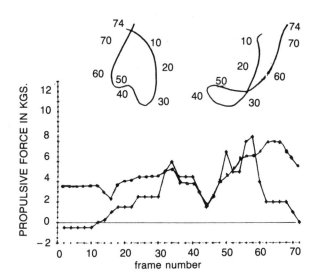

Figure 8 Propulsive forces for a hypothetical swimmer created by combining the most propulsive stroke phases of the 3 female distance freestylers studied.

Figures 7 and 8 depict hypothetical male and female swimmers, respectively, who combine the most effective sweeps of the subjects in this study. The strokes of the 3 male distance swimmers are combined in Figure 7, and the strokes of the female swimmers are combined in Figure 8.

These fictional swimmers could attain large propulsive peaks during the downsweep and maintain approximately that same peak until their hands neared the surface of the water at the end of the underwater part of the arm stroke. Obviously, a competitive swimmer who could combine the best propulsive characteristics of the world-class swimmers in this study would establish World Records in the freestyle events. A swimmer who could utilize all four sweeps to advantage should be able to generate a large amount of propulsive force for a little over 0.5 s during an underwater stroke that would require approximately 0.8 s to complete.

It is surprising, therefore, that none of the distance swimmers in this group were able to maintain a propulsive peak for longer than 0.15 s, and most were only able to do this twice during each stroke. One possible explanation for this result is that it might be too fatiguing to try for major propulsive peaks in all four phases of the arm stroke. Perhaps swimmers utilize their energy more efficiently by working hard only during the most effective portions of their underwater arm stroke while minimizing those sweeps where they are less effective.

Another possible explanation is that swimmers may not be able to maintain propulsive peaks for more than 0.15 s before accelerating the water beyond their ability to maintain pressure against it. Figure 9 shows the hand velocity of one of the subjects superimposed over the propulsive force that he produced during the various phases of his arm stroke. The propulsive peaks occurred during periods when the hand was accelerating, which is in agreement with the information presented by Counsilman and Wasilak (1982). Notice that a deceleration occurs between peaks (see Frames 36 to 42). This deceleration occurred when the swimmer's hand was changing directions from an inward sweeping to an outward sweeping motion. Perhaps, as Counsilman (1977) theorized, this deceleration is necessary in order to find relatively slow moving water that can be accelerated in a new direction. On the other hand, it may be a result of the normal slowing that must take place in order to change directions.

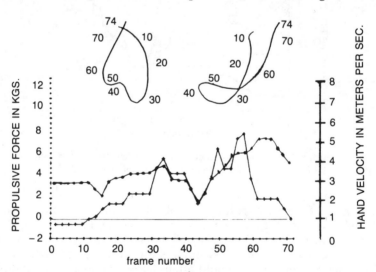

Figure 9   A comparison of changes in hand velocity and propulsive force for a male distance swimmer.

Regardless of the reason, the swimmers in this study tended to emphasize only two of the four sweeping motions available to them. Perhaps, through training, they intuitively learned to emphasize those phases where they were most effective while de-emphasizing and therefore saving energy during stroke phases in which they were less effective. An interesting question for future researchers would be to determine if swimmers can be taught to use all four phases of the stroke effectively. If it is possible to do so, future swimmers might be considerably faster than contemporary athletes. On the other hand, swimmers who were taught to emphasize all four propulsive phases of the stroke might only be able to generate four minor propulsive peaks that, when combined, would not equal the magnitude of the two major peaks.

Summary

Four phases of the freestyle arm stroke can generate a considerable amount of propulsive force. These phases are the downsweep, insweep, outsweep, and upsweep. No swimmer in the present study was able to generate large propulsive peaks in more than two of those phases. This may be because generating the hand velocities and/or force required to maintain propulsive peaks during all four phases is impossible. Therefore, these world-class swimmers may have intuitively learned to use the two sweeps that were most effective for them while minimizing the effort expended in the remaining two stroke phases. It is interesting to speculate as to whether swimmers of the future should concentrate on learning to use all four phases of the underwater arm stroke or whether they should elect to use only the two sweeps that are most effective for them.

References

Alley, L.E. (1952). An analysis of water resistance and propulsion in swimming the crawl stroke. *Research Quarterly*, **23**, 253-270.

Barthels, K., & Adrian, M. (1974). Three dimensional spatial hand patterns of skilled butterfly swimmers. In J.P. Clarys & L. Lewillie (Eds.), *Swimming II* (pp. 154-160). Baltimore: University Park Press.

Counsilman, J.E. (1977). *Competitive swimming manual for coaches and swimmers*. Bloomington, IN: Author.

Counsilman, J.E., & Wasilak, J. (1982). The importance of hand speed and hand acceleration. In R.M. Ousley (Ed.), *American Swimming Coaches Association World Clinic yearbook* (pp. 41-55). Fort Lauderdale, FL: American Swimming Coaches Association.

Plagenhoff, S. (1971). *Patterns of human motion*. Englewood Cliffs, NJ: Prentice-Hall.

Schleihauf, R.E., Jr. (1974). A biomechanical analysis of freestyle. *Swimming Technique*, **11**, 89-96.

Schleihauf, R.E., Jr. (1978). Swimming propulsion: A hydrodynamic analysis. In *American Swimming Coaches Association 1977 World Clinic yearbook* (pp. 49-86). Fort Lauderdale, FL: American Swimming Coaches Association.

Schleihauf, R.E., Higgins, J., Hinrichs, R., Luedtke, D., Maglischo, C., Maglischo, E., & Thayer, A. (1985). Biomechanics of swimming propulsion. In T.F. Welsh (Ed.), *American Swimming Coaches Association World Clinic yearbook* (pp. 19-24). Fort Lauderdale, FL: American Swimming Coaches Association.

The Evaluation of Highly Skilled Swimmers via Quantitative and Qualitative Analysis

Christophe Loetz
Klaus Reischle
Gerhard Schmitt

Highly skilled swimming is characterized by an extraordinarily high frequency of events. Within a second in time the swimmers must solve the difficult task of coordinating the motions of their body segments, for example, when swimming the crawl: (a) the pull-push phase of the right arm with the pull-push phase of the left arm; (b) the rolling motions pivoting on the longitudinal axis with the pull-push phase, the recovery phase, and breathing; (c) arm strokes with leg kicks; and (d) head movements when the swimmer inhales and exhales. Moreover, during different movements (e.g. during a pull-push phase), the geometric and dynamic movement pattern changes continually.

The high frequency of events and the dynamic and geometric variations make subjective evaluation difficult even for the most observing and experienced coach, unless he or she has a method for obtaining objective data to support subjective conclusions. These data are achievable by quantitative measuring and scanning consistent with a theory-based conceptional model (Barthels, 1979; Brown & Counsilman, 1970; Schleihauf, 1977, 1979). In this way, the motions can be evaluated both qualitatively and quantitatively.

Being norm-oriented, the evaluation of the movements involves a comparison between the factual values, or actual motions, and the "statistical" or "ideal" norms (Ballreich, 1976; Letzelter, 1985). The diagnosis of the performance levels must consider two elements: the ability of the swimmer and his or her developed skills. Although an evaluation of abilities can furnish useful knowledge for orientation and training, this study was limited to the evaluation of skills.

The evaluation of swimming motions is based on a number of criteria, videorecordings (slow-motion and frame advance), and quantitative biomechanical parameters. Velocity-time and pressure-time are recorded, graphed, and measured via biomechanical methods that will be described later. The horizontal intracyclic velocities are gauged by means of an impulse light method and electrical resistance variation method; the pressure-time graphs are recorded by the difference-pressure method. Using the difference-pressure method, it was possible to measure the amount of *time-dependent resultant* of lift and drag. The different bio-

361

mechanical methods are synchronized by a sensor-video personal computer (PC) unit in order to evaluate swimming skills qualitatively and quantitatively. This evaluation system offers the advantage of delivering objective and subjective knowledge of results simultaneously to the trainer and the swimmer.

Measuring Procedures

Difference-Pressure Method

To measure the fluctuations of pressure on the hand, the difference-pressure method (Loetz, Reischle, & Albrecht, 1984) was used. The pressure-time graphs were synchronized with the swimmer's motions or vice versa, by means of the sensor-video PC unit.

For this purpose, 5-mm thick piezo-resistive pressure sensors were attached to the palm and the back of the hand. These sensors measured both hydrostatic and hydrodynamic pressure based on the movement of the athlete's hand. The hydrostatic pressure was eliminated by analog subtraction, leaving the effective hydrodynamic pressure. This measurement was made on the swimmer without hampering him by tethering. He was able to swim freely and still provide the required data. The analog signals were put in a PC via an analog-to-digital (AD) converter.

When tested initially on 40 female swimmers of the A-, B-, and C-squads of the DSV (German National Swimming Team), the measuring apparatus turned out to be fundamentally applicable. It has been further improved by the addition of an electronic calibrating system, so it was possible to calibrate the entire measuring apparatus.

In an exemplary study, the pressure-time graph of the stroke was measured for a male individual medley swimmer and for 8 female breaststroke swimmers. The athletes were asked to simulate competition and sprint speed on a 25-m lap. The pressure-time graph was recorded for the whole lap, but only three strokes from the middle of the lap were evaluated.

Impulse Light Method

Initially, the intracyclic velocity fluctuations were measured and recorded by the impulse light method. But because this process was not electric, it is not capable of recording the intracyclic velocity fluctuations and the pressure-time fluctuations simultaneously.

To remedy this situation, an electrical-resistance variation method was developed. With this method, it was possible to synchronize the data of the intracyclic pressure-time fluctuations with the video picture or horizontal intracyclic velocity-time fluctuations.

Electrical Resistance Variation Method

The water of the pool constitutes an electrical resistance in accordance with Ohm's law. This electrical resistance, measured between two electrodes submerged in the water, is proportional to the distance from one electrode to the other.

One electrode was attached at the side of the pool, the other was fixed to the swimmer. The swimmer's electrode stayed immersed throughout the measuring process. As the swimmer advanced in the pool, the distance between the two electrodes was continuously changed.

The change in distance was proportional to the change in resistance between the two electrodes. However, this variation was small, and direct measurement of resistance change (RC) would have been very difficult. Therefore, what was measured was the time constant of an RC component. To do this, a constant frequency was modulated by the RC component in such a way that the frequency time quotient was proportional to the distance variations. These modifications of relationship could then be transformed into velocity units by further use of electronical systems.

Results

Two minima and maxima were typical for the velocity time graph of a breaststroke swimmer. The amounts of the minima and maxima are described in Table 1.

The pressure-time graphs during the pull-push phases had several peaks: The breaststroke was characterized by two pressure peaks during each half cycle per arm; the butterfly, front crawl, and backstroke by three pressure peaks per half cycle (Figures 1, 2, 3, 4). As an example in breaststroke swimming: During the pull and the push phase, an increase of pressure on the hands of the swimmer was recorded. The first peak was reached after 35%; the second peak was reached at 64% of a half cycle (compare Figure 1 and Table 2). The change in direction of the hand movements from outward/downward/backward to inward/downward/backward caused a reduction of pressure.

Table 1 Horizontal Intracyclic Variables of Hip Point in Female Breaststroke Swimming

Variable	n	Mean	Minimum	Maximum
$\bar{v}$ (m/s)	16	1.10	0.94	1.21
c_v (%)	16	0.41	0.33	0.48
$v_{min\ 1}$ (m/s)	16	1.28	1.11	1.56
$v_{min\ 2}$ (m/s)	16	0.26	0.11	0.42
$v_{max\ 1}$ (m/s)	16	1.72	1.43	2.00
$v_{max\ 2}$ (m/s)	16	1.39	1.27	1.69

Note. $\bar{v}$ = average velocity; c_v = coefficient of variability; $v_{min\ 1}$ = velocity at the beginning of the pull-push phase of the arm stroke; $v_{min\ 2}$ = velocity at the beginning of the leg kick; $v_{max\ 1}$ = velocity at the beginning of the arm stroke recovery; $v_{max\ 2}$ = velocity at the end of the leg kick.

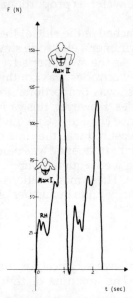

Figure 1 Force-time graph of the pull-push phase in breaststroke swimming. RH = recovery; MaxI = force peak before the end of the outward/downward phase; MaxII = force peak before the end of the inward/downward phase.

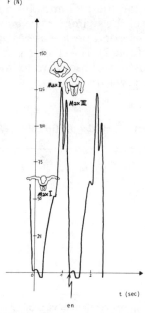

Figure 2 Force-time graph of the pull-push phase in butterfly swimming. en = entry; MaxI = force peak before the end of the outward/downward phase; MaxII = force peak before the end of the inward/downward phase; MaxIII = force peak before the end of the outward/upward phase.

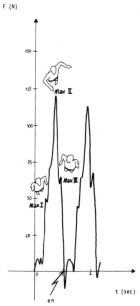

Figure 3 Force-time graph of the pull-push phase in crawl swimming. en = entry; MaxI = force peak before the end of the outward/downward phase; MaxII = force peak before the end of the inward/downward phase; MaxIII = force peak before the end of the outward/ upward phase.

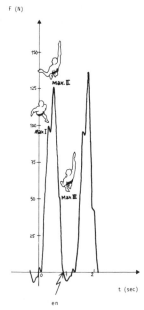

Figure 4 Force-time graph of the pull-push phase in backstroke swimming. en = entry; MaxI = force peak before the end of the downward/outward phase; MaxII = force peak before the end of the inward/upward phase; MaxIII = force peak before the end of the downward phase.

Table 2   Force-Maxima and Their Time Relation During the Pull-Push Phase

Event	n	Max$_1$ (N)	Max$_2$ (N)	Max$_3$ (N)	t_0 (s)	t_1 (s)	t_2 (s)	t_3 (s)	t_{cycle} (s)
Male Swimmer									
Crawl	1	78.50	126.20	60.00		0.40	0.55	0.75	1.15
Butterfly	1	55.00	130.00	121.20		0.40	0.60	0.75	1.30
Breaststroke	1	61.20	133.70	—	0.5	0.25	0.45	—	1.20
Backstroke	1	42.50	127.50	5.00		0.20	0.55	0.75	1.55
Female Swimmers									
Breaststroke	8	32.98	75.34	—	0.5	0.18	0.37	—	1.48

Note. The forces are calculated as product of the difference pressure and area of the palm. Max$_1$ = force maximum during the outward-downward phase; Max$_2$ = force maximum during the inward-backward phase; Max$_3$ = force maximum at the end of the push phase; t_0 = time of the recovery phase; t_1, t_2, t_3 = time of the maxima in relation to the entry; t_{cycle} = time of a cycle.

Typical pressure and time values taken from 8 female breaststroke swimmers and 1 male individual medley swimmer are shown in Table 2.

Conclusion

The procedures described enable one to ascertain the rate and the amount of the minima and maxima during each stroke cycle as well as the corresponding times at which each minimum and maximum occurred on the velocity-time and pressure-time curves. Thus, norms for an objective evaluation of swimming motions corresponding to the level of skills can be developed.

References

Ballreich, R. (1976). Biomechanische Normen, Gesetze und Prinzipien [Biomechanical norms, foundations and principles]. In M. Letzelter & Müller (Eds.), *Sport und Sportwissenschaft* (pp. 19-25). Berlin.

Barthels, K.M. (1979). The mechanism for body propulsion in swimming. In J. Terauds & E.W. Bedingfield (Eds.), *Swimming III* (pp. 45-69). Baltimore: University Park Press.

Brown, R.M., & Counsilman, J.E. (1970). The role of lift in propelling the swimmer. In J.M. Cooper (Ed.), *Selected topics in biomechanics* (pp. 179-188). Chicago: The Athletic Institute.

Letzeltcr, M. (1985). Soll- und Ist-Werte in der Trainingssteuerung [Debit and net worth in controlled training]. In Hagedorn, Karl, & Bös (Eds.), *Handeln im Sport* (pp. 142-148). Clausthal-Zellerfeld.

Loetz, C., Reischle, K., & Albrecht, C. (1984). Die Dynamik von Teilbewegungen beim Schwimmen [The dynamics of movement patterns in swimming]. *Leistungssport*, **6**, 39-43.

Schleihauf, R.E. (1977). Swimming propulsion: A hydrodynamic analysis. In *American Swimming Coaches Association 1977 World Clinic yearbook* (pp. 49-86). Fort Lauderdale, FL: American Swimming Coaches Association.

Schleihauf, R.E. (1979). A hydrodynamic analysis of swimming propulsion. In J. Terauds & E.W. Bedingfield (Eds.), *Swimming III* (pp. 70-109). Baltimore: University Park Press.

A Rating Scale for the Evaluation of the Breaststroke Technique in Pedagogical Situations

Johan Pion
Patrick Devos
Walter Dufour

It is difficult to be objective about the quality of movement. Most observations are used to evaluate sports skills. These observations can be free or structured. The first type of observation is often used in pedagogical situations; the second one is more experimental and often too complicated to use at school. One can observe by means of structured processes or rating scales that are mainly objective, although the results can never achieve the same objectivity as objective measuring instruments. In contrast, free observations utilize no measuring devices. Both types of observation need to be made more useful in pedagogical situations. There must be a way to utilize them in the observation of sport skills at school.

Table 1 shows that free observations are practical, made in real situations, not structured, not objective enough, and not expensive. On the other hand, scientific observations are structured, more objective, conducted in experimental situations, expensive, and time-consuming. The practical rating scale should be structured, feasible in real situations, not expensive, not time consuming, and most of all, objective.

Table 1   A Comparison of Free, Practical, and Scientific Observation

Free observation	Practical observation	Scientific observation
Not structured	Structured	Structured
Field situations	Field situations	Experimental situation
Subjectivity	Objective/subjective	Objectivity
Not expensive	Not expensive	Expensive
Practical	Practical	Time-consuming

Procedures

In order to design a rating scale, descriptions and analysis of the breast-stroke were completed. The techniques of the breaststroke were established using six movement descriptions from the existing literature (Counsilman, 1968; Gierhl, 1983; Jiskoot, 1975; Lesneuck, 1975; Maglischo, 1982; Persyn, 1984). The obtained prototype description was presented to six specialists in order to detect possible errors. This movement description was necessary to obtain the clearest possible description of the movement. The better the description, the more readily it will be understood by the teacher and the better the evaluations.

In the second phase, attention was given to the scoring form. One of the first criterion was the need for simplicity. The data must be clear to the observer. The objective was to obtain a well-structured scoring form using the comprehensive, clear descriptions. The information had to be objective, relevant, and complete. The illustrations had to attract full attention. On the one hand, one can compare student performances with the pictures, and on the other hand, pictures can evoke different ideas. They represent a language of their own. In other words, instead of explaining something with a large number of words, sometimes one single picture is even more clearly understood. Due to the complexity of the breaststroke movement, a distinction was made between different items. By evaluating each part of the movement separately a more valid assessment could be obtained. Figure 1 illustrates the scoring form on which the correct form is shown.

The authors wondered if a positive rating scale would yield the same results as a negative one. The positive protocol was in accordance with movement descriptions, the negative protocol was useful for error analysis. Both protocols were identical to each other. Thus, the description was subdivided into movement characteristics for a positive protocol and into error descriptions for the negative protocol. The scheme presented in Figure 2 is in accordance with Persyn (1979) and includes both protocols. Persyn (1979) subdivided these movement items even further as mentioned in the figures. This led to the overstructuring and was only useful for top-level swimmers.

The number of categories chosen was based on the visibility of each item. Therefore, the authors assumed the place of the teacher was by the side of the swimming pool.

In the protocol of the present study, the observer was able to score performance items on a scale from 1 to 5, each of which was multiplied afterward by a coefficient of importance. Due to the fact that not all the items were of equal significance, the scoring possibilities were not always the same. In some cases two categories (yes/no) were sufficient.

Methods

A total of 38 students in physical education and physiotherapy were evaluated by four physical education teachers. The validity of the rating scale was determined by comparing the scores with an external criterion,

1	Stretched body	Position head/trunk	Head/trunk horizontal		−	±	+		8
2	Arm pull	Hands	Water resistance		−	±	+		8
3	Arm pull	Hands	Hands in front of shoulders		−	±	+		9
4	2nd part contra	Hips	Trunk/legs angle = 135°		−	±	+		9
5	Extension legs	Feet	Leg flexion		−	+			8
6	Extension legs	Feet lower limb	Acceleration leg kick		=	−	±	+	‡	7
7	Extension legs	Arms	Maximal extension of the body		−	±	+		6
8	Arm pull	Hand/elbow	Arm flexion elbow high		−	±	+		6
9	Arm glide	Hands	Acceleration of arm		=	−	±	+	‡	7
10	I, II, III and IV part	Coordination arm/legs	Alternation of arms/legs		−	±	+		8

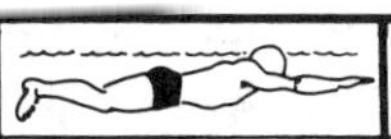

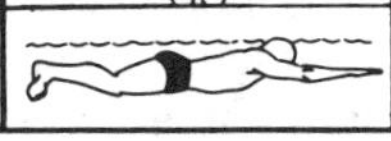

Figure 1 The scoring form. Column 1 indicates the phase of the movement; column 2 , the part of the body that is to be observed; column 3, information about the movement; column 4, figures; column 5, score possibilities; column 6, individual score is inserted; and column 7, coefficient of importance.

Positive RATING SCALE

Head/trunk horizontal

Water resistance

Hands in front of shoulders

Trunk/legs angle = 135°

Leg flexion

Acceleration leg kick

Maximal extension of body

Arm flexion elbow high

Acceleration of arms

Alternation of arms/legs

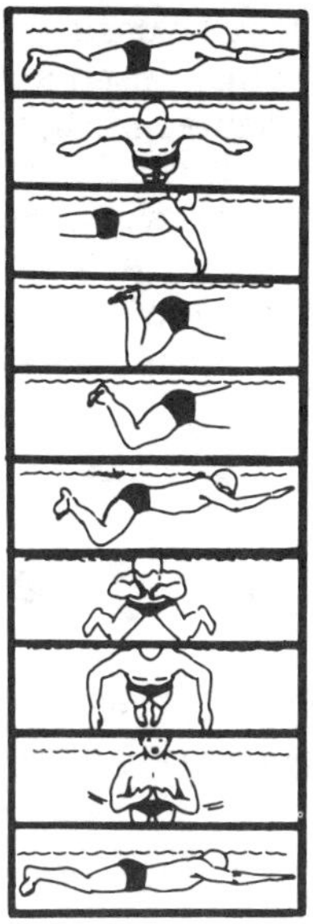

Negative RATING SCALE

Trunk not horizontal

Slipping (hands)

Hands behind shoulders

Trunk/legs angle < 135°

Leg flexion not optimal

Without leg kick

Extension not maximal

Arms too wide

Acceleration arms not optimal

Alternation legs arms too short

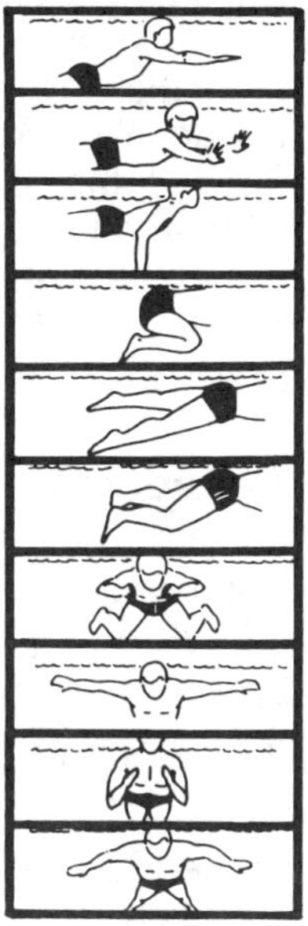

Figure 2 Movement characteristics for a positive protocol, error descriptions for a negative protocol.

which was the time for the 20-m breaststroke. It was assumed that a fast swimmer would utilize good techniques. The second criterion was the number of repetitions of the movement attempted in 20 m. It was hypothesized that a small number of repetitions were an indication of good technique. Finally, the product of both factors were chosen because of the same type of ordering of the factors.

To check reliability, the parallel-test method was used although the circumstances were not optimal because of small differences between the positive and negative protocols. The objectivity for both of the protocols was determined by an interobserver analysis.

Results

The validity of the rating scales based on the external criteria yielded an r of .68 for the negative and $.54 < r < .78$ for the positive rating scale. Pearson product-moment correlations were employed to determine these validity coefficients. The reliability was measured by means of the two identical protocols. The Kendall correlation coefficients were used to obtain reliability coefficients of $.50 < r < .74$ for the 10 substructures of the breaststroke movement. Finally Kendall correlation coefficients were used to obtain the objectivity of the rating scale. A correlation coefficient of .75 was obtained between the scores of the four observers.

Discussion

The obtained protocols were more appropriate as a means of observation than as an evaluation method. The test may be used as preparation for an evaluation. The scoring form is the instrument used during a lesson. The teacher observes the 20-m swims; at the same time the number of repetitions of the movement are counted (with the help of the students). Although there are only small differences between the positive and the negative rating scales, both scales are presented because often teachers are used to noticing errors and correcting them. Therefore, it is possible to use either the positive or the negative scale in school situations.

References

Coünsilman, J.E. (1968). *The science of swimming.* Englewood Cliffs, NJ: Prentice-Hall.

Gierhl, J. (1983). Sport in beeld, zwemmen. Amsterdam: B.V. Elsevier.

Jiskoot, J. (1975). *Een didactiek voor het zwemonderwijs in schoolverband.* Groningen: Regenboog.

Lesneuck, J., et al. (1975). Leren zwemmen, zwemonderwijs voor school en vereniging. *De Sikkel*, 121.

Maglischo, F.W (1982). *Swimming faster. A comprehensive guide to the science of swimming.* Palo Alto, CA: Mayfield.

Persyn, U. (1979). De observatie van de Zwembeweging, *Hermes, (Leuven)*, **12**, 231-248.

Persyn, U. (1984). *Clubtrainer zwemmen.* Brussels: LCK ministerie van nederlandse cultuur.

PART IX

TRAINING DEVICES

Added Mechanical and Physiological Loads During Swimming With a Drag Suit

Nobutaka Taguchi
Hidetaro Shibayama
Mitsumasa Miyashita

While swimming at a constant velocity, the swimmer must exert a propulsive force to overcome water resistance. Therefore, numerous studies have reported on water resistance in the static position in relation to velocity, body size, and so forth (Alley, 1952; Clarys, Jiskoot, Risken, & Brouwer, 1974; Karpovich & Millman, 1944; Miyashita & Tsunoda, 1978).

Competitive swimming has developed rapidly, partly because of the marked increase in the volume of training (Holmer, 1979). In addition, various devices for training may have contributed to the development of world records. Recently, a swimming training device called a drag suit has been developed to increase drag force.

The purpose of the present study was to investigate the differences in water resistance and physiological responses such as heart rate (HR) and blood lactate (La) while wearing a drag suit and a normal suit. This study was pretested on December 23, 1985, and the actual testing was performed from December 24 to 26, 1985.

Methods

The subjects were 7 male swimmers, ranging from 18 to 49 years of age. Their average height and weight were 170.3 cm and 65.3 kg, respectively. They were not well trained at the time of the experiment but were highly skilled swimmers.

The drag suit was originally developed in the U.S.A. and was constructed of 100% nylon. The nylon was perforated to allow water flow. Various sizes were used in order to fit each subject, but the four drag-producing pockets attached to the outside of the suit were of the same dimensions. There was 1-cm difference in the pocket sizes between the two front pockets and the two back pockets (front: $15 \times 3 \times 14$ cm; back: $16 \times 3 \times 15$ cm).

Drag Measurements

The drag measurements were performed in a specially designed swimming flume, in which water was circulated in a deep loop by a motor-

Figure 1 Test subject resuming prone position, partially submerged.

driven propeller. The water velocity in the swimming flume could be varied from 0 to 2.5 m/s, and the temperature was kept at 27 °C in this experiment. One end of a cord (about 1 m in length) was attached to a load cell; the other end was held in the hands of the swimmer who was lying in a prone position with arms outstretched above the head and submerged (see Figure 1). The load cell (measuring range: 0 to 50 kg) was fixed at the edge of the flume ahead of the swimmer. The tension of the cord was recorded by a pen-writing recorder (Polygraph RM-6000, Nihon-Koden) through the load cell, which was calibrated with a known weight before and after the measurements.

The drag in the normal suit and the drag suit was measured at four constant velocities (1.2, 1.4, 1.6, and 1.8 m/s).

Blood Lactate and Heart Rate Measurements

Each subject was asked to swim at three velocities—1.0, 1.1, and 1.2 m/s—using the crawl stroke. The subjects swam 200 m twice at the same speed following a pace-maker system (Pace-making System 1289, Takei and Co., Japan) mounted on the pool floor, once while wearing a drag suit and the other time wearing a normal suit.

The HR was monitored throughout the test and recorded for 10 s immediately following each trial (Life Scope 11, WEP-7201, Nihon-Koden). A blood sample was taken from the fingertip 1, 3, and 6 min after swimming, and La concentration was determined by the enzyme electrode method (Omron-Toyobo Lactate Analyzer, HER–100). The highest value was used for the results.

Results and Discussion

Takahasi, Nomura, Yoshida, and Miyashita (1983) have already reported that the differences between the passive drag with a drag suit and a normal suit increased with water velocity. The present experiment, showed nearly the same trend in that drag increased with velocity from a mean of 12.0 N at a velocity of 1.2 m/s, 10.0 N at 1.4 m/s, 21.4 N at 1.6 m/s, to 24.1 N at 1.8 m/s. However, when calculations of drag percentages were made between the normal and drag suit for each velocity, there was no significant increase in drag with an increase in velocity. In Figure 2, individual values are shown related to velocity using a bar graph. It can be noted that drag rose as velocity increased.

These results indicate that the swimmer must overcome a 30 to 40% increase in water resistance when swimming with the drag suit. According to the theory of fluid dynamics, the hands must be moved faster to create a greater reaction force from the water. In other words, even when swimming with the drag suit at slow velocities, a swimmer must move the hands relatively faster resulting in the recruiting of more muscle fibers, especially fast-twitch fibers (Type II). This also results in an increase in stroke frequency (see Table 1).

In Figure 3, HRs show definitely higher values when using the drag suit at lower velocities. However, at higher velocities, even when using the normal suit, HR increased to a point at which it leveled off in most subjects.

The drag suit increased La levels above 4.0 mM/l, when swimming at the lowest velocity tested (see Figure 3). Therefore, it can be said that the drag suit elicited anaerobic metabolism (Sjodin, Schele, Karlsson, Linnarsson, & Wallensten, 1982). This was particularly noticeable in the less skilled subjects (C, D, and E) in Figure 3. In the more skilled subjects (G and B), anaerobic thresholds were barely reached at a velocity of 1.1 m/s.

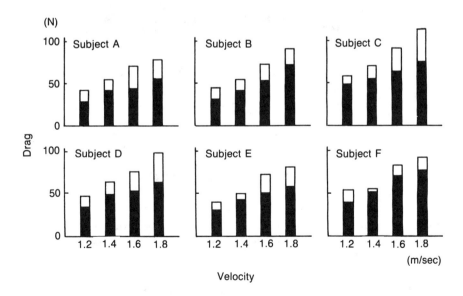

Figure 2 The passive drag with and without the drag suit in relation to water velocities. The darkened area indicates the value without a drag suit, and the lighter area indicates the increment of drag.

Table 1 Increment in Number of Strokes During a 200-m Swim With the Drag Suit

Swimming velocity (m/s)	Subject				
	C	D	E	G	B
1.1	5.5	20.0	20.0	11.5	13.0
1.2	27.0	34.5	18.0	11.0	17.0
1.3	—	—	22.0	13.0	24.5

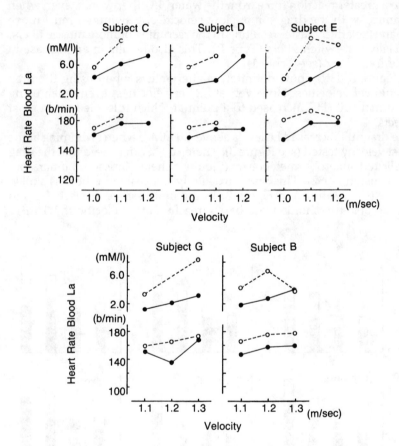

Figure 3 Physiological responses of HR and and blood La while swimming at three constant velocites. Swimming with normal suit is indicated by •——• and with drag suit by O---O.

The less skilled swimmers showed anaerobic levels of lactate (4.0 mM/l) at higher velocities when wearing a normal suit. However, the more skilled subjects did not achieve an adequate level of blood lactate to elicit a training effect unless higher velocities were emitted.

Summary

In the last two decades, dryland strength training has become popular among competitive swimmers in order to develop their anaerobic swim capacity, which might account for the frequently changing world and national records. On the other hand, equipment has been devised for strength training in water such as the swim training paddle attached to the palm of the hand, drag suit, and so forth. Few scientific papers consider the former situation, whereas a similar investigation was conducted on the drag suit in the present study. One interesting finding was that the blood La increased over 4.0 mM/l, though HR remained submaximal at relatively low swimming velocities. Therefore, it might be hypothesized that Type IIb fibers were recruited to overcome the added water resistance, in addition to Type IIa fibers when swimming using the drag suit.

References

Alley, L.E. (1952). An analysis of water resistance and propulsion in swimming the crawl stroke. *Research Quarterly, 23*, 253-270.

Clarys, J.P., Jiskoot, J., Rijken, H., & Brouwer, P.J. (1974). Total resistance in water and its relation to body form. In R.C. Nelson & C.A. Morehouse (Eds.), *Biomechanics IV* (pp. 187-196). Baltimore: University Park Press.

Holmer, I. (1979). Physiology of swimming man. In R.S. Hutton & D.I. Miller (Eds.), *Exercise and sport sciences reviews: Vol. 7* (pp. 87-123). Philadelphia: The Franklin Institute Press.

Karpovich, P.V., & Millman, N. (1944). Energy expenditure in swimming. *Research Quarterly, 15*, 140-144.

Miyashita, M., & Tsunoda, R. (1978). Water resistance in relation to body size. In B. Eriksson & B. Furberg (Eds.), *Swimming medicine IV* (pp. 395-401. Baltimore: University Park Press.

Sjodin, B., Schele, R., Karlsson, J., Linnarsson, D., & Wallensten, R. (1982). The physiological background of onset of blood lactate accumulation (OBLA). In P.V. Komi (Ed.), *Exercise and sport biology* (pp. 45-56). Champaign, IL: Human Kinetics.

Takahasi, G., Nomura, T., Yoshida, A., & Miyashita, M. (1983). Physiological energy consumption during swimming, related to added drag. In H. Matsui & K. Kobayashi (Eds.), *Biomechanics VIII-B* (pp. 842-847). Champaign, IL: Human Kinetics.

The Effects of a Device to Provide Feedback on Learning in Relay Starts

Klaus Nicol
Dirk Clasing
Klaus Tubessing

When motor learning is considered as a continuous process of trial and error, a feedback system of some kind has to be established in order to prove the success and/or the errors involved in one trial. Usually the athlete uses his or her acoustic, visual, vestibular, or tactile system for feedback by judging the movement or uses feedback information supplied by a coach. These biological feedback systems provide a wide range of information, that is, the athlete utilizes many different kinds of information from which to judge. In contrast, technical devices used for supporting motor learning processes often supply limited types of feedback—a few variables are output that precisely describe some important aspects of the movement. Both kinds of feedback must be precise, reliable, and fast enough so that the athlete can recall the pattern of the previous movement and thus use the feedback for planning the next trial.

One study (Nicol, Henning, & Huber, 1980) showed that amazing success was sometimes possible using feedback devices. A physically handicapped man had to learn to avoid excessive loading of the big toe while walking. This previously had turned out to be the reason for his unusual walking style. A force transducer was fixed under the big toe; for feedback an impulse was sent to an earphone, if a certain limit of force was exceeded. It turned out that this person was able to reduce the force to a given level within a learning phase of 10 min. When the earphone was removed, the corrected movement was maintained, which indicated that the external feedback system had been replaced by an internal one. So it was hoped that a similar procedure could also be successfully used for learning to minimize the exchange time in relay starts in swimming.

Methods

For time measurement, waterproof switching mats were used that are commercially available. They were fixed on the starting block and at the wall of the pool and were connected to a battery-powered microcomputer for exact measurement, convenient storage, evaluation, and printout. Ten members of a swimming club served as subjects, 4 of whom were mem-

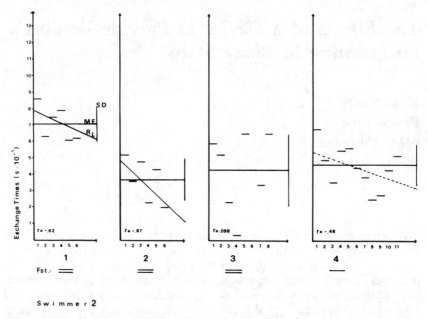

Figure 1 Exchange times of different trials (small dashes). M = mean, SD = standard deviation, and RL = regression line for Swimmer 2. U = training unit 1 to 4, various trials, numbers of early starts (Fst.). RL solid lines: $r > .50$; broken lines: $.30 \leqslant r \leqslant .50$; and no RL drawn: $r < .30$.

bers of a female elite relay crew. For this crew, nearly 200 exchanges were recorded. They were informed about the exchange time after every trial.

A similar system was recently used for up to six channel measurements in swimming (Nicol, Clasing, Thayer, & El-Din, 1987). Due to its acoustical output capability, the system may be used as an automatic trainer for starting time and exchange time, so that the coach will no longer be completely occupied by one single event. Moreover, the switching-type sensor mats can be replaced by force-measuring platforms, so that the pressure level can be adjusted to the force applied. These platforms are similar to the type used for the study of force applied to the wall of the pool while performing different types of turns (Nicol & Krüger, 1979). For further extensions of the system, a photoelectric cell system was designed to measure intermediate time. In order to avoid well-known problems of this procedure, the following principle was used. Waterproof photo sensors were placed on the floor of the pool. They were supplied by a tube so that the sensor received light emitted by a 10-cm × 100-cm section of the water surfaces, the long side of which was arranged orthogonally to the swimming direction. When the swimmer passed by, a signal was generated that was proportional to the cross-section of that part of the swimmer's body that was just above the sensor. From this signal, the time interval from the start until the head or feet passed the sensor was derived.

Results

According to the considerations outlined, it was anticipated that the device would generate a considerable improvement in exchange times. This turned out to be true in many cases, but there were exceptions. The members of the 4 × 100-m relay crew happened to represent three different classes as far as their learning behavior was concerned.

The data of the first exchange (Swimmer 2) are represented in Figure 1 for training units 1 to 4 (U1 to U4). It can be noted that (a) the average exchange time was reduced from U1 to U2 and remained at a lower level in U3 and U4 than in U1; (b) the average standard deviation (SD) was smaller than the rates of exchange for swimmers 3 and 4 (see Figures 2 and 3); (c) the correlation coefficient of the correlation: exchange time versus learning time is better than − .48 for U1, U2, and U4; (d) the first trial of each session was one of the worst ones and the second through the fourth trial showed a considerable improvement; and (e) the number of early starts was low and almost constant. It seems that this swimmer adapted herself well to the situation: She learned quite readily during one session, in particular during the first trials. She was consistent and stabilized her performance at a high level.

Swimmer 3 showed a quite different behavior: (a) Starting with low exchange times, the times increased on an average during the study; (b) SD was higher than Swimmer 2: (c) correlation factors within sessions varied between + .35 and − .59; (d) the first trial of each session was one

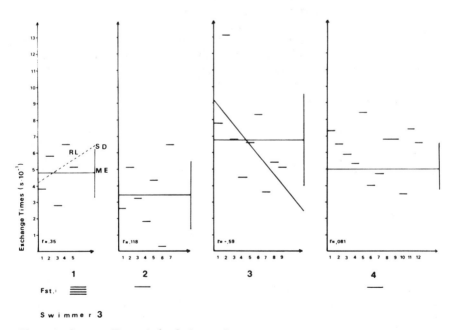

Swimmer 3

Figure 2   Same as Figure 1, for Swimmer 3.

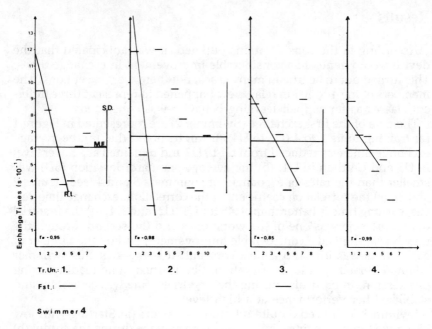

Figure 3 Same as Figure 1, for Swimmer 4.

of the best, the following trials were worse; and (e) Swimmer 3 also succeeded in reducing significantly the number of early starts.

The data of Swimmer 4 significantly differed from the previous ones. The average exchange times were higher and *SD* rates were by far the largest ones. Although all four sessions show a small negative correlation coefficient, indicating a small improvement during sessions, this subject's performance increased considerably during the first few trials, then the performance deteriorated.

In U5 and U6 (figure not shown), the advice was given not to care about early starts and to realize as short exchange times as possible. Swimmers 2 and 3 adapted themselves to that advice: Most of the starts were early, but the late ones showed very short times. In contrast, Swimmer 4 was not able to adapt her behavior to the new situation; data corresponded to U1 to U4. She claimed that she was afraid to hit the feet of the incoming swimmer if she started too early. This attitude seemed to explain the result that she obviously was not able to take advantage of the feedback information.

Conclusion

The results indicated that only a part of the final goals of this research was achieved. Swimmer 2 improved in the exchange times, but did not reduce the number of early starts. For Swimmer 3 the situation was reversed. Swimmer 4 showed no improvement at all. On the other hand, some interesting and seemingly stable structures in the individual learning processes were encountered that will provide a basis for future research in this area.

References

Nicol, K., Clasing, D., Thayer, A., & El-Din, A. (1987). Time characteristics in swimming. In B. Jonsson (Ed.), *Biomechanics XB* (pp. 757-766). Champaign, IL: Human Kinetics.

Nicol, K., Henning, E., & Huber, G. (1980). Meßsohle Vermittlung von objektiver Ergänzungsinformation [Measuring arrangement of objective feedback data]. In R. Ballreich & A. Kuhlow (Eds.), *Beiträge zur Biomechanik des Sports* (pp. 288-297). Schorndorf: Hofmann.

Nicol, K., & Krüger, F. (1979). Impulses exerted in performing several kinds of swimming turns. In J. Terauds & E.W. Bedingfield (Eds.), *Swimming III* (pp. 222-232). Baltimore: University Park Press.

Biomechanical Signals for External Biofeedback to Improve Swimming Techniques

Didier Chollet
Jean Paul Micallef
Pierre Rabischong

The present research was the result of a number of practical questions with direct applications: How can one analyze and then provide a swimmer with information on his or her motor patterns during swimming?

Swimmers have an objective means for evaluation at their disposal, but this is available only after the performance is completed. They may also estimate their efficiency in real time, but their biological perceptions are not very precise or objective.

The aim of this research was to develop an experimental device that would permit the measurement of the force or pressure on the hand during the propulsive action in crawl swimming and to transform this information into an audible signal that could be transmitted to the swimmer while swimming.

Justifications

A very brief ballistic motion cannot be modified once it has begun, whereas a motion that requires sufficient time to permit adjustments can use feedback. That is, by giving cues to the central nervous system, external or internal biological systems can modify and therefore improve the motion while it is being performed.

Biofeedback was originally used in fields that were remote from physical practices but now is applied in numerous ways to sports. The main point in using biofeedback is to learn how to control a movement. For example, Gauthier (1985) used such methods in order to improve the rowing stroke of oarsmen. The method consists of providing subjects with some indications on their behavior that they may not be aware of, by transposing these movements into audible or visible signals.

The major principles of biofeedback are characterized as follows: (a) objective criteria for estimation, (b) feedback during the task, (c) consideration of the performance as a whole, (d) perceptions of information previously ignored, and (e) actual involvement of the subject with the training device.

An Experimental Instrument for Auto-Control of Propulsion in Swimming

The starting point of this research was the improvement of performance and the idea that technical skill can be improved by auto-control of motor actions. This idea led to a simple device that was adaptable to individuals and that took into account the specificity of the task (swimming motion). The idea was to try to transform the vague, subjective feelings and delayed information into precise, objective, and immediate perceptions.

The hand action was assumed to be the most representative segment to estimate the efficiency of the stroke pattern in crawl swimming (Stoner & Luedtke, 1978). However, this pattern was actually very difficult to control. It was hypothesized that the subjective sensations provided by the biological sensors on the hand could be instantly transformed into audible objective perceptions by means of force transducers.

The purpose of swimming paddles is to increase the surface in contact with the water during a propulsive movement. Paddles are different in size and shape and increase the sensation of a stroke, but primary function is greater force propulsion.

Belokovsky (1971) used a pressure transducer fixed to the hand in order to analyze the variations of the propulsive forces in speed crawl swimming. The resulting information was not initially intended to be available to the swimmer, however. Svec (1982) used the same kind of hydrodynamic pressure sensor. The signals were recorded on a strip chart recorder where the swimmer could use them a posteriori.

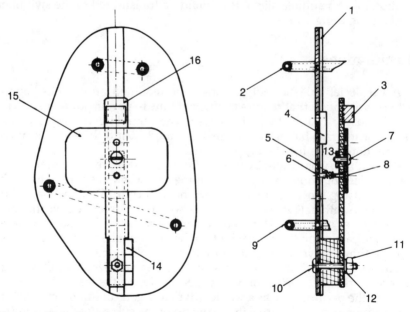

Figure 1   Biofeedback swimming paddles (face and profile).

Description of the Experimental Hand Paddles

The device consisted of paddles as well as force sensors, sound generators, and an electric power source (battery) (see Figures 1, 2, and 3).

The swimmer fixed the instrument to his hand, by means of an elastic band (see Figure 1; nos. 2 and 9). The stiff paddles (no. 1) were approximately the size of the surface of the hand. The transducers that were attached to the paddles were either analog (directly proportional) or on/off

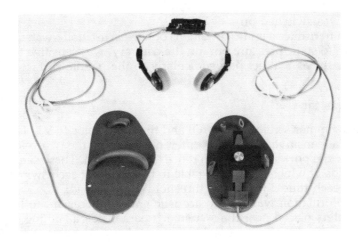

Figure 2 Experimental waterproof device composed of paddles, wires, sound generators, and an electric power source.

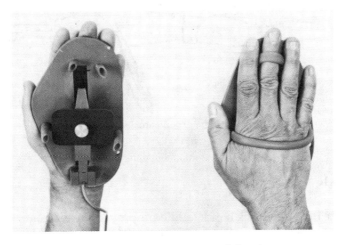

Figure 3 Biofeedback paddles mounted on a swimmer's hands.

ones. In the on/off situation, the threshold was adjustable either continuously by means of a screw (no. 8) acting on a spring (no. 5) or in regular steps (no. 14).

The device for force measurement included a plane, a moveable, stiff plate (pressure plane no. 15) placed on a flexible beam (no. 16), the displacement of which was in direct proportion to the perpendicular force applied at the surface of the paddle. A permanent magnet (no. 3) was fixed at the end of the flexible beam, and a reed ILS relay (no. 4) was waterproofed and sensitive to the magnetic field generated by the magnet. A hydrodynamic force applied at the level of the pressure plane brought the magnet close to the sensitive plate, which emitted a signal (when the contact was switched on).

Such a transducer, under conditions of normal use underwater, was not sensitive to static pressure but, on the contrary, was sensitive to hydrodynamic forces that act perpendicularly to the paddle surface.

Directions for Use

The swimmer's velocity was V0 and the hand velocity V1. The transducer was sensitive only to the difference between the two velocities or to one of the powers of this difference (see Figure 4). These sensors, the thresholds of which were adjustable to the ability of each swimmer, indicated each time a top-speed threshold was reached.

The information was sent to acoustic and, on occasion, to luminous transmitters placed near the swimmer's ears inside a bathing cap. The swimmer was fitted with a paddle on each hand that was connected to an acoustic transmitter to each ear by a wire. The optional luminous transmitter provided the same information to poolside (e.g., to the coach).

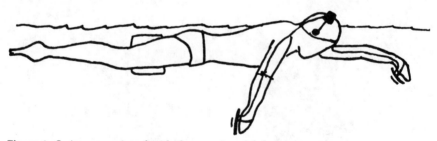

Figure 4   Swimmer equipped with the experimental device.

Methods

The use of biofeedback hand paddles improved the efficiency of swimming when used over a reasonably long period of time. For this, the device provides a real time evaluation of the stroke and an external biofeedback loop under the control of the swimmer, and therefore it improves his or her strokes.

Subjects

The 25 subjects belonged mainly to local academic or national competitive swimming associations. The experiment included 34 tests (trials for the swimmers). The division of subjects into the control group and the experimental groups was made at the end of the first test. The groups were equated on objective variables. Two categories of variables were used: (a) variables that did not depend on the result of the first test series (sex, age, school level, number of training sessions per year, number of training sessions per week, and records on 400 m); and (b) variables depending on the results of the first test series (average time for 50 m, maximum deviation [time], amount of the variation in the deviations, number of arm cycles per lane, and maximum deviation of the arm cycles).

Three groups were employed: Group A—control subjects; Group B—experimental subjects; and Group A'—experimental subjects having already performed the test as control subjects. During the training sessions, the control subjects used neutral hand paddles, whereas experimental subjects used the biofeedback swimming paddles. During the test series, all the subjects used neutral swimming paddles.

Tests

After a standard warm-up, the test was to swim 5 × 300 m with arms alone, equipped with hand paddles, while the legs were restrained by means of an elastic band and lifted with a pull-buoy.

The first and last 300 m were utilized as tests: T1 and T2. The second, third, and fourth 300 m were training sessions: E1, E2, and E3 with rest intervals (1 min) between swims.

The evaluation of the results consisted of a comparison of the second test (T2) to the first test (T1), based on the criteria of time in seconds for 50 m and the number of arm cycles for the second 25 m of each 50 m.

Results

One must keep in mind that the differences between the first and second test (T2 − T1) were a function of both time of performance and the number of arm cycles per lane. The difference between the deviations, when estimated by number of arm cycles, was highly significant (Figure 5 and Table 1). The quality of the performances also improved as a result of using the experimental device, whereas the mean velocity for all trials in a session was not improved by the use of the experimental device (see Figure 6 and Table 2).

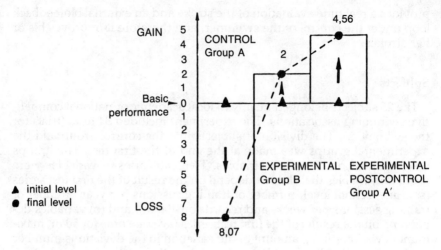

Figure 5 Schema showing the variations of the variable: mean number of arm cycles per lane between T_2 and T_1.

Table 1 Experimental Results—Variable: Number of Arm Cycles

Group	T1	T2	T1 – T2	% (T2 – T1)	Relation to Group A
		Means*			
Control (A)	142.86	150.93	+ 8.07	Decrease 5.65	—
Experimental (B)	140.00	138.00	– 2.00	Increase 1.43	Increase 7.08%
Experimental postcontrol A'	141.44	136.88	– 4.56	Increase 3.23	Increase 8.88%

*$p = .01$.

Conclusion

The crawl swimmer, even a highly skilled one, finds it very difficult to maintain the propulsive efficiency, especially related to the rhythm. Controlling the stroke once in the water is difficult for the swimmer as well as the coach. The pattern of the test series was mainly directed toward the evaluation of the experimental device in order to validate the external biofeedback loop.

The results of this study can be summarized as follows: A subject during a training session without any biofeedback, from the beginning to the end of training, has a tendency to have his or her efficiency regress when estimated in velocity (for the entire session) and in number of arm cycles (evaluation of the technique). When a subject uses the test device, the number of arm cycles and an optimum stability in velocity is reached.

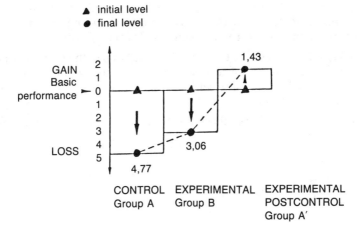

Figure 6 Schema showing the variation of the variable: mean chronometric performance between T_2 and T_1.

Table 2 Experimental Results—Variable: Chronometric Performance for 50 m

Group	T1	T2	T2 – T1	% (T2 – T1)	Relation to Group A
Control (A)	5.03.6	5.08.4	+ 04.8	Decrease 1.58	—
Experimental (B)	4.47.3	4.50.4	+ 03.1	Decrease 1.08	Increase 0.50%
Experimental post-control (A')	4.42.2	4.40.8	– 01.4	Increase 0.50	Increase 2.08%

This stabilization may be regarded as an improvement inasmuch as the control subjects recorded a regression in their performance. If this difference was not significant, it would have some value considering the number of arm cycles. The fact that the number of arm cycles increased was not the result of increased velocity, which was one of the major points of this experiment. This is a stage of relative improvement of the performance by use of the external biofeedback information.

References

Belokovsky, V. (1971). An analysis of pulling motions in the crawl arm stroke. In L. Lewillie & J.P. Clarys (Eds.), *First international symposium on biomechanics in swimming* (pp. 217-222). Brussels: Université Libre de Bruxelles.

Gauthier, G.M. (1985). Visually and acoustically augmented performance feedback as an aid in motor control learning: A study of selected components of the rowing actions. *Journal of Sports Sciences, 3*, 3-26.

Stoner, L.J., & Luedtke, D.L. (1978). Variations in the front crawl and back crawl arm strokes of variety swimmers using hand paddles. In J. Terauds & E.W. Bedingfield (Eds.), *Swimming III* (pp. 281-288). Baltimore: University Park Press.

Svec, O.J. (1982). Biofeedback for pulling efficiency. *Swimming Technique, 19*, 1, 38-46.

Primary Authors

Erik Bollens
Vrije Universiteit Brussel
Dept. Experimental Anatomy
Campus Jette
Laarbeeklaan 103
1090 Brussels, Belgium

Jan M.H. Cabri
Vrije Universiteit Brussel
Inst. Lichamelijke Opvoeding
Dept. Experimental Anatomy
Laarbeeklaan 103
1090 Brussels, Belgium

Georges Cazorla
Departement Recherche
Creps Aquitaine
653 Cours de la Liberation
33405 Talence Cedex, France

Jean-Claude Chatard
Laboratoire de Physiologie—GIP Exercise
U.E.R. de Medecine—30, rue F. Gambon
42023 Saint-Etienne Cedex, France

Didier Chollet
Unite de Formation et de Recherche in Sciences
  et Technique des Activites Physique et Sportives
700 Avenue du Pic saint coup
34 100 Montpellier, France

Jan Pieter Clarys
Vrije Universiteit Brussel
Inst. Lichamelijke Opvoeding
Dept. Experimental Anatomy
Laarbeeklaan 103
1090 Brussels, Belgium

James E. Counsilman
Assembly Hall, Dept. of Athletics
Indiana University Bloomington
Bloomington, Indiana 47405

Albert B. Craig, Jr.
University of Rochester
Rochester, New York 14642

Daniel Daly
I.L.O. K.U. Leuven
Tervuursevest 101
3030 Heverlee, Belgium

Brigitte De Witte
Vrije Universiteit Brussel
Inst. Lichamelijke Opvoeding
Dept. of Experimental Anatomy
Laarbeeklaan 103
1090 Brussels, Belgium

Gert de Groot
Universiteit Amsterdam
Werkgroep Inspanningsfys. en Gezondheitk
Meibergdreef 15
1105 AZ Amsterdam, The Netherlands

James G. Hay
Dept. of Physical Education
University of Iowa
Iowa City, Iowa 52242

A. Peter Hollander
Universiteit Amsterdam
Werkgroep Inspanningsfys. en Gezondheitk
Meiberrgdreef 15
1105 AZ Amsterdam, The Netherlands

Ulrich Hüellhorst
Rt. 2 Box 4A
Homerville, Georgia 31634

Peter A. Huijing
Vrije Universiteit
Interfac. Lichameljke Opvoeding
P.O. Box 7161
1007 MC Amsterdam, The Netherlands

Kari L. Keskinen
Dept. of Biology of Physical Activity
University of Jyväskylä
40 100 Jyväskylä, Finland

Henryk Kuński
Dept. of Sports Medical Academy
AI. Politechniki 4
Hula Sportowa
90–532 Lodz, Poland

Christophe Loetz
Ziegelhäuser Landstr. 45
6900 Heidelberg, West Germany

Cheryl W. Maglischo
Department of Physical Education
California State University
Chico, CA 95926

Ernest W. Maglischo
Athletic Department
California State College, Bakersfield
Bakersfield, California 93311

Richard M. Montpetit
Department d'education physique
Université de Montréal
C.P. 6128, surrursale "A"
Montreal, Quebec H3C 3J7
Canada

Yoshiteru Mutoh
Laboratory for Exercise Physiology and Biomechanics
Faculty of Education
University of Tokyo
7-3-1 Hongo, Bunkyo-ku
113 Tokyo, Japan

Klaus Nicol
FB 20 University Münster
Horstmarer Landweg 62 b
4400 Münster, West Germany

Reinhard Nimz
Deutsche Sporthochschule Koln
Abt. Schwimmsport
Carl-Diem-Weg
5000 Koln 41, West Germany

Jan Olbrecht
Deutsche Sporthochschule Köln
Inst. f. Kreislaufforschung und Sportmedizin
Carl-Diem-Weg 1
5000 Köln 41, West Germany

Ulrik Persyn
Unit Aquatics
I.L.O. K.U. Leuven
Tervuursevest 101
3030 Heverlee, Belgium

Johan Pion
Inst. of Physical Education and Physiotherapy
Vrije Universiteit Brussel
1090 Brussels, Belgium

Annie H. Rouard
Centre de Recherche et d'Innovation sur le Sport
  (C.R.I.S.)
U.F.R./A.P.S.
27-29 Bd. du 11 Novembre 1918
69622 Villeurbanne, France

Robert E. Schleihauf
Hunter College
Dept. of Health and Physical Education
695 Park Avenue
New York, New York 10021

Dietmar Schmidtbleicher
University Freiburg
Inst. for Sport und Sportwissenschaft
Schwarzwaldstr. 175
7800 Freiburg, West Germany

Werner Skipka
Institute of Physiology
Deutsch Sporthochschule Köln
Carl-Diem-Weg 6
5000 Köln 41, West Germany

Dieter Strass
University Freiburg
Inst. for Sport und Sportwissenschaft
Schwarzwaldstr. 175
7800 Freiburg, West Germany

Adalbert Szögy
Inst. for Sportmedicine Frankfurt/M.
Otto-Fleck-Schneise 10
6000 Frankfurt 71, West Germany

Nobutaka Taguchi
National Institute of Fitness and Sport in Kanoya
Shiromizucho 1
Kanoya Kagoshima, Japan

Miwako Takamoto
Laboratory for Exercise Physiology and Biomechanics
7-3-1 Hongo, Bunkyo-ku
113 Tokyo, Japan

Richard D. Telford
Dept. of Sport Science
Australian Inst. of Sport
P.O. Box 176
Belconnen A.C.T 2616, Australia

Huub M. Toussaint
Universiteit Amsterdam
Werkgroep Inspanningsfys. en Gezondheitk
Meigergdreef 15
1105 AZ Amsterdam, The Netherlands

Bodo E. Ungerechts
University Bielefeld
Abt. Sportwissenschaft
Postfach 8640
4800 Bielefeld 1, West Germany

Peter J. Van Handel
U.S. Swimming Sports Medicine
United States Swimming
1776 East Boulder Street
Colorado Springs, Colorado 80909

Luc Van Tilborgh
Unit Aquatics
I.L.O. K.U. Leuven
Tervuursevest 101
3030 Heverlee, Belgium

Michael Weiss
Bundesleistungszentrum
Abt. Sportmedizin
Im Neuenheimer Feld 710
6900 Heidelberg, West Germany

Yoshiharu Yamamoto
Laboratory for Exercise Physiology and Biomechanics
Faculty of Education
University of Tokyo
7-3-1 Hongo, Bunkyo-ku
113 Tokyo, Japan

4/24

DATE DUE

DEMCO 38-297